FAMILY THERAPY
AN INTIMATE HISTORY

BOOKS BY LYNN HOFFMAN

1968: *Techniques of Family Therapy* (with Jay Haley)
1981: *Foundations of Family Therapy*
1987: *Milan Systemic Family Therapy* (with L. Boscolo, G. Cecchin, and
   P. Penn)
1993: *Exchanging Voices: A Collaborative Approach to Family Therapy*

A NORTON PROFESSIONAL BOOK

FAMILY THERAPY
AN INTIMATE HISTORY

LYNN HOFFMAN

W.W. Norton & Company
New York • London

For information about permission to reproduce
selections from this book, write to
Permissions, W. W. Norton & Company, Inc.,
500 Fifth Avenue, New York, NY 10110

Composition and book design by Ecomlinks, Inc.
Manufacturing by Haddon Craftsman
Production Manager: Leeann Graham

Library of Congress Cataloging-in-Publication Data
Hoffman, Lynn
  Family therapy: an intimate history/Lynn Hoffman.
    p. cm.
  "A Norton professional book."
  Includes bibliographical references and index.
  ISBN 0-393-70380-0
    1. Family psycholotherapy. I. Title.
RC488.5 .H599   2001
616.89'156--dc21   2001044331

W. W. Norton & Company, Inc., 500 Fifth Avenue, New York, NY 10110
www.wwnorton.com
W. W. Norton & Company, Ltd., Castle House, 75/76 Wells Street, London W1T 3QT
3 4 5 6 7 8 9 0

To My Family

Contents

Acknowledgments

How does one acknowledge an entire field? I feel that my book represents "a great cloud of witnesses," as it says in the Bible: pioneering psychotherapists who insisted on working against our most persistent illusion, the stand-alone self. I wanted particularly to honor three people who are no longer with us: Virginia Satir, whose boldness started me off, E.H. Auerswald, who offered me protection along the way, and Harry Goolishian, who drew me into his enthusiasm for postmodern ideas. I also acknowledge my debt to the mentors who led me through difficult terrain, and the families and couples who helped me to critique my own myths. This book is composed of their stories. In a way, it is a version of my earlier book, *Foundations of Family Therapy*, except that it is written from a much more personal point of view.

Thanks also to Mary and Kenneth Gergen and Sheila McNamee for their encouragement, and to Mary Catherine Bateson for her inspiring example. I must also mention the American Society of Cybernetics, which has continued Bateson's tradition of inquiry under the aegis of its three wise men: Heinz von Foerster, Humberto Maturana, and Ernst von Glasersfeld. Other inspirers include artist Richard Baldwin, who was a longtime partner in unorthodoxy; Cathy Taylor and the MOSAIC mothers; Michael White, a tender therapist but a tough theorist; and Tom Andersen, Peggy Penn, and Judith Davis, wonderful practitioners, beloved colleagues, and unfailing friends. Readers of this book will meet many other unusual talents who contributed to my education. An alternative subtitle for the book would be *A Family Therapist Learns How*.

As for the people in publishing who helped me, I want to thank Jo Ann Miller for keeping a place at the table for me at Basic Books until that place expired, and Susan Munro, for leading me to Norton, and being my editor. As for the process of putting the book into print, let me thank Professional Books director Deborah Malmud, associate editor Regina Dahlgren Ardini, and editorial assistant Anne Hellman, who have managed to compress the bookmaking time to a fast six months. I also want to thank my writer friend Jane O'Reilly for leading me to computer wizard Craig Smith, who created the original idea for the cover design, and poet/painter Cooper Edens, who gave permission to use one of his pictures.

Lastly, I want to thank my daughters, Martha and Livia Hoffman, who read parts of the manuscript and gave me good advice, and my ex-husband, Ted Hoffman, for his unceasing moral support. I have one more daughter, Joanna, who is estranged from me, but her clear spirit lives at the heart of this book and gives me hope.

—Lynn Hoffman, Northampton, Mass.

Introduction

My Mother's Ashes

This book traces my journey from an instrumental, causal approach to family therapy to a collaborative, communal one. When I first became acquainted with the field in 1963, I assumed that a therapist was supposed to fix a system that was in trouble. Over the course of time, the description of the problem changed from a maladaptive behavior to a dysfunctional family structure to an outmoded belief. In all these cases, however, the therapist placed herself outside the arrangement in question. This assumption of objectivity led to a therapist stance that was aloof and distancing, but it was congruent with the rational, scientific norms of the day.

By the seventies, I became aware of a shift in the zeitgeist. Anthropologist Gregory Bateson (1972) had already cast aspersions on the Newtonian mind-set, with its dreams of controlling the physical universe. Cognitive researchers like Humberto Maturana, Heinz von Foerster, and Ernst von Glasersfeld went on to challenge the idea that we can ever know what is really "out there," because our perceptions are filtered through the sensory screens of the nervous system. Paul Watzlawick (1984), one of the early researchers in family communication, summed up this situation by describing the knower as the pilot of a ship that is navigating a difficult channel at night. If he gets through successfully, he does not know what was really there, only that he has not hit a rock.

By the eighties, this skepticism was amplified by an intellectual movement called postmodernism that had a long history in European thought.
Its adherents were a brilliant group of linguists and literary critics that were
influenced by philosophers Ludwig Wittgenstein (1953), Jacques Derrida
(1978), Michel Foucault (1972), and Jean-Francois Lyotard (1984). Put all
together, the effect of these writers' work was to undermine the truth
claims of philosophy, the objective standards of science, and the assumptions
of social and psychological research. The postmodernists accused the mod-
ernists of believing in "totalizing truths" and "grand narratives." The mod-
ernists declared their opponents to be relativists without values. The quarrel
spilled over from the academy into other fields, including family therapy,
where it created much argument but also an explosion of new energy and
ideas.

Meanwhile, out in the real world that some of us no longer believed in,
family therapy was losing its borders and becoming a goal-oriented, short-
term type of work. The managed care movement, with its demands for
accountability, had pushed the field up against the wall. Our research results,
although not any worse than other brands of therapy (Shadish, Ragsdale, &
Glaser, 1995), were not outstanding, in part because our approaches had not
emphasized outcome. Despite years of experimentation, family therapy had
reached no firm conclusions and seemed mainly fortified by the assumptions of popular psychology and the loyalties of small believing bands. I was
shocked when, as recently as 1994, I began taking one of the new drugs that
alter serotonin levels and experienced immediate and lasting relief from cat-
astrophic fears that had crippled me throughout my entire life.

This experience left me more confused than ever before. Even if emotional suffering were partly a matter of brain chemistry, there were obviously
other influences. How did one decide what they were? In a kind of mission
creep, each successive approach to family therapy had added a rich new bank
of suspects to the roster. Starting modestly with schizophrenia, we moved on
to parent-child problems, marital woes, developmental lacunae, traumatic
events, life-stage stuckness, gender discrimination, sexual abuse, violence,
addiction, poverty, and all the injustices of race, ethnicity, and class. Following
an increasingly medical vocabulary, every difficulty was being turned into a
disease, a deficit or a disorder, and claims and counterclaims were proliferat-
ing within what was now calling itself behavioral health.

This seemed like a good time to assess the family therapy field. As it
evolved, it resembled a version of the scissors, stone, paper game of my
childhood, except that it kept marching up a set of stairs. Family therapy
trumped individual therapy, systemic therapy trumped family therapy, feminist therapy trumped systemic therapy, multicultural therapy trumped feminist therapy, and so on. But this formulation implied an upward and

onward progression, which I distrusted. Also, each of these models pointed to a different location for distress, as well as a different recipe for how to handle it, and each had enough good points to make it hard to choose between them.

One solution was to set aside the models. In explaining why, I find myself revisiting the story of my mother's ashes. My mother, Ruth Reeves, was a textile designer, one of the first artists to put modern design on cloth. Equally in love with folk design, she spent the last ten years of her life in India, creating a catalog of village crafts and textiles for the Indian government. In 1966, having been diagnosed with cancer, she was sent back to the States. Her young Indian assistants thought they would never see her again, but after only three months of treatment, she came back, appearing to have risen from the dead and eager to complete her work.

She died a year later of a heart stoppage. Her Indian friends took half her ashes and sprinkled them in a place reserved for highly evolved persons where the Jumna and the Ganges rivers meet. The other half was sent back in care of my sister. Shortly after that, I was cleaning out Ruth's studio with a friend and came upon some metal canisters containing powdered colors: blue, red, yellow, white, gray. I checked each one and then set it aside to throw out. My friend was struck by the intricate design chased onto the copper surface of one of the cans. Looking inside, she said, "I don't think this is powdered paint." I looked too. It was my mother!

Thus began a family quandary. We knew she wanted to be buried on the land where she had built her house, but I was afraid that some future developer might come and bulldoze it up. After talking to a number of people, an anthropologist friend came to my rescue. He said, "Look, your problem is not the ashes but the urn. All you have to do is take the ashes out and you can do what you like with them." This suggestion brought immediate relief. Once her ashes were out of the container, it seemed no problem to bury them in her favorite spot: a mossy place where two streams flowed together, surrounded by ferns and presided over by a tall tulip tree.

I used this story to explain the liberation that comes from throwing away the container. Not only was I leaving the container behind, but I was also abandoning the container that contained the container: in my case, the "modern" worldview. So I asked myself, "What are the biggest hits of family therapy?" I thought that if I just listed some important examples of what therapists did, I might get useful answers. My list of favorite ideas and techniques included triangles, genograms, boundaries, paradoxes, secrets, circular questions, externalizing questions, reflecting teams, and more. It kept getting longer until it began to remind me of a tower of Babel. Baffled, I asked myself how I could reconcile these competing practices, each of which was attached to a competing point of view.

Then I had a rescuing thought. Perhaps the real biggest hit of the family therapy movement was its power to fold back upon itself and change. An evolutionary image came to mind. I began to think of the field as a Jewish challah, or braided Easter bread, with early strands forming, then disappearing, then reappearing in a changed position or on another side. A later strand might compensate for a deficiency in an earlier one, but it was the conversation between the strands that made the entire braid so special.

This analogy had room for innovation and continuity both. Not only was there a place for new strands, but there was a place for new loaves. What particularly interested me about the idea of family therapy as a braid was that, in its self-revising journey, it had become able to critique itself at the level of its own premises. I have always been impressed by the number of family therapists who have used the insights of each new development to rethink their theories and practices rather than getting fixed in one particular school. Interestingly enough, postmodernism has played a helpful role in this process. Let me try to explain how.

In the history of large-scale literate frameworks, Western culture has had at least three: Augustine's City of God, which defined the place of humans in the heavenly order; the Enlightenment framework, which followed the assumptions of the natural sciences; and now the postmodern view, according to which reality is constantly woven and rewoven on social and linguistic looms. Each framework is true within its own boundaries. Each allows things to be seen that are outside the purview of the others, and one can move back and forth between them, just as one can choose to speak another language. But let's not forget that the modern framework dates back only to the 18th century, and that postmodernism has existed for scarcely any time at all.

So how has postmodernism changed the landscape of family therapy? As I have said, the ascendance of systems theory in the middle of the 20th century encouraged a theory of dysfunctional family structures and an active technology of change. The technical-rational point of view (see Schoen, 1984) had found a new beachhead in the budding field of family therapy. Then, just as this perspective solidified, an iconoclastic backlash hit. From Plato's idea that we must learn to "carve nature at the joints," we moved on to seeing that our conceptual systems create the joints we erroneously think we carve. As a result, the objectivist, one-way approaches of modernism began to be challenged by an interest in self-reflexive, open-ended processes that included therapists as well as clients in the loop.

It has been an engrossing experience to watch all this happen. Holding in mind my braided challah, I want to describe my own sense of how the various strands of family therapy evolved. An article by psychologist Margaret Singer (1997), one of family therapy's foremothers, inspired my thinking. When I first met Singer in Palo Alto in 1963, she had recently performed a remarkable feat. The research group that had formed under Jackson had proposed that communication patterns in a family with a symptomatic child could be "read" by specialists in family communication. It should be theoretically possible to tell, on the basis of a conversation between the parents alone, whether the symptomatic child was a "schizophrenic," a "delinquent," or a "normal." Singer was the only member of the group who was able to predict the correct diagnosis from a blind sample beyond the effects of chance, and she only did it once. However, rather than tag the theory incorrect, the experimenters preferred to assume that Singer had unusual psychic powers. Various family researchers continued to try to typologize families based on the symptom of the child for many years thereafter.

Later, in her book *"Crazy" Therapies* (Singer & Lalich, 1996), Singer compares a number of recent psychotherapies to cults or witch hunts. During the first part of the 20th century, she observes, the treatment of emotional illness moved from a rehabilitative framework based on the work of German psychologist Adolf Meyer to an etiological or causative one based on Freudian psychodynamics and developmental theory. This shift, according to Singer, had unfortunate consequences. Freudian theory had fostered an emphasis on the family as a source of psychic injury, and this view, backed up by developmental research on children, created a hostile environment for parents. In time, we began to see what Singer (1997) and others have called the "blame and change game." In other words, if you can find somebody in your family to blame, you can change. This idea was key for many individual therapies, but it was often disastrous in family therapy, as a host of humbled parents can attest.

The Mental Research Institute's interactional view (Watzlawick, Weakland, & Fisch, 1974) was a happy exception to this blaming bias. From the beginning, the MRI emphasized a rhetorical rather than an etiological stance. If you believe that reality is constructed in the eye of the observer, you will naturally try to alter perceptions. As a result, instead of looking for causation and cure, they used language and suggestion to shape a different world of meaning. This approach was a welcome corrective to the blame and change game. For one thing, not only did you avoid pathologizing your customers but you liked them better too.

Another good aspect was the witty, hopeful character of this work. Paradoxical tasks became a way to play-act a problem and have it come out differently. Directives not to change took the customer's so-called resistance and turned it into a wind at her back. This entire method, in fact, was an intervention into a field that took itself much too seriously. Once you began telling people to do more of what they were already doing, you adopted a habit of acceptance. People might look askance if told to practice stuttering really well for five minutes every day, but there was something about it that was an antidote to fear. Psychiatrist Richard Rabkin (1968) put it best when he said, "I believe that patients come by their problems honestly."

The downside of this rhetorical strand was the way the customer was perceived. Family therapy was compared by theorists like Paul Watzlawick to a game of chess. The therapist, who knew the rules of the game, was the master player, while the family members were the pieces on the board. Not only is this picture condescending, but it is easy to see that therapists who bought into it would want to hide the thinking behind their moves. If customers knew the reasons behind paradoxical maneuvers, they might object. As a result, the proponents of this view sometimes seemed to be conducting guerilla warfare, not only against a psychotherapy establishment that didn't take them seriously, but against the families who were coming to them for help.

The third strand to appear, the Milan systemic approach (Selvini Palazzoli, Boscolo, Cecchin, & Prata, 1978), blended elements from both etiological and rhetorical camps. The Milan team targeted a relationship knot which Mara Selvini, the founder of the team, described as an "imbroglio." This was clearly a causal notion. But the team used a rhetorical technique to untie the knot: the famous counterparadox. One or two persons would interview the family, while the others watched from behind a screen. At the end, the observers would join with the interviewers to compose a paradoxical message to leave with the family. The formal separation between observers and families was further widened by the apparently illogical nature of the message.

In any case, the systemic strand modified itself. The invention of "circular questioning" (Selvini, Boscolo, Cecchin, & Prata, 1980c) gave Luigi Boscolo and Gianfranco Cecchin, who in 1980 started their own training institute, a tool for placing family members outside their accustomed places. It was then easier for them to become aware of the patterns they were caught in. As this form of questioning took off, the systemic hypothesis, with its somewhat accusatory feel, began to be replaced by open-ended reflexive formats. Cecchin's special interest in qualities like curiosity and irreverence (Cecchin & Lane, 1991) was part of this trend, which focused on an inquisitive hopefulness rather than on descriptions of what was wrong.

In their invention of solution-focused therapy, Steve de Shazer (1985) and Insoo Berg (1994) now brought in a fourth strand. With the help of other colleagues (O'Hanlon & Weiner-Davis, 1989), they replaced the field's historic interest in problem-talk with what they called solution-talk.

Both kinds of talk depended on the use of rhetoric, but solution-talk emphasized possibility rather than pathology and had a vastly more sympathetic feel. In operationalizing this technique, de Shazer and Berg offered some simple and elegant suggestions for covering the grit in the oyster with pearl. "Exception" questions were used to look for any proof that things had changed, and the "miracle question" invited people to imagine how their lives would be if the problem disappeared. As a result of this optimistic outlook, the therapist became an ally and a friend.

Thinking back, the emphasis on solutions was a huge corrective. It counteracted the negative effect of the etiological view while adding humanity to the rhetorical one. However, there was a larger difficulty. Where in family therapy was there any awareness of gender? Feminist theorist Rachel Hare-Mustin (1988) accused systemic therapists of practicing therapy within the "mirrored rooms." Her objection, it's only fair to say, was part of the powerful movement of critical feminism that was challenging the masculine bias built into fields like developmental psychology (Burman, 1994), language studies (Crawford, 1995), and sexology (Tiefer, 1995), to name only a few. Writers like Elaine Showalter (1985) exposed male dominance in fields like mental health, and journalist Barbara Ehrenreich (1978) took on male arrogance period. Into this battle stepped the Women's Project (Walters, Carter, Papp, & Silverstein, 1988; see also Goodrich, Rampage, Ellman, & Halstead, 1988), which attacked the gender-blindness of family therapy head on. Another strand was born.

Culture and race were the logical next issues. A lively multicultural movement started up, led by writer-therapists like Monica McGoldrick (McGoldrick, 1988; McGoldrick, Anderson, & Walsh, 1989; McGoldrick, 1998), and Celia Falicov (1998). Ethnic groups were asking to be treated with respect and to be allowed to treat their own. African-American family therapists threw their special agenda on the table (Boyd-Franklin, 1989), and some of them pointed out that using the term "multicultural" could be seen as a way to avoid taking a stand on racism. Amid this useful ferment, leaders of academic family therapy programs like Kenneth Hardy (Hardy & Laszloffy, 1995) developed the "cultural genogram," which punched more holes in the mirrored rooms. Hardy was one of the first African-American family therapists to bring postmodern social criticism to bear on issues of race.

Then came the narrative approach, which placed privilege itself under the microscope. The originators of this approach, Michael White and David (1990; White, 1995), exchanged the metaphor of systems for the metaphor of stories. Taking their cue from the ideas of Foucault (Rabinow, 1984), they redefined therapy as helping people "re-author" their lives. Foucault had identified some of the institutional and cultural discourses that invisibly constrain and oppress people. White and Epston saw these as discourses of entitlement: the belief of whites that they are superior to non-whites; the belief of men that they have the right to dominate women; the belief of heterosexuals that homosexuals are abnormal; and so forth. Training in narrative therapy began to serve as a re-education movement for professionals who wanted to move out of the solipsism of culture, race, and class. Dismaying in some ways, this proactive stance was a relief after the neutrality of the systemic years.

Another strand now appeared that tucked itself under a postmodern banner and called itself a collaborative approach. Led by the late Harold Goolishian and Harlene Anderson (Anderson, 1997; Anderson & Goolishian, 1988), this group turned for support to the constructionist framework proposed by social theorists like Kenneth Gergen (1994) and John Shotter (1993b). Following Lyotard's dictum of "incredulity toward meta-narratives" (1984), these therapists also began to question the assumptions that underlay the practice of present-day professionals: the idea of the expert, the idea of objectivity, the idea of control. If you watch collaborative therapists at work, you will see that they do not seem to care about goals and methods. The not-knowing stance of Anderson and Goolishian (1988), the reflecting team process of Tom Andersen (1991), and the poetic activism of Peggy Penn (Penn & Frankfurt, 1994) are examples of a style that prefers to follow openings as they surface rather than imposing a predetermined scheme.

Although my own work seems to belong in this category, I am unwilling to leave other outlooks and methods behind. Many stay with me, if only as presences in my mind. This is why I like the image of the braided challah. It allows me to float in and out of the many currents of family therapy and to reflect back on what Katz and Shotter (1996) call the "arresting moments" of the field. Since the beginning of my immersion in this enterprise, I wanted to see what people did, not what they said they did. The late Donald Schoen's unusual treatise *The Reflective Practitioner* (1984) offers many good reasons for watching therapeutic practice from within. Let me explain.

The Swampy Lowlands

Donald Schoen (1984) was a questioning organizational consultant who asked why the technical-rational view of modern science should be the preferred framework for all professional fields. This framework did well in the case of medicine and engineering, but was not so good when applied to what Schoen called the "swampy lowlands" of such areas as theology and social work. So Schoen did something unusual: he watched in person, for hours at a time, while practitioners and students in "soft" sciences like city planning or organizational consulting engaged in their teaching or their craft. Stranger yet, he paid little attention to the times when the practitioner was working smoothly, only to the times when she changed direction or hit a wall.

In a chapter with the nice title "Design as a Reflective Conversation with the Situation," Schoen described standing behind a student of architecture while she sketched in the plan for a building project. Every once in a while, he noticed that she stopped short, erased lines, or crumpled the paper and started over. At these moments Schoen would ask her, "Why did you stop? Why did you go in another direction?" Generalizing from cases like this, he said he would first get what he called an "espoused theory." The student would give a cursory but conventional answer. However, if Schoen persisted, the student would usually come up with a reply that was more fine-grained and thoughtful. This he called a "theory-in-use." It was the kind of theory that arose from the operational level and was usually accessible to the practitioner's consciousness only when she was experiencing a breakdown.

Schoen called the process of getting at these subterranean theories "reflection-in-action," meaning that you generalize from your experience within the activity. This mode, he said, puts a high value on metaphoric frameworks like "as if" exercises and the use of "virtual worlds" like sketch pads and stories. Simulated actions like "seeing as" and "doing as" were other examples. Schoen says that this activity is not like ordinary research because the inquirers have no objective quarry in mind but are looking for something far more elusive: *the situation's potential for transformation* (1984, p. 166).

I felt that this type of inquiry, which Schoen called "reflective conversation," was exactly the kind I wanted to undertake in the present book. I wanted to revisit the experiences, ideas, and influential relationships that informed me during my journey, and present them from two vantage points: as I perceived them at the time and as I perceived them looking back. I wanted to create a legacy out of those situations that had acted on me most powerfully, that had wrenched my thinking and my practice out of their usual groove, and that I felt would most interest a beginning practitioner in any number of helping fields.

It is true that I have been selective in the tales I have included and the persons whose work I have highlighted. For instance, I have not included the important solution-focused approach of Berg and de Shazer, or given space to the imaginative tradition blazed by followers of Milton Erickson, or expounded on the remarkable contribution of feminism to family therapy. If I took a third-person descriptive view, as most histories of the field do and as my own books have done, I felt I would be violating my contract with myself. I wanted to include only firsthand materials and focus on the reflective conversation between myself and the ever-changing environment of my profession.

Another reason for being selective was more programmatic: I wanted to create a counter-tradition to the strategic approach that had influenced me so strongly early on. I once asked family theorist Jay Haley why he never told a trainee in one of his teaching tapes the reasons for the directives he gave. He said, "I'm not interested in 'why.' I'm only interested in 'what.'" Then he added, as if he needed an exclamation point, "Dogma!" At the time, I felt that Haley was excluding the student from the process on principle, but I began to think later that this posture had something to do with the deliberate masquerades of hypnotic technique. Partly in reaction, and partly under the influence of Gregory Bateson's (1972) notable distrust of "conscious purpose," I began to move toward a more open, more mutual, and less controlling style.

The stories in this book document my trajectory, seeking out those experiences and events that led to the stance I think of as a "different voice" (Gilligan, 1982). At the start of my journey, as I say in the first chapter, I felt like an arrow shot from a great bow. I had no idea what it was aimed at or where it would fall. At the time, I said to myself that I was crazy, that after a period of madness I would wake up and find myself back in the sane world. To my amazement, that never happened. I continued to experience the sense of being on some meaningful trajectory toward some unknowable destination. Only recently did the arrow fall to earth. Then I finally did begin to feel sane, but only because the perceptions of those around me began to match my own.

In a recent paper, social performance therapist Fred Newman (2000) describes postmodern therapy as a study of the unknowable, meaning the domain of things that cannot be "discovered" in the same way that things in the physical universe can. For this reason, he states that storytelling should be seen as "a non-explanatory mode of understanding the activity of human life." I like that idea. I want to continue to be not-knowing at the level of the road map while still exploring the road. If you are like me, you will remember the sand tunnels we used to dig as children at the beach, and that delicious final moment when the sand began to crumble and our fingers touched.

FAMILY THERAPY
AN INTIMATE HISTORY

1

group of family therapists that meet

The Mermaid Tavern

Days with the Magicians

I was born an artist's daughter. In our self-conscious American community of painters, writers, and composers, forty miles up the Hudson River from New York, everyone was by definition a little crazy. Most of the individuals I knew as I grew up had been the black sheep, scapegoats and rebels of the families they had left behind in communities in the middle or far west. We knew nothing of mental health or emotional illness, at least as those terms might apply to us.

We did know some psychiatrists. They could be met in the summer communities like Provincetown our members frequented, and it was often they who bought our paintings or commissioned us to design their houses. My mother, who was a textile designer, saw a Jungian psychoanalyst for a year, with the result that the words "introvert" and "extravert" entered the family vocabulary (I was the introvert, my mother the extravert). Then there was the psychoanalyst who was the second husband of a neighbor who was a costume designer; we pitied him as a kind of businessman who had to work in New York.

Growing up, I never had any dealings with social workers, although I had the vague belief that becoming one meant going downhill in the social scale. Neither did I ever see a psychologist except in connection with my invariably progressive schools. These persons were in the same category as the school nurse and did a mysterious kind of testing to which you never knew the score. Most striking, from my later point of view, was that none of us ever used psychological phrases when we gossiped about each other.

We did have colorful ways of describing whatever we found odd or unusual. A neighbor told me that she had once asked my father what it was like to be married to my mother. My father said, "It was like swimming behind an Olympic swimmer and having water kicked up in your face." Another family friend told me that my two younger sisters and myself were known in the community as "the Bronte sisters," and there were powerful beliefs enshrined in sayings like "Those who can, do; those who can't, teach." Our terms for people who didn't fit our norms were political, not psychological. I remember my mother calling certain persons "reactionaries" or "philistines." These epithets were applied (quite unfairly) to my mother's missionary relatives in Redlands, California, as well as people like businessmen or right-wing publishers. Rich people were especially suspect unless they could be viewed as patrons of the arts or "fellow travelers" who donated time and money to left-wing causes.

With an upbringing like that, it was no wonder that I found psychology, when I ran into it in college, an alien science. A strange new terminology had infiltrated the language of social relationships. Phrases like "she's repressed" or "you're just projecting" were used to gain traction over others and were considered very sophisticated. A variant was the use of a Freudian vocabulary as an aid to courtship. I had read a selection of Freud's work at college and was fascinated by his Sherlock Holmesian case histories and by the fact that he had taken on the Dark Continent of sexual development, which gave a heady excitement to the whole enterprise. Young men I went out with would tell me that I suffered from this or that "complex," or that I had a secret desire to possess a certain part of a man's anatomy that did not at the time interest me at all.

I had dreams of being a writer, but along with the dream came the burden of living up to my parents' generation. I was also unwilling to adopt the escape hatch of teaching (those who can't), so I entered an ambiguous world where I excelled at studies and little else. I remember being puzzled at my second-class citizenship when I walked to classes at Harvard, where women could not enter the Widener Library Reading Room or wear pants in the Harvard Yard. The mentor system did not apply to women either. The only literature professor who paid any attention to me was a poet named Theodore Spencer, who once said of me that I was like "a clear door with fog in front." In spite of the fog, I was awarded a Summa Cum Laude in English literature, and after graduating took a secretarial job for which I was supremely unqualified. Then, like most of my bright female classmates, I married a young man who was clearly destined to rise in the world.

Firmly in the grip of post-war feminine mystique, I worked at my lowly job until my husband got a higher degree than my own, and then we had three children. Years later, my daughters were amazed when they came across the one article I ever sold commercially. It was a piece for *Mademoiselle* called "Your Husband Is an Investment." I had interviewed four young wives who worked while their husbands developed their careers, and the proceeds paid for my husband's M.A. at Columbia University. He quickly got a teaching job in the theater department of Bard College up the Hudson River from New York. For a while, I continued to commute to my job. I was the "reader" at a good, grey publishing house, meaning that I read all the unsolicited manuscripts. It was the job of a bright young thing. Then I quit in order to become pregnant. To my surprise, I experienced a huge fall in status after I stopped working.

By 1963, my family had become a group of human fleas. During the previous decade, we had followed my husband from Bard, where he built a new theater; to Oxford, England, on a grant from the *Kenyon Review* to study drama; to a year at the theater department at the University of California at Berkeley; to Carnegie Mellon in Pittsburgh where my husband became head of its famous drama department; and three years later to Stanford University. Every time we moved, my self-respect dwindled. It was like one of those cotton T-shirts that shrinks every time you put it in the wash. My life had become an endless series of new schools, new supermarkets, and new "playpen pals," as my writer friend Alison Lurie put it. "Here I am again," I would muse self-consciously, "Ruth amid the alien corn."

After a year at Stanford, my husband got involved in the regional theater movement and began to travel around the country on a grant from the Ford Foundation. We had a late night talk, which my husband later referred to as the beginning of our "emotional divorce." I had not thought of it that way, but I would grant that I too was unhappy. I had no work except for home editing jobs (I specialized in psychologists who couldn't write), and I developed few friendships outside the network of faculty wives that came with each new campus. I felt guilty about being overly wrapped up in my children, and also guilty because my heart wasn't in the job. From graduating at the top of my class at Radcliffe, I had sunk to a low level indeed.

At this point, I entered a peculiar psychic state I called "verging." It was as if I were gliding down a tranquil stream in a canoe, all the while being conscious of an ominous roar ahead. I knew that I was heading for some momentous life upheaval, but I was puzzled about what that would be. Actually, I thought I was going to have a love affair. Never one for flirtations, I nevertheless cast my eye about and it fell on the caretaker of the grounds of the house we were renting in Menlo Park. Poor Mr. Willie. He was a middle-aged spinster, spare and taciturn and good at fixing things. He had become caretaker for the whole brood of us while my husband traveled, and I was inordinately grateful to him for putting up an old tire as a swing for my children. He seemed to be fixed on me, staring at me whenever we met in a stubborn, glassy way. I decided he was my Fate and asked him over for supper during one of my husband's trips. It turned out that he was not my Fate after all. At the last minute, after the children had gone to bed, I found myself steering him to the door. Relieved and disappointed in equal measure, I decided that whatever was in store for me would have to happen of its own accord.

In this mystical mood, I answered the telephone one day and heard from another faculty wife that a woman named Virginia Satir wanted an editor who could help her with a book. This Satir person was something I had never heard of: a family therapist. The young freelance editor helping her had quit and two others had turned the job down. My prejudice against psychotherapists and psychologists had, if anything, hardened. Whatever their gifts, none of them could write and they could also be hard to work with. Then I heard a voice in my head saying, "This may be your big chance." In a bemused state of mind, I said I would call.

So it was that when I went to my first meeting with Virginia, as she was known, I was bristling with premonitions. There was nothing special about the building that housed the Mental Research Institute where she worked. It was an old wooden house on a shady street in Palo Alto with lots of offices warrened away. A list of denizens hung in the hall, and I picked out one—Jay Haley—as seemingly full of promise. I still felt, you see, that I was going to meet my prince. But here I must make a digression. There is something about conversion experiences and sudden personal turnabouts that stamps the ordinary as miraculous. What happens is that the victim-to-be falls into a state of readiness and then throws her net out at random. Whoever and whatever gets caught in the net and meets certain specifications is imbued with supernatural properties from the start. Connections seem divinely preordained. Persons materialize and turn out to be a long-lost twin or soulmate. These co-victims, so to speak, are often innocent bystanders who experience nothing miraculous at all. But I am getting ahead of my story.

I was charmed by Satir. Looking back at a description I wrote at the time, I find this paragraph: "It is safe to say that Mrs. Satir does impress people. She is physically imposing. She glitters with jewelry and she likes bright, clear colors. She has a look which fits (forgive me, Virginia) the stock image of the 'sexy blonde' in America, with earth mother overtones. And she is warm. She genuinely likes her patients and her sympathy is not cloying or overdone."

I also began to hear many stories about Satir's famous optimism. An Irish colleague told me that she once met Satir at the airport in Dublin when it was raining, and her car began to leak. When the woman apologized, Satir said, "Never mind. It's only God's water." Another time Satir and my husband were on the same flight to New York. When the plane got stuck in Chicago, they found seats together in the airport. As my husband shrank into his chair and wearily contemplated the long hours between one and six in the morning, Virginia looked down at him and said cheerfully, "You know, this could be a joy!" Pretend cynic that he was, he never tired of telling this story.

Satir was also very funny. She told me about the courtly man who would find out when she was going to do a workshop in Milan and then walk ten steps behind her holding his penis in his hand. I said, "Virginia what did you do?" She said, "I thanked him for the compliment and walked on." Another story I heard was that Satir, who was very tall, was dining at a conference next to a well-known therapist who was very short. They had a pleasant conversation, and she went up to bed. At midnight, she heard a tap at the door and it was the short family therapist. He said to her, "Virginia, we had such a nice time at dinner, why don't we finish the evening together?" Virginia said to me, "You know, I was tempted. What stopped me was the discrepancy between the navel and the nose."

At our first meeting, Satir showed me the manuscript she had been working on. It was called *Conjoint Family Therapy* (1964) and was mostly finished except for a disheveled middle part. Satir told me that Don Jackson, the psychiatrist who was the director of the Mental Research Institute where she worked, intended to publish it under the stamp of his new publishing house, Science and Behavior Books. Apparently, Jackson had come to Palo Alto in 1959 as a part-time consultant to the Bateson project, and had at the same time started the Mental Research Institute. Being interested in clinical research, he had asked Satir to join him and direct a pilot project in family therapy.

During our conversation, I learned that the editor I was replacing was a writer who had already published some articles about the work of the MRI. She had become imbued with the wish to spread the family therapy word, but before the book was finished, she brought her parents and herself into therapy with Satir. Until then she had been "the favorite," but Satir was a sternly neutral therapist. The shift in relationship placed everyone in a difficult position, and she and Satir had decided they could no longer work together. I could only guess at the shards of feeling that might be lying on the floor along with the pieces of manuscript. Clearly, this place was a weather vortex with winds that could blow a person down.

Another reason why the book had fallen apart was a weakness in the theoretical chapters. Satir came from a humanist psychology background, and the feelings-oriented language of that world conflicted with the language of the MRI, which was drawn from General Systems Theory, communication theory, and cybernetics (Buckley, 1968). However, she was the kind of odd genius who used bits and pieces from the most disparate universes in her work. Sometimes, she would take on the manner of a communications engineer, asking a surprised couple, "How many value messages have you exchanged this week?" At other times, she would talk about concepts like personal growth and self-esteem. As a result, many of Satir's colleagues at the MRI were slightly embarrassed by her. One psychiatrist I spoke to told me that they felt about Satir as they would about a little girl who ran out of the house without any clothes on.

While I was working with her, I was unaware of these currents, and within three months the book was patched together and ready to go. I had put in a new paragraph that explained a concept that both puzzled and intrigued me: the double bind. Jackson told me that he was very impressed with the way I had described it. In the meantime, I was watching Satir interview families from behind a one-way screen and what I saw made me very dissatisfied. The book didn't come close to presenting what she did in all its glory. At that moment, I too became filled with a John the Baptist fervor. There was Satir, who would sail like a stately three-master into the midst of a family stormwracked by the problems of a troubled child. What she did not only calmed the waters, but gave hope and meaning to the entire scene.

Up to that time, I had assumed that there was such a thing as mental illness and that it was just like any other disorder or disease. In talking with the inhabitants of the MRI and reading the many articles produced by the Bateson group, I found that they did not believe this. The "identified patient," as the child with a problem was called, was not so much sick as unable to communicate directly. There were many secrets in these families, and many hidden rules that kept these secrets from surfacing. This explained the peculiar use of language and gesture that characterized the so-called schizophrenic. These strange behaviors were like messages sent by semaphore.

At the MRI, as I discovered, there was a presumed link between the communication style of the family and the problem of the child. Research was being done comparing "schizophrenic" families to "delinquent" families, "normal" families to "abnormal" ones. If you analyzed the conversation between a pair of parents, you supposedly could tell whether a new baby would become schizophrenic by the age of twenty. This idea led to attempts to create a typology of families that would predict for various kinds of symptoms in children. Research on this idea was suggestive but never proved, and it had pejorative implications. Just think of the "alcoholic family" and its list of losers: the "addict," the "lost" child, the "parentified child," the "codependent spouse," the "enabler," and so forth. At the time, however, I saw only a rescue operation.

This idea was typified by the operation called "taking the label off the I.P." I once saw Satir interview the family of a disturbed boy who made a "cocktail" out of condiments he found on the table in a restaurant: ketchup, salt, worcester sauce, and so forth. Satir connected this odd behavior to the feelings about drinking in the family. It turned out that the father drank, and the mother disapproved, and that this disagreement festered even though the parents never brought it up. Satir suggested that the boy's cocktails were a message, not only about the hidden conflict but about what she saw as the prohibition in the family against joy of any kind.

The intention was noble: to rescue the family's problem member from being stigmatized. Unfortunately, the opprobrium merely shifted to the family. Jackson (1957) and his colleagues had been trying to study "family homeostasis," under the assumption that the family was like an aquarium, with fish and weeds and water operating as a self-maintaining whole. When someone in the family was symptomatic, this meant that some event was threatening the balance of this world. If an older girl were about to go off to college, and if she were indispensable to the mother, a younger brother might develop symptoms. The older girl might then drop back from college to help the mother out. The implication was that the family (for which read "mother") was to blame for the problems of the child.

A related idea, shared by many early family therapists, was that behind the child's symptoms was a conflict between the parents. Whatever the presenting problem might be, it was only a cover-up for this deeper split. As Satir put it, "the child's problem hides the parents' pain" (1964, p. 4). Although it didn't occur to me at the time, the pejorative bias of psychodynamic theory had crept into this strand of the family therapy movement. The term "dysfunctional" was much valued by Satir and became one of her major legacies. She used it to replace the labels "mad" or "bad," but it put the entire family under a cloud. It is not for nothing that in some quarters family therapy has become known as "therapy against the family."

So I would like to offer another legacy for Satir: her ability to make a silk purse out of a sow's ear. We have seen a wave of interest in strengths and resources sweeping across the family therapy field, in contrast to the problem-oriented approaches of the pioneers. Satir's work was a forerunner of this trend. Realizing this, I decided to exhume a paper of mine that had lain unpublished in my files for 35 years. Written in 1964, it was called "Another Version of Virginia Satir."

Re-reading this article was a revelation for me. Having by then become aware of the implications of social construction theory, which I will describe in Chapter 12, I began to see Satir's work as a brilliant example of constructionism in practice. With language as her medium, Satir helped people to build an alternative relational world. Instead of referring to a problem, she would speak about "an accident in the interests of the self." She would say of a child's disruptive behavior, "Perhaps this is a way that he is asking that room be made for him in this family." Or if the child was seen by the parents as good, she would say, "Perhaps he is making room for everyone else's needs and not his own."

The MRI researchers called this type of move "positive reframing" (Watzlawick et al., 1974). It was supposed to counteract the resistance to change that families, being stubborn, obdurate, and mule-like, were expected to present. In the interview with Satir that Haley and I did together ("A Family of Angels," *Techniques of Family Therapy*, 1967), he repeatedly tried to get Satir to admit that her emphasis on the positive was strategic. There was a famous story about Satir's response to a man who had chased his wife around the kitchen with a hatchet. She had said to him, "You are really trying to tell your wife that you want to be closer to her, but you don't know how." Satir refused to admit that such statements had anything strategic about them. All she would say was, "You catch more flies with honey than with vinegar."

Satir did have one major enemy, which she called the "morality play." By this she meant the ideas of right and wrong that set up barriers between people and the morally loaded words that expressed them. So she created a special vocabulary. "Love" became "a value message"; "your moral duty" became "what fits"; "what are you doing wrong in this family?" became "what hurts in this family?"; "what is good?" became "what is feasible?"; "a bad thing to do" became "a distorted growth attempt"; and terms like "crazy," "sick," or "bad" became "dysfunctional." Instead of asking, "Why did you steal?" she would ask, "Why did you rob yourself?"

With this language, Satir altered relationships. For instance, she would insist on helping people listen or be listened to. She asked that, at home, they make sure that the person they were talking to heard them, by touching the person and then asking, "Are you feeling the touch?" Or she would explain that she had a "paper eardrum," a hearing device she wore, and would ask people to speak louder. If a daughter spoke in a small, insignificant voice, she would act as an amplifier. If a father used loud angry tones she would say, "I think Dad is feeling hurt inside."

Another of her techniques was to take a criticism that one person made about another and generalize it. In an interview where a sister complained about her brother's swearing, Satir went round the room and everyone but the brother agreed that swearing was hurtful, vulgar, and wrong. Going round again, she found that everyone in the family did swear, including the offended sister. Then she pointed out the "discrepancy," saying, "Isn't it funny how everyone in this family swears yet everyone agrees it is a harmful thing to do? This is one of the ways people in the family hurt each other." Later, the brother explained why he thought swearing was okay: "I thought all men swore when they got together over a highball or something. Like my Dad and Mr. H., they'll be talking, and one of them will say 'Balls,' or something." The father protested that not all men felt they had to swear; he was shocked that his behavior had given his son this idea. By labeling the confusion as a "discrepancy," Satir was able to validate the boy's perception while not putting the father in the wrong.

I will end this reminiscence of Satir with an anecdote that impressed me very much. This was an interview she did with the family of a policeman whose son had stolen a car. The boy was on probation and living with a foster family. He told Satir that he knew he was doing wrong when he stole it, but she countered him, saying, "I don't believe that. I think you had a different purpose in mind, that you saw it fitting you in some way that was good." The boy agreed, and said, "Well, my friend's relatives had this ranch up near Sonoma, and he told me a lot about the town. It sounded real nice, with all those hick policemen and women and all. We were going to saw wood and make money that way, and I wasn't ever going to come back."

The boy had broken probation by seeing some members of his old gang. He explained that they had been meeting and getting away with it so he thought he could too. So Satir said to him, "You, of all those boys, must be careful about getting caught because you are marked out, made special, by your talent, your intelligence, your good looks. The people who are trying to help you, myself included, will be angry if you disappoint them to the same degree that they are attracted by your potential." As I watched, I saw the boy's head lift sharply and the depressed-looking policeman father straighten his back, as if to look the world in the eye.

Most early family therapy had been aimed at locating a cause for the problem, but Satir went in a different direction from the start. She gave all her attention to leading families out of the shadow of blame, coming as close as anyone did in those days to inventing a no-fault type of practice. She also showed me what a therapy that created possibilities rather than correcting pathologies might be like. She was a skillful weaver who asked the family to join her in making handsome, useful textiles from the most unlikely threads.

The Inner Sanctum

While I was working on Virginia's book, I found much else to interest me. I had begun to read reprints of the more than 70 articles produced during the ten years of Bateson's research project. I also got a copy of a book by Haley that had just been published called *Strategies of Psychotherapy* (1963). This was the first book on a psychological subject I had ever read that was written in ordinary English. I felt like a medieval monk getting hold of the Bible in the vernacular. Instead of hiding behind a screen of jargon, this book spoke straight to me, and the ideas it held amazed me. Haley not only criticized the insight-oriented approaches of that time, but also made a hit list of psychological abstractions like "affect" or "drive" that were to be banished from the kingdom. In one chapter that dripped with irony, he described psychoanalytic practice as a particularly gifted example of humorist Stephen Potter's theory of gamesmanship. In my eyes, he demolished its claims for good.

I also had lengthy talks with Jackson, a tall, fair-haired man who looked more like a tennis pro than anyone's idea of a psychiatrist and seemed to reign over his little principality like a god. His visions regarding his publishing enterprise were extremely grand. Like many people who had become infected by the concept of the family "system," he was convinced that he had stumbled on a true revolution. *Pragmatics of Human Communication* (1967), which Jackson co-authored with Paul Watzlawick and Janet Beavin (now Bavelas), summarized much of the original thinking and research that had come out of the years of the Bateson group.

One of Jackson's best traits was his acceptance of people who did not have the right credentials, as long as they were bright. He liked the work I had done on Satir's book and invited me to the Thursday bag lunch meetings where the house researchers presented their findings. I was thrilled to be part of these events. The people who attended seemed to be neither scientists nor artists, but some combination of both species, like a mermaid. I had been looking for a Mermaid Tavern to belong to, a place where I would be allowed to hang out with sweet Will Shakespeare and rare Ben Johnson. Even though the MRI was basically a boys' club, Satir's project offered me the opportunity to converse with Mistress Quickly as well.

Jackson continued to employ me to edit books on his list. Overwhelmed by a longing to be more than just an onlooker, I began to set down my own opinions about Satir's work. This turned into the paper that I spoke about before. It was tortuous and inelegant and far too long but when I showed it to Jackson he said it showed promise. He suggested I let Haley read it for possible inclusion in a magazine he edited called *Family Process*. Offhandedly, he told me that Haley had recently separated from his wife. As there was no context for this remark, I was astounded that he would say such a thing, but it did tell me that I was part of the inner sanctum. And needless to say, it played into the many schemes and fantasies that were budding in my mind.

By this time I had become intensely curious about the now-defunct Bateson project and had decided to go around and interview everybody who had belonged to it. Jackson's suggestion gave me a good excuse to visit Haley. From attending the Thursday bag lunch meetings, I had found that he was a tall, stooped man of about forty with a forelock perpetually hanging over one eye. He stayed in the back of the room and looked very gloomy, exciting all kinds of questions in my head. He also had an air of untouchability. "Don't bother me," his demeanor seemed to say and, but for my article, I never would have dared to do so.

So one morning I went round to the discontinued church where Haley had his office, gave him my article, and made a date to return. At our next meeting, he told me he liked it and if I rewrote it to be more in line with a professional journal, he would run it by the editors. I remember being overjoyed and incredulous. This forbidding man, whose unorthodox mind had so greatly impressed me, thought that my paper was worthy of his attention. Haley might not remember details like this, but the times he praised me stood out for me like meteors in a night sky. Once he said, "You have thoughts that never even cross my mind." And on another occasion he said that what he most appreciated about me was that I was naive. Statements like that evoked in me sheer gratitude.

At that point, I asked Haley to tell me about the Bateson project. He obliged; it was obviously a period that he looked back on with interest and pride. The somber gentleman of the bag lunch meetings vanished and in his place was a lively and engaging raconteur. It was like seeing a dark, untrimmed fir tree turn into a Christmas tree with lights. Our conversation touched on a dizzying range of topics: from schizophrenia to otters, from play to paradox, from movies to hypnosis, and back in time for tea. By this time, of course, I was deep in some kind of trance. Before I knew it, it was noon. I got up to go, swimming on a cloud of air, and heard myself asking Haley a peculiar question: "What am I going to do with you?" He, in turn, acted as if he had merely been waiting for me to say that. He suggested that I help him do an interview project that he had begun with John Weakland. It had been shelved because neither of them wanted to do the dirty work.

Readers, I grabbed gladly at the chance. Haley explained his idea for a book of interviews he wanted to do with a number of pioneering family therapists of his choice. He would ask each of these people to select an audiotape of a first session. Then he would play it back to them, asking them why they said what they said, step by step, and what they thought was going on. That discussion would be taped too and somebody (me) would edit the results. Hopefully, a product would fall out of this process that would lay bare the mysteries of family therapy for all to see. I went out of

that office feeling that the Christmas tree had just given me all its orna-
ments. But the terrible thing was: I was in love.

Now when I say "love," I do not mean puppy love or infatuation love or
worshipful love or lustful love or platonic love, although my love felt at
times like all of these. It was something I will call a change-of-state love.
The effect was of a lightning bolt splitting my life as if it were a big oak,
and one half falling one way and the other half the other. At other times I
imagined that I was being shot like an arrow from a great bow. I felt that
some mysterious force had launched me upon a trajectory whose destination was as yet unknown. From then on I walked into the Thursday meetings with the secret knowledge that I was a mysterious lady who was going
to do great things. On the other hand, I knew that I was crazy, since none
of these possibilities had been credible a short time before. The downside
of my elation was confusion and despair. My idol seemed even more unap-
proachable now that he seemed to welcome me into the magic circle, and
a band of invisible iron seemed to keep the two of us apart.

Looking back with the wisdom of hindsight, I have to admit that thirty-
five years later most of the prophecies have come true, although after many
turns in the road and in radically different forms than I ever imagined. The
story, as it unfolded, was a wonderful illustration of the idea that the lunacy
of today may make tomorrow's sense. But I did not then know this, and in
between the times when I was congratulating myself with idiot abandon, I
was muttering, "Those whom the Gods wish to destroy, they first make
mad."

Let me dispose once and for all the idea that Haley and I ever got
together except in the most business-like, collegial sense. There seemed to
be a prohibition against intimacy, which on my side came from a deep wish
to avoid embarrassment. I was married; Haley was married. Our relationship was limited to two or three meetings a week when I would bring over
the parts of the interview book I had worked on. Then I would sit back and
listen to tales about Bateson and Erickson and all the other memorable
characters of those days. But there was one story that stood out for me, and
here it is.

The Smile of the Mona Lisa

Since I was not sure that I understood the double bind, I asked Haley to
explain its history. He told me that Bateson was interested in messages that
were delivered on two levels—one consisting of a statement and the other
indicating how the statement was to be understood. Examples of such dou-
ble-level messages could be found in areas like play, paradox, and animal
communication. In the case of otters, a creature Bateson would watch at the

San Francisco Zoo, the message "This is play" was embedded in gestures that resembled an attack but then did no harm. The bite would be a play bite, so that both animals would know what was going on. But what happened in cases where the qualifying cue was self-contradictory or confusing and an important relationship was at stake? Bateson surmised that there might be a breakdown and peculiar behavior might result. This was why he and some of his younger researchers began to visit the Palo Alto V.A. Hospital to study what they called "schizophrenic communication."

Here is where my memory of Haley's story becomes apocryphal, a product of too many tellings, but I will repeat it anyway. Bateson had received an initial grant to research paradoxes in communication. In two years, the grant ran out. The group had studied and written about subjects like ventriloquism, or the training of guide dogs for the blind, but nothing had really come together. Bateson's young researchers went to him and said, "Gregory, we need another grant, but this time we have to be more specific." He said, "Let me think about it," and went off. When he came back he said, "I know what we can do. We can study the double bind." They asked, puzzled, "What is the double bind?" He said, "That's what our grant will find out." So they got a grant to study the double bind. A couple of years later, the money ran out again. The young men went back to Bateson and said, "We need another grant, but this time we need to come up with an example of the double bind." He said, "Let me think about it," and went off. Finally he came to them and said, "I have an example of the double bind." They said, "What is it, Gregory, what is it?" He said: "It's the smile on the face of the Mona Lisa."

Stories about Milton Erickson were another staple of our conversations. If Virginia's accent on the positive was astounding, Erickson's was even more so. Erickson's work modeled for Haley a new kind of therapy based on a directive, strategic stance. This was part of Haley's war against the psychoanalytic establishment. Where analytically-influenced therapists sat back and said little (and, according to Haley, did less), Erickson busily sought out a person's area of resourcefulness and put it to work. I particularly remember the story of the elderly woman who was illiterate but wished to learn to read. Erickson helped her to read by using analogies from carpentry, because that was one thing she could do very well.

Erickson's most famous device was to give people paradoxical tasks. He would tell them to fight on purpose, stay awake on purpose, and stutter on purpose. When these directives worked, they worked with extraordinary swiftness. Clinicians who had spent a lifetime helping people gain insight into symptoms that stubbornly refused to disappear tried paradox and they suddenly vanished. Many years later, I met MRI psychiatrist Richard Fisch at a workshop we were both attending, and I decided to interview him in *wetting herself*

front of everybody. I asked him what had led him to leave his psychoanalytic roots behind and become an interactional therapist. He said he had
heard about the exploits of Milton Erickson and decided to try a paradox
with a woman who lived in dire fear of wetting herself whenever she went
out. Nothing had worked and she was becoming unable to leave home, so
Fisch suggested that before going to work the next morning, she stand in
the bathtub, urinate while fully dressed, then go to work. She never wet
herself again and was able to resume a normal life. This so astounded the
young psychiatrist that he became an immediate convert.

There were many explanations for the success of these moves. In this
case, you could say that the woman's fear of wetting was the problem—
once she had wet herself, the fear was gone. Others took the position that
paradoxical directives were instances of reverse psychology. Yet others
turned to game theory. Haley believed that people with problems were
playing a control game. If the therapist prescribed the symptom, the client
would have to abandon it in order to "win." After years of thought, I have
come to a simpler conclusion. A therapist who encourages a symptom promotes a habit of acceptance, which is in itself helpful. In Virginia's work, and
also I suspect in Erickson's, a key element lay in preventing everyone, especially the therapist, from pulling any tighter on the Gordian knot.

As I said in the introduction, the rhetorical emphasis of the Ericksonians
was a clean break with the etiological bias of most other psychotherapy
schools. It was also a great step forward. In return for giving up the com-
forts of causality, you increased the chances that therapy would be a blame-
free environment. Even so, I was not totally comfortable with the emphasis
on outwitting people for their own good, nor did I see therapy as a struggle for control. The belief that the clinician had to conceal her working
assumptions seemed wrong too. This mystique might protect the therapist,
but it put the client at a disadvantage. Satir had showed me that it was possible to be open about what you were doing without lessening your influence. Without realizing it, I was already selecting the strands of transparency
that were to crystallize later on.

But at that time, I had no idea that I would ever do therapy myself. I busied myself with the interview book with Haley, which immediately ran into
snags. I had assumed that we would include Satir but Haley doubted that
she would agree. He had just published an article in *Family Process* (1962)
in which he had described Satir's work as the "Great Mother" school of
family therapy, and he had heard that she was miffed. So it was up to me to
play mediator. I went to Satir and told her that Haley had heard that his
article had upset her, but that he very much wanted to include her in our
book. She was surprised and doubtful, but I talked her into accepting our
offer. Then I shuttled back to Haley and told him that she didn't feel hurt

at all and was very pleased to join us. Lies in the interest of science, as I told myself.

So we lugged Haley's big Tandberg audio machine with its old fashioned reels over to Satir's office and recorded what we both thought was a magnificent interview. But when we went back to Haley's office to listen to it we got—nothing! Haley had forgotten to punch the "on" button. He wanted to abandon the interview then and there but I convinced him to give it another try. Back we went, improving on our previous performance greatly. I have always thought that this interview, which is called "A Family of Angels," is one of the best portraits of Satir at work that I know.

My next attempt to enlist a notable pioneer fell flat on its face. Without telling Haley, I decided to visit Nathan Ackerman, the founder of the Ackerman Institute for Family Therapy in New York. Way back in the thirties, Ackerman had written about the family as a "social and emotional unit" (1937), and by the sixties he was inventing a brilliantly novel approach to working with families (1966). Even though I knew that Ackerman and Haley weren't close, I assumed that Haley would go along with me if I captured him, just as he had done with Satir. Since I was going on a trip to New York anyway, I phoned Ackerman, explained who I was, and asked if he would see me. Of course, he said he would.

I found Ackerman to be a sturdy, cigar-chomping little man who didn't waste his time on useless politeness. When I explained about our interview book, he told me that he and Haley had long been at odds and that there was a long-standing feud between the "warmhearted clinicians" of the East Coast and the "coldhearted researchers" of the West Coast. They certainly came from different worlds. Ackerman used the more insight-oriented language of psychodynamics in working with a family. Haley, as I have said before, openly ridiculed psychoanalysis, and his approach was more that of a social engineer.

After much doubting on Ackerman's part, I prevailed upon him to become part of our book, but when I went back and told Haley, he refused to agree. He gave what seemed to me a spurious rationale. Ackerman was famous for his demonstration interviews, after which the family's primary therapist, who in most instances was a psychiatrist named Paul Franklin, would continue with the case. This meant, Haley said, that Ackerman didn't really do family therapy, only "family demonstrations." No matter how hard I tried, I couldn't get Haley to change his mind. I don't remember what I told Ackerman, but I do remember feeling frustrated and annoyed.

The other problem was the matter of publication. By the time the book was finished, I had taken the first two chapters (the interviews with Satir and Jackson) to Basic Books and they had agreed to publish it. I felt this was a real coup and hastened to let Haley know. Haley then notified Jackson, who refused to give us permission to publish with anyone but himself. He wanted to create a series of monographs, one for each therapist we interviewed, which were to be printed on tinted paper. Also, he objected to the inclusion of "unknown" family therapists like Charles Fulweiler (one of Haley's discoveries) in a series that included Satir and himself. Haley wasn't too happy about Jackson's reaction, but told me he didn't want to alienate him.

I had always deferred to Haley before, but I told him that I would throw the manuscript, of which I had the only copy, into the trash rather than let Jackson publish it. Tinted paper, indeed! Why not toilet paper? In any case, Jackson had not contributed anything but his interview to the preparation of the book and I was no longer working for him. Then Satir told Haley that she was upset because Jackson had been funneling her royalties back into his publishing operation. Haley wrote Jackson a very stiff letter complaining on her behalf and refusing to publish with him. So we went ahead with Basic Books, and in 1967, four years after its inception, *Techniques of Family Therapy* appeared.

Alas, the world took no notice, not even the miniscule family therapy world. Even before it was published, Haley told me he was disappointed because the book was only a portrait of five master therapists at work. He had hoped that a theory of family therapy would fall out of it, and when it didn't, he refused to write a theoretical introduction. But I was not disappointed. I knew of no other account that led readers step by step through such a secret world as the therapy process had always been, and allowed them to come to their own conclusions, uncontaminated by the opinion of an expert.

In 1966, well before the book came out, my Palo Alto connection came to an end. I moved to New York City, where my husband, Ted, was starting a theater program at NYU. Not too long after, Haley was invited to join Minuchin at the Philadelphia Child Guidance Clinic. At that time, as I remember, the great dream of my life was to stand on the same stage with Haley at a family therapy conference. It turned out that the publication of the book marked the end of our collaboration, but our lives had touched and the arrow was still speeding on its way.

2

Outdoor Therapy Eco-system view · person in environment

Ecologies of Hope

During the four-day cross-country drive from California to New York, with my husband at the wheel, I found myself prone to fits of silent weeping behind my sunglasses. I realized that these fits occurred around 10:30 in the morning, the time I was usually sitting with Haley and talking or working on our book. I supposed the tears were a kind of temporary mourning that brought us back together. In California, I had inhabited a reality-based dream that rescued me from my isolation and made it tolerable. In the defunct church with Haley, I could fly, but I feared that once I no longer had that place to spread my wings in, I would crash.

As a result, I began to search for a substitute for my vanished world. It never occurred to me that my children might also need a world. Heaven knows how they experienced the situation, with a father absorbed in a demanding job, and their mother an absentee landlady whose spirit was never at home. I had also begun to rely on prescription drugs. A doctor had prescribed Miltown for me, and I went around trapped in a haze of self-medication until I found out that the drug was addictive and quit it cold.

This was altogether one of the worst periods of my life. Unfortunately, there were no support groups in those days for crazy, despairing mothers, and my distrust of the psychiatric profession was so great that I refused to go near it. My connection with family therapy only fed my fears. During the late sixties, there was a growing sentiment against conventional psychiatry on the grounds that, by diagnosing mental illness, doctors created it. Haley had once said, "There is no such thing as a schizophrenic in the wild, untouched by the hand of a helper." I was sure that I myself was a schizophrenic in the wild, and the hand of a helper was the last thing I wanted to touch.

This book may be criticized on the grounds that its author was not successful with her own problems, but this was also a reason for writing it. Looking for help as an individual sufferer in my early thirties, I found only hindrance. After my first child was born, I had what felt to me like a nervous breakdown, and went to see a psychiatrist in a small city near the college where my husband was teaching. He was a former dermatologist from England who worked with the unfortunate poor in a local hospital. Physically unattractive, he reminded me of a blown-up version of Alfred Hitchcock, protruding stomach and no chin, but I had no other standards to judge him by. It turned out that his approach was to prescribe reserpine, a recent discovery that turned me into a jittering zombie. If that didn't work, he offered to enroll me in his "little shock club," which met every Friday afternoon. He was also very frank in telling me that I was "too bohemian," and that I should find a hobby, like flower-arranging.

My next experience, after the birth of my second child, was with a psychologist. He was a fatherly, pleasant person who seemed very interested in my story; in fact, he recorded it all on an old-fashioned tape machine. I remember talking about my sexual fantasies and disappointments in great detail. Then he started to touch me, asking about the material of my jacket, for instance, and rubbing it between his fingers. When he started to give me a lingering hug at the end of each session, I realized this wasn't so innocent. I wondered how to get out of the situation. If I faced him with my fears, he might tell me I was "resisting treatment." So I wrote him a letter and said that I had this fantasy that he had a "case" on me, and that even though I was probably wrong, it would do little good to continue. He never charged me for the last session.

So by the time I hit New York, I knew better than to look for a therapist. Instead, I went looking for another Mermaid Tavern, but as New York was an analytic town, most of the people I knew were in emotional bondage to shrinks. Nobody had ever heard of family therapy, let alone Gregory Bateson or Jay Haley. I lent my autographed copy of Haley's *Strategies of Psychotherapy* to a college friend in the publishing world, hoping that she would recognize the genius of the work, and she returned it in damp condition, explaining apologetically that it had fallen into the bathtub. My poor mutilated icon! But I persisted. I remember going into Barnes & Noble on Fifth Avenue and looking through all the sections: psychology, social psychology, sociology, anthropology, philosophy, religion, even mathematics, biology and engineering, and finding nothing except some texts on computing. I went out of that store weeping with frustration. It wasn't until I accidentally stumbled onto Walter Buckley's *Modern Systems Research for the Behavioral Scientist* (1968) that I realized that what I had caught by the tail in Palo Alto was not a new comet; it was just one that had not yet appeared in New York skies.

In the course of my search for "systems" people, an acquaintance introduced me to the late Edgar H. Auerswald, who was starting an Applied Behavioral Sciences Program at Gouverneur Heath Services on the Lower East Side. Auerswald, a child analyst turned community psychiatrist, had been working with the families of poor, minority children at the Wiltwyck School for Boys in New York state. The signature book that came out of that work was *Families of the Slums* (1968), written by a team that included family therapy researcher and psychiatrist Salvador Minuchin and psychologist Braulio Montalvo. Auerswald would have been one of the authors if he had not left Wiltwyck to go to Gouverneur. I began to think that Wiltwyck had been the East Coast equivalent of the Palo Alto group. When Auerswald asked me to join his program as staff historian, I jumped at the chance.

In this way, I fantasized, I could continue my link with Haley. I had left California thrilled by my discoveries about family communication. I had learned that everyone lived in what I thought of as loyalty fields, webs of sympathy and antipathy, exerting pulls and counterpulls. Family therapy too was such a web, and it comforted me that Haley and I were both part of it. Auerswald's ideas were particularly interesting because he was using a Batesonian ecological metaphor that both supplemented and challenged the family systems one. Family therapy had taken the onus off the person only to put it on the family, and the enlarged scope that ecology brought in felt to me more just. However, I knew little about the community mental health movement. I simply called what Auerswald did "outdoor therapy," in contrast to the "indoor therapy" that took place in a clinician's office.

Just to bring back some picture of this generous man, imagine an office door always open to a busy hall where the Applied Behavioral Health Program's staff had their offices. Auerswald's ample girth was always displayed at an angle to his desk, which faced the door, and he sat with a phone to his ear. He was always accessible, always willing to talk with you about ideas, projects, a new article, a difficult situation, family therapy gossip. His office was a combination telephone central, from which he maintained his connection to the far reaches of his Lower East Side empire, and the entrance to a hive, with bees constantly buzzing in and out.

One example of Auerswald's ecological thinking was the Mobile Crisis Unit: a Volkswagen bus and a team comprised of a community psychiatrist, a social worker, a social health technician from the community, and a

Spanish-speaking driver. The Crisis Unit defied the usual limitations of bureaucratic time and space, offering round-the-clock availability and on-site service anywhere in Gouverneur's catchment area. It embodied a term that we used much later, "problem system," because it placed the dilemma and everyone connected with it in one large, ambulatory package. Auerswald did not think of himself as a family therapist, because with poor populations so much else was in play. He did not hold with group therapy either, because groups were artificial and based on notions of individual pathology. The Crisis Unit was his wide-angled way of handling the clashing of persons and environmental forces that were our daily fare.

Related to the Crisis Unit was Auerswald's Family Health Team, a pilot project in which families in a given district were assigned to a team of medical and behavioral professionals who acted as a collective general practitioner. As all family members would be seen by the same group, there would be a shared knowledge of the connections between the health events of family members and other factors in a family's life. In an important paper, Auerswald (1968) compared the usual "interdisciplinary team," in which each specialist works in an isolated manner with a person or a body-part, with an "ecosystemic team," where information is exchanged across disciplinary lines and across the conceptual boundaries that isolate the individual. In the team's weekly meetings, the interplay between a child's hearing problem, a mother's depression, and a father's job loss could be laid out and understood in a holistic way.

One of Auerswald's best ecological inventions was his "chairman of the case" conference for multisystemic problems. I have found gatherings of this kind consistently useful in cases when many levels of authority, representing many agendas, are trying to cope with a family in trouble. We used to say in family therapy, "If you're stuck, add more bodies." In ecologically complex situations, Auerswald would simply widen the scene to include as many of the key players as possible: the symptomatic person, the relevant family members, important outsiders like a minister or a teacher, agency people such as the welfare worker, the welfare worker's supervisor, and so forth. Auerswald would meet with all of them in one large room.

The way Auerswald conducted a chairman of the case conference was this: he would ask each person present to explain his or her stake in a case, and describe what he or she thought should be done. Then he would ask the group to come up with an ad hoc "chairman" to coordinate the various lines of attack. A meeting like this was crucial in that it exposed contradictory views that otherwise would remain hidden and forestalled interventions that might conflict. Once out in the open, these differences could be dealt with. In addition, Auerswald often dealt with city bureaucracies, where a welfare worker would have to get permission from a higher-level person to do something useful but unconventional, so he often included supervisors.

In general, Auerswald acted more as a presiding genius than a clinician. On the rare occasions when I saw him interview a family, I noticed that his work had certain trademarks. The most notable one, aside from his reluctance to use medication, was his war against diagnostic labeling. He foresaw the inexorable creep of the system of nomenclature that has now captured the institution of psychiatry and did what he could to undermine it. If he could find any environmental or cultural reason for someone's unwanted behavior, no matter how far the reach, he was a happy man. He would gladly accept a cognitive disability if it got a child off the hook of being "bad."

For this reason, Auerswald did not disdain biology. He had an abiding interest in contemporary research on cognition and felt that cognitive deficits might account for some of the lacks and limitations shown by inner-city children. Despite my not having a postgraduate degree, he asked me to lead a group of students from the Yeshiva School of Social Work in a seminar called "The Ecosystem of a Child." In Auerswald's view, it wasn't enough to see the child in the context of the family. For him, children's cognitive territories were shaped not only by their intimate relationships but by the environment they grew up in. I am always reminded here of writer Annie Dillard's phrase, "The river fits and shapes its banks as the mind fits and shapes its world" (1994).

In line with his interest in cognitive studies, Auerswald hired a young French psychologist, Mireille Demeuron, who had trained with Jean Piaget. Children were often sent to Gouverneur by the local schools to be tested for "minimal brain damage" or MBD (the acronym of the day), so that they could be transferred out of mainstream classes. Demeuron tested these children with Piagetian instruments that often showed that their stage of cognitive development did not match their grade level. As a result, they would be unable to do certain tasks required by their teachers. Alternatively, she might find that they had dyslexia or trouble with hearing or sight. In the case of Hispanic children, there was always the problem of language. For instance, Demeuron found that a question on an intelligence test used in the local secondary schools asked the test taker to distinguish between "huckleberries" and "blueberries." These were fruits a Hispanic child might never have seen.

Another feature of Auerswald's practice was his attention to cultural differences. He believed that what looked like crazy behaviors could often be seen as responses to cultural or social dissonance rather than evidence of an inherent disorder. He would see a Puerto Rican woman who was acting hysterical and refusing to go out of her apartment because of "the junkies outside the door," and instead of medicating or hospitalizing her for agoraphobia, he would get the Welfare Department to prescribe her a telephone. His reasoning was that somewhere in the city lived a friend or relative with a telephone who came from the same village. Chances were that once the person's natural network was activated, the appearance of craziness would melt away.

One interview I will never forget involved a staff psychiatrist named Robert Ravich who used a "train game" to predict patterns of relationships between couples (1974). A Puerto Rican mother had consulted Ravich because she was afraid that her fourteen-year-old son was taking drugs. She would come into her son's room unannounced, the boy would get angry with her, and they would quarrel. Learning that she had a spiritual advisor, or priest, Ravich asked her to bring the advisor and his wife, who acted as his medium, in for an interview. The advisor, his wife, and the mother came in first. I was behind the one-way screen ready to videotape, but they refused to give us permission. Then the boy arrived. When he saw the priest sitting there, he bolted. His mother explained that he was terrified of the priest. We went ahead with the consultation anyway.

The advisor at first doubted that his wife would go into trance in front of strangers. All of a sudden her head dropped onto her shoulder and the "spirits" began to speak. All I heard was garbled sounds, but her husband translated. What the spirits advised the mother to do was to buy a can of "Aerosol de Poder" from the local Puerto Rican drug store and spray it around the boy's room. This would deter the evil spirits, but the spray was so powerful that it could be dangerous for the mother to enter the room herself. At the end of this message, the wife came out of what seemed like a trance state and looked about in confusion. Her husband said she usually did not remember what the spirits had said. Ravich told us later that the mother had obeyed their instructions and that the quarreling had stopped. At the time, I assumed this was because the "spirits" had blocked the intrusive behavior of the mother but in retrospect I see that I was thinking with a causal, Western mind.

A more debunking story about the world of the spiritual advisor was told to me by Gloria Cruz, a gifted social health technician who worked at Gouverneur, and whose aunt was one of this elite group. One time a woman had come to see her aunt because she kept getting into fights with her husband. The aunt had given the woman a vial of holy water and told her that when her husband came home from work, she must fill her mouth with this water and hold it there for a long time without swallowing it, otherwise it would make her sick. Gloria had asked her aunt if this water was special or if it had been blessed by a priest. Her aunt said, "It's only tap water, but as soon as that woman's husband comes home, she opens her big mouth, and from then on you know there's going to be trouble."

While working at Gouverneur, I documented many situations that exemplified an ecosystemic approach. Part of my job was to write about and videotape the program's work. However, I had no license that allowed me to work with clients directly. I was fairly naive about the caste system of mental health until I began to study the pecking order of the weekly meeting of the staff. My "results," statistically insignificant though they might be, were stark. Auerswald, as the director, had only to lift his head and the Red Sea parted. The staff psychiatrists raised a finger and they were recognized. The psychologists raised their hands, and the social workers raised their arms. The social health technicians, who were African-American or Hispanic women from the community, never raised anything. They only spoke when spoken to, and the same rule seemed to apply to me.

However, as staff historian I had great freedom. The Crisis Unit's first director was a psychiatrist called Richard Rabkin who had worked with Auerswald at Wiltwyck. He had written a witty, philosophical book called *Inner and Outer Space* (1968), which poked holes in several articles of psychiatric faith. After we met, I shared my dark secret, which was that I didn't know the meaning of the word ecology. Rabkin went into a long digression about an afternoon sitting on a Fire Island beach watching the various species—sandpipers, crabs, seagulls—as they came and went with the tides, prospering together in a mutually regulated way. Rabkin's erudition was a blessing for me. I rejoiced when I had the privilege of videotaping the only family therapy interview on which he and Auerswald ever collaborated.

The Father of His Country

This story concerned a six-year-old African-American boy named Washington, who had been referred to the Crisis Unit by the school because of his clowning and his disruptive behaviors. His mother, Mrs. J., a handsome, educated African-American woman, was a single parent with a full-time job. Wash, as her son was called, had two older sisters, but their father had been out of the home since the parents had divorced, two years before. After the Crisis Unit made an initial home visit, the family came in for a consultation.

Present were the family, Rabkin, and a Gouverneur social worker. Behind the screen were Auerswald, an African-American social health technician, and myself. Wash put on an extraordinary show of strutting and posturing, while his older sisters giggled and egged him on. Mrs. J. sat very calmly, only saying "Wash" in a low, admonitory voice when the noise level got too high. Rabkin asked a few questions, then came behind the screen to watch the family. This intermittent observing was something the staff used to do at the Wiltwick School. When Rabkin went back into the interviewing room, he asked the family to explain an exchange that had mentioned George Washington. The older sister said that Wash had said he wanted to go to Washington state. Wash broke in to explain that he really wanted to go live with his father, whose name was George Washington. Mrs. J. pointed out that this was not his father's real name, but the day before had been Washington's Birthday and Wash might have been thinking about that.

Then Wash said he wanted to "skip some numbers," which his sister translated to mean that he wanted to be grown up. He elaborated, saying, "I'm going in the Army and win the war." Rabkin asked him about his father, but he refused, saying "I don't want to open my big mouth." He pulled his sweater over his ears and sat mute and all bunched up. The girls went on giggling to each other. Mrs. J. said, "He does that because he thinks the girls are making fun of him." Rabkin asked her to explain to Wash that his sisters weren't really trying to be mean. Instead, she asked him if he felt bad because his sisters were teasing him. He only pulled the sweater higher over his head. Rabkin said, "Sure he does." Then he said, with emphasis, "I'm on Washington's side."

Rabkin then asked Mrs. J. to sit next to Wash and tell him three good things about himself, which she did. Next he suggested that Wash ask his mother to tell him about the divorce. Behind the screen, Auerswald saw that the sisters were jiggling up and down and giggling. He went into the room and pointed out that, at the precise moment when Wash and his mother began to talk about the father, his sisters began to make a lot of noise. He wondered if this topic might be frightening to them. Rabkin turned to Mrs. J. and asked her if she thought Wash might be afraid to ask questions about the divorce. This bit of transcript followed.

MRS. J.:	Why do you think we broke up, Wash? (*tries to make him sit up*)
WASH:	I can't, because it's going to make me cry. (*starts to sob*)
SISTER:	I know, I know. Because you get angry.
MRS. J.:	Why don't you want to hear it, Wash?
WASH:	Because it makes me cry.
AUERSWALD:	Do you think it's your fault, Wash? (*nods yes*) Because it isn't, you know.
MRS. J.:	Do you think your father and I broke up because of you, Wash? Are you going to talk to me? Hm? (*Wash continues to sob.*)

AUERSWALD:	I think he thinks that in some way he had something to do with it. I don't think that's true, Wash. I think that is a mistake.
MRS. J.:	Actually, he hadn't anything to do with our breaking up. Only I don't know what could have happened that would give him this idea, you know?
AUERSWALD:	Children try to explain something they don't understand, and very often they'll make up some explanation that involves themselves. But I think you can tell him he had nothing to do with it.
RABKIN:	Tell him that by being friendly. I don't think you have to discuss it at any great length. You just have to hug him and say, "Oh, that's silly!" Can you give him a hug right now? (*Mrs. J. starts to embrace Wash, who turns away and breaks again into a loud wail.*)
MRS. J.:	(*laughing apologetically*) He acts even sillier when I try to do it. Wash, no, come on, seriously. (*Wash is still wailing loudly and wriggling away.*)
RABKIN:	Even if he doesn't want it, it's very important.
MRS. J.:	Wash, you *know*, I don't have to tell you, you *know* you had nothing to do with it.
WASH:	(*weeping*) I *didn't* know.
MRS. J.:	What do you mean, you didn't know? I want you to tell me why you thought you had anything to do with it. Huh?
RABKIN:	Just tell him it's silly. There's no why in it.
MRS. J.:	I just want to know what he's feeling, why he thinks he had anything to do with it. (*turns to Wash again, questioning him gently*)
SISTER:	(*in a hushed voice*) Mommy, want a tissue? (*She brings one over. Mrs. J. dries Washington's nose and eyes.*)
AUERSWALD:	(*to Mrs. J.*) Is he OK? (*to Wash*) Isn't it nice to have sisters who love you?
WASHINGTON:	No! I hate girls! They just get you in trouble.
RABKIN:	(*who has been talking to the two girls*) Mrs. J., you have to tell Wash that the girls have been trying to help you make Wash feel better. They can also help Wash if they can stop getting in between you.
AUERSWALD:	(*to Wash*) You know, I was watching your sisters when you were feeling bad, and they were feeling bad for you, they weren't giving you a hard time. They certainly weren't laughing at you. They were feeling very sad.

Shortly after this, Rabkin suggested ending the interview, and the family left after agreeing to a follow-up interview at home the next week. What fascinated me was a later discussion between Auerswald and Rabkin. Auerswald, speaking from a cognitive framework, said that it was crucial to correct the child's erroneous belief that it was he who had caused his parents to break up. He felt that without this shift in perception, nothing would get better. Rabkin disagreed. For him the important thing was to build up the affection and support between Wash and his mother and sisters, and he was extremely directive on that score. It was interesting to me to see how Rabkin zeroed in on the emotional connections between people, pushing them in a more positive direction, where Auerswald focused on changing perceptions and beliefs. Both had the same goal, to take the pressure off the little boy, but they used different modalities for their interventions. This was the first time I had seen such a vivid clash of practices in a family therapy session. The odd thing was that when the two psychiatrists conversed theoretically, they sounded as if they were coming from the same page.

However, the differences between their therapeutic models were soon rendered moot. Shortly after the Gouverneur interview, Wash began attending a new school—preceded by his record. Knowing his reputation as a classroom terror, the school already expected the worst. As if to confirm their fears, Wash went up to his teacher on his first day and pronounced triumphantly, "My mother's *on my side!*" Of course the teacher assumed that the rest of the sentence was "*against you.*" Hackles rose all over the place, and the mother was called in, after which she contacted Gouverneur. Luckily, Rabkin recognized the origin of the remark. He and Auerswald asked the principal of the school and the guidance counselor to see the videotape, with the family's permission of course. The tape, with its explicit drama, made clear to the school authorities the self-accusation Wash had been laboring under. The principal informed Washington's teacher, and the teacher, a seasoned woman who had been in the same school for thirty years, acted on this new information by making Washington the "class greeter."

An effort to do a follow-up the next spring elicited a vividly irritated response by the school counselor: "I hope you people didn't think that boy was going to be cured by one videotape." He added that Wash was "in great need of agency help," and that the mother "had not improved." It did not help that the community was just recovering from the long, disastrous teacher's strike of 1968–69, and that tensions between the mainly African-American parents and the mainly white teachers had still not simmered down. Worst of all, since the family had moved and was no longer in the Gouverneur catchment area, there was little we could do.

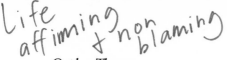
Life affirming + non blaming)

By the next year, Rabkin had left and the Crisis Unit had outgrown its early experimental stage. I remember wanting to accompany the bus on one of its trips into the field, as I had done previously, and being told by a new social worker that I couldn't because I had no professional degree. It seemed that I was not even allowed to "touch" a client, as they were now called. From then on, my exposure to the events I was trying to write about became extremely limited. I was dependent on intelligent collaborators like Rabkin and Emery Hetrick, the psychiatrist who replaced Rabkin as clinical director of the magic bus. Here, as the narrative that represents the heart of this chapter, is an article I wrote about Hetrick's work.

The Broome St. Network

Hetrick was one of the first gay psychiatrists I knew to come out of the closet. After he left Gouverneur, he became well-known for the part he played in establishing the Gay Men's Health Alliance. Like Auerswald's, his perspective was life-affirming and nonblaming. Both were ingenious at creating bridges to the diverse communities they worked with. On the Lower East Side, where Gouverneur was situated, there were several such communities: Puerto Rican families creating beachheads in the U.S. while their extended kin stayed home; Island families from the Caribbean who were moving in as the sons and daughters of Jewish immigrants moved out; and a small remnant of elderly Jews who were left behind.

Hetrick began telling me about the predicament of one such group of people who lived in a block of condemned tenements that lay in the path of an extension of the Brooklyn-Queens Expressway. I asked if I could write about their story, and he began to provide me with audiocassettes in which he described events as they took place. *The Broome Street Network* was originally published in an anthology of social work practice (Hetrick & Hoffman, 1982), but it is such a good illustration of Auerswald's ideas about ecology that I wanted to use it here. When I finally looked up the etymology of the word "ecology" in *Webster's*, I found that it came from the Greek "oikos," or house, and that "ecology" was "the study of the relationships between living organisms and their environment." It was no accident that one of the most complex situations the Crisis Unit handled while I was at Gouverneur had to do with relocation.

Our first inkling of this situation was our encounter with Mrs. Pearl. She had come to Gouverneur health center with many problems. Even after they were taken care of, she would haunt the corridors, bending the ear of anybody she could find with long, rambling monologues about impending disasters. For a while, nobody dared to keep their office doors open. I'm sorry to say that I, too, listened for her onset with dread, but Saint

Auerswald, with his ever-open door, spent hours with her. She rambled on in disconnected sentences like, "It's the end of the world! There's going to be a terrible flood! We'll all be washed away." Auerswald finally asked the Crisis Unit to pay her a home visit. They discovered that she and her husband were in poor health and that their building was about to be torn down. After the team assured her that they would not be turned out into the street and brought in the department of relocation to help them, she only visited us occasionally, and the oracular monologues became a thing of the past.

Hetrick discovered that there were a number of other elders at risk. There was Clara Bercowits, who had been living in the streets since her building had been vacated. She had refused six perfectly good apartments and was in the process of turning down a seventh because it was "too high up." There was old Mr. Klugman, who was afraid of going into public housing and was thought to be incapable of living alone in any case. And finally, there was Miss Sadie, a recluse who had not set foot outside her apartment for twenty years and who had not allowed any garbage to go out for five. The relocation people felt that she would not survive a transplant, and they turned to the Crisis Unit for help. Hetrick was intrigued and asked who else was involved with her. He was given the name and address of Mrs. Klosky, the wife of the owner of the grocery store across the street from Miss Sadie. On investigating, Hetrick found the store boarded up, but he located Mr. and Mrs. Klosky in their apartment next door.

Once she was reassured that the team had Miss Sadie's best interests at heart, Mrs. Klosky was quite willing to talk about her. She had known Miss Sadie, the daughter of a very fine and respected rabbi, for many years. When Miss Sadie's mother had died, some twenty years before, she had sat shiva according to the orthodox Jewish rite. However, she had been somewhat more orthodox than usual and had never stopped sitting shiva. Her father knew this was not right, but he had not been able to get her to leave the house.

For the next ten years, she stayed at home, caring for her father and watching TV. One day, her father came into the Klosky's store and ordered ten dollars worth of groceries. Mrs. Klosky, who knew the grocery-buying habits of most of her clients, was alerted to an unusual situation by the rabbi's large purchase; he had never before shopped for more than two days at a time. He was apparently ill, for he took himself to Bellevue Hospital, without telling his daughter where he was going, and died.

When his death became known, Mrs. Klosky and other neighbors began to worry about his surviving daughter. In order to force her out of seclusion, they decided not to bring her any food. Days passed, and Miss Sadie did not appear. Finally, Mrs. Klosky broke the well-meant siege. She found

Miss Sadie lying in bed, faint with hunger but stoutly refusing to believe that her father was dead. She had settled on an alternative explanation for his absence by saying that he had been spirited away by his sister in Brooklyn. Mrs. Klosky took pity on her and brought her food. She also got her on welfare, something of a feat considering that she had to do it without Miss Sadie's applying in person. From then on, she managed Miss Sadie's life for her. She cashed her welfare checks, even getting a new lock so that she could take Miss Sadie's check out of the mailbox and bring it to her to sign.

For the next ten years, Mrs. Klosky took Miss Sadie's shopping lists and filled her orders. Mr. Klosky carried down her garbage and brought up her supplies. After he could no longer negotiate stairs, Mrs. Mandelbaum, who lived with her retarded daughter down the street, took up the groceries. Mrs. Klosky arranged with the iceman to take the garbage until the icebox was replaced by a refrigerator and the iceman stopped coming. After that Miss Sadie collected the garbage and stored it. She resisted all efforts to have it removed, saying that she was collecting it for a prize: "The garbage goes when I go, not before."

In spite of these peculiarities, Mrs. Klosky insisted that Miss Sadie was no fool. She had held an office job before her mother's death, and she was still very good with figures. "People are not so stupid or crazy as you think they are at first encounter," Mrs. Klosky told Hetrick. "Sadie knows what she's about. I once made a mistake in her favor and she wrote down, 'Shame, shame, you made a mistake.' I wrote her back, 'To err is human.' She answered me, 'To forgive is divine.'"

By this time, Hetrick told me, he was anxious to meet this interesting person. He asked Mrs. Klosky if she would arrange a meeting, and some days later she took Hetrick over to the building where Miss Sadie lived. When Mrs. Klosky got underneath Miss Sadie's second floor window, she called her name, and soon a dim face framed by long, untidy hair peered out. Mrs. Klosky told her she had some visitors. Miss Sadie raised the window, which apparently meant that she was receiving. "Tell her you're from 'the Office,'" Mrs. Klosky said to Hetrick. "She thinks she's employed by the FBI, and if you say that, she may let you in." Hetrick followed this advice. After Miss Sadie had sized him up severely for a moment, she said, "Well, I guess you must be from a different office," and told them to come up.

Hetrick said that her apartment was unusual, even for the apartment of a recluse. It was crammed full of garbage, but it was far from disordered. The bags of garbage were neatly stacked against the walls to a height of four or five feet. Even though they contained materials that would not decompose, bones picked clean and empty cans, the smell was intense. Only the front room had no garbage; it was filled with dust-covered furniture and was apparently never used. The rest of the apartment could only be described in terms of ribbons of space: the narrow passage down the hall; the window sill that served as Miss Sadie's larder; the trailway to the bed; the route to the bathroom, where even the bathtub and the sink were filled and only the toilet was accessible.

Miss Sadie's appearance was in harmony with her surroundings. Hetrick described her as wearing a torn and dirty sweater, an old black skirt, and a blouse of filmy, rotted material. Her hair was hanging in loose strands about her face, and she had one eye that kept swerving off. But despite her suspicious manner, she took to Hetrick and he to her. He asked whether she understood that she would have to leave her apartment. She said yes, but that she was not going to do anything until the Office gave her instructions. The Office was preparing an apartment for her and would let her know when it was ready. Explaining the situation to the workers at the department of relocation, Hetrick said he thought that once they found her an apartment, she would agree to live there. He recommended that Miss Sadie be found temporary accommodation in Mrs. Klosky's building, as it was not being torn down right away, and he promised to help.

When an apartment in Mrs. Klosky's building was found, Hetrick worked with the relocation workers to furnish it. Hetrick had noticed that the only mirror in Miss Sadie's apartment was one in the unused front room, which was covered with a cloth, presumably to conform with the ritual of sitting shiva. Thus she had no way to see how ragged and filthy she looked. Hetrick made sure that there would be a mirror in the bedroom of her new home, and requested a radio and a clock to clue her in to the rhythms and events of the outer world. To make up for the glaring deficiency of the new place—it had no window on the street—Hetrick requested a TV from the department of welfare on medical grounds.

The relocation workers got into the spirit of the event and contributed many details of their own, like a bright-colored housecoat, a pretty nightgown, and a modish black dress for Miss Sadie on moving day. In one respect they went beyond the call of duty. Hearing of furniture left by a tenant in another building, they had a bedroom set of fine mahogany Chippendale delivered to Miss Sadie's apartment. During this time, an incident occurred that disproved the myth that Miss Sadie was totally helpless. Mrs. Klosky was visiting her daughter-in-law in Brooklyn, and Miss Sadie had no one to get her groceries up to her. According to the relocation workers, she had leaned out of her window and commandeered the help of some boys playing in the street. Until Mrs. Klosky returned, they brought up her supplies.

The date set for the move, July 18, finally came around. Mrs. Klosky had come back from her trip the night before, but refused to exert any influence on Miss Sadie for fear of alienating her. Another friend of Miss Sadie's, Mrs. Hirsch, showed up too, and a variety of housing agency persons were on hand. A social worker from the British West Indies and a psychiatrist from Gouverneur were also present and acted as ad hoc members of the Crisis Unit team. I wanted to be there too, but my nonprofessional status prevented it, so I relied on Hetrick's eyewitness account.

At around 11:00 A.M., Mr. and Mrs. Klosky, Mrs. Hirsch, and the relocation worker went up to fetch Miss Sadie. They found her sitting on her bed, refusing to move, and saying that they would have to wait till Monday. A two-hour period of negotiations followed, while everybody took turns trying to dislodge her. The relocation worker got her to put on the new dress by pointing out that her usual ensemble, which showed her bare, dirty midriff, was a bit immodest to go out in, but her cooperation ended there. She said that the Office was fixing her a place in the Bronx and she was going to sit where she was until it was ready.

After consulting with the others on his team, Hetrick gave Miss Sadie ten minutes in which to take one of three options: (1) to call upon the Office to see if it would come across with the alleged apartment before the deadline was up; (2) to stay where she was until the workmen came to demolish the building; (3) to walk across the street. This tactic didn't work either. The people in the apartment were discouraged, sweating, and nearly asphyxiated by the smell. Finally Hetrick went to phone the local precinct station, asking them to send an ambulance and some policemen to "take an old lady to Bellevue."

But before they arrived, one of the relocation workers fell upon the clue that saved the day. She had heard Miss Sadie say, "I will be *carried* across the street." The worker interpreted this to mean that as long as Miss Sadie did not have to go on her own two feet, she would not resist. She went out to tell this to Hetrick. He, in turn, was ushering in the policemen who were looking for the female psycho they were taking to Bellevue. Hetrick explained that this was no psycho but an elderly lady who needed a wheelchair and a gallant escort to help her to cross the street. The two policemen were willing, but the police car had no wheelchair. Hetrick ran down to call the health center ambulance service to ask for one, and it arrived shortly and was placed in the hall outside the apartment. One of the policemen said to Miss Sadie, who had come over to the doorway, "Hey, Sadie, look here—I've got something to show you." Miss Sadie stepped across the threshold for the first time in twenty years.

After that, there was no further problem. Miss Sadie did not resist being lifted into the chair. The policemen strapped a belt around her waist and used Hetrick's necktie to secure her arms and upper body to the chair so she would not fall out. It was only then that she gave a cry of alarm. The policemen carried her down the steps, out the door, and across to the new apartment. Once set loose from the wheelchair, Miss Sadie went over and sat down on her new divan, looking around at the attractively furnished living room and breaking into a smile. By this time, many people had tears in their eyes, and the relocation worker and Mrs. Klosky were openly weeping.

A celebration seemed in order. Hetrick dashed out and got a bottle of champagne and a Sabbath tablecloth as housewarming gifts. Mrs. Klosky had brought seltzer water. Mr. Klosky had rescued the mizuzahs from the door of the old apartment and now placed them on the door of the new one. Then the mystery of Miss Sadie's reluctance became clear. Telling Hetrick that she had to go downstairs to her apartment because she was cooking for the Sabbath, Mrs. Klosky said that Miss Sadie might have been especially resistant to moving that morning for religious reasons. Even though there was no infringement of orthodox law in moving before sundown, Miss Sadie had been known to stretch a point of ritual before.

In the days after the move, Miss Sadie began to respond to her changed circumstances. Visiting her some time later, Hetrick said that she must have taken a look in the mirror, because her face and her arms up to the elbow were clean. She had also asked the relocation worker to buy her two new house dresses. Most impressive of all, she was taking her garbage out into the hall and dumping it into the incinerator. Hetrick discussed with her the final move to an apartment in one of the projects. He reported that she seemed quite accepting of the idea, as long as she had a home-care person available to see to her needs.

Oddly enough, it was not Miss Sadie but Mrs. Klosky who was most upset by the move. When the Crisis Unit social worker called her to ask how Miss Sadie was doing, she was distant and unwilling to talk. Miss Sadie, she said, wasn't too happy. She had never received the promised TV set or the electric clock and radio. In addition, Mrs. Klosky disapproved of the telephone that had been installed. She said that Miss Sadie was not used to having people phone her, and when the phone rang she would worry that it was somebody who wanted to break in.

Mrs. Klosky also complained that the relocation department had asked for her help in moving other old people. She wanted Hetrick to tell them to stop bothering her because she didn't want to get mixed up in any more operations like that. It had angered her to see Miss Sadie treated with disrespect. Apparently, one of the policemen who tied Miss Sadie to the wheelchair had said to Mrs. Klosky, "Are you her friend?" When Mrs.

Klosky said "Yes," he said, "Then why don't you tell her to wash and get clean?" Mrs. Klosky retorted, "Young man, if my friend were able to wash and get clean, you wouldn't be tying her to a chair."

At last Mrs. Klosky came out with the real hurt. After the move, she had gone in to see Miss Sadie, and Miss Sadie had accused her of "going over to the enemy." Always ready with a tart answer, Mrs. Klosky said, "Well, if I'm the enemy, perhaps you don't want me to bring the groceries." Miss Sadie quickly said that wasn't what she meant, but the barb had stuck. Mrs. Klosky ended the conversation with a remark that startled Hetrick. She said she had run into an acquaintance who had asked her about the young psychiatrist from Gouverneur that everybody had been talking about. Mrs. Klosky said, "I told her I didn't know him." This was a curious and sobering reaction. It led the members of the Crisis Unit to realize that what for them was an occasion for rejoicing, namely, Miss Sadie's move, was not necessarily the same for everyone else. In a network where some are caretakers and others are taken care of, a move toward independence on the part of the one who is taken care of affects the relationship with the other, whose life is just as surely changed.

The story of the Broome Street Network did not end there. Other elderly people who were in the same boat were also helped. Mrs. Bercowits, despite her initial reluctance, was successfully introduced to life in a highrise building. Mr. Klugman, whose feet were in a bad way from diabetes, was moved into a nursing home. Mrs. Pearl and her ailing husband were found another apartment. Eventually, the Mobile Crisis Unit earned some recognition. As a result of the incident with Miss Sadie, the Commissioner of Relocation wrote the team a letter of commendation. In it, he said:

> To my knowledge, this is the first time my Department has ever faced the relocation of an absolute twenty-year recluse. The successful transfer of this withdrawn person into a viable apartment rather than a hospital ward is something at which we wonder and applaud.

At around this time, Gouverneur and I were coming to a parting of the ways. Together with a talented community organization major from Adelphi named Lorence Long, I had written a paper called "A Systems Dilemma" (1974) and had sent it to Haley for *Family Process*. It was accepted, but when I told Auerswald about it, he vetoed the idea, saying that anything I wrote was to be part of the book he and I were writing together. Book? What book? I was shocked, as this had never been a part of our contract. Later, I found out that he felt that in publishing this piece on my own, I was purloining his ideas. Unfortunately, he did not say this to me directly. Not understanding his feelings, I resigned.

However, one lesson was clear. The only way I could own the material I wanted to write about was to get a degree myself, so I decided to apply for an M.S.W. at the Adelphi School of Social Work. At the same time, Gouverneur was getting picketed by people from the local health council, with signs that said "Doctors Go Home." The Hispanic community resented the fact that they had so few good jobs at an institution that served their district. The Health Center's well-meaning efforts to empower the community had succeeded so well that Auerswald was in the painful position of having to cross a picket line that protested his own job. Soon after I left, he left too, going to Maui to run a community mental health center on the slopes of Haleakala. I was happy to think of him applying his visionary brand of caretaking in a setting that hosted so many cultural groups.

As I look back on my experiences at Gouverneur, I ask myself which of them have passed the test of time. Auerswald gets star credit for applying an ecosystemic view to community psychiatry. Owing to his influence, notions like the "interdisciplinary" approach to public health, or the "person-in-environment" of social work, seem narrow and dated. One has only to look at Auerswald's insistence on working with the cultural ring around the family to see how much his work foreshadowed the current multicultural trend. For family therapy to be useful in a broad sense, it had to add a wider template to the narrow family one, and it had to begin looking at the implications of issues like environment, economics, ethnicity, race, and class. And so it was that instead of working with bounded units like the individual or the family, relational therapists began increasingly to experiment with shifting, looser forms like assemblages and nets.

And what about my own network? That web was still there, still active. In 1969, Haley told me that Don Jackson had died, and that he was thinking of moving on. I promptly told Auerswald, and he went looking for funding so that he could offer Haley a position. Before he could do so, psychiatrist Salvador Minuchin, who had just been made the Director of the Philadelphia Child Guidance Clinic, hired him for his own training staff. My heart was glad; a continent no longer sat between us. I left Gouverneur and was accepted at the Adelphi School of Social Work. Then our book, *Techniques of Family Therapy*, came out. It dropped down a well so deep that not even the splash was heard, but I still loved it for capturing so many early moments in the history of the field.

In ending, here is a letter that Mrs. Pearl gave to Dick Auerswald, in thanks for his perpetually open door. I put it into lines so that it would read like poetry:

This 9th Day of April, 1968,
To precious Dr. Auerswald.

When I first met you
And asked if I may take a few minutes,
To tell you of my difficulties,
You did not refuse.
And this is the real reason why I take time now,
Before Passover,
When everything has to be cleaned
So Matzohs have to be on the table,
I cannot wait, but wish for you
With all my heart,
"A Healthy, long life."

I had a song for you
while I was putting up my cooking at an early hour, 3 a.m.
(I average from 2 to 4 hours of sleep)
And read the following:

My brother had a wonderful voice.
Two of them took vocal lessons.
Papa with a big hammer and chisel used to make "Etz Hayim" _____
    for Synagogue.
There are two at the House of the Sages at Broome and Willett Streets
which we held for about fifty years.
He made them in a large city of Russia, Odessa, where Papa was born,
Forks, spoons, knives, all by hand.

And I keep up my life, and like to stand and look at the painting of
    Mother and Father together on the wall,
One cannot miss when I enter the door of my so-called dinette.
I have only two rooms.
The melody is what my brother sang:

Sunset, Sunrise, Sunrise, Sunset (not these words)
My room here is quite dark.
Thank the Lord I have an attic,
So I could see early the Sunrise.

I get ready for the Synagogue,
And proudly take the prayer-book in hand.
To the Synagogue I am going,
Dressed in black from toe to neck (imagination).
And the Torah is my love and life,
The Tallis _____ is a precious shawl,

Which I put on my bent shoulders,
And this is my life, and my joy.

On my table I see a Talles,
Skull Cap, Prayer Books, and all, the Tefillen, _____
In memory of those innocent, who fell.

And now you know the kind of girl I am.
This is my reference.

★ The wooden handles attached to the scrolls of the Torah
★★ Prayer shawl
★★★ Phylacteries

3

The Year of the Rabbit

The Little Black Dress

In the fall of 1969, I found myself taking an M.S.W. at the Adelphi School of Social Work. The dean, Joseph Vigilante, was an outstanding progressive who had made great efforts to enroll older minority persons as well as women in midlife like me. As a result, the school had become a haven for political activism and social thought. Amazingly, Vigilante had persuaded the Welfare Department to pay for its case managers to get a social work degree, although this soon ended because the department decided that the managers were coming back too radicalized. Reconnecting with my left-wing roots, I decided to become a community organization major like the students I admired at Gouverneur. A lesser agenda was to keep from getting entangled with case work or group work, which were too individually oriented to satisfy my family systems mind. I thought, "I'll keep my head down and burrow through without being noticed." A social work degree seemed to me like the legendary little black dress: you could dress it up or dress it down; it would take you anywhere.

I immediately ran into a hail of bullets. My first field placement was at a mental health center way up in the Bronx. It was going to take me hours in the evening to return to my family in Brooklyn, where of course I was expected to go on making supper. Although I asked the administrative people to reassign me, they were used to the complaints of student mothers and turned a deaf ear. So I found my way to the cement shoebox that housed the service and the small office I shared with several other women, most of whom had just gotten out of college. The atmosphere felt very precious, and I kept hearing the word "supervision" pronounced in extremely religious tones. Somebody asked who my supervisor would be. When I told them her name, there was a sigh of approval, even envy. This only heightened my anxiety.

By the time my first supervision hour came round, I had met with my first "case," an Irish-American widow of small means whose chart said she was a character disorder, whatever that might mean. She didn't seem disordered to me, just worried, and she had good reason. Her grown-up son, who had a habit of beating her up, had just been let out of jail, and as she was the one who had jailed him in the first place, she was worried about what he might do. Feeling that I was not competent enough for this situation, I welcomed the idea of getting some advice. My supervisor was a mature woman and pleasantly authoritative. She seemed to be eagerly awaiting me, so I began to lay out my concerns about the unfortunate widow. To my surprise she did not seem interested. Instead she said, "I see that you are sharing an office with several younger women. How do you feel about that?" I was stunned. What business was it of hers? I told her that if it became a problem to me, I would take it to my therapist (not that I had one). She persisted in her questions. I felt trapped and panicky. We talked about how it felt to be an older student.

The next morning, I phoned the administrative office at Adelphi and announced that I was dropping out of my placement. They called me in and told me that I was being manipulative, social work's equivalent of a dirty word. Since I wouldn't budge, they sent me to a Bureau of Child Guidance in a school way out on Long Island. I thought it might be a punishment placement, but it had two great virtues: my supervisor was not invested in turning me into a patient, and even though I had to get up at five in the morning three times a week, I was able to leave for home by 3 P.M.

Except for this bumpy beginning, my experience at Adelphi surpassed all expectation. I learned more about welfare policy and social affairs in those two years than I had in all my previous life. In my field placements, I got to champion African-American children whose white teachers were trying to push them into special classes. I worked at a crisis clinic that was instrumental in closing down a Mafia-owned, drug-dealing welfare hotel on New York's upper west side. My most memorable experience was going in a bus to Washington, along with classmates and teachers, to protest the Kent State killings. The time favored such actions, coinciding as it did with the cresting of the baby boom and the terrible questions of the Vietnam War. When I got my degree, I felt I had earned it.

However, an M.S.W. did not a family therapist make. Adelphi offered two evening electives in family therapy in the second half of the second year, and my schedule wouldn't let me take them. If anything, I felt even more ignorant than before. Despite all my hobnobbing with people who did family therapy, I had never done any myself. Nonetheless, I received an invitation from Salvador Minuchin to join the staff at the Philadelphia Child Guidance Clinic. Haley had already been employed there for a year, giving me hope that I would have a chance to work with him again. And since my husband was taking a sabbatical, I persuaded him that we should sell our house in Brooklyn and move the whole family down to the Pennsylvania countryside.

What a harebrained idea! We bought a house with a fatally inadequate sewer on a street prophetically named Swamp Road. It was a beautiful antique-store house with pre-revolutionary fireplaces and deep Pennsylvania Dutch window sills, but nothing in it worked. The powder room flooded every time a toilet was flushed anywhere in the house, and the barn-paneled kitchen stank like a fox stall on a wet day. Out back was a little pony barn filled with manure because nobody had ever taken it away. The owner, we found out later, had lived in the remodeled barn and used the house as a display case for her antiques and a kennel for her dogs.

But the house was the least of our troubles, and I am bitterly sorry now that I subjected our family to this move. Our oldest daughter, Martha, was just going off to college, and Joanna and Livia, teenagers who had been attending a small, private school in Brooklyn, had a hard time adjusting to Bucks County public high schools. They were used to a city neighborhood where they could walk to friends and school, and now they were stranded in the Pennsylvania countryside on a country road where huge trucks came and went from a nearby gravel pit. To compound the problem, I was commuting daily to Philadelphia and my husband was traveling about doing a report on regional community theater for the Ford Foundation.

Joanna spent an unhappy year being mocked for her unfashionable straight jeans (the boys still wore "bells" and the girls wore high boots, miniskirts, and white lipstick), so we transferred her to a nearby Quaker school. Livia ran into even more troubling experiences at her junior high. A boy on her school bus tormented her constantly, and one day punctured her thigh with a soldering wire. She fought going back to school from that time on. We looked into a Quaker school for her too, but it didn't take. Unnerved, we finally sold the house and moved everyone back to Brooklyn. I wish I could say that this repaired the damage, but it didn't. Livia refused to return to her old school, although she finally found an alternative school on her own, and it became clear to me and my husband that our marriage was in trouble. We struggled on together, fixing up yet another old house in Brooklyn, while I continued to commute to Philadelphia part time. But that was two years later. Let me go back and pick up the thread of my tale.

When I first got to the Child Guidance Clinic in 1971, Minuchin told me that the clinical director, Harry Aponte, would be my supervisor. He himself was going to be in Sweden on a sabbatical, so I never worked with him. However, I did get to watch some of the tapes he and his child psychiatry residents did as part of a remarkable research project on families with psychosomatic children (Minuchin, Rosman, & Baker, 1978). I tried to make training tapes out of these interviews, and actually did produce one, featuring child psychiatrist Ron Liebman's work with a touching anorectic teenager and her Orthodox Jewish family. These interviews could be edge-of-your-seat enthralling. Life and death issues were involved, and Minuchin played a dramatic, high-stakes game. Watching tapes and trying to make training materials out of them was the major part of my connection with him while I was there.

I didn't work with Haley in Philadelphia either, although that was my dream. At first he invited me to be in one of his research cases. In these videotaped sessions, he would sit behind the screen and supervise a chosen therapist, giving her directive tasks of his own devising. If the case turned out well, he would add a commentary and edit it for a teaching tape. If it didn't, you never heard of it. These became known as miracle tapes and at first he said he wanted me to be in one of them. Then, suddenly, he withdrew his offer. When I asked why, he said, "Because you are no longer naive." He explained that he preferred to work with beginners, and of course I was no longer in that category. I was crushed, but at least we still worked in the same place, and other chances might arise.

Then, as I was commuting every day with my umbrella and briefcase, I noticed another woman commuting with umbrella and briefcase. She lived in Washington and her name was Cloe Madanes. I learned that Haley had met her while at a conference abroad, and that he and Cloe had just become engaged. I now felt displaced not only as a trainee but as a disciple. Luckily, Aponte had just been made director of a satellite clinic a few blocks away, so I asked if I could transfer. From then on, Haley and I took diametrically different paths. As I nursed my negative transference over at the other clinic, Madanes and Haley became the stars of a gala training conference. I sat glumly in the back of the audience, while Madanes, in the most beautiful fitted dress you can imagine, glittered on the stage. I had plenty of time to ponder why I ever wanted to be a disciple. Not surprisingly, I became less and less enchanted with Haley's ideas and more and more determined to develop my own.

Aponte's "ecostructural"

So it was Harry Aponte, not Haley or Minuchin, with whom I worked during the Philadelphia years. Aponte was younger than I, very intelligent, very reserved, and he bore with conscious dignity the mandate that came with being a Black Puerto Rican professional. His work with poor families (the only families we ever saw in that satellite clinic) was filled with a generosity that was rare by any standards. Haley's strategic approach, based as it was on the extravagant genius of Milton Erickson, attracted me by its inventiveness, but it seemed to work overtime to avoid heart. Aponte's style was the direct opposite. When he listened to the stories of the families that came our way, he did so with an empathic quietness that impressed me greatly. Although I would not know this for many years, he made the most lasting imprint on my style of any of my teachers.

If I Don't Get Simple, I Cry

One of Aponte's most important contributions to family theory was to challenge the cliché that poor African-American or Hispanic families were disorganized. The term had become a stigmatizing code word, and Aponte dealt with this injustice by looking at the larger picture. Calling his approach "ecostructural" (1976), he showed that if you took into account the social and material factors that impinged on these families, they were structured very logically indeed. You will see that clearly in the story I am going to tell below. He and I had drafted a discussion of this interview, but after I left Philadelphia the project got shelved and Aponte wrote it up on his own and published it in 1986. However, I continued to show the tape at workshops and, despite the dimness and graininess of the old reel-to-reel, each time I saw it I found more meanings in it. For me, it is still a stellar example of what therapy ought to be.

This was an interview with the kind of inner-city family that middle-class white therapists like me feared, because we did not know what to do with them. The cast of characters included an African-American mother in her fifties, six of her eight children, and two grandchildren. When the group came trooping in, the boombox was blaring, the baby was shrieking, and everybody was talking at once. The seventeen-year old daughter, Carrie, whose problems with school had prompted the mother to make the appointment, was rushing around trying to get everyone organized. The mother, a solidly built woman with a very sad face, sat seemingly removed from all this activity. The phrase "like pity on a monument" came to my mind, except that she wasn't smiling at grief but weighed down by it. Carrie, in contrast, was a bustling mass of energy, with bright, observant eyes that took in everything.

Aponte started by telling everybody about the one-way room and the video camera and asking for permission to tape. Then he went round the room and connected—no, "docked with" is a better term—each child in turn. He repeated their names, asked where they went to school, found out how old they were. What interested me was the time he took with each. He was like a spinner, twisting and thickening the threads between the children and himself, and this ceremony seemed to calm everyone down. Finally he went to the mother, who was reading a magazine. "Mrs. H.," he said, "everybody looks pretty happy except you." Carrie broke in to say, "She ain't got no sleep, that's why." Mrs. H. gave him a knowing, weary smile, and explained that she had just come home from work.

Aponte got up and sat next to her, asking, "Did you really just get home from work?" She told him that she had a night job cleaning buildings. He said, "And you have all these children to take care of by yourself?" She nodded. There was a general cacophony of fingerpointing and disclaimers with regard to who did and didn't cause problems. Aponte listened, then turned back to the mother and asked, "Are you just tired or are you as unhappy as you look?" She said, "No, just tired," but Carrie interrupted, saying, "Yes she is unhappy, she just don't want to tell anybody."

Carrie then launched into a recitation about who was contributing to her mother's unhappiness and in exactly what ways. Trying to lessen Carrie's centrality without alienating her, Aponte trolled back and forth across the group, checking on her information. He found out that Carrie's eighteen-year-old sister Toby was working in a bar with a bad reputation; Jack, sixteen, was getting involved in street dangers; Mark, twelve, lived with an aunt, but she and he weren't getting along; Earl, eleven, had a job, but when he was at home he got on people's nerves; Vera, twenty, was the mother of the two little ones, Rita, three, and Curt, two. She and her husband had been living with her mother until recently, and then her husband had moved out. There were two older brothers who weren't there.

All this time, the mother was quietly reading a magazine. I later asked Aponte why he did not try to activate her, as I thought Minuchin might have done. He told me that this was a very powerful mother. If he went to her before getting established with the children, she would jump in to control them and he would lose his connection with them. The scenario was familiar to him: a strong but exhausted parent whose many dependents were at risk for one reason or another, and whose main helper was threatening to fall apart. His job was to find out if there were any structures among the siblings that he could build on.

Speaking to the older children, Aponte found that there were no strong alliances, just as there were no strong antagonisms, except between Carrie, the seventeen-year-old, and Toby, who was a year older. The children would fight, take sides, make up, forget, in a perpetually shifting sequence. Jack, the sixteen-year-old brother, and Carrie attacked Toby for working at the problematic bar; then Jack and his younger brother Earl criticized Carrie for being fat. Carrie said that the only people in the house she liked were Vera and her two children, but when Aponte asked Vera who she liked, she said she liked everyone equally and Carrie chimed in, saying, "I love them all." Aponte described the loose character of the family relationship connections to me thus:

> What structure there was has collapsed, and they are desperately brewing a little ritualistic touching and connecting to keep themselves going. You can compare it to a good swimmer who has an automatic stroke that keeps up steadily as opposed to the person who doesn't know how to swim and is constantly improvising, making movements, just to keep his head above water.

Having checked out the courtiers and finding them without much power, Aponte now went to the Queen. He asked her, "How do you handle all this?" She smiled and said, "Just put on my gorilla suit, that's all." The children immediately broke into shrieks of laughter and displays of mimicry. Carrie said, "She gets violent!" and Vera said, "Everybody running every which way!" Aponte said to Mrs. H., "I imagine you have to get violent to keep things under control." She said, "I'd better. If I don't get violent, they'll put me out of my own house."

Aponte then said, "Tell me something. If you work all night how do you rest in the daytime?" She replied, "I don't. I only get about two or three hours of sleep." Aponte learned that she had been working for about three months. Before that she had been on welfare, but, she said, she needed more money. He asked why she didn't work days, and she explained that her father was living with her: "He's seventy-seven and senile." "How's your health?" Aponte asked. She said it was fine, but Carrie broke in to say "except for her nerves." Mrs. H. admitted that she was seeing a doctor and that he had given her some pills.

At this point, we saw Mrs. H. put on her gorilla suit. While she and Aponte were talking, the baby was standing on a chair and the younger boys were teasing him. Annoyed, he began to scream. Vera, the baby's mother, did not respond, even when Aponte asked her if she thought he would stay with a babysitter downstairs. Mrs. H. then rose from her seat, sternly swatted the child's behind with a rolled-up newspaper, and told him, "You better shut it up." The baby sat down with a thump and stopped crying. It was a dramatic moment. The other children talked and laughed excitedly, relishing the spectacle of their mother on the march. Aponte asked Vera if the little boy would listen to her the way he listened to his grandmother. She said, "Nope." Aponte then observed to Mrs. H., "So you're a kind of mother to everybody." And she replied, with feeling, "I'm the mother of all of them."

Aponte sat back with a sigh and said to Mrs. H., "You know, they said that Carrie here was the one with the problem. I feel more for you than I feel for anybody else in this family. I'm not kidding you. Don't you have sisters or anybody else who can help out?" She said, "Sure I have sisters, but they're busy with their own problems." He said, "Okay." After a short pause, he asked, "Tell me, what was the problem with Carrie?" Mrs. H. said, "Carrie has repeated tenth grade three times."

This was a kind of turning point. Now that Aponte had made an alliance with the mother and showed that he understood her situation, Carrie's smoke-screen behavior tapered off. He learned that she had started out doing well in tenth grade, but then she got sick and lost so much ground that she was kept back a year. She said that having to repeat lessons that she already knew bored her. Then, when she handed in work that was good, she was accused of cheating. She said, "I got mad and didn't care." Toby, the next oldest girl, came in to support her, saying, "What you get in elementary school you get in junior high school. Even the math, like, they give you one and one in junior high school."

Vera, the oldest, agreed: "They're giving her stuff that she already knows. Like she wants stuff higher, that she can learn, so when she gets out of school and has kids and everything, she'll know what it's all about." Vera said that she had dropped out in tenth grade because she was pregnant. She could not look for a job because she needed somebody to watch her children, and her mother couldn't take care of them because her nerves were too bad. So, even though she wanted to get out on her own, she was hesitating. She didn't know if her husband, who was living elsewhere, was going to live with her, and she was afraid to live alone.

Now an extraordinary story came out. Vera said, "Like if it ain't nobody home but us kids, and I know they are all there, I will sit up all night long and watch the door, the cellar, everything, because I am scared to be in there by myself." Aponte asked, "Are you scared even though they're all home?" She said, "Yes," and added that once, when they were all there, a strange man came into the house and went upstairs to look around. When she yelled, "Who's that?" he fled. Aponte discovered that Toby felt afraid too. If their mother was home, they weren't afraid, but if she wasn't, none of them could sleep.

Carrie joined in dramatically and said, "One day I killed everybody in my family." She said she was in the house at around 11:30 at night, and in her imagination she pictured everybody getting killed: "Jack got shot, Curt was clubbed to death, Rita got shot, and Earl got smothered." After that she said to herself, "I ain't getting killed," and went to sleep. Aponte asked, "Why were you scared?" Carrie said, "I don't know. Cause before I went to bed I locked all the doors, checked all the windows, everything." Aponte repeated his question: how come they were so afraid when they were all at home? Vera explained that the boys were no help. "You can tell them the house is burning, and they don't care—they'll cover up and go back to sleep." Aponte turned to Jack and asked if he were afraid too. He said, "I ain't afraid of nothing." Aponte then asked Mrs. H. if she were afraid. When she said, "No," everybody started to joke and giggle. Jack said, "My mother's not scared of nothing." Vera said, "If you mess with her, she don't care what you do, she's going to get you."

Aponte asked Mrs. H., "How come you got all the courage and the girls have all the fear?" She answered that she didn't know, but everyone agreed that none of the boys was afraid. Aponte said to me later that it seemed as though a vicious cycle were operating: the more the boys ignored danger, the more the girls feared it. In part this was because if the boys got into trouble on the street, it could follow them into the home. Homes were very vulnerable where they lived. A contributing factor to the confusion was that instead of keeping watch in turns, which would have been a logical way to organize things, the girls all stayed awake together.

At this point, Aponte told me, he felt that he had gone as far as he could with the whole family present. Once he started focusing on Carrie, it would take too much energy to control the younger children, who were already getting restive. So he asked everybody but Mrs. H. and Carrie to go downstairs to the waiting room. When they had left, he sat down in front of them and said, "Mrs. H., I don't know how you do it. You know, you really have more than one problem at home." She nodded, saying, "The whole batch is a problem." Aponte asked her why she had picked out Carrie to bring for help. The mother replied, "This is suppose to be my sensible one, and when she starts goofing off, I know the whole house is crazy." Aponte asked, "She helps hold things together?" and Mrs. H. concurred: "When she's blowing her stack and falling apart, it's time to find out what's the problem." Aponte said, "Okay, you need her to help you."

Carrie now came in to say, "That's why I fall apart." Aponte asked her, "Because she depends on you?" She said, "No, because when she wants me to do something and I can't do it." She suddenly started to cry. Aponte looked at Mrs. H. and said, "She's upset," and Mrs. H. nodded her head in response. After a long pause, Carrie wiped her eyes and giggled. "I got tears," she said, "I don't like to cry." After she had found some tissues and pulled herself together, Aponte said to her, "Now let's talk." Then Carrie came out with something that amazed both Aponte and me: "*If I get simple, then I can tell you what's wrong with my mind. If I don't get simple, I cry.*" In other words: "As long as I act crazy, I can tell you about my problems, but if I stop acting crazy, I'll break down, and then I won't be able to talk at all."

Aponte asked her what was wrong with her mind. Carrie told him that she worried too much: she worried that her mother would have an accident going to work; Jack would get shot in the street; Earl would have a train accident; Rita and Curt would choke to death; Vera would get shot by her husband. She ended by saying, "And me, I'm going crazy." Aponte commented that she hadn't always been this crazy, and asked how long things had been so bad. She said, "Since June." Aponte asked her why it had gotten worse then. She said, "They don't listen to what I say."

Aponte then turned to Mrs. H. and asked if she knew what Carrie was talking about and Mrs. H. said she did. She looked at Carrie and said, "Vera and her husband fighting, right?" Mrs. H. said that she had given the couple a date for moving out, but instead they just kept quarreling. She explained that Carrie was upset that Vera and her children were still there. Carrie added that Vera came to her to complain about her problems, but when she tried to help her, Vera didn't listen.

More things tumbled out. Carrie said she "hated" Toby, the next older sister, but she didn't know why. When Toby had gone into the hospital a year ago, her mother had said, "Pray that she don't die," and she had tried to pray but said that she really didn't care. Her mother told Aponte that this feeling might go back to the time when Carrie was five years old and some boys had tried to rape her. Toby was with her, but wouldn't come to her aid, and she had said to Toby, "I'll always hate you." Mrs. H. said, "That could have been back there in her subconscious mind."

Aponte, choosing not to delve into this bit of history, asked Carrie if she had any other worries and she brought up the subject of her oldest brother James, who was twenty-five. Carrie told Aponte, "Somebody's going to kill him yet. He runs around with sixty million women at one time and all of them know it." She gave another example: "This dude was cussing at his mother, my brother walked up to him, and my brother was drunk as a skunk and beat this dude up for cussing at his mother and walked away." Aponte said, "He's taking a chance." Carrie said, "Yeah, and don't care. Somebody's going to kill him." Mrs. H., looking somber, nodded assent.

Aponte, who saw that Carrie was caught in the role of assistant mother, intervened. He said to Mrs. H., "She's really been like a part of you, to take care of things and hold them together. You can't possibly do this by yourself, and she's been the only one you could really depend on to handle things." The mother answered, "Right." Then Aponte said to her: "You know, when you first came in here, you looked very tired. You looked out of it. The kids have all left and I can really see you now and your eyes are very clear, and I think they're very clear because you see a lot. I think maybe your nerves are as bad as they are because you see too much and there's nothing you can do about it."

There was a pause. Mrs. H. raised her head, her eyes opened wide, and she said to Aponte, looking straight at him, "I'll go along with that." He added, "And she is trying to carry this burden with you. I can understand why she can't worry about school, she's got the worries of any woman, not a seventeen-year-old kid. She couldn't have any more worries if she had ten kids of her own." Carrie broke in with yet another worry, this time about her grandfather, but Aponte ignored her and asked Mrs. H., "You really don't have any help from outside?" She said, "No, they don't even care." "You don't have a man to help you?" Mrs. H. shook her head. He asked, "How long has it been since you had a man to help you?" She said, with a wry grimace, "Too long to remember."

There was a long pause. Aponte said "Vera doesn't talk like she's going to leave." Mrs. H. now came in strongly, emphasizing her words, "Right! Now you understand. Right, right, right!" Carrie started to explain how she had tried to help Vera get a job, but this time her mother brushed her aside, saying to Aponte, "I feel like this. If Vera was to find a place and get a job, take her children—and I don't know what Toby is going to do—and just leave the household to my five dependent children, four dependent children, which I do have, I think things would be better, I really do." Aponte said, "You may be right." She went on, "I told them, 'Look, you got your problems, I have mine. Pack your problems up and go ahead for yourself and leave me with my four dependents, that's all I ask.' "

Carrie suggested that Vera wouldn't have to be alone if she took an apartment, but Aponte again ignored her and asked Mrs. H. if she had any relatives Vera could live with. Mrs. H. said her two sisters had no extra space. In that case, Aponte said, Vera posed a really difficult problem and her children were a problem, too. Mrs. H. agreed that they were hard to control, and Carrie said, "I mind them more than Vera does." Another worry was that when the little boy got upset he would hold his breath. "That boy sure keep me on roller skates," Mrs. H. stated. "He'd turn all blue and his eyes go off in the back of his head." Then Carrie described the time Rita, the three-year-old, had a convulsion. She was about to go on to something else, but Aponte stopped her. He checked out the story with Mrs. H., who said that two years ago Rita had two convulsions, had been seen by a doctor, but was now fine.

Aponte then apologized to Carrie and asked what she had been going to say. She answered, "I just forgot," and then said, "I do that a lot too. I make myself forget stuff." Aponte answered, "Carrie, you have so much on your mind that I think you need to forget a few things. You can't keep all these things in your head at once or you'll go crazy." Carrie said, "I know

I'm crazy, that makes me mad, cause I can't do nothing about it." Aponte agreed, saying, "This kind of thing would drive anybody crazy. You're not crazy in the sense that you're just crazy. You're crazy because you have too much to deal with."

Again there was a pause. Aponte said to Mrs. H., "I guess that what you're saying is what we really should be concentrating on first is Vera and her kids. If we can get something done for her and her kids, we could relieve the rest of it." Mrs. H. said, "Right," adding that she thought that the other problems would fall into place if this one were taken care of. Aponte turned and checked this out with Carrie. Carrie said she thought her older sisters should move out and that her mother should find another place for her grandfather. She said she didn't get along with him because "he throws them riddles at me and I don't know what he's talking about." Mrs. H. asked her, "And where am I going to put him?" Carrie explained that her mother had taken her grandfather out of his nursing home after there had been a big fire and the Health Department had declared the facility unsafe. Aponte observed to Mrs. H. that life in the city wasn't helping, and they both agreed that nobody should be poor.

Then—and this was a notable first—Carrie broke in to complain on her own behalf. She said, "You know, I think things will never go my way." Aponte told her that she couldn't live for herself because she was living for so many other people. Her mother came in strongly at this point, saying, "Right! And that will make you sicker than anything in the drugstore. Because you can't solve everybody's problems. We just have to make arrangements with them, and if they can't solve the problem, I can see if I can help them and get them off your back." Aponte echoed her, saying, "I'm listening. I'm with you one thousand percent."

This moment always moved me. Together, Aponte and Mrs. H. had just lifted a huge burden off Carrie's back. The effect was almost palpable. Carrie, who could now return to her own concerns, said that she wanted to get training for some kind of job. Aponte said that they had to deal with the other problems first, but she objected, saying, "I don't want to stay home and do nothing." Aponte picked up on that, saying, "No, really, you're too smart for that. Actually, your family is smart. People are bright in your house. Nobody should be doing nothing, but if you have all these worries, you can't do a lot of things." Her mother chimed in, saying, "You can't. You can't really remember what is one and one."

Aponte now turned to Mrs. H. and said, "And you can't help her if you're overwhelmed. See, right now you're calm, you think very clearly about what she needs. But when they were all there, you know, you were out of it." Mrs. H. said, "Right." Aponte continued, "I would have been out of it too. I was having a hell of a time myself, keeping everything straight in my head. Worrying about Vera and worrying about her kids and worrying about Toby and watching Earl causing trouble. Everything was just—." Aponte here clapped his hands together.

This was the signal for a shift. Aponte shared with the family that he too had been puzzled and confused, but to me, watching, he had tracked all the pieces of this immensely complex jigsaw puzzle and put them together so that they made sense. I was especially impressed by how strongly he connected with the mother, freeing Carrie to ask for something for herself. So Aponte laid out a plan: first, to help Vera take charge of her life, then to see what could be done about the grandfather. He told Mrs. H. that he had medical people available, a team to fall back on, and that once they could take care of those two things, they would get going on Carrie's school. He said he wanted to move fast, before she missed too much of it. Carrie said, "That's okay. I know everything they got," but Aponte told her that the school might not have handled things right and he wanted her to get to the right grade in the right school "so that you can do something with your head." Mrs. H. exclaimed, "Oh, that would be beautiful," and for the first time she smiled.

The session ended with Carrie saying to Aponte, "You want to know a little secret?" and when he nodded yes, she told him about the song that she had been singing on the way to the clinic: "When the Nuts, Oh when the Nuts, When the Nuts come marching in, All the Psychs going to jump out the windows, When the Nuts come marching in." Aponte smiled and said, "Nobody's going to jump out the window. What's going to happen is that you're going to get more people connected with your family and we're going to try to get things in order." And he made good on his word.

Every time I watched this tape, I was struck all over again by the humanity of Aponte's manner. As his former supervisee, I remembered how often he would insist that the therapist check in with her own feelings—or what we might now call "inner voices"—as a way of determining direction. It was as though he had a gyroscope inside, a touchstone that told him if he were hot or cold, connected or losing ground. Using this process as a sort of feedback instrument, he took tremendous care to stay close to what Michael White calls the "lived experience" of people, moving together with them against the forces that diminished them. I was later to speak of a "different voice" for therapy, but I think my early exposure to Aponte's thought and practice laid the groundwork for this idea. Aponte (1985) himself has explained it within a frame of spirituality. It fit that, when I recently asked him if he knew what had happened to the people in the family, he told me that the mother had become a minister.

So, to the humanistic optimism I took from Satir, and the wide-angle generosity I took from Auerswald, I added Aponte's genius for emotional connection. Despite its disastrous consequences, my move to Pennsylvania was not all wasted. However, returning to New York dropped me into a cauldron of new circumstances. I first got a job teaching family therapy to the child psychiatry residents at Downstate Medical Center in Brooklyn, which was essentially a psychoanalytic training program. The residents were all young male princes, and even though the head of the program hopefully asked me if I couldn't act more authoritative, I failed to live up to the challenge. He quietly replaced me with a male family therapist who took over with the princes. By this time, I was busy introducing family therapy to the Child Outpatient Department of Kings County Hospital, Downstate's training site, and in this role I flourished.

At the same time, my husband and I were trying to rescue our marriage. We were stuck together by such infernal glue that we needed a dose of magic, so we went to see family therapist Olga Silverstein at the Ackerman Institute, who was known as the Wonder Rabbi of New York. Rather than bringing us closer, the process moved us toward a separation. Around this time, Olga asked me if I would like to join the staff at Ackerman and work with the new Brief Therapy Project that had been started by Peggy Papp and herself. What an opportunity! Of course I said yes.

But I must include one more piece before I end this chapter, and incidentally speak about my love affair with the I-Ching. I had long admired the special quality of Chinese thought, based as it was on the belief that polarities mutually arouse each other rather than compete. If you cast your fortune or "Kua" from the I-Ching, it always had a double meaning. You might get a positive reading like "The Creative," but attached to it would be one that counteracted it like "Youthful Folly." Conversely, a reading like "The Darkening of the Light" might give you as an upside "The Creative."

On January 1, 1975, the Year of the Rabbit, I bought an I-Ching diary. For each week, there were spaces to fill out indicating your plan for the week, any special events, and your Kua. At the bottom of the page was a box entitled "The Unexpected." During the first week of the first month of that year, my father died. During the first week of the second month, my husband's mother died. I put both these events into "The Unexpected." Although I had never been able to keep a diary, I faithfully continued with this one until the following fall.

On the first of October that year, under the sign of "Splitting Apart," my husband and I decided to put 25 years of marriage behind us, and he moved out. Our oldest daughter was living on her own; our second daughter was still in college; and our third daughter, who was attending an alternative high school, put a tarpaulin over the circular staircase that led down to her room and told me to keep out of her life. Then the living room ceiling fell down. Covered with plaster dust, I felt as if I were camping in a bombed-out city. I put my last entry in the diary for that year: "I am really alone."

For the first three nights of my separated life, I slept in the conservatory off the parlor floor with all the lights on, while the ancient Jamaican plasterer I had located went about carefully repairing my ceiling, grape leaf moldings and all. He never went home to sleep, although he occasionally took naps in a chair. When I asked him why, he said he had quarreled with his wife. I woke up on the third morning and the ceiling was finished but the plasterer was gone. He never asked to be paid and I never could find him again.

4

The Ugly Duckling

The World of Paradox

In 1978, after getting a divorce, I joined the faculty at the Ackerman Institute for Family Therapy. I had sold our house in Brooklyn and moved into Manhattan to be closer to work, but the divorce still cast its somber light over my life. I felt as if I had murdered a child, and living alone in a white brick high-rise only compounded my pessimism. I was an older woman, a social worker, and single, three strikes right there. On the other hand, I had found another cradle of creativity. When I arrived at the Upper East Side townhouse that held the Institute, with its rickety elevator from Old Vienna, I found its training program in the midst of change.

This was particularly welcome because Peggy Papp and Olga Silverstein, redoubtable stars in what had by now become a performance field, were striking into new territory. In their work at the Brief Therapy Project at Ackerman, these two pioneers merged Palo Alto's paradoxes with their Bowenian interest in the family of origin. They had also been influenced by the work of a research team in Milan headed by child psychiatrist Mara Selvini Palazzoli. This group's seminal book, *Paradox and Counterparadox* (Palazzoli et al.,1978) had been translated from the Italian by Gillian Walker, one of our team members, and I read it with intense interest and admiration.

However, doing therapy and reading about it are not the same. Papp and Silverstein's brand of brief therapy was very different from the structural approach I had cut my therapist teeth on, and training in this new model meant unlearning what I had worked so hard to know. Ackerman's client population was at that time mainly white, middle-class, and educated, where the Philadelphia satellite clinic served people who were African-American, Hispanic, and poor. I was used to sympathizing with my families and advocating for them, where at Ackerman, many of the families we encountered were wealthier than most of the staff and I found them somewhat intimidating.

As a result, I was glad I had a team to back me up, and welcomed the paradoxical messages so pungently described by the Milan team as "bombs." This work reminded of a TV program I once saw on opal mining. The miners lived in man-made tunnels underground, and every once in a while they set off small blasts of dynamite at the end of their burrows, hoping to dislodge precious stones. But this is too violent an image. Papp and Silverstein added a softening influence by linking the presenting problem to the thematic metaphors of the family's history. Their work had a quality of poetic resonance that appealed to me. Papp, in her earlier life, had been an actress, and Silverstein a "poet of the revolution," and under their regime I found that my gift for images was appreciated and extended.

When I joined it, the Brief Therapy Project consisted of two teams of four persons each, one headed by Papp and one by Silverstein. Periodically the teams would change leaders, but the teams remained the same. The following story concerns one of the first families I saw during my sojourn on Silverstein's team. But before beginning, I must mention one huge blind spot. The family sessions in this project were videotaped but the conversations of the team were not. Not only was there no video camera in the room where the therapists met, but there seemed to be a covert policy that said "clients visible, therapists invisible." Whenever we videotaped a family, the lens was focused on the faces of the family but only picked up the back of the therapist's head. Although these one-way practices were challenged in later years (see Chapter 9), in the present narrative I have had to become a kind of spectral "we," standing in for discussions behind the screen that were never recorded. But on to the story of my beloved thirteen-year-old Harry and his family. They gave me a run for my money but ended up lodged in my heart.

The Ugly Duckling

Harry's family was first assigned to an Ackerman staff member who saw them for four sessions, then decided they would be perfect for the Brief Therapy Project. I was the therapist who drew the lucky card. This family had contacted Ackerman because Harry had been suspended from school for unruly behavior, including biking home from school whenever he felt like it. The spring report card was succinct: "During the course of the school year, Harry moved on to oppose teachers, all phases of the curriculum, established practices, and the principal." The school held a meeting with Harry's family, and an agreement was reached that he would be readmitted only if he went to therapy. Since he refused to do this, family therapy was the only other choice.

There was a lot of background information of course. The family consisted of Harry, who was adopted; Michael, sixteen, also adopted; and a natural daughter, Laura, twelve. Laura was conceived just as Harry, then a baby, was brought home. Even though from early on Harry had learning problems, the family perfected its own ways of dealing with the situation. They found a school that worked well for him, and he and they prospered. Then the family moved from the country to the suburbs. Accustomed to a school that sounded like a protracted kindergarten, Harry now faced one that emphasized responsibility and rules. The parents were accepted warmly by the old school while the new school had a policy of "parents stay out." As a result, they did not even know Harry was in trouble until he was abruptly suspended. They were understandably upset and questioned the school's ability to motivate their son. The school had its own side of the story, but the upshot was a tense school-family interface.

This was an attractive, accomplished family. Despite having to tell their story all over again to another group of professionals, they were extremely cooperative, and I was correspondingly grateful. The father, in his late forties, was an investment banker with a reassuringly thoughtful manner, and the mother, also in her forties, was a handsome, lively woman who was getting an advanced degree in English literature. Michael struck me as unusually good-natured for a teenager, and Laura, pretty and bright, shared her mother's challenging mind and her enthusiasm for Women's Lib.

Harry, in contrast, looked as if he had been dropped into this family by mistake. His clothes were sloppy; his hair stood up like straw; he interrupted conversations at will. During the interview, he created a constant rumble of distraction, drumming on the mike, banging on the radiator, humming, talking. This noise was punctuated by occasional witty remarks at my expense. When I used the phrase "I may be barking up the wrong tree," Harry cut in to say, "Dogs don't climb trees." Later, when his father was speaking about him, Harry reminded him of something he knew his father disliked by saying, "The camera's on you, Dad."

With tactics like these, Harry wiped me out in the first round. I could hardly ask a question without his making some idiotic wisecrack that broke everybody up, including me. But, as you can imagine, the audience I was really concerned about was the one behind the screen. One feature of our strategic teams was the freedom to express ourselves backstage, sometimes at the family's expense. The therapist was not exempt either. At times I was sure that I heard, despite the one-way glass, the sound of laughter. Hiding my discomfort, I steeled myself to endure what felt like an initiation rite.

Despite Harry's constant intrusions, the parents made clear their disappointment with the school. They admitted that Harry had learning problems but said that it was the school's job to teach and manage him. I learned that he had been in individual therapy since age six, and that during the previous summer he had become a "therapy drop-out." I wondered whether the family might have agreed to family therapy as a way to track Harry back into a therapy of his own. We were all afraid that if the present school, which seemed to be a school of last resort, expelled him, he was headed for a locked facility.

When I took a break toward the end of the session to talk with my team, I was relieved to find how supportive they were. Far from laughing at me, they commiserated with me and praised me for my persistence. As a final task, they suggested that I ask the parents to make separate lists of the strategies they used to manage their irrepressible son, and to share these lists with us when we met again in two weeks. The parents did not want to bring Michael and Laura back in, but we had insisted on this for the first session, and we insisted on it again. One of the guiding rules at this stage of the family therapy movement was that the whole unit should be seen. We assumed, you see, that the family was benefiting from the problem because it served some important function, and if everyone wasn't there, we couldn't find out what this function was.

I myself was pondering how to understand Harry's extreme behavior. Many factors obviously fed into it—the adoption, the learning impairments, Harry's life stage, the new school—but I was convinced that it acted as a coded message that pointed to some feared event. My rationale was that if a therapist could figure out this message and find a more direct way to transmit it, the anxiety behavior would calm down. I had a bit of time in which to do this, as it was the spring break. So what I did during the following two weeks was to ask myself: "How is this problem a metaphor for something else?"

As I ruminated, I kept coming back to the theme of liberation, so often mentioned in a half-joking, half-serious way by various family members. Everybody paid it lip service, yet everyone in the family seemed enslaved. I initially thought of likening the household to a well-run hospital ward in which Harry was a patient, but that would have been terribly offensive. Liberation, on the other hand, was an image that was both affirming and ambiguous. I fortified myself with a plan of action that centered on this concept. All the same, I dreaded the next interview, and knew that with Harry around, I would never be safe from surprise.

The awful day came. I listened carefully as the parents read their lists, trying to block out Harry's efforts to create turbulence. The father's list was a long one. He said that seating was ruled by the need to "minimize disruption or maximize control." In the car, Harry sat in front while the other two, despite Michael's longer legs, sat in back. At the movies, Harry sat between his parents, "to minimize poking." His father also gave him considerable private time. He would play games with Harry or sit and chat with him at bedtime. Last but not least, Harry cost more. He went to private schools while the others went to public schools and, because Harry was a "Hebrew school drop-out," the family had to hire a tutor to prepare him for his bar mitzvah. In general, his father said, less was expected of him than of the others.

The mother recited her list next. She seemed to be the one who was most affected by Harry's misbehaviors. He would wake up the whole household early in the morning by calling "Mom, Mom," from his bed. She said she had to ignore him for a long time before he would finally stop. She was infuriated by his constant biking home from school, because she was writing her dissertation and he made it impossible for her to work. Another annoyance, she said, was his "allergy" to soap and water. Since she sat next to him at meals, she said, she occasionally had to ask him to leave and take a bath.

I then asked Michael and Laura about their part in the effort to minimize Harry's disruptive behaviors. Michael said that it was hard for him to have friends over because Harry interrupted their activities. He also resented having to do chores like shoveling snow while Harry was exempt. Laura said she often had to share her bike with Harry because his was always broken, and he would also come into her room and take things. If she objected, he would punch her in the stomach. However, if she screamed loudly enough, her father would come and remove Harry bodily.

During this part of the conversation, Harry moved to the seat next to Michael and began to trade punches with him. Tired of being constantly interrupted, I temporarily moved back to a structural approach and used an "enactment." I asked to see an example of the family's system of control. The mother told Michael to move to Harry's vacated chair, which was next to the father on the outside of our semicircle. Michael, uncharacteristically, I thought, refused, and the father gently manhandled Harry back to his original seat. While Harry was sitting there, muttering to himself, I complimented the parents on being a "good team." They looked a bit insulted and said they had always been a good team. I remarked that Harry was certainly giving them the chance to demonstrate it. The mother smiled and said, "We were a team before Harry came along. When he's away at camp, we're still a good team."

I confess that part of my plan was to expose the way the problem influenced the family and then uncover the ways the family kept it going. White and Epston (1990) were to employ a version of this technique some years later in their "relative influence questioning," but here I went in paradoxically, complimenting Harry for his bad behavior and implying that the family should be grateful to him. I turned to him and said, "You know, Harry, if you became an angel overnight, I don't think that would be so good." Harry started up in exaggerated shock and said, "Angel! Are you sick?" I said, "No, I really think the family would miss you." He snorted. Then I pushed my luck. I said, "You're an ugly duckling and an ugly duckling implies swans. And I think that what your family did just now was extremely graceful, they looked like swans."

Michael rushed in to disagree, saying, "No, it's ugly, it's not graceful at all," but the mother, who knew what I was doing, said, "If you mean that we need that to look good, I think you're wrong." I pointed out that I wasn't talking about things they consciously did. For example, when Harry was acting up just then, Harry looked bad and Michael looked good. I added that Michael would have looked even better if he had given up his seat to Harry, and that I was surprised that he didn't. There was a general family murmur against this idea, but Michael looked quizzically at me and began to smile.

The Prisoner

The next bit of conversation with the family allowed me to use the liberation image I had so carefully chosen beforehand as my weapon of choice. Here is a transcript of that passage.

LYNN: You have a remarkable family. You've organized yourselves in such a way as to minimize the way Harry can disrupt things, though at some cost, and I ask myself, is this family like a sort of prison where Harry is the prisoner and the rest of you are the attendants, or are you the prisoners and is Harry the attendant?

HARRY: (*for once listening attentively*) I'm in prison. I'm stuck with this family.

LYNN: I don't know. Maybe you're the one that holds the key to the door and maybe not—it's hard to say.

HARRY: If I hold the key, then I'd be able to get out—I mean, isn't that dumb? I don't want to be in jail no more.

LYNN: Well, it's funny—maybe you do have the key, Harry, because (*Harry tries to interrupt*) no, you're the attendant and all these people are in jail.

HARRY: If I say I'm in jail, I'm in jail.

FATHER: It may sound organized—it sounds organized to me when I make a list—but of course these things evolve out of what seems necessary. I don't look at it as a system, it's just things that keep happening. It's become a system.

MOTHER: Did you say there was a cost involved? Because that's certainly the way we feel.

LYNN: Well, I just meant a price—absolutely a price. That's why I asked all of you to come here, even though I knew you didn't want to inconvenience Michael and Laura one more time, because I felt they were paying a price too, and if we were going to put our heads together they might as well be part of it, because they are.

What was interesting to me and the team about this jail analogy was the way everybody chimed in to comment on it. Unlike the kind of interpretation that "points things out," which often alienates people, this sort of metaphor gets them thinking. The father, who looked as if he were less burdened by Harry's behavior than the mother, dismissed it as "things that keep happening," but the mother zeroed right in on the cost. I had the impression that she felt particularly oppressed, even though I was not sure why this should be. But what was really striking to me was the experience of being directly connected to Harry for the first time. No longer deflecting, intruding, disrupting, he seemed to speak from his heart, and for the first time I got a sense of the enormous sadness in this boy who was "stuck with this family."

Shortly after this, I took a break to meet with the team. The hypothesis we came up with was a version of the belief that the child's problem mediated a struggle between the parents. I suggested the idea of mother as a kite, with Harry, who represented father's interests, holding onto the string. If she started to sail too far out or become too "liberated," Harry would do something to pull her back. But Silverstein, with her usual (or unusual) intuition, thought we should stay with the metaphor of liberation. When we crafted the final message, she suggested we express our belief that someone in the family wanted to escape and that it was Harry's job to prevent this. The message below was thus our version of "prescribing the system"— a statement from the team that made Harry the protector of the family and cheered him on.

LYNN: My team was struck by the way in which it is confusing
            whether the family is like a cage, or a prison, and it's unclear
            whether Harry is the person you're keeping watch over, or
            whether it's he who's keeping you locked up.

HARRY: They're keeping me locked up.

LYNN: It's a kind of game of jailers and prisoners, and we're not sure
            who is which—and I think a lot of the pain that everyone
            experiences comes from that. The other thing the group
            noticed was that somebody here, secretly in their heart,
            might want to escape (*Harry makes an abrupt hiss*), but this
            might be very devastating to the family because it's a very
            close family . . .

HARRY: I can run away—I can run away . . .

LYNN: . . . and in a sense, Harry, your job is to keep this game of
            prisoners and jailers going (*Harry makes a snorting noise*),
            because otherwise that person might in reality try to make
            a break for it.

HARRY: I'm the one that's locked up.

LYNN: I don't know, I'm not so sure.

HARRY: I know. I can see . . .

LYNN: I think it's very important for you to play the part that you
            play, whether it's the one of being locked up, or the one of
            being the one who's locking everybody else up.

HARRY: Do you have the rules?

LYNN: I think those are the rules of the game, that you play that
            part.

HARRY: To keep it going?

LYNN: Yep.

HARRY: Those are dumb rules. (*starts talking to Michael about how
            dumb they are*)

MOTHER: (*looking thoughtful*) Are you saying that the group felt that the
            family is constricting maybe for some or all of us at some
            time, or that there's somebody in particular?

LYNN: I wasn't sure. They felt that it might be more than one per-
            son, but at least probably one person might be feeling par-
            ticularly constricted and—they weren't so sure—Harry says
            he'd like to make a break for it, but they weren't so sure, they
            weren't so sure. And so their admonition, really, was for
            Harry to continue playing this game, certainly until we find
            out a little more about it and (*to Harry*) what the conse-
            quences might be if you stopped. Okay?

HARRY:	Excuse me . . .
LYNN:	Will you agree, Harry, to continue playing this game of jail?
HARRY:	Maybe. Uh . . .
LYNN:	Please, will you agree?
HARRY:	Maybe.
LYNN:	Maybe? Oh, that's very noncommittal. Yes or no?
HARRY:	What college did you go to?
LYNN:	Yes or no? Will you agree to play this game?
HARRY:	(*quickly*) No. (*louder*) Where did you go to college?
LYNN:	That makes me a little worried. Harry said that he wouldn't agree to play this game. However, I think that he probably has no choice.
HARRY:	(*gasping indignantly*) Hah!

At this point, I made a date for the next session and the family left. Our team felt that the mother's curiosity about who might want to leave, and Harry's concerned response, confirmed our hypothesis, which was that Harry's behavior was keeping his mother in line. Two weeks later, although Harry was reportedly behaving better, it was Easter break, and when I spoke to the mother on the phone, she sounded particularly angry. She felt that the school had mishandled Harry from the beginning. I asked what might happen if the school refused to keep him. Would the next step be to send him away from home? The mother answered with an emphatic, "Yes."

However, we were not yet at that point, and so we decided to set up a meeting between Harry, his parents, and the school, to try to get him back to school as soon as possible. The meeting seemed to go well. The school agreed to share information with the parents on a weekly basis, Harry agreed to try to limit the number of misbehaviors per class, and the parents promised that if Harry left school without permission, they would impose a consequence. This was all written down in contract form, signed, and Harry was readmitted on a half-day basis.

All the same, I was uneasy. I kept feeling that there was some rhyme, some reason, for Harry's incessant need to bike home, which was as yet opaque to all of us. Worse yet, the school contract seemed set up to be broken. Harry was unlikely to turn into a good citizen overnight and the parents were tired of being told to impose consequences. Some huge anxiety, whatever it might be, kept pulling at Harry, and the school had made it clear that he would not be given another chance. I was sure that if he were to be placed in a facility that he could not leave at will, he might begin acting in such a disturbed way as to bring a heavy label on his head.

The Secret

Into the general blackness of my mind came a ray of light. I had been re-reading *Paradox and Counterparadox*, and had been transfixed by the para-doxical letters the Milan team sent to their families. These messages seemed to have a powerful effect in depriving symptoms of the oxygen they needed to grow. So I devised a Milan-style letter and showed it to my team. Silverstein added the bit about Harry, but otherwise they approved and accepted it intact. I sent it to the parents and told them that my team would like the father to read the message to the family some night at dinner or whenever they were together. The message, dripping with positive conno-tation, read as follows:

Dear Family:

There is a secret in this family which Harry is part of and is pro-tecting. Because of this secret, he refuses to leave home the normal way. The secret has to do with mother, who lovingly puts her family before her own self-interest or liberation. Taking care of Harry is the best way she knows to prove that fact. Father knows this and lovingly helps mother to fulfill her task. Laura and Michael know this too, and do their part to show mother they truly appreciate her sacrifice. And Harry knows this best of all.

At the bottom of this mutual concern is a secret that may be painful but keeps the family together. Under no account do we believe that this secret should be revealed.

The Ackerman Team

At the next meeting, attended by the parents and the two younger children (Michael was off somewhere), I encountered a nest of polite hornets. The father asked if we were playing some kind of a game, and Harry made a rude comment. But the mother said that, although the note had angered her, it also made her think. In the car the day before, she and the father were having a "mild" argument, and Harry, as he often did, got upset and told them to stop. She had asked him if he were afraid they would get a divorce. He said yes and that he would not like it. According to the father, Harry had said that if they got a divorce, he'd be "split." Harry, who was then sit-ting between his parents, corrected them: "No, I'd be in the middle." I asked Laura, who was sitting apart, if she had the same fears, and she said, "No."

Harry immediately began to disqualify what he had said, saying he had "made it up." The mother came in to say, "It's his reality, it's not our reality." Her own hypothesis was that because Harry had been adopted, he was especially sensitive to anything that was going wrong in his family. The father had another explanation: he had been tougher on Harry since they had been in therapy and that was why he was acting up. It seemed that Harry had asked him one day if they were going to get rid of him, something that was very hard for this father to hear.

Since the subject of divorce was not going anywhere, I asked how Harry was doing in school. Not well. He was coming home at all hours, and the school was threatening to expel him for good. The mother said that, if they threw Harry out, it was his responsibility—she had ceased to care. At this point, I was responding to a sixth sense that told me what a disaster it would be for her if she gave up on Harry, and I decided that I must challenge her statement at any cost. So I said that of all the persons in the family, she was the one who would most resist sending him away. She disagreed sharply with me, and I backed off.

The interview ended on the subject of consequences, which the school was insisting on. Richard said that Harry could not be punished because there was so little he cared to do or have. I remarked that the only thing he seemed to care about were his parents. I also wondered if he might not continue to make trouble to keep his fears from coming true. The mother asked, "Do you mean his greatest fear is that we would get divorced?" Harry exclaimed, "Damn right!" He added that an even greater fear was that he would be sent away. I said that if he were sent away, it would probably be to a place he couldn't run away from every time he wanted to check things out at home. At that point he said, "That's why I run home, to see if my parents got divorced yet."

Despite Harry's validation of our hypothesis, I was discouraged when I went backstage for our team discussion. But Silverstein, as she so often did, provided an idea that opened the path forward. She told me to say to the family that the team agreed with my statement that the only thing Harry cared about was his parents. But then she added her trademark leap: I was to say that the team felt that the only way the parents could punish Harry for infractions like biking home from school would be to openly disagree about the consequences if he did. Arguing about their differences in front of him would be the ultimate deterrent.

I was amazed at the effect of this simple suggestion. Harry became extremely agitated and kept repeating, "If I did something bad they'd *both* get mad, right?" The father said that they hardly ever disagreed. The mother said she did not agree that they did not disagree. She said that she took the position that Harry should be held more responsible for his actions than his father did. She also said that it would be a good idea for them to discuss this issue in front of Harry, rather than going behind closed doors to make their decision, as they usually did.

Harry was now beginning to interrupt, drum on the radiator, and show other signs of restlessness. I feared that the small disagreement that had already surfaced was too much for him, so I swung into a digression with the hope of calming him down. Here is a rough transcript of this conversation, which ends the interview. Harry's father had just said that even though it was an article of faith that they shouldn't let the kids play one of them against the other, maybe that wasn't right. In reply, I said that things that were right for one point weren't always right for another. Then I turned to Harry, who was pulling the window curtains over himself.

LYNN: Harry, you're not at fault, you're standing on a fault. Do you
           know what a fault is?
HARRY: Yes.
LYNN: A fault in the crust of the earth, two platelets, like the San
           Andreas fault?
HARRY: (*indignantly*) I know what it is!
LYNN: Well, in a family that has two parents, there's two people
           who are moving through life and they can't possibly be
           moving at the same rate. And I have the feeling that you are
           supersensitive to the rate of movement, especially of people
           in your family, and to these slight differences, which are so
           minute but which creep from year to year. (*to parents*) He's
           like those people who can put their ear to the ground and
           hear a storm far off or an army many miles away. (*to mother*)
           And I really feel that it would help if you would air some
           of your thoughts about his misbehavior—not about per-
           sonal things but when he misbehaves—I don't mean play-
           act.
MOTHER: I don't think we'd have to play-act.
FATHER: No, but we'd have to create divisions where they don't really
           exist. We react spontaneously to what Harry does—at least
           we react without having a conference on how to react. And
           he hears us.
LYNN: But do you comment on what each other is doing? (*to
           mother*) Do you comment on whether you think your hus-
           band is behaving correctly?
MOTHER: No.
FATHER: (*to mother*) When I think you're too tough, I just keep quiet.
MOTHER: And when I think you're too soft, I tell you later, privately.
LYNN: I would say have it out right there. Would you give that a try
           anyway?
MOTHER: Okay.

HARRY:	Okay. Goodbye.
LYNN:	And Harry—
HARRY:	What do you want?
LYNN:	If you hear of any earthquakes, let me know.
HARRY:	*(patting Lynn on the shoulder as he went out)* You're right!

This was the first time I had any sign of acceptance from Harry, and I wanted to hug him. As for the metaphor of the fault, I had used it before in writing about the position of the "identified patient." I believed that this person was literally standing on a fault or split in the family, but that the practical effect on the other family members was to make them feel that the fault was within him.

The next session was a tense one. Only Harry and his parents were present. The parents said they had not done the homework, so the team suggested that I ask them to discuss the issue of whether or not they should impose consequences right there in the room. The mother started out by saying that in the past, when she and Richard discussed whether or not to punish Harry for something, she was for punishing him and he was against it, and ninety-eight percent of the time he won.

She then mentioned a recent infraction (she had caught Harry smoking) and stated her opinion that they should impose a fine. She asked the father, "What would happen if for once you backed me two hundred percent and we did impose a fine? Then maybe he wouldn't do it again." The father said, "That would be papering over our differences. I can't do something I don't feel like doing. I have to be me." The mother replied, "But when I agree to do what you want, isn't that papering over our differences?" The father said, "You're saying 'Just agree with me,'" and began to talk about family bylaws and constitutional differences.

The mother began to look confused and turned to me, explaining, "Well, that's the problem. I want to do the harsher thing and he wants to do the softer thing, and I feel that I'm wrong, so I give in." I confess that I had a feeling of sympathy for this mother, knowing from my own experience how easy it is to "give in." If we had seen this case in a stronger feminist environment, 1990 instead of 1980, we might well have supported the mother more openly, but at that time we believed that taking sides would jeopardize our effectiveness. In this particular situation, I think that, if I had sided with the mother, the family would have swung to the father's defense and the "differences" we were trying to get at would have vanished.

So all I said to the mother was, "If you only win two percent of the time, that must make you feel pretty ineffective." The mother replied, "Well, at least we can air our differences, even if we don't do anything about them." Then she came out with a rather astonishing statement: "I'm not sure why, but even the little bit of disagreement that we had in front of Harry last week seems to have taken an enormous burden off my shoulders. I feel that the world won't fall apart, and Harry won't fall apart, if we don't speak in one voice." I had noticed that Harry, for the first time ever, was lying on the couch next to his mother, leaning against her and frowning tenderly. With the disagreement between the parents so openly stated, I was worried and launched once more into prophetic mode. I told Harry that there might be some kind of earthquake ahead, but that if he were to deliberately make some small explosions, maybe he could avert the big one. I said that I had full confidence that he would protect the family by doing this. I wanted to prescribe what I was worried about in the hope of preventing it, but I worried that it would happen anyway.

It did. A week later, the mother called to say that Harry had brought his bike into the classroom every day that week and would not let anyone else take it; also that he biked home every chance he got. The school decided they had had enough and expelled him. But here was the surprise. The mother stated that I must have had a crystal ball when I predicted that she would never agree to send Harry away. She said she had made a 180-degree turn and had decided to keep him at home if she had to tutor him herself. She also said that she wanted to continue with family therapy as she, at least, had profited greatly from it. Now it was the mother I wanted to hug.

Armed with this encouraging news, I called the school psychologist, with whom I had been careful to maintain a good relationship. I said I thought that Harry's behavior was a temporary aberration and that the family had made a real shift. Since it was now the end of the school year, I hoped that the school would re-think their decision and that maybe we could work something out for the fall. I added that the mother wanted to continue with family therapy and was prepared to cooperate fully with the school. To my relief, the mother and the school worked out a half-day tutoring schedule for the coming fall, and the crisis was averted. Laura and Michael went off to camp, and Harry, who was shortly going to camp too, came in with his parents while we discussed the new arrangements.

During the session, we asked Harry to sit behind the screen, which he did. Amazingly, he stayed quietly glued to the mirror the whole time. The mother wanted to try to convince the father to commit himself to therapy. She said that she was now a true believer and hoped he would want to continue too. The team got nervous and called me out to discuss how we might get the father out of his bad position. Here were two females, both favoring family therapy, ganging up against him. So they told me to go back in and tell the father that I valued his skepticism much more than his support because I too was a family therapy doubter (which was true). The team also suggested that the mother explain to her husband what changes she wanted to work on. So she said to him that she felt they should be firmer in disciplining Harry when he misbehaved. The father, in what felt to me like a outstanding concession, agreed to do this.

In regard to meeting again, I said that I would not even consider it if the father were not involved. The father asked why Harry couldn't go back into individual therapy, since he had apparently already agreed to do this. I felt that I was in a delicate position, because I might lose the father if I pushed to see them all. So my team came to the rescue. They sent in a message stating that "the men in the group" didn't think that I really understood what an important role the father played for his son, and how important it was for the father to help the boy "in his struggles against authority," meaning, of course, female authority. The father smiled and said that he had never for a single moment thought of not being included.

Dr. Harold

After this, we adjourned for the summer. Harry went to camp, and nothing was heard from the family until the middle of the summer, when Michael suddenly surfaced as the new identified patient. True to our theory that the family "needs" its symptom, the team had already stated that if Harry ever did vacate his position of troublemaker, Michael might very well take his place. The mother had called around mid-August, saying that the crystal ball had worked again and that they were now worrying about Michael.

Despite my prediction, I was surprised. From being a wonderful, helpful teenager, Michael had become a sullen, long-haired hippie. His "bad" behaviors were surprisingly similar to Harry's. He was staying out all night without telling his parents where he was (actually, he was at the home of his girlfriend), and had announced that he was not going to college. At Michael's request, I saw him a couple of times. He was worried about himself, felt quite depressed, and had lost interest in school. I tried to normalize this state of affairs and to point out that it had been topsy-turvy for his younger brother to be a rebellious teenager before he was. After all, he needed a chance to rebel too. I hoped that this way of prescribing the problem would work. At any rate, something did. His grades had gone from good to failing that fall, but he made such a quick recovery that by spring he was accepted in the college of his choice.

But an even bigger surprise was Harry. When he came back from camp, he was truly a changed character. He had won the camp award for Most Personal Improvement. He was acting responsible, behaved with decorum, and was no longer harassing people in his family or anywhere else. The main problem was that he had become his older brother's ferocious little watch dog, yelling at his parents when they reprimanded him, and at the same time telling Michael to start working at school or else he would end up a bum.

That fall, Harry's own school career began to go well. He had the good fortune to be assigned a tutor who was a natural therapist, and came into the few sessions we had calling himself "Dr. Harold," and saying things like, "Dr. Harold says you mustn't smoke." The only time he reverted to his former behavior was when his father's father died. Harry was impossible at the funeral, creating disruptions and clowning around in the most appalling way. But this behavior was short-lived. By the end of the year, Harry was routed into a normal tenth grade. He had some trouble at first, but soon adjusted.

There was one more tiny eruption that threatened to occur. Just when Harry and Michael were straightening out, the mother called to say that she was worried that Laura was not pursuing her studies as assiduously as she should. However, before a meeting could be set up, Laura had promised to reform. The major regret I had was that I had never made any real connection with Laura, the natural child. Not having any problems, she became invisible to me.

My experience with this family caused me to question some of my beliefs. Some family theorists predicted that if the problem child got better, the marital relationship would get worse. This did not happen. When asked about their personal issues, the parents said they had no substantial concerns and I believed them. However, I had read some research showing that older people give off clues about their death during the year before they die. The death of a grandfather will set all sorts of bells tolling, and I wondered if Harry's rambunctious displays were not in response to a premonition of this sort. The mother's father had died in 1978 and the father's mother in 1979, just before we saw the family, so there was already a plague of deaths. Also, I thought that Harry was particularly sensitive to the vulnerability of his father. One comment jumped out at me while I was going over the tapes. When I asked what would happen if Harry became an angel overnight, Laura had jokingly remarked that "Dad would have a heart attack," and Harry had passionately concurred.

In our last session, we asked a question of each family member except Michael, who was away at college: "What would each of you have to do to bring the situation back to where it was when you first came into this room?" This was a strategic intervention based on the idea was that if you prescribed a relapse, it was less likely to happen. It was also a way of obtaining evidence of change, and the answers were interesting in that respect. The mother said she would have to go back to thinking she could handle everything. The father said that he would have to go back to not airing disagreements openly. Laura said that she would have to scream whenever

Harry came near her. And Harry said that he would have to go back to being a "nasty rotten kid," but added that this would be difficult because of "Dr. Harold."

One interesting difference was that instead of doing everything as a bloc, with Harry as a centripetal force, there was a marked weakening of fixed alliances. Michael, when not at college, was often at the house of his girlfriend. Laura and her mother had taken a trip together. The father and Harry had gone off together too. There seemed to be greater flexibility for all. I wondered if this were not the hallmark of the elusive "happy family." The coalitions, as we called them then, seemed looser, and the individuals seemed freed up too.

In saying goodbye, I thanked Dr. Harold for taking such good care of Harry, and was rewarded with a manly handshake and a charmingly exaggerated "God bless me!" When we contacted the family a year later, everyone was doing well. The entire course of these conversations had lasted over a period of a year and a half and included thirteen family sessions and two couple sessions at approximately monthly intervals. There were also two individual sessions with Michael.

So much for brief therapy. The Milan team was now describing its work as a kind of long brief therapy, with separations of two weeks to a month between sessions. If the family was indeed a many-layered kinship system (as it certainly was in Italy), an intervention would take a much longer time to percolate through it than conventional therapies allowed for (Selvini et al., 1980b). I myself had become more and more enthralled with the unusual thinking and unorthodox practices of this group. I began to make yearly pilgrimages to Milan to sit behind the one-way mirror at the Centro per lo Studio della Famiglia in Via Leopardi, No. 19, and watch the team at work. In the next chapter, I will describe the way Peggy Penn and I developed a new team at Ackerman, which was organized more strictly along Milan lines, and which allowed us to explore the strengths and also the limits of this fascinating approach.

5

Magnificent Obsessions

When I first read *Paradox and Counterparadox,* I was inspired. Here at last was a theory about therapy built upon the systemic vision that Bateson was trying to describe. Better yet, I was in a setting that welcomed it. Peggy Papp and Olga Silverstein had already seen Selvini's team in action, and in 1978 they were invited to pay a visit to Ackerman and to the Brief Therapy Project in particular. Both teams were among the first to take up the ideas of the MRI, particularly their emphasis on paradoxical interventions, and both had expanded the model to include formal observer groups behind the screen.

So this was a momentous occasion. You have to imagine a small room on the fourth floor of the Institute behind a one-way screen, video cameras at the ready, packed with people who were sitting on bleachers or standing, waiting for the Milan team to appear. Even though our expectations were high, they did not disappoint us. Selvini came in as if she were a court visiting another court; despite her short stature, she held herself as regally as Queen Elizabeth. "I am Dr. Mara Selvini," she informed us. Then, treating us to her famous throaty laugh, she introduced the rest of the team: psychiatrists Luigi Boscolo, Guiliana Prata, and Gianfranco Cecchin.

There was an interesting wrinkle to this situation. Family therapy interviews had traditionally included the basic family: the child with the problem, the parents, and the siblings. Grandparents didn't have to be present unless they were living in the same household. But the Milan group was part of a growing movement in the field to include not only kin groups, but also people from systems outside the family: those who might hold a stake in the outcome of the work, like the "referring person" or helpers from other agencies (Selvini et al., 1980a). We knew that Joel Bergman was bringing in not only a young man who was severely agoraphobic and his parents, but also a female social worker who had become very close to the young man and whom Bergman called the "significant other." In due time, our receptionist phoned Bergman to say that the family had arrived and he went down to bring them up.

So we waited. And waited. And waited. I remember Mara sitting coolly expectant, with her trademark large purse on her lap, while the watchers fretted and muttered behind the screen. Finally a frustrated Bergman came into the interviewing room. He explained that the young man's agoraphobia prevented him from using the only elevator, and the group had only managed to get to the second floor. Despite exhortations from his parents, the social worker, and Bergman, the young man had plunked himself down on the staircase and refused to go any further.

In such a case, the members of the Brief Therapy Project usually spent the time allotted analyzing the family's "resistance" and trying not to feel unhappy. Imagine our surprise when Selvini took the news with great relish. Addressing Bergman, she said, "Very good! Tell the family that the Milan team will hold a consultation anyway. They can go now, but tell them that we will compose a message for you to give to them at your next session." We all watched, fascinated, to see what message they would come up with. How could the "experts from Milan" come to a conclusion without even meeting the family?

This question was answered when the group addressed themselves not to the situation the family was in but to the situation *the professionals* were in. The young man's disability had prevented him and his family from meeting with the experts from Milan, disappointing not only them but much of the teaching staff of the Ackerman Institute. Now it seemed that the team was not going to let the family "win." The wording of their message, in which optimism and pessimism were curiously mixed, was extremely provocative. It sounded as if the Milan team were going up a level to engage both the family and Ackerman on the question of therapy itself. The content of the message was of far less importance than the relational aspects. I think this was the first time that I had ever experienced from the inside what we were later to call a "second order" move.

The statement the team composed went generally as follows (my memory is not exact):

Here is the message from the experts from Milan: In Milan, we see many, many young people who cannot leave home but live with their parents or remain supported by them, not leaving their room, not getting a job, not having friends. In most cases the reason for this is the fear that if they did so, they would leave their parents in a state of intolerable loneliness. In Milan, we have found that eighty-five percent of these young people eventually get a job, move out, and so forth, but fifteen percent fail to do so. If we were in Milan, we would know what to say, but here, as we cannot predict which percentage this particular young man might fall into, we cannot make any further statement. Thank you very much. The Milan Team.

This statement was conventional in one way, being a positive connotation of the young man's problem, but what about these mysterious percentages? It was Cecchin who explained them as a fiction that was thrown in to provide an incentive. They hoped that the young man would resist being lumped with the fifteen percent that failed. According to Bergman, who continued to pepper the family with letters containing similar paradoxes, the young man got angry and told Bergman that he intended to sue Ackerman and use the letters as evidence of malpractice. The clinic director declared Milan-style letters henceforth out of bounds, but before this rule came down, social worker Gillian Walker, who was consulting with Bergman, wrote the man a letter that said the team was happy that he had conquered his agoraphobia, and cited his intention to go to court as evidence of success.

But let me go back to the Milan team's consultation. We could not know how the family received the intervention or if it had any effect, but its influence on the community of therapists who witnessed it was profound. I began my annual pilgrimage to Milan to watch the work of the team, and after Boscolo and Cecchin launched their own training institute in 1980, several of us attended their yearly "teams" meetings. I think it was Selvini who first used Bateson's word "systemic" to describe their work, but I picked it up and pushed it, just as I had done with Minuchin's use of the word "structural." Systemic therapy went on to become a huge influence on family therapy worldwide.

Through all these years, Selvini, who recently died, remained an enthusiastic and endearing friend. She was one of those women I now call "scholar-therapists," innovative practitioners who valued ideas as much as techniques and whose work was as much a calling as a profession. Cecchin used to say, "Never marry your hypotheses," and Selvini was a remarkable example of a person who came up with brilliant ideas, held onto them tenaciously, and yet was willing to drop them when experience proved her wrong. Her pursuit of the secrets of family systems resembled that of a big game hunter stalking his prey, and her spirit inspired many others. She also inspired a rare affection. Unlike other research teams, which often broke apart in acrimony after their work was published, Selvini's former partners never stopped loving and respecting her, nor did any of her students and colleagues.

Let me share one more example of her vivid presence. In 1978, on one of my early visits to Milan, I was sitting behind the screen with Cecchin and Selvini while Prata interviewed the mother of a six-year-old boy. He was referred to the team because since the previous Christmas he had refused to talk. In the interview, he kept running around the room, and if anyone addressed him he would stop and say, "Si," then continue running. Prata, who was trying to find out what had happened during that Christmas, learned that the family had spent Christmas alone. Backstage, I noticed Selvini get up to watch more closely. Then she said, "A family—in Italy—having their Christmas dinner alone? Without any relatives? Impossible!" Then she intoned, sounding much like the Giant in "Jack the Giant-Killer": "I smell the rotten meat." And she asked Prata to find out more about the family's recent history.

Prata discovered that before Christmas the couple had moved from an apartment that was near the wife's mother to an apartment nearer the father's mother. As a result, the wife's mother refused to join them for Christmas dinner. On Christmas Eve, after a horrible quarrel with her husband, the wife had put the little boy in bed between them and from that time on had refused to have sex. In the final message, Giuliana asked the little boy if he knew how important it was for him to keep his parents from quarreling at night by getting into bed between them. The little boy looked up, smiling, said, "Si," as if he totally understood, and for the first time stopped running. I don't remember much else about the case, but I took away, and still keep, a strong impression of Selvini's active mind, her generous presence, her expansiveness, her humor. Someone once said that the painter Picasso was a "discontinuous genius." In the field of family therapy, Mara was the same. But on to my exposition.

Davening at the Window

The Milan team felt that a child's symptoms arose from a pathological tangle that resembled the Bateson group's double bind. In one of her presentations, Selvini described this syndrome as an "imbroglio," and gave an unforgettable illustration. When she was a young woman in Italy, just after the war, there was a black market in cigarettes. She went to buy a pack from a street dealer and gave him a large bill, which he went off to change. When he came back, he only returned part of what he owed her. Seeing a policeman nearby, Selvini ran up to him and informed him of the dealer's attempt to cheat her. The policeman told her that it was she who was guilty of criminal behavior, by buying cigarettes on the black market, and threatened her with a fine. As she stood there, shocked, she watched the dealer and policeman walking away arm in arm.

Selvini and her team assumed that some version of this confusing relationship pattern could be found in families with a symptomatic child. The job of the interviewer was to ask questions that would cast some light on how the symptom protected the relationship system. After a discussion, the group would deliver a "counterparadox" that positively connoted and/or prescribed the problem but would touch all members of the group. For instance, the family might be given a ritual to be carried out at supper in which each person ceremoniously thanked the person with the problem. Mother would say, "Thank you, Anthony, for refusing to go to school because that insures that your grandmother will remain close to me." Father would say, "Thank you, Anthony, for refusing to go to school, because that keeps me and your mother from fighting." The brother would say, "Thank you, Anthony, for refusing to go to school because then nobody notices what I do." The family might be very upset at such a directive, and might not carry it out, but often the boy would go back to school.

As one might imagine, the Milan approach did not transfer too easily to the U.S. For obvious reasons, the team's deliberations were held in secret and the rationale for their seemingly sarcastic messages was never shared. Usually, the interviewer wrote them down, took them back to the family, read them out, and fled. But we were not in Italy, where the public treated medical professionals like priests, so we had to be more careful about what we told our families or asked them to do. We believed that this verbal shock therapy would cause the family to recoil against the symptomatic behavior, but it just as often caused them to recoil against us.

In 1980, I left the Brief Therapy Project and asked Peggy Penn, who had just been asked to be a member of the faculty at Ackerman, to join me in setting up a Milan-style team. Penn had a background in theater, a degree in social work, and in later years became a published poet. She was a striking person to look at: you saw flyaway reddish blonde hair framing a narrow face with great violet eyes, and then she surprised you with her incisive intellect. I also admired her ability to think in images. We spent a year working as a pair. The following year, psychiatrists John Patten and Jeffrey Ross, hypnotherapists who had studied with John Grinder and Richard Bandler, asked to join us. Then Joel Bergman and Gillian Walker, original members of the Brief Therapy Project, asked to come in too. We became an unwieldy busload of six.

At this time, Penn and I were moving from the idea of changing behaviors to the idea of changing meanings. In this we were following Luigi Boscolo and Gianfranco Cecchin, who had separated from the original Milan team. They were exploring the idea of a family myth (Boscolo et al., 1987), which, if it became too rigid, might require crazy behavior to keep it going. Penn and I were taking a similar view, but used the word "premise." If you said that a family was operating in the service of an outmoded premise rather than playing a psychotic game, it seemed less pejorative. The problem was that we were still using a reified language. We were talking as if a premise sat inside a family the way a message sits inside a fortune cookie. In the grip of what I now think of as a modernist persuasion, we spent endless hours trying to find patterns in our families that matched those that were operating in our minds.

During this time, Penn would every once in a while come up with what I called "blue lightning" questions. There was one family where a young pianist of twenty, a former child prodigy and star at Julliard, had a nervous collapse. He had been hospitalized for several weeks and was now at home with his mother and father, both émigrés from Poland. His mother, a talented painter, had invested many hopes in this son, and his father, also a musician, was equally proud of him. The mother's mother, who lived in the family, was a gracious woman in her seventies who couldn't speak English very well, so her grandson would translate for her. The parents argued over any issue that came their way, and it was hard for myself and John Patten, as the interviewers, to detach them from their perpetual bicker.

During one session, when John Patten and I must have looked particularly stymied, Penn called from behind the screen and told us to ask the following question: "If Grandmother were to say to either Mother or Father, 'You are right, I love you the best,' what would happen?" I fielded this question to the family. To my astonishment, it provoked a kind of pandemonium. After it was translated for her, the grandmother said that she was always trying to tell her daughter not to favor her son so much because this made his father jealous. The mother said her husband was foolish to feel this way. The father announced loudly, "I am Public Enemy Number One, and I will leave this family." And the young man, who usually did not say much, declared to everyone: "There, you see, that was why I had to go to the hospital."

For us systemic thinkers, with our belief that disturbed behavior in a child was tied to a multigenerational struggle, it was an amazing scene, as if the inner politics of the family had been unfurled before us. Penn's question seemed to hit at the heart of the "imbroglio," to use Selvini's term, and lay it out for all to see. Of course, knowing what was causing trouble did not tell us how to deal with it, but our new team members brought in new capacities. Walker's intense interest in the spoors of family history added depth to our work. Bergman brought his dramatic appreciation of craziness. Patten, who later started an AIDS project at Ackerman, offered his fine sense of irony, and Ross, a colleague of Patten's at Payne Whitney, contributed an empathic common sense. This was lucky, because the team rapidly became the hit squad for some of the clinic's most difficult referrals. Here is a story about a family we found particularly endearing.

A school psychologist had recommended Delia, seventeen, and her family to Ackerman because she was plagued by lurid thoughts that interfered with her school work. The father, who taught high school history, and the mother, who tutored homebound children, were both in their forties and they had two other daughters: Leila, nineteen, and Reba, fifteen. They were Jewish but not particularly religious and not a Holocaust family either. John Patten and I were the interviewers, and the other four were behind the screen. As was customary with the Milan approach, we saw them on a monthly basis. In the following account, I often say "we" when either John or I was speaking, because my notes did not always distinguish between us. Also, due to the fact that there was no behind-screen recording system, I can represent the thinking of the group only in a general sense.

The family charmed us with their eager interest in Delia's "case." The mother, a short, bubbly woman with bobbed hair, waved and smiled at "the mirrors" as she called them, whenever she came in. The father was a high school teacher, but the family agreed he should have been a rabbi because of his serious intellectual tastes. Leila was small, dark, and intense; she too had a formidable mind and was taking pre-med classes. Delia was a Pre-Raphaelite beauty with a flair for drama and the arts. Reba was in junior high school and possessed contagious curiosity and enthusiasm.

Our first meeting was a general intake, and my notes on it are sketchy, but we learned all about Delia's obsessions. A few years earlier, she had begun seeing images of "old dead rabbis," and went on to even more grotesque thoughts about her dead great-grandmother. More recently, she kept seeing Leila's face covered with peanut butter, in which she, Delia, would make "sick designs." Delia at one point said that her obsessive thoughts were like a cork on a bottle, prompting her father to wonder what would happen if it ever came off. In our second interview, we zeroed in on the family of origin. Gillian Walker, an indefatigable student of intergenerational themes, told John and myself to ask when the obsessions had begun. The mother said that the thoughts of old dead men had started with the death of her father five years before. The thoughts about the great-grandmother occurred two years later, when she in turn died. The peanut butter thoughts coincided with the partial departure of Leila, who had been living in a dorm at medical school except for weekends.

It became clear that this series of deaths impacted family members profoundly. Twelve years before, when the mother's own mother died, her younger brother had apparently "gone berserk." The mother had an equally intense reaction to her father's death. He had remarried late in life, gone to live with his new wife in Florida, and died shortly thereafter. The mother then began to berate herself, saying over and over that if she had only stopped him from leaving, he might still be alive. The father had told her it was wrong to carry on that way and refused to let the family sit shiva. When the great-grandmother died, the father again forbade the ritual. He explained: "My attitude was, 'Let's get on with education.' " We asked the daughters how they felt about the death of these people. Delia said that even though she was an emotional person, she had never been able to mourn them. Leila said that she avoided thinking about them—"otherwise I would go under." Reba wished they could go back to the past when everybody was still alive.

As you can imagine, this story activated a lengthy team discussion. Family theory at that time suggested that obsessions like these might be connected to incomplete mourning, so we decided to give the family a paradoxical ritual. We explained that the obsessions rose from Delia's belief that she must divert attention from the deaths in the family that had not been properly mourned. To help her with this important task, we asked the family to sit together every Friday evening during the next month and pass around photos of the people who had died. If Delia noticed anyone looking sad or upset, she was to offer one of her obsessions. Our theory was that the obsessions served a diversionary function in the family, and we hoped that if this function were made overt, the obsessions would die down. We also wanted to honor the prohibited feelings of grief.

During the third meeting, the family said they had done the ritual but that, despite pressure from Leila, Delia had refused to offer any obsessions. Of course, this was what we had hoped for. The father discounted this result, but Delia looked and acted calmer. It was the mother who now complained, saying that her daughters were criticizing her for sloppiness and that she was beginning to feel like a "battered mommy." It seemed that Leila objected to her mother's table behavior, especially to her eating noises. Defending her mother, Delia countered that Leila had a habit of bringing up food at meals and spitting it into a napkin. Leila (who later became alarmingly anorectic) dismissed this as her "slight regurgitations." Despite their irritation with their mother, Leila said they loved her for her "happy little ways." It seemed that when she got home from work, she would stand in front of the kitchen window, swaying and humming and waving her hands. She would thank God over and over for her wonderful daughters and her wonderful husband, mentioning each by name. "She sings with her mouth," Delia told us. Leila explained that "Even though supper never gets made, it's a beautiful, beautiful thing."

In our team discussion, we noted the similarity of the mother's behavior to the practice of saying Kaddish, the yearlong, daily prayer for the dead. The mother had told us that indeed she had first started practicing her ritual at the window after her father's death. Our new hypothesis was that Delia's obsessions obscured the conflict between the parents around the expression of grief. We composed a "sacrifice intervention" that put Delia's thoughts about the vanished relatives and the mother's mourning behavior in the service of the father. It read as follows:

> The meaning of all of Delia's obsessions became clear in the session. Most importantly, the team understands that Delia and her mother are selfless women who believe that father has never been able to mourn the people in mother's family whom he truly loved, because mourning would be too painful. Therefore, to protect father, mother must continue to daven at the window and Delia must continue to obsess about death until both women receive a signal from father that he is ready to mourn—only then will it be safe for the cork to come off the bottle.

In the fourth session, the father chided us for this interpretation and stated that Delia still had obsessions even though she didn't talk about them. However, even though our messages might be experienced as strange or sarcastic, we felt their shock value was worth it if they produced a change. And there was one. Delia told us that she was now seeking a "new image" by throwing out everything in her room. She had gone back to her classes at college and she was dating. At least the obsessions were no longer getting in her way.

In this same meeting, we found that food was a major preoccupation in the family. Delia said that when she attempted to feed her father "creamy snacks," Leila would snatch them out of his mouth because she feared he would have a heart attack. "There's a heart condition somewhere," Leila said ominously. Reba added that the father's mother had sustained a slight heart attack that previous summer. This was a premonition we ignored at the time; we were so focused on the past that we didn't worry about the future. It was only later that we realized that we should have picked it up.

When we asked about the father's family, the father said that his parents had "stifled" him as a child and Delia told us, "They took away his blocks." The father said that he had been very fond of his wife's family because it was more warm-hearted than his own. It turned out that his own mother was not very tolerant of his wife's personal habits, so the family only made ritual visits to those grandparents. With the older generation gone on the mother's side, it was easy to see why Reba said she longed for the "good old days" when these important and affectionate people were still alive.

At this point, we asked the daughters how they would describe their parents' relationship. Leila said that their father had been attracted to their mother because she was "uplifting" and would tell him, "You must have been a poet in a former life." However, there was a drawback; as Delia put it, "Mother builds you up, but builds you up to the unattainable." When we asked the father about the relationship, he said that he once had dreams of romance but that this marriage was a compromise. I didn't keep the message at the end of this session, but I think we described the marriage as an unusual one in which romantic expectations were deferred. I came later to feel uncomfortable with such frank intrusions into the personal lives of the parents, especially when they had come in about a child.

A word of explanation. The Milan group often asked children how they perceived their parents' sex lives. The group was not so attached to the content of the children's answers as to what it could tell them about alliances. If a husband and wife were not close, they might hypothesize about a "marriage" between the mother and sister that excluded the husband. Or they might find that such a marriage existed between a father and a child. In their eyes, such ties had less to do with sexuality than with family politics. An odd wrinkle came in here. Trying to escape these politics themselves, the group aspired to a "neutral" stance. This stance was seen by the growing feminist presence in family therapy to be immoral if not worse, but systemic principles prevented Milan-style therapists from aligning themselves too directly with any person or side. As a result, they came in for much criticism during the eighties and nineties, when families were being scrutinized for child sexual abuse and therapists were being scrutinized for any kind of boundary violation at all.

The Spinster Child

When we met for our fifth session, a month later, the father said he had been confused by the message and the mother disagreed with it. However, Delia's obsessions had more or less dried up and the father said that the problem now was that the mother was trying to match Leila up with boys. Ominously, Leila's spitting up had gotten worse. Her mother said she was eating nothing since she was living away from home and Leila agreed that she had had a depressing year and had lost weight (she now weighed 88 pounds), but she resented her mother's attempts to bring her food. She complained, "If my mother could, she would breastfeed me."

It seemed that Leila had finally gone to see their family doctor, who had dismissed the problem, but her mother was pushing her to see a specialist in "bularexia." We supported this idea, as Leila looked alarmingly pale and thin. We then asked Leila what her parents would worry about if she were not the new focus of concern. She said, "My mother would propagate something. They'd pick a dog up off the street or my mother would start to worry about her homebound children, maybe adopt one." When asked what she thought of her mother taking in homebound children, she said it would be wonderful, but she wished her mother would leave her alone.

Moving off this topic, we asked the daughters if they thought their father felt neglected by their mother's involvement with them. The father said that perhaps it was the other way around and that his wife was involved with the girls because he wasn't doing his job "as a husband, as a lover." He confessed that he wanted her to stay involved with the girls. "If she got too concerned with me," he said, "she'd be pushing and pulling at me, "Let's go here, and now we're going to adult education, and why don't you study this, and why don't you get involved in community theater?" I said, "So better she be concerned with her children," to which the father replied, in heartfelt tones, "Right, right."

In our message at the end of this interview, we elaborated our original hypothesis, namely, that the parents had always been assisted in their relationship by other family members, some of whom were now gone. Fearing that their parents would be in trouble if they were left alone, we said that each of the three daughters was vying to be the spinster child. We noted that Leila, since she was having trouble with her weight, was now making more of a sacrifice than the others, possibly even to the point of becoming anorexic, and that because of this imbalance we would like to see the daughters alone.

The sixth meeting was with the three girls. Leila said that she was feeling happier and that she was enjoying school more. She was still spitting up, but her weight had stabilized. We asked the daughters what they thought would happen when they all left home and they told us that their mother was talking about having another baby. They also mentioned the possibility of divorce. We asked which daughter the parents would choose if one of them had to be "homebound." They agreed that it would be Delia. Our message said that we had the faith that if at any time the homebound sibling decided to leave, another would make the sacrifice and take her place.

The father called to reschedule the next meeting, saying that the girls were all busy with summer plans: Reba was going to be a counselor at a camp for six months, Delia was going on a trip to Israel, and Leila had applied to six medical schools. I asked the father how he thought things would go with him and his wife that summer. He said that Delia had sat down with the two of them and played marriage counselor, pushing her father to take her mother out. He said that he had refused and then asked wistfully if I thought it possible that he really didn't like his wife. I told him that these kinds of thoughts were common when children start to leave home. I also spoke to Leila, who said that ever since she had realized that her regurgitations might keep her at home, she had made successful efforts to control them.

The seventh meeting, which we held before the daughters left for the summer, focused on the parents' relationship. The father came in very angry with his wife because she hadn't got the daughters ready to come in on time. We brought up the question of how the parents would fare with their children gone. Delia worried that they would have more confrontations, but Leila said that they complemented each other: "My mother would take care of all the world if my father didn't keep them out, and my father would never come out of his bedroom if my mother didn't drag him." I was impressed with Leila's perceptiveness.

Here the normally gentle father became vehement, saying, "I want more out of life. I want romance, not outside, but inside, with my wife." I turned to the mother and asked how she felt about her husband's complaint. She laughed and made light of it, but her husband said he was insulted that she took him so for granted. Here the team called me and John Patten out and suggested that we sit the parents together and ask the father to convince his wife of his seriousness, otherwise one of the children would have to stay home to be a therapist. We did this. An intense conversation ensued while the daughters listened. The father asked his wife to make some changes like dressing more attractively and eating less sloppily at meals, and the mother, a little too dutifully, agreed to try.

The summer intervened and a meeting in the fall was cancelled because the father's mother had a stroke and was in the hospital. When our eighth meeting was finally held, in November, the mother was again complaining of being a battered mommy. Her husband and Delia were ganging up on her and telling her she was too involved with her daughters. The session seemed to become stalled in trivia, and the team called John and myself out, instructing us to tell the family that the team felt we were failing to help them. This was another Milan maneuver. In response to such an accusation, the family would usually side with the therapists against the team and produce evidence of progress. Sure enough, the family told us that Delia was no longer overwhelmed by her obsessions and that Leila had gained some weight.

However, even when a family's therapists knew the rationale for this intervention, it usually upset them. Boscolo and Cecchin were famous for consultations in which they would interview the family themselves, ignoring the therapist. When they took a break to discuss the intervention, they would leave the therapist sitting with the family. Then, in the message to the family, they might commend the therapist for protecting the family by not producing any change. I knew therapists who had been reduced to tears when this happened to them. In my case, even though I knew the reason for this move, I nevertheless felt upset and abandoned. I don't remember how John Patten felt.

But when we came back in, the mother surprised us. Sounding unusually strong and clear she said: "It's my husband and me. I think he has to change." She complained that he was becoming "like a block of ice," playing with his computer all night, and refusing to go out with her. She said that if he weren't always pushing her away, she wouldn't have to get so involved with the girls. The daughters were delighted with her and cheered her on. In our message we asked the question, "What would light a fire under father?" and came up with the suggestion that until something did, Delia might have to be the coals that kept the marriage warm.

The Cork Comes Off the Bottle

At our ninth meeting, in January, the couple said they were getting along better. Leila had been accepted at a nearby medical school, and Delia merely complained about being nervous. In her colorful way, she said, "I think I'm the product of a brilliant mind gone berserk." We began to think we were ending with them. Then disaster struck. The father's mother died in January, and by April the mother phoned in with a new concern. She said that Delia was weeping day and night and threatening to commit suicide. Her mother said the obsessions had nearly disappeared when the father's mother died, and then "it was as though the cork was off the bottle." Delia had signed herself into a hospital for a short time, then left, and now she was sitting at home, pulling her hair out and neglecting herself.

In our tenth session, Delia did indeed look a picture of dishevelment and sorrow. She kept saying things like, "I'm such a pain, I bite off my nails, I am garbage." The father showed us the hole in her scalp. He seemed furious with her, calling her a "fine actress." He had ordered her to get out of the house and look for a job, but when she went out, she called hot lines, telling them she was going to kill herself. "They grab me for therapy," she complained. Often the father was called at work and he or both parents ended up taking her to an emergency room. They couldn't go out together anymore for fear of what Delia might do. The mother said she didn't feel

Delia was psychotic, just suffering from hysterical anxiety, but a psychiatrist at one hospital had put her on medication for depression.

We asked about the difference between the death of the mother's father, which had been so troubling, and this death. The father said that for this one they had sat shiva. His own father, who was now seventy-six, was a man who had always left decisions to his wife, so the son had to take over his affairs. Now the grandfather sat in the house brooding, always talking about the past. The strange thing was that Delia was behaving similarly. The mother said it was as if she were taking on her grandfather's personality: "She looks like him, acts like him." Delia broke in to wail, "I turn to stone—I'm empty inside—I worry about myself." The mother added that the subject of Delia was the only thing that brought the grandfather's mind into the present. Our theory, of course, was that Delia's problem served exactly this function, to distract the family members from the impact of the death.

At this point, an incident occurred showing how a hypothesis can take hold and crush out any wider inquiry. We had been working from the notion that the latest death in the family was a trigger for Delia's extreme behavior, but Penn, behind the screen, remembered that the mother had previously spoken of some Canadian boy that Delia had met and liked. In response to this prompt, I asked about him, and the mother said that the boy had returned to Canada and hadn't come back. Delia started to wail and weep again, saying that he had wanted her to join him before he left, and that she couldn't do so because of her grandmother's death. "It could have led to something important," she said pathetically.

So I asked her, "If this boy called now, how would you respond?" She said, "I don't know. The way I am now, I'm not a prize. But I might try as hard as possible to fix myself up." I asked, "Would you say you were in love?" She nodded, saying, "There was a spark." I asked if she would say that her heart was broken. She agreed, sobbing more quietly now. She said she would see her friend, as if in a picture, three or four times a day, then would get very angry at herself and start to pull her hair out. I asked if this was the first romantic attachment that had appeared among the girls, and they all said yes.

In our message we said we felt that Delia's behavior was not so abnormal; after all, she was pining away for love, and not just for herself but for everyone in the family. Through her exhibition of grief, she helped Grandfather to live in the present, Father to pay less attention to his own mortality, Mother and Leila and Reba to go on with their own lives. We also said we felt she should sit shiva every evening for the next month, with Reba bringing her food and Leila calling from her dorm. The parents could use that time to go out together and get a rest. We said that it was premature for Delia to try to contact the young man, and she also had to refrain from going out with friends. She could do so only when the work of mourning was done.

A month later we saw the family again. This was the eleventh meeting and little had changed. Delia sat looking uncombed and miserable. The father said they had not sat shiva very much. Whenever Delia went out to job hunt, she continued to call hot lines or accost strangers, making threats of suicide and giving her father's work number. One night at 3 A.M., she called 911 with a suicide threat and two policemen came to the house, rushed upstairs, and took the phone away from her, asking her father if they should hospitalize her. The father, deeply embarrassed, told them he did not take her threats seriously and sent them away, but in recounting this escapade he sounded as if he were at the end of his rope. The mother added wearily, "When she talks about suicide, I act like she's saying, 'It's a rainy day.'"

It turned out that Reba had offered some comic relief to this exhausting drama. The family good girl had gotten herself suspended from high school by wearing a "Sex on Sunday" T-shirt to an outing, and had worked an obscene message into the artistic border of the yearbook. It was picked up by the printer in time, but she was forbidden to go to graduation. This caper occurred the day after the police had descended on the house. The father then told us that one of the doctors Delia had seen had recommended intensive psychiatric treatment and asked us what we thought. John and I took a break to talk this over with the team. We knew that we were using an unconventional model, but we eventually decided not to change our tack with Delia, as she was seeing a psychiatrist for medication and that seemed sufficient backup for now.

While we were conferring, a noisy scene erupted in the family room. The father had started yelling at Delia that she had a responsibility to the family to stop acting crazy. Leila joined in, saying, "You're not sick, you're blocking your beautiful real self and showing outwardly only ugly things. We are denying that you are mentally ill. You're just proving that you're weak." When John and I came back in, our message linked Delia's phone calls to the original obsessions. We said that these behaviors protected the father, since this time it was his parent who had died. We prescribed the mourning ritual again, on a weekly basis. The grandfather was to be brought to their house every Friday night, and if he started obsessing about the past, Delia was to talk about her own suffering to distract him. If she forgot, Leila and Reba must remind her.

The father objected. He didn't want the phone calls to continue because then people would be constantly telling him to put Delia away. We added the suggestion that each day Delia made a phone call, the mourning ritual should take place that night as well. The father said they would have to go to the grandfather's house because he wouldn't leave home. Delia said the only reason she wanted to die was to relieve her family. We replied that she must keep making her phone calls to keep their minds off their sadness. Perking up a bit, Delia asked "Should I go out with friends?" We said absolutely not, because that was part of the sacrifice she was making. The fact that the family did not appreciate her sacrifice was part of the sacrifice. We then made a date for the following month. As we went out, the father said angrily to Delia, "You're in control. You're coming out ahead in this game. You're coming out with more freedom than you had before."

This was in June of 1982. The father left a message telling us that they were cancelling the next session, as the family wouldn't be together again until fall. After two and a half months of silence, I made a follow-up phone call and spoke to Delia. She sounded perfectly calm and composed and said everything was fine. She told me that Leila, after our last meeting, had said to her, "I'm going on a trip for three weeks and I want you to be back to normal by the time I get back." Delia said that was good advice because it gave her a deadline. By the time Leila returned, Delia said she was her old self again. She had gone back to school and was going out with "a Shakespearean actor." I asked how everyone else was doing. Leila was doing well and finishing up her medical studies. Reba was in her first year of college and planning to be a psychiatric nurse. The parents had "mellowed out." Most amazing of all, the widowed grandfather was seeing a woman who lived nearby and had been a close friend of his wife. She was always in his house and the grandfather was happy because with her he could talk about the past. There were even hints that she would move in with him.

Theories of Change

We had our twelfth and last meeting with the family later in the year. It was two and a half years since we had first met them. Delia now looked very artistic, decked out in flowing scarves and bangles. She had a new boyfriend, a cabinetmaker. The mother said Delia sometimes reverted to her "thoughts" when she was under stress but not otherwise. Delia said she was teaching school now and told us that the children had called her a witch. In reply she had said, "I'm not a witch, I'm a gypsy." Then she frowned and said to us, "It's not such a Jewish value to be a gypsy." Everybody laughed.

The mother was still worried about Leila being too thin, but Leila was very pleased with her school and was studying hard. She hardly ever came home now. The father's only complaint was about Delia's makeup, which was heavy, with kohl around her eyes that did indeed give her a gypsyish look. Reba was homesick. Even though her college was not far from home, she had come back for intersession so she could see how her parents were doing. She reported that her father was immersing himself in Hebrew studies, which pleased her mother, and that her mother was involved with all kinds of committees and volunteer work, which pleased her father. More than anyone else in the family, the mother had changed. When we first met her, no one seemed to take her seriously, not even herself, but the volunteer work seemed to have given her a new lease on life. Delia gave her an accolade: "Here is a Woman of Valor."

We asked the family what they thought had happened to allow these changes to take place. Delia told us that after the last visit she had taken a vow to do something new every day because the things she was already doing weren't working out. In addition, her father had given her some useful advice. He told her that if she wanted to see really hopeless people, she should volunteer at the state mental hospital, which she did. She told us that it had impressed her enormously to see how much these people did with so little. One elderly woman with no hair insisted on Delia's giving her a new hairdo and, when Delia "finished," thanked her and said she was "so happy." Another lady showed her a dead geranium in a pot and said, "See, it has a new bud." The family was not, however, inclined to give us credit. The father said that even though they liked us as people, they didn't take our messages very seriously because most of the time they were wrong. Only Leila gave us a tribute. She said that we had seen the way everything in the family connected "like a big knot," and had helped them to undo it. I felt inordinately grateful to her. All along, she had seemed to understand where we were going, even in our most confused moments.

The moral of the story was a sobering one. I began to wonder whether our elaborate system of hypothesizing served any purpose other than to entertain ourselves. Our interventions, too, were at times questionable, even when they seemed to work. Other objections arose: was our team reacting too mildly to conditions that in other settings would have attracted a serious diagnosis like anorexia? Perhaps we should have taken conventional precautions like hospitalizing Delia or setting up a suicide watch. All I can say is that the family never felt that Delia's threats were that serious, and our own bias made us reluctant to push her in the direction of a promising mental illness career.

So what did this family teach us? As I have said, we were enamored with the "sacrifice intervention," which meant putting the person with the problem in the service of other people in the family. This sometimes produced a backlash, but was just as often taken as sarcasm by the family or dismissed. Worse yet, such messages kept putting the family in the wrong. When we connected Delia's obsessions to the father's refusal to mourn, we put the father in the wrong. When we made the daughters into caretakers of the parents' marriage, we put the parents in the wrong. Our messages were full of humiliating implications: that the parents "needed" a homebound child, or that a daughter might have to stay home to be a parent's therapist. This father, at least, had no trouble disagreeing with us to our faces; in other cases, families simply left. I was left with an enormous appreciation of this family's tolerance and good will.

That said, let me underline what we did accomplish. The task our team undertook, to positively connote a constantly changing situation in session after session, and to apply this effort to family after family, was in retrospect a most important education. Long after I no longer believed that a symptom served any kind of function in a family, one habit stuck. I had learned how to open my arms wide enough to encompass whatever came at me and to find meaning in it. For years I had talked about the "presenting edge," because the problem had seemed to rotate from session to session, always facing up a different way. The task was to find a way to describe this moving edge, and then to find a larger universe in which all the contradictions would make sense.

Let me cite an example of this idea. Some while ago, I was doing an online email consultation with a colleague from Austria, psychologist Gisela Schwartz, who was seeing a woman whose son had died in a car crash. For years, this woman had suffered with the fear that a combination of reckless driving and drinking would end her son's life, and when it finally happened, it was nearly too much for her to bear. She told Gisela that every day in the morning this trembling would start inside her and then her face and hands would tremble so that she could hardly bring a cup of coffee to her mouth. This trembling stopped only when she walked to the grave and talked to her son. She said that her heart had gone into the grave with him.

When Gisela shared this story, I felt great sympathy with this mother, and an image came vividly to mind. I asked Gisela to tell her from me that what had really happened was not that her heart had gone into her son's grave, but that his had joined hers. Now she had a "double heart." Gisela reported that this image had a positive effect. The woman told her that it was comforting "to get this picture from another mother." Gisela had also showed her a picture of me. Two weeks later, the woman came back in and told Gisela that this idea of the double heart had calmed her down so that she no longer trembled and shook and she didn't feel as if she would fall apart. Looking back, I believe that the ability to pick up encompassing ideas like this one was a direct result of the practice of positive connotation, which had come to seem so questionable at the time.

Here, then, was a stellar example of the reflexive impact of practice on theory. It was this family that helped our team to move away from the belief that the behavior of the troubled person serves a protective function in the family. In the next chapter, you will hear how we began to see through another myth: the linear causal bias of the models most therapists are trained in. This was also the beginning of an acknowledgment that while we might try to influence families, the families no less surely influenced us.

6

A Magic Happening

The Little Princess

At the beginning of 1981, a family was assigned to our team that challenged one of my core beliefs. Up to then, I had automatically assumed that therapies were all about change and that the primary weapon of change was the intervention. For example, in Haley's training video, "A Modern Little Hans," issued in 1976, a little boy who was afraid of dogs was told to adopt a puppy who was afraid of humans. His father, who was a postman of course, was to help him find a dog that was suitably afraid, and then to help him cure it of its fear. Of course, in so doing, the little boy would have cured himself. For structural, strategic, and systemic therapists, the word "change" was the signature of their work.

Leaving this concept behind, although I didn't think of it then, turned out to be one of the ways I began to distance from an instrumental approach. By this time, the team at Ackerman had shrunk from six to four persons and now consisted of Peggy Penn, John Patten, Jeff Ross, and myself. This was a relief. Too many cooks didn't necessarily spoil the broth, but it often came out too rich to digest. Some operational changes had also taken place. For instance, we had stopped asking at the beginning of a first session, "What is the problem?" because that would imply that we were looking for some kind of objectively knowable condition, and we were moving away from the "essentialist" position of modernism (see Chapter 8). Instead we asked, "What is your idea of the problem?"

We also moved toward a stance of more spontaneity. We no longer wrote out our final messages but spoke them extemporarily. The team had stopped interrupting the interviewer during the session, except in times of need, and our brainstorming at the end was far less formal. In addition, we were relying less on the intervention and more on circular questioning (Selvini et al., 1980c). These questions built in a sensitivity to many kinds of difference: more vs. less, agree vs. disagree, before vs. after, now vs. then. Cecchin, who had a Jesuit schooling, was brilliant at this rhetorical method, which was designed to show the hidden connections between seemingly unrelated events. He would ask questions like, "Did you have this problem before or after your grandfather died?" "When did your husband become boring? Was he born that way or did he become boring after you married him?" "Is he a real idiot or just a 'systemic' idiot? Maybe the system made him that way."

Penn (1985) became interested in expanding these questions toward the future. Depending on her analysis of the "problem premise" in the family, she would ask: "Would your relationship with your husband be different if you had had a daughter rather than a son?" Or, to a child whose conduct was upsetting her mother, she might ask, "When you are grown and have children of your own, which of your parents would you turn to for help?" Penn called this process "future-questioning," and it often released surprising and informative replies. In the first case, the mother had said that if she had a daughter, she would have someone to turn to in the family, which was at present dominated by her husband and her mother-in-law. In the second case, the child, whose authoritarian father ruled the home, didn't have to answer. Instead, her father said, with tears in his eyes, "I hope she wouldn't choose either. I hope she would choose her husband."

An early generative tactic was what the Milan team called "gossip in the presence of the family" (Selvini et al., 1980c) They would ask a husband about the thoughts or feelings of his wife, even though she was sitting right there. This might prompt the husband to say, "Why don't you ask her yourself?" However, if he did answer, the husband and wife frequently learned something new. Little did we know that this idea would have an important flowering later on. The discovery of the power of listening in on a conversation, and the alternation between speaking and listening, became greatly expanded in the later work of Tom Andersen (1991) and his idea of the reflecting team (see Chapter 9).

But here I was in 1982, awkwardly attempting to insert circular questions into my clinical toolbox. I confess I was not entirely comfortable with them. They seemed designed to hunt out evidence for a hypothesis that the therapists already knew, and they channeled the conversation into a narrow path. As a result, I felt I was standing on a cusp, not comfortable with our current approach but not sure what direction to go in next. Enter Melanie, with her bright spirit, dark tangled locks, impudent smile, and saucy answers. Melanie and her family became a pivot around which I began to abandon many therapeutic assumptions. This was the family that changed my attitude toward change.

Melanie's mother, Ellie, had called the clinic at Ackerman saying that her thirteen-year-old daughter was having suicidal thoughts and that the two of them were constantly fighting. The family was assigned to our foursome, and I was the interviewer. Again, here was a family we really liked. The parents, in their forties, were concerned, caring people, who spoke affectionately of their nine-year-old "model divorce." Melanie lived with her mother and spent every other weekend with her father, and up to now this arrangement had been peaceful and stable. Ellie, who was dark, intense and quick-witted like her daughter, gave the impression of Dresden china tempered with Arabian steel. Melanie's father, Lennie, was a lawyer. Although his demeanor was reserved, you could tell that he was deeply fond of both his daughter and his ex-wife. It was he who had suggested family therapy.

The princess who was the recipient of this joint concern seemed impervious and vulnerable in equal parts. Though pretty, her face was smudged by irritation and her hair had a deliberately not-brushed look. She had not wanted to attend this meeting, and when I greeted her, she gave me a rebellious "don't care" stare, signaling her opposition by keeping her ski jacket on and disappearing within it as often as she could. She reminded me of my own youngest daughter at that age, so fierce yet so tender.

I asked the family what they thought the problem was. Lennie asked guardedly what I had been made aware of. I shared the mother's concern about the fighting and about Melanie's "depression." Lennie didn't think depression was a factor, but he was troubled by the fighting. Ellie explained that the relationship between herself and Melanie had gotten so bad that the man who had been living with her for four months had decamped. As a result, she suggested that Melanie go live with her father. He, in turn, had said he was uncomfortable with such a precipitous decision and had suggested they go to family therapy. I then asked Melanie what she thought the problem was. Melanie said, "We don't get along." I asked, "Who doesn't get along most?" She said, "I don't get along with her and she doesn't get along with me." I asked, "Fifty-fifty?" and she said "Yeh."

It turned out that the worry about depression came mainly from Nana, the mother's mother. When Ellie suggested that Melanie live with her father and her father objected to the move as too precipitous, Ellie said that Melanie had told her grandmother she didn't want to live. Melanie cut in to correct this; she had only said that her life "wasn't happy." Ellie replied that a couple of times she had found Melanie under the covers crying.

Melanie said, "That's not anger, it's upsetness." I asked Melanie which of her parents was more upset by the fighting. She said both. I again asked, "Fifty-fifty?" She agreed. I turned to Ellie: "Would you say fifty-fifty?" After a pause, Ellie said that it wasn't an immediate problem for Melanie's father, and added, " He sees my daughter—*his* daughter—only every other weekend." Melanie interrupted, "Yeh, but I talk to him about these things on the phone." Ellie continued, sounding angry, "I don't believe that anyone could empathize on a day-to-day basis with something that isn't even going on in their own house."

It was interesting to me to see the effect of these simple questions about difference. It seemed that Melanie, despite the fighting, was intensely loyal to her mother. On the other hand, when her mother challenged her father, Melanie came to his defense. I found myself going back to my structural roots. If, as the wording "fifty-fifty" indicated, this daughter were at the nexus of a closely contested triangle, her situation might well predict for unhappiness. However, it did not seem that she was in any great danger. What seemed more salient was the tension between the parents, which was coming to the surface very fast.

The quarrel now broke out openly. Responding to Ellie's doubt that he could understand her situation, Lennie said, "I think she's wrong." Melanie, the girl in the middle, gave a funny little chuckle. Lennie emphasized how concerned he was with his daughter's well-being and added that even though he wasn't there to witness the fights, he knew what was going on. Ellie said heatedly, "I said I think it's *affected* me more." Melanie interrupted, saying, "That isn't the question." She was truly torn.

During this session, I asked about the other family members who were involved. The father described Ellie's mother, whom they called Nana, as "no match" for Ellie, who often criticized her, but Ellie said they were very close and that she often felt like a mother to her mother. Lennie explained that he and Nana both hated confrontation, where Ellie thrived on it. Ellie responded that Lennie never showed his emotions and would walk away from her rather than fight. All the same, they agreed that they got on better now than when they were married. The father observed that they were a "statistical oddity" in that after nine years of being divorced, they were still close.

I went on to find out that Lennie's father had died when he was little and his mother, whom he described as an emotionally distant person, was living in Florida. However, his sister lived near him and Melanie got on well with her two female cousins. It was at this point that we learned that Lennie's girlfriend had moved in with him while Melanie was away at camp that summer. When she came back, Melanie found not only her mother but also her father absorbed in new relationships. I ended by asking everyone's views about therapy. Ellie had trained as a psychiatric social worker even though she now ran a small import business, and she was also involved in sensitivity training. Lennie said he had no faith in individual therapy but thought that family therapy might help. Melanie said, "I'm not for it, I'm not against it." Again, that fifty-fifty position. I said, "You're a swing vote," and she agreed. I excused myself to meet with the team.

When I came back into the room after the team break, I brought a message which I read aloud. My team had agreed with my structural interpretation, but decided to base a paradoxical prescription on it. The exchange went as follows:

LYNN: I have a fairly short message. We don't know the family very well so we can't say too much—I'll give you another date so we can get to know you a little better. But the group does agree that you are a statistical oddity in the sense of being cohesive in the midst of all separations, and that Melanie is a pivotal person in the whole picture and does many things for the family—not only in her own self-interest, of course.

MELANIE: (*frowning*) What do you mean?

LYNN: One of the things you do is to make absolutely sure that your mother will find a man who is a good match for her . . .

MELANIE: What do you mean?

LYNN: Because if somebody is not a good match, you will warn your mother.

MELANIE: Oh yeh, I tell her . . .

LYNN: And, in return, until she finds that person, you are a good match for her.

MELANIE: Yes, but she has other ones, she doesn't listen to me . . .

LYNN: Not good enough, not good enough. Furthermore, as a good daughter, you make sure that your mother stays close to your grandmother, because when you are too good a match for her, your mother can turn to her own mother. Finally, you keep your mother and father close too, because whenever you and your mother fight, your father comes in to help your mother . . .

MELANIE: No, to help me . . .

LYNN: And you—and this is what makes you pivotal in this family, and we just want to give you a hand for that.

Melanie seemed to be puzzled but amused by this idea, and the family promised to come back in about two weeks. As the reader can see, this was a Milan-style positive connotation, praising Melanie for connecting everybody through fighting with her mother. The hypothesis we based this message on, although we didn't share it with the family, was that the model divorce had outrun its usefulness. The parents were now experimenting with new partners and Melanie, feeling displaced, was worried about this sudden change in the status quo and was sending up flares.

In the next interview, Ellie said she had seen that the quarreling between herself and Melanie was a vicious cycle, so she broke the pattern by backing off. As a result, no quarreling had occurred during those two weeks. During the interview, I asked more questions about the mother's family of origin. Ellie said she had a conflictual relationship with her father, whom she and her mother called "the Grim Reaper." During her own childhood, her parents were always bickering and threatening to divorce but never did. The model divorce looked now like a compensatory comment on the far-from-model marriage of her parents.

At the end of this interview, we decided to "prescribe a relapse," a technique I mentioned previously as a way to guard against backsliding. I told the family that the team was worried about the fact that the fighting had stopped because this might threaten the model divorce. In Ellie's family, I said, the father was the bad guy, always fighting with the mother and always threatening divorce. Since Ellie usually took her mother's side, she had a poor relationship with her father. Because of this, we were convinced that one of her dreams for Melanie was that things should be different between Melanie and her father. Melanie immediately objected, saying, "Yes, but she's always telling me that my father is trying to be better than her." I said that might be so, but that we were picking up on something deeper, which was Ellie's dream for her daughter. I added, "That's why we think you should go back to fighting with your mother and then calling your father. We feel it would be too soon to stop."

Melanie looked puzzled and said, "But I don't like fighting—why should I?" Starting to feel confused (did I really want to be defending this prescription?), I said, "Because it somehow rights ancient wrongs. It rebalances things in the past, in the memories of your parents, certainly in your mother's family." Melanie said crossly, "That's not going to do me any good." Her father joined in, saying, "You can't turn it on and off." At this point, the team knocked, seeing that I was getting into a muddle, and told me to say that we had another family waiting. I did so, apologizing for my confusion, and made a date for the following month.

Looking back on this message, I am struck by its disingenuous, almost deceitful tone. I had said that we had been made fearful by the change in the problem when privately we were glad. I had said that we thought that it would be helpful for Melanie to go back to a behavior that made everyone unhappy, which was also not true. Finally, I pretended to be confused when I knew perfectly well what I was doing. Again, it was only worth it if it brought results.

This time it didn't. When the family came in again, the situation had escalated. Ellie told us that she had deliberately set out to be nice to Melanie, but the nicer she was, the more unpleasant Melanie became. She repeated her belief that it would be best for Melanie to live with her father. Lennie said that he would welcome her moving in with him as long as everyone understood this was only until a "real" decision could be made. Ellie, who was going on a month-long business trip with the grandmother, said, "Fine, she can stay with you while I go to Europe," adding, "And I may never come back." Melanie countered with the statement that she too might never come back. In fact, she said, she might run away from home.

This was not good. Something very like Mutual Assured Destruction was going on between mother and daughter. I asked what they thought the effect would be on the other people in the family if Melanie did go to live with her father. I was surprised at the dire predictions that surfaced. Ellie said that Nana would feel that Melanie was lost forever. She might become ill, might even have a nervous breakdown, and the fights between the grandmother and grandfather might get worse. We found out at this point that when Ellie and Lennie broke up, Ellie's father was so angry that he wouldn't speak to her for a year and a half.

I left to have a discussion with the team. With Ellie about to leave for a month and a crisis brewing, we rejected anything too paradoxical because it tended to heat things up. Instead, we decided to endorse the plan to have Melanie stay with her father. I came back in and said that we thought that Ellie's idea seemed like a natural way to try out the change of domicile without having to make a decision. Melanie could even go on staying with her father after her mother came back. That way her mother could be the parent she could feel romantic about, the parent who was not in charge.

At this point my nervous team knocked from behind the mirror and told me to remind everyone that Melanie's mother was, after all, coming back, and that she and Melanie's father still had to decide about her future. I repeated this to the family, and Ellie responded tartly, "Of course I'm coming back—my *cats* want to live with me." My heart sank and I heard myself saying, "I'm sure Melanie will know how to translate that statement." It was obvious that Melanie did, because she was looking daggers at her mother. I closed the interview down very quickly and made a new date for a time after the mother's return.

The Decision

The next interview tested our fortitude and skills to the utmost. Ellie had been back in the U.S. for two weeks and Melanie was still living with her father. According to Ellie, she and Melanie were fighting more than ever. During the meeting, Melanie sat in the lee of her father, as if taking up psychological residence with him. Lennie looked protective and glum, and Ellie, sitting on the outside of this welded pair, seemed to feel keenly the sting of her position. In addressing the primary topic, which was where Melanie was to live, Ellie said that Melanie had made the decision to stay with her father even before she went to Europe. Melanie's rejecting behavior, she said, indicated that she no longer wanted Ellie as a parent. I asked Lennie if he agreed, and he said he didn't, adding that while Ellie was away Melanie had kept alluding to the temporary nature of the situation. He didn't think she had made a decision.

Ellie explained that the reason Melanie couldn't make a decision was because of the "destructive behavior pattern" she was caught up in. Ellie said, "She's a thirteen-year-old, this is her world, this is all she's known. For her to say, 'Wait a minute, my reality is destructive to me and it's making my mother miserable, it's turning me into a horrible person, and I hate my mother' is impossible for a child to admit to. And her father can't admit that he wants to save her—how can he be put in that situation?" She seemed close to tears.

I was beginning to feel very sorry for Melanie. However, I was equally constrained by the Milan principle of neutrality: never be judgmental, never take sides. So I continued my effort to get clarity on the issue of the decision. I said that my team and I felt that at this point nobody could really decide anything. The mother, sounding really anguished, came in to say, "No, I have to, I have to. Her father keeps saying 'If you really love her, how can you give her up?' but when she left—here was my own daughter who was leaving me for at least a month, who couldn't even say goodbye to me. She kissed the cats goodbye but she couldn't kiss me goodbye. I mean, this is my only child!"

Melanie was looking extremely sad, so I asked for her reaction. She said she hadn't made any decision. I asked, "You didn't decide to leave your mother and live with your father?" She said, with a hint of a smile, "Guess so." I said, "But your mother thinks that you made a nonverbal decision." "Guess so," Melanie said again. Trying to pave the way for the parents to decide, I said to Ellie, "If you believe that Melanie has made some kind of nonverbal decision but still can't decide for herself, what are you going to do about it?" She replied, "Well, I have to make some kind of decision." I asked, "Independent of Melanie's father?" She said, "I've discussed it with her father. He doesn't give any feelings, he doesn't say anything one way or another." Melanie broke in to say, "He's spoken to *me*."

Ellie now turned to Lennie, saying, "I've told you how I feel and I ask you how you feel, and you say, 'It's okay—she can live with me.'" She was mimicking the tone of someone who didn't care one way or another. Lennie, showing considerable emotion, said, "Far from that it's just okay. I think it's in her best interest to live with me. However, I think that we should understand where this thing emanates from, in terms of how any kind of agreement comes about." I was getting more and more frustrated. The parents were basically fighting over who would be held responsible if Melanie went to live with her father, thus stalemating any reasonable negotiation. So I sat there, paralyzed, while the invisible octopus that seemed to have all of us in its clutches squeezed ever more tightly.

Ellie now spoke to Lennie very passionately indeed. Defending herself, she said, "I can no longer put up with being kicked in the face on a day-to-day basis. I regained my own self-respect in Europe and I don't think there is any other way to break this pattern than for Melanie not to live with me." I asked Ellie if she were speaking in her own interest. Ellie said quickly, "And hers." Melanie said, "No, yours." Ellie said, "I don't think it's healthy for you to live in a hostile environment, Melanie, because it isn't good for me, it's killing me, and it isn't good for you."

Melanie, who had kept up a pretty tough front until now, lowered her head and began to weep. I felt totally sorry for her but refrained from showing her any outward sympathy. Instead, I asked if anyone knew why Melanie was crying. The father said he thought she was feeling rejected. He added, "It's difficult to actually come to grips with this thing and make a decision. It's a tough transition." The mother said, "It's very tough." I asked her why she thought Melanie was crying. She said, "Because I don't think she's been responsible for her own behavior in the past couple of years. I think she has acted irresponsibly."

The Thing in the Bushes

I want to stop here and make a confession. In all the years I consulted with families, I often sensed that I was in a powerful and potentially fatal relationship field. Researchers like Bateson (1976), who speculated on double binding communications in families, or Haley, who spoke of children being "at the nexus of warring triangles" (Watzlawick & Weakland, 1977, p. 44), or Selvini, who used the phrase "the imbroglio," were all attempting to capture what I myself once called the "thing in the bushes" (1981, p. 146). And you know, there is a "thing in the bushes." You can experience it, but you can't nail it down by explanatory words. This is what structural and systemic therapists tried to do, where strategic therapists, being more interested in change than explanation, got off the hook. I am taking the chance of being called essentialist if I talk about it.

However, at that moment in the interview, I was caught. Despite my aversion to pathologizing descriptions, there lurked in this family, as in any family, the type of relationship eddies that could overwhelm and drown. When I summered with my children on Martha's Vineyard many years ago, there was an undertow off the Atlantic side of the island called locally a "sea-pussy." Despite the unintended humor of the idea of the sea having a you-know-what, this was a real hazard. I remember once going to one of those places alone with my two young children. I told them to sit on the beach while I took a swim.

The beach sloped steeply where I went in. I was soon out of my depth, but I was a decent swimmer and had no fears. Suddenly, I noticed that the more I tried to swim back to shore, the more the ocean dragged me out. I realized I was caught in one of those terrible currents. Looking at the two babies playing innocently on the beach, my heart nearly stopped. Nobody ever came to that deserted place. I swam with all my strength, to no avail. Then I remembered being told that these eddies were strong but narrow, and that if one swam to one side, one might escape their grip. I did this, and found no further barrier to getting back to shore. Needless to say, I never took this chance again.

But floundering around in the session with Melanie and her parents, I felt as if I were caught in a similar undertow. And if I felt that way, what must Melanie feel? What must her parents feel? We had no language to depict such fluid but devastating environments. As soon as we posited some abnormal structure or system, we became outsiders pointing the finger. Even here, I would hesitate to do more than offer the story I have just recited, which uses an anecdote as a parable for what I have in mind.

Immobilized by this dilemma where explanations dared not go, I stumbled across a saving grace. Family theorist Evan Imber-Black (1993) believes that secrets in families can be toxic to relationships. In an article in *Family Process* (Imber-Coppersmith, 1985), she described an exercise that presents this theory experientially rather than verbally. From a training group, she chooses three persons to be a father, a mother, and a child (in my version usually a teenager). The mother can be a stepmother, too. There are three acts to this play, and at the end, the role-play family is asked to share with the class their reactions to each. In the first act, three messages are written on a piece of paper and given to the appropriate persons, with the instructions not to show them to anyone. Here are my versions of these messages:

1. You are the father in this family. You have an alliance with your daughter. This alliance is open and can be revealed.
2. You are the mother in this family. Your husband and your daughter have an alliance that is open and can be revealed.
3. You are the daughter in this family. You have an alliance with your father that is open and can be revealed.

Imber-Black then asks the threesome to plan an outing together. In this version of the exercise, the planning usually takes place quite easily. There seems to be no real stress, except that the mother may feel left out. The next set of messages to be given out reads:

1. You are the father in this family. You have an alliance with your daughter that is secret and cannot be revealed.
2. You are the mother in this family. Your daughter and your husband have an alliance that is secret and cannot be revealed.
3. You are the daughter in this family. You have an alliance with your father that is secret and cannot be revealed.

In this new situation, planning an outing becomes more complicated. Very often, the price of coming up with a plan is that one of the participants will explode unexpectedly or "act out," and the secret may come to light. However, with suitable bargaining, the outing sometimes does take place. In the third act, the messages change again:

1. You are the father in this family. You have an alliance with your daughter that is secret and cannot be revealed.
2. You are the mother in this family. You have an alliance with your daughter that is secret and cannot be revealed.
3. You are the daughter in this family. You have alliances with both your mother and your father that are secret and cannot be revealed.

This time the atmosphere in the group changes strikingly. It is as if everyone is held down by a multitude of tiny strings, like Gulliver in Lilliput. There is no conflict, but each suggestion is countermanded by another one, and no group decision seems possible. Sometimes a pseudo plan is arrived at, but another outcome is that the trainer simply imposes a mercy killing. Debriefing takes a long time, as the class and the "family" exchange observations on this strange and rather chilling experiment. The old-fashioned term "schizophrenic family" may be used.

What is not included in this exercise is the "schizophrenic therapist." In the session with Melanie, I too felt tied down by a multitude of tiny strings.

I am including this version of my "thing in the bushes," because the exercise makes it so clear that the "thing" is not a thing at all, but more like some kind of invisible loyalty field, with sympathies and antipathies forming and reforming and flowing together and apart. I decided to talk about this loyalty field, because if you asked me which one idea I would keep from my structural and systemic training, this would be it.

But loyalty fields and their effects—fighting, scapegoating, and splits—are not easily reducible to words. Some communication specialists use Wittgenstein's (1953) concept of "language games," but this is, as Michael White (1995) would say, a thin description. I believe that the category of communication is larger than language, and that words like "text" or "narrative" or "story" are inadequate descriptors when relationships are in question. You can't resolve a conflict between a husband and wife unless you realize that this abstract, pallid word is in fact awash with blood. Think of blood ties or blood feuds or even bloody mindedness. Constructionist John Shotter (1993b) is eternally eager for us to admit that language games are matters of guts, gore, and bickering over prizes. At least that is how I felt while our princess sat sobbing in the corner.

The Mantra

To my infinite gratitude, the team knocked at this point and I excused myself and went out. All I remember is that I wanted to interfere directly with this unhappy child, put her behind the mirror, force her parents to make a decision, act like the Grim Reaper. My team, not being hampered by my structural background, vetoed these moves and kept on looking for a message that would positively connote the situation. We were at least hoping to reduce the amount of anger, grief, and blame that everyone was feeling, including me.

Then one of those "blue lightning" ideas came to me in the form of a Selvini-style ritual. The Milan team once saw a couple where the husband accused the wife of taking advantage of his impotence by being unfaithful. The wife, in turn, accused the husband of looking for a lover who could arouse him. The message, to be read every night by each spouse to the other, went: "*Thank you, dear wife (or husband), for believing that I could be unfaithful to you, because in that way I know that you will never break the bond that binds me to you until death.*" This statement positively connoted the couple's mutual distrust as a way they would always stay together. I remember that it had an explosive effect. I was in Milan observing the team during one of my pilgrimages to Milan, a week after the message was given, when a call came from the wife. Selvini told us that the wife was upset because her husband was in the bathroom threatening to cut off his penis, and she wanted an appointment immediately. Selvini told her that they were sorry but they could not change the appointment, which was now three weeks away. I was shocked. Mara told me that the couple's reaction only justified the correctness of the team's hypothesis. In a sentence that was characteristic of their entire stance, she said, "It's only information."

My message, though it did not have such an intense effect, was similar. It went: *Thank you, mother (or daughter), for loving me so much, because if I left you I know that I would hurt you so much that I will never have to leave you.* I don't think I knew clearly at the time what it meant, but it felt right. It described the threats to leave as a way mother and daughter guaranteed their closeness to each other. The team, luckily, admonished me not to ignore the father, which I probably would have done had they not reminded me. So I went back in, armed with my fragile saying, which was written on two slips of paper, and hoping for the best.

I sat down and said to the family that their problem, though seemingly simple, defied logic. It would be logical for the father to take Melanie to live with him, but he couldn't because he was too sensitive to the very strong bond between mothers and daughters in this family. That was why he hadn't taken a stand all these years and wouldn't now. Lennie said, strongly, "I already have," adding that it was a different ballgame now that Ellie herself had recommended this change. I pointed out that the mother could change her mind, or that her feelings could show that she had, and that this would prevent him from making a decision. I said, "It's a decision that has to be made by the two of you as parents, and we're not convinced you're together."

Then I launched into a clumsy attempt to explain what I meant. I told Lennie that he had gone along only after his wife had made a decision, so it was not his decision. And Ellie had said that Melanie's "destructive behavior" had made the decision, so it wasn't Ellie's decision either. Then I held up the pieces of paper on which my mantra was written and, turning to Melanie and her mother, said that we felt that they were caught in a loving bind that would make it impossible for anyone to make a decision. In order to make this more explicit, we were giving them a message. I handed them each a copy. I said that we wanted them to read this message to each other every night until we saw them again. Since Melanie was not living with her mother, they could read it on the phone. I then asked them to read it out loud right there.

Melanie, looking over the message, giggled and asked, "What if I don't believe this?" I said, "It doesn't matter, just read it." Melanie asked, "Then what's the point?" I said the point was to have them exchange those thoughts, and asked her to read it right away. Melanie gabbled her way through the letter, continuing to laugh self-consciously: *Dear Mother, Thank you for loving me so much, because if I left you I know I would hurt you so much that I will never have to leave you.* While she was reading, Ellie simply stared at her, totally bemused. She stared so long that I had to remind her that it was her turn to read. Ellie then read her sentence, which was the same as Melanie's. She said, looking puzzled, "That's the same thing." I nodded and said that it was a statement of what was binding them. Melanie asked again, "Then what's the point?" I said, "Because it just makes it clearer and clearer and clearer." I then gave them a choice of dates for the next meeting. The father, who had been looking perplexed all this time, said, "You're advising us not to make a clear decision." I cheerfully agreed with him and we said goodbye.

At our fifth meeting, a month and a week later, Melanie came in astoundingly, wonderfully different. Her hair was shining and bouncing about her face and she had the smug expression of one who has completed a daring secret mission. After much laughing back and forth, the news came out: mother and daughter were back together. I asked the mother what had happened. She said that Melanie had told her that if she didn't take her back, she was going to run away. The father explained: "She said she was going to go to New Jersey and live in a tent." Melanie went off into peals of embarrassed laughter.

I asked about the fights. Apparently they had stopped. Melanie was still calling her father, but she wasn't crying on his shoulder any more about how bad things were at home. Lennie, looking genuinely confused, confirmed this report, saying that he wasn't getting any negative feelings from Melanie since she had gone back to her mother. More poignantly, Lennie expressed his disappointment at not having his daughter live with him. I asked him if he thought the change would last, and he said he hoped so but wondered what would happen the next time his ex-wife brought another man into her life.

I wanted to find out if Ellie and Melanie had read the mantra, so I asked them about it. This brought another round of giggles from Melanie. Lennie asked her, "You didn't stop reading it, did you?" Ellie said, "No, but she's gotten so good at reading it fast that I can't understand a word, it's just gibberish." I asked Melanie if she would show me herself, and once she got out from under her laughing fit, she agreed. It sounded like this: "Deemoth—hanoofohlovmesomush—beekfaylevyoo—wdhuryoosomush—nevhavlivyou." Ellie sat transfixed, as before. "Isn't it amazing?" she asked. I agreed, adding, "It's like a prayer."

Ellie then said, "After two weeks, she had the whole thing memorized." I asked, "Did you read it over the phone?" Ellie said, "Yes. I don't know what the dynamics are, but it worked. When Melanie was finally able to verbalize that she wanted to come home, and I expressed some doubts, she asked, 'Aren't you listening to the words of that note? Well, it's all true.'" Melanie protested: "I didn't say that." Ellie continued, "I said, 'How come in the session when you read it you said to Lynn, "How can I say this when it's not true?" and two weeks later you told me it's all true?'" I asked Ellie, "And you believed her?" and she said, "Yes."

In our end-of-session message, we basically complimented the family for its achievement, even if it was only temporary. We told them that it was important for Melanie and her mother to spend a little time together because eventually both of them would be reaching out to other people and they would start to grow apart in the normal way. We also said that Lennie was to be commended in supporting them through this difficult time. We gave them a date for six weeks later, saying we wanted to give them time to see what kind of change had taken place, because the father might be right and the whole thing could fall apart.

But it didn't. This was one of the seductive features of this kind of work. Every once in a while, the original complaint that brought the family in would dramatically disappear. Not only the family but our team would be confused as to what had really happened. Was it, as we liked to think, our wonderful messages, or simply that we had furnished an accepting environment in which people had the freedom to try new things? There was never any way to tell. I felt that any positive message we asked mother and daughter to read when they were at such dagger points would have at least temporarily reconnected them. In any case, Melanie had boxed herself into such an extreme position that she probably welcomed a face-saving way to get back. And Lennie, who could have been much more active in insisting that Melanie live with him, was extraordinarily sensitive in not forcing the issue. So whatever happened only happened because the family had figured out a new kind of cooperation. That, at least, was what we hoped.

But in the next and last session, something unusual happened. Ellie had a dream that pushed me toward a position of "causal agnosticism" in regard to therapeutic change. This phrase was invented by a Nobel prize winning economist named Ronald Coase, in work that challenged the need to determine individual blame in pollution cases. But I bent his idea to my own purposes. For me it meant not believing in simple chains of cause and effect because in human affairs there are so many other pulls. Ellie's dream, which I will describe below, reinforced my growing suspicion that if we really gave up a control-centered logic for our work, our simplistic ideas of change would be one of the first things that would have to go.

Was It Change?

When the threesome came in for the next meeting, I noticed not only that Melanie's hair was still gloriously coiffed, but that Ellie was looking like a bride in a flowing white dress. When I complimented her, she said she had made it out of a bedsheet (shades of my own bohemian past!). I asked them how things had gone. Lennie said that everything seemed to be substantially better. Melanie was going off to camp soon, and there was a hint somewhere of a boy. Ellie added breathlessly, "I can't believe how wonderful she is." Melanie, using her ironic look, asked, "What do you mean?" The mother backed off, saying, "No, she's really not, she's just the same old bratty kid, but we just really get along."

I asked them how they explained this shift. Melanie gave a sharp glance toward her father, and I added quickly, "If there is one." Lennie said, "I don't know what happened. Her mother would know." I asked if Melanie was different with him, or if the phone calls suggested any difference. Lennie said, "I would say that the phone calls are maybe a little less frequent, which is probably a function of the fact that there are no problems. Which is okay." I turned back to Ellie and asked if she agreed. She said, "Yes, I love her very much and I let her know it and she shows me that she cares." I asked, "How does she show you?" and she said, "She does things to help me." When I asked Ellie to elaborate, Melanie cast her eyes up to Heaven, exclaiming "Oh, God!" I said to her, "Let's get a list, then you can be a brat again." She snickered charmingly. Ellie said, "Well, last night she had cleaned up the whole living room." (Lynn: Good Heavens!) And she does the dishes. (Lynn: Oh, my!) She's sensitive, she's caring." Melanie glanced uncomfortably toward her father with a peculiar scowl on her face.

In the type of therapy we were doing, we would often go for a change statement or "testimonial." So I asked Melanie, "Do you think your mother sees you differently?" Melanie said, "Yes." "Do you see your mother as having changed?" She said, "No." I persisted, "Does she see you as having changed?" Melanie said, "I didn't change." I said, "So there was no change but your mother feels happier?" Silence. "Some kind of piece of magic happened?" Melanie, finally agreeing, said, "Okay, but nobody changed." The mother said, "Yes, but aren't you happier?" Melanie repeated, "Yes, but nobody changed."

Finally I got the point. To claim a change often puts people in the wrong, because it assumes things were bad before the change. Also, the change may be good for some but not for others. I had noticed that the father seemed quieter than usual, even somber. I wondered whether Melanie feared to give the impression that she no longer cared for him as much, now that she had chosen to stay with her mother. It was at that moment that the word "change," a badge of identity for so much of the family therapy movement, began to tarnish before my eyes.

But I had one more lesson to learn. Not only was the idea of change on the chopping block, but the idea of the therapist as the source of change was too. The bearer of this second tidings was not Melanie but her mother. Sitting there resplendent in her white, bedsheet dress, Ellie delivered the final blow. I had asked Lennie's opinion about this change that seemed to have taken place, and he had replied, "Here is the question: when we came in we were in very difficult circumstances, which seem in great measure to have changed. However, the major change that's taken place along with this one is that my wife is no longer involved with someone. So the question I come to now is what's going to happen the next time? We're apparently in much better shape, but I don't know if that's true."

When I looked to Ellie to respond, she put her two hands to her head and looked off into the distance. Then she said, "I had a dream that we had another session, right after the last one." She paused for what seemed like an eternity, until Melanie, impatient, said, "Aren't you going to tell us?" Ellie continued: "We were sitting in the waiting room and waiting and waiting for you [we were famous for keeping families waiting] and this man came out and said, 'I'm sorry, Lynn won't be here today, but I'm aware of everything because I'm on the team, so I'm taking her place.'" There was another pause while Ellie seemed to be trying to recall the dream. She finally went on: "So we went in and what happened was he said he didn't really think everything was fine. He felt that Melanie was still running my life, and that I was afraid to exert my role as a parent and it was about time that I made the decisions about my own life, and about my role as a mother in relation to her, and that was what was left for me to do."

My inner response was: What was Salvador Minuchin doing in Ellie's dream? It seemed uncanny that even though I was trying to work in such an opposite way, this straightforward structural directive should have appeared. I also wondered why the idea of a decision, which had been such an elusive quarry in former sessions, took that occasion to appear. One hypnosis-minded Ericksonian who saw this tape felt that this was an example of an "embedded suggestion," but at this point in my evolution, I was not looking for methods that depended on manipulation.

Ellie went on, "Then another girl came in and she was counting and the whole thing took place in a gymnasium and I looked at the wall and there was this grid. It looked like shadows from grillwork that had been illuminated onto the wall—it looked like two grids on top of one another—and I looked closer and it was painted, it was a trompe l'oeil." I translated: "Something that looks real but is painted." Ellie said, "Yes, and this girl said to me: 'The answer of how to do that is there.' I didn't understand what that meant, but that was the dream." Despite my fascination, I thought I should remind Ellie of what we had been talking about earlier. I asked her if she agreed with Lennie that there was still some unfinished business that might arise. She replied that this was why she remembered the dream.

It seemed that there were two parts to what the dream told her. The first was that she and Melanie had to build a good foundation for their relationship, and this part was already done. The second part had to do with her authority. She said, "Through this dream I have an awareness of what I need to do. I'm not afraid to let Melanie know how I feel and she doesn't react to me in the same rebellious way. So even in the househunting that I'm doing, she knows that even though I'll take her wishes into consideration, I'm going to make the final decision. When I first told her this, she balked, but now she's accepted it. I think that once I get the house, and we have separate quarters and more privacy, when I do start bringing men into my home, her reaction will be different."

Melanie came in teasingly and said, "It's not going to be different." Ellie replied, "It better be, or you'll find another place to live!" After that shocking statement, she turned to me and said, "That's how I feel. I'm not afraid to tell her that and I'm not afraid of her rejecting me. I'm sure about her loving me and she knows that I love her."

Melanie said with a wicked smile: "You're sure?" and the mother, smiling back, said, "Yes." I turned to Lennie, who was sitting outside all of this sunshine, and said that we were glad to be hearing his perspective, too. My fear was that too much triumphalism on the mother's part would make Melanie feel disloyal to her father and all this good work would be undone.

This felt like a natural breaking point, so I went back to see the team. They warned me again to pay attention to the father. It was he, after all, who had initiated the idea of family therapy, and he had been looking uncommonly sad. So in giving them our message, I started by saying that we agreed with him that this better relationship might not withstand the intrusion of another man into the mother's life. I said we were impressed with the shift, but also didn't understand how it came about. Then I said that Melanie was right to say that she would tell her mother if she didn't like someone Ellie might get attached to, and that Ellie was right when she talked about the good foundation that had been put down. I ended by saying that she would know that their relationship was strong enough when she could choose a man that Melanie would like and Melanie would like a man that she would choose.

Both Melanie and her mother were looking perplexed and repeated what I had said, so I said it again, feeling a bit uncertain about my phrasing. Did it equalize them too much? I closed by saying to Ellie, "I think that's about it, so let me thank you on behalf of the team, since they somehow got into your dream." At this point Melanie went off into another one of her raucous peals of laughter. The father now said, "Are we thinking of this being our last session?" Melanie said firmly, "No." I had got up to say goodbye and now sat down again. I said, "Well, for the moment we see no problem. Melanie is going to camp, so it's up to you. If we hear from you again, we will certainly be able to see you then."

Melanie was looking dismayed, so her mother asked her, "Is there something else you want?" Melanie said, "Well, what about the problem that's supposed to be cleared up?" Lennie said, "You mean the next time your mother is involved with someone? We'll have to see what arises in regard to that. Maybe you are going to be more accepting, or maybe your mother is going to be involved with some different kind of person. Maybe all this has been accomplished and we don't know it yet." I said, "We don't know. We're agreeing with your mother that it's mysterious." Handshakes all round, and the family left.

This abrupt ending was par for the course. In the Milan model, as soon as the family no longer complained about the original problem and as long as there were no new ones, we would simply close shop, with the understanding that we could always open up again. I have kept that feature in my current work, and find that the idea, "Come when your toe hurts, not when it doesn't," is very welcome to people who don't want to be drawn into a process of indeterminate length and uncertain outcome.

However, my experience with this family gave me a sense of a less purposive way to work. The message at the end of the first interview, where we told Melanie to go back to fighting with her mother, had strategic overtones, but I had become aware of moving toward a more general type of affirmation, as when we spoke about the mother's dream that her daughter would be closer to her father than she was to hers. This kind of positive description felt helpful to me, because it said, "Whatever is happening here, no matter how strange it seems, makes sense in some larger universe."

But let me come back to Melanie's objection to the idea that anything "changed." If you look at some of the early books on family therapy, you will find that this word is often featured in their titles. It became a way to distinguish the interactional and strategic therapists from the psychodynamic practitioners they opposed. And yet, experience shows that the hardest way to bring about change is to try for it. The paradoxical strategies of the MRI and the Milan teams were a partial answer in that they recommended that people do not change within a context that indicated that they should.

However, this answer leaves untouched the emotional consequences that change brings with it. For this reason, it is valid to ask why we cut the father off at the end. Part of it was that I identified with the triumphant mother; she won me with her dream. That may have been a mistake. But another aspect was at play: our model had no theory of suffering. If I were in that same session now, I would be much more attuned to feelings. I not only would have clued into the father's disappointment but would also have found an active way to acknowledge his sense of loss.

Six months later I called the mother to ask if I could use clips from the videotapes of the sessions in a forthcoming workshop. She gave me permission on her behalf and on Melanie's, but when I asked her about Lennie, she said, "We're not talking." It seemed that all along he had been handling her financial affairs. The week before I called, she had told him she no longer needed his advice, and he had most uncharacteristically slammed down the receiver. The model divorce was at an end.

7

The Continental Divide

The Death of Bateson

The period leading up to and away from 1983, when I decided to move up to New England, has always felt to me like a continental divide. It is the place at the spine of the continent where the flow of water reverses course. When, in 1980, Gregory Bateson died, the event intensified a malaise I had already been feeling. I had often observed that a death in a family released upheavals, like underwater tsunamis, that could impact shorelines far away. In the family of family therapies, Bateson's death seemed to identify a schism that had always lurked within its history but was never sharply perceived. In trying to understand this rift, a position became clear to me that deeply challenged the way I thought about my craft.

My devotion to the field of family therapy had been channeled through the persons who introduced it to me. When I was eight, I played Miranda in a children's theater version of *The Tempest*. I never forgot the emotions of wonder and awe (my own emotions, surely) that went with the line Miranda speaks on first seeing the shipwrecked nobles: "Oh brave new world that hath such creatures in it." I bestowed upon the survivors of the Bateson group, gathered under the roof of the MRI after Bateson's departure, the same type of uncritical admiration. Thinking at first that the group was united in the glow of a common achievement, I later realized that they had many philosophical differences among them. The discord between Bateson and Haley had been sharp enough that Bateson referred to it in later writings (Sluzki & Ransom, 1976, p. 106).

I first realized this split in the late '70s, when I had the chance to meet Bateson for the first time. He was speaking at Roosevelt Hospital to a group of psychiatry residents. I remember their confusion when he challenged the term schizophrenia. He told them it was a "dormitive principle," using the tautology that Molière's learned doctors employed to explain sleep. The hostile residents threw dart-like questions at him, and he deflected them with his usual rambling indirection. Squatting on a low set of steps at the end of the room, rather than standing behind the podium, he seemed to care nothing for the rules of academic dignity. I noticed that his shirt had a triangular gap where it met his belt buckle. Beguiled by the flow of words and the swirl of smoke from his cigarette, I waited with fascination to see how long the ash would get before falling on his chest.

After the talk, I took my courage in hand and went up to introduce myself. You have to remember that for me this was the equivalent of being presented at court. Doing the honors for myself, I said, "Mr. Bateson, I wrote a book on family therapy with Jay Haley, and I wanted to meet you. My name is Lynn Hoffman." I am fairly tall, but he was even taller, and I felt him considering the top of my head. Then he said, referring to our book, "Oh, Haley and Hoffman. *That* Hoffman." And he turned to the next person. I was perplexed. Being connected with Haley was not the right letter of introduction, but I had no idea why.

The answer came much later from a young newcomer to the Ackerman staff, Bradford Keeney, who had just published a book on cybernetic epistemology called *The Aesthetics of Change* (1983). I thought of Keeney as a Fourth of July sparkler. He was a captivating talker and despite the fact that you couldn't always remember what he had just said, you wanted to listen to him anyway. Keeney had visited Bateson in California shortly before he died and had published some of their conversations in the form of metalogues. When I told him about my disappointing meeting, he told me that Bateson still carried strong feelings about his disagreement with Haley, and that I shouldn't take it personally.

Around this time there came an event of the sort that congeals one's loyalties. Keeney had written a paper critiquing the "pragmatic" point of view in family therapy because it was based on a strategic rather than an aesthetic set of values (1982). He cited Bateson for support, and his paper was published along with two other pieces that took a similar view. A number of defensive comments came rushing back to *Family Process*, mostly from supporters of the strategic schools of thought. Then Haley sent in some pages of a manuscript that he claimed to have found stuck to the bottom of a chimpanzee cage. His "sample" consisted of sentences taken in alternating order of appearance from the three first pages of each article. Because the articles were written in an abstract latinate prose, this patch job was almost believable. Of course, you had to assume that the author was a mad philosopher with a tin ear and very poor writing skills.

Haley's pastiche rather cruelly ridiculed Keeney and the two other writers, whose language seemed to come from the same New Age science vocabulary, but for me the event was useful because it opened up the schism in the field. Haley (1968) had placed power at the center of his theories about family systems. He believed that in "pathological" family systems, each family member tried to control the behavior of the others, forcing the therapist to take control at the level of the therapeutic process. Bateson had disagreed with the emphasis on power. In a comment on Haley's history of the Bateson project, he says,

> As I saw it, he [Haley] believed in the validity of the metaphor of power in human relations. I believed then—and today believe even more strongly—that the *myth* of power always corrupts because it proposes always a false (though conventional) epistemology. (in Sluzki & Ransom, 1976, p. 106)

In other words, "power" was the kind of abstraction that did not mean anything in itself. You had to specify: is it power over? power that enables? the power of faith? of force? Words like "crime" and "play" were similar abstractions. Bateson called such words epistemological errors because they turned complicated processes into noun-like abstractions while ignoring the context that gave them their meaning. Bateson's position had an incendiary effect on feminist critics of family theory, who naturally wanted to defend the concept of power. They kept asking, "What do you mean, the myth of power? What about battered women? That's not a myth." They liked Haley's problem-solving approach because he acknowledged power and believed in directives for change.

But the feminists' objections melted in the face of my commitment to Bateson's views. Just before he died, he gave a lecture in a huge barn-like structure on Union Square in New York. It was raining and the roof leaked. Bateson, looking very tired, produced his usual seamless stories like colored scarves out of a magician's sleeve. During intermission, he sat behind his table, looking down at his notes. I felt that this was my last chance to present myself. I came to the far edge of the table, kneeling down to be more in line with his face, and said, "Mr. Bateson, my name is Lynn Hoffman, and fifteen years ago, in Palo Alto, you changed my life." He looked at me, puzzled, and then he smiled and said, "Why thank you, lady. Thank you." That was it, and I went back to my seat. He died a year later.

But I was back on track. The idea of a less-purposive therapy had once more taken me by the hand, and this was when I thought of moving away from Ackerman to pursue what I thought of as "religious freedom." I also wanted to renew my life in a country community like the one I grew up in, where small was beautiful and I could live by my wits. I had read in the paper that the five college area around Amherst, Massachusetts, was a newly popular spot for retirees. My youngest daughter was about to finish up at Hampshire College, and a number of colleagues who lived in New England were pressing me to come there. In deference to my daughter's request to "stay out of her back yard" until she graduated, I waited until 1983 and then bought a Greek Revival farmhouse near the University of Massachusetts.

It was the sort of obliging house that crumbles one bit at a time so that you can keep up with the repairs. I was particularly pleased by the two huge weeping willows that flanked it. Nobody told me that its immense branches would keep falling down in windstorms, endangering my house and that of my neighbor. I was afraid that the rare Greek Revival barn in back would fall down too, but it just swayed in place like a quiet drunk. I loved that house because it was so different from my Upper East Side efficiency apartment, which never needed me to care about it and never gave anything back. Not only the house but the university community around it seemed to welcome me with open arms.

When I arrived in Amherst in the spring of 1983, someone told me that, "The concrete never sets on the University of Massachusetts." This saying alluded to the building programs that were constantly tearing up the campus, but it seemed also to apply to the School of Education, which had a particularly powerful history of tearing down traditions and building up new ones. It had been revitalized in the '70s under the aegis of educator Dwight Allen, who actively sought out African Americans and other minorities for the faculty, played down the necessity for advanced degrees, and created a renaissance in teaching and consulting.

Fortunately, I did not arrive at the University of Massachusetts as a total stranger. In 1978, the Chairman of the Department of Psychology, Harold Raush, had asked me to attend a conference he had designed called "Close Relationships." Himself a pioneering researcher on the interaction patterns of couples (1974), he had read my paper on "Deviation-Amplifying Processes in Natural Groups," and was sufficiently impressed to ask me to be one of the discussants. This was the first time that I had been noticed by anyone from the academic world, which I always stepped into with the awe of the outsider. Later acquaintance with the Psychology Department was disappointing, however. Except for a few social psychologists like Raush, it consisted of a psychodynamic clinical wing and a very behavioral research wing.

It was the School of Education, not the Psychology Department, that was the birthplace of the University's outstanding family therapy program. Family therapist Evan Imber-Black, its founding mother, had been asked by psychiatrist Karl Tomm to teach at the University of Calgary in Alberta just before I arrived, and the vacuum she left behind suctioned me in. There were many gifted family therapists working all over the Valley, and many gifted teachers like Janine Roberts, the director of the Family Therapy Program at UMass, who had replaced Imber-Black. Soon after I arrived, social work educator Ann Hartman came to Northampton as dean of the Smith School of Social Work, along with her partner, researcher Joan Laird. I became an adjunct lecturer, first at UMass, then at Smith, and later at psychologist Catherine Kikoski's Marriage and Family Therapy Program at St. Joseph College in West Hartford. I continued to give workshops in the U.S. and abroad, and I always had a study group going on in my home.

I also set up a private practice. The Valley was well known for its thriving cottage industry of therapists of every stripe. A young woman called me while I was still in New York, saying she had heard I was coming to the area and asking if I could see her. When I said that I wouldn't be arriving for some months, she asked for a recommendation. I gave her the name of a man I knew. She said she wanted to see a woman. I told her that I had heard that there were 400 women family therapists in the Valley alone. She said plaintively, "I am one of the 400 women therapists." She didn't want to go to any of them because she knew them, and because they were young like herself. I realized that it would be a plus to be the Oldest Living Woman Family Therapist in the Valley.

What I appreciated most, however, was the social justice bias of the Family Therapy Program. Soon after I arrived, I asked Roberts if we could create a Milan-style team at the University's Clinical Services Center. Alexander Blount, who was the director of an innovative halfway house called Crossroads in Holyoke, also joined us, as well as the late Stuart Golann, who taught in the Psychology Department at UMass and was a pioneer in the community mental health movement. As the project did not pay anybody, it collapsed into myself and Roberts during its second year, but I still felt privileged. Roberts was a brilliant hands-on practitioner whose work reminded me of raisin bread, because it was so stuffed with rituals, tasks and stories. Roberts and Blount had been hosting a yearly participants' conference at the University, where the many family therapists working and studying throughout the Valley presented their ideas to each other, and by attending them I got to know my new community in record time.

It was at a special workshop hosted by the Family Therapy Program that I was "presented." I was the therapist for a role-play mother and daughter.

The daughter's symptom was intractable asthma, and soon after I started the interview she began very realistically choking to death. It was a bad moment, as I saw my entire reputation going down the drain. In the nick of time, William Matthews, an Ericksonian hypnotherapist who taught in the School of Education, saved the day. He crashed the interview and calmed the daughter down with an elegant hypnotic induction woven around the metaphor of a jazz riff. This was my introduction to another gifted colleague. For several years we did co-therapy and workshops together, each learning from the other.

My move, however, placed me in a new period of uncertainty, much like the time twenty years before when I had jumped into an unknown field with no institutional support. Now, as then, I felt only a vague connection with my guiding star. I had let go of the entire objective universe in the hope that a "zen" of family therapy would appear. Of course it didn't, but the answer was spinning away behind my back, like those times in the wash cycle when the machine is silent and you think it's turned off. Unbeknownst to me, the road was readying itself below my feet.

The Different Voice

A year after I came to Amherst, I attended a conference at the University of Massachusetts called "Is the Earth a Living Organism?" I had the uncomfortable feeling that this was going to be the New Age equivalent of four days in church. I could not have been more wrong. Among the speakers were Lynn Margolies, the molecular biologist; chemist James Lovelock, creator of the Gaia hypothesis; physicist George Wald, the Nobel prize winner; and writer Mary Catherine Bateson, who was at the time dean of Amherst College. This stellar cast held a large audience of fuzzy-looking people spellbound for four days. They told story after story until science began to look like legend and magic began to sound like common sense.

It was at this event that I first met Catherine Bateson. She invited me to her home and showed me sections of *Angels Fear* (1987), the book she and her father were co-authoring at the time he died. Daughter Catherine was now composing the metalogues (the imaginary conversations between father and daughter that the elder Bateson had created for *Steps to an Ecology of Mind*, 1972), but this time it was the daughter who put words in the father's mouth. In "Persistent Shade" the last metalogue in the book, a ghostly father complains about the misuse of his ideas, and says, "The engineers get hold of them. Look at the whole godawful business of family therapy, therapists making 'paradoxical interventions' in order to change people or families, or counting 'double binds.' You can't count double binds."

Here was yet another message about the dangers of conscious purpose. For both Batesons, schemes designed to control human behavior were as chancy as schemes to control nature. As I knew from experience, such schemes often backfired in serious, unexpected ways, but since they bolstered up many forms of psychotherapy, they persisted. The first inkling I had that any other theorists were thinking along similar lines was when I read *In a Different Voice* by Harvard psychologist Carol Gilligan. This book gave me an experience of sudden light. Let me explain why.

Gilligan was a different feminist from the kind I knew. I had danced around the edges of the Women's Movement of the '70s, amazed at the insights it produced. However, as with the Marxism of my youth, there was too big an element of "Who is not with us is against us" to make me happy. Gilligan, in pointing to the idea that women have an epistemology of their own, offered me another way to think. Of course, Gilligan did not act in a vacuum; she was influenced by innovators like Nancy Chodorow (1978) and Jean Baker Miller (1976), who had created what Miller called a new psychology of women. Miller observed that where men tended to view their relationships as adversarial in nature, women viewed them in a framework of connection. Failure to recognize this difference, Miller said, had seriously distorted the field of psychology and done great injustice to the study of women's lives.

Like the Minoan female athletes who somersaulted over bulls, Gilligan took these ideas by the horns. Noting that the classic study on stages of moral development by Harvard psychologist Lawrence Kohlberg (1981) was based on respondents who were all men, she set out to replicate this study in a format that included women, too. In so doing, she got some strikingly different results. At the highest stage of moral development, Kohlberg had found that his subjects followed abstract principles of truth and justice. Gilligan found that this was true of her male subjects, but not the women. It seemed that women would bend principles into pretzels to protect relationships.

The famous stimulus story, used by Kohlberg and borrowed by Gilligan, went thus: if a man needed a drug costing a thousand dollars to save his dying wife but was unable to pay for it, and the druggist refused to lower the price, what should the husband do? The men in Gilligan's study gave answers that fit with a logic based on principles: since they put the principle of life above that of money, they thought the husband should steal the drug. The reason this answer was obvious to them was because it was congruent with the way they reasoned. One of the male subjects in Gilligan's study described issues of morality as "sort of like a math problem with humans."

When Gilligan's women subjects were asked to solve this dilemma, they were far less sure of the answer. The question about stealing did not fit into their moral universe, which was based on what Gilligan called an "ethic of care." In accordance with this different ethic, they felt that stealing the drug would endanger the relationships touched by this action, and they looked for a solution that preserved them. One woman, for instance, suggested that the husband "talk it out" with the druggist in the hope of getting him to be more charitable. Where the men resorted to clear rules of logic, the women saw the solution embedded in negotiation and communication, a much murkier context. Gilligan compared these two types of response by using the image of a hierarchy versus a network.

In addition to suggesting that the moral attitudes of men and women were different, Gilligan pointed out what feminists have been hammering at for a long time: women's customs are treated as inferior to those of men. To quote a particularly nice statement of hers, "In the life cycle, as in the Garden of Eden, the woman has been the deviant" (1982, p. 6). Of course, being thought a deviant when your own perceptions tell you that you are right is a crazy-making situation. In the book *Meeting at the Crossroads* (Brown & Gilligan, 1992), Gilligan expands her critique to include the field of psychology as a whole. I was struck by one passage that prefigures the more communal practices I will be describing later on:

> A relational practice of psychology moves beyond a revisionary interpretation of voices or texts. Such interpretation, in fact, ought to mark only the beginning of a dialogue, the initial move by the listener toward the forming of questions and ultimately toward a relationship in which both people speak and listen to each other. (p. 39)

These assertions by Gilligan and other feminist psychologists had enormous relevance for therapy. Theories of development based on research conducted by men, usually on other men, have created misleading myths about normal functioning. The concept that maturity is a matter of achieving individual autonomy is only one example. For years, individual therapy has been predicated on the idea that the differentiated self is the pot of gold at the end of the rainbow. Popular notions of mental health follow this line, and dependency, often seen as a female trait, is devalued. Witness the derogatory label "codependent" for the mostly female spouses of alcoholics.

Another consequence has been to impose expectations of independence on women whose identity is defined by the web of obligations in which they live. Women are apt to be extremely responsive to family ties and influenced by sanctions against breaking them. They may find it difficult to leave a violent partner or denounce an abusive father. Women who come for help with such situations are often perceived by therapists as uncooperative, but they have their reasons. Because the act of leaving may jeopardize them and their children even further, they often fall into a confusion between loyalty, honesty, and survival as soon as therapy begins.

This dilemma is beautifully spelled out in the article "Love and Violence: Gender Paradoxes in Volatile Attachments" (Goldner, Penn, Sheinberg, & Walker, 1990), which addresses feminist issues in the context of battering but does not favor unilaterally taking sides. Similar perceptions resulted in the revolutionary work of the Stone Center at Wellesley College (Jordan & Surrey, 1986), which puts the quality of empathy center stage. Its practitioners have tried to follow the stories of their clients and really hear them, rather than imposing expectations from above. Their meetings often take the form of therapists sitting with groups of women as they share stories and sympathy together.

Family therapy opinions were also due for an overhaul. The early schools of family therapy had painted a particularly damaging picture of mothers. They were "overinvolved" if they were seen to be too concerned about their children, "disengaged" if they left them too much alone. Family therapists, like the courageous foursome who developed the Women's Project at Ackerman (Walters, Carter, Papp, & Silverstein, 1988), began to address these injustices and call for changes in the language and practices of the field. Other feminist family therapists (Goodrich, Rampage, Ellman, & Halstead, 1988) put together case books that laid out clear differences between pre- and post-feminist ways of working.

Many of these writers saw therapy as a tool for the liberation of women. They attacked Gilligan's approach as "difference feminism" and said that it trivialized women by treating them as superior servants. The law weighed in on the debate too. In some states, laws were passed forbidding therapists to see couples in cases of battering as long as the violence continued. When there was a question of sexual abuse of a child, family members would be siphoned off to individual therapists and kept apart, damaging functional family relationships as well as bad ones. Family therapists were often called to account if they presented a systemic framework for such problems at national meetings.

Mine was a different battle, however. It energized me to think that the customs of women could influence the customs of men. Mary Belenky and her colleagues Blythe Clinchy, Nancy Goldberger, and Jill Tarule (1986) had recommended that teachers allow students "to glimpse the process of their thinking, to see them groping in stages of imperfection." In a woman-centered university, they wrote, fewer courses would be conducted in the "masculine, adversarial style of discourse" and more would rely on what Belenky called "connected teaching." This was especially true in social and psychological studies. Morawski (in Hare-Mustin & Marecek, 1990) attacked conventional psychology, saying that,

> feminist scholars have shown that what is reflected in the structure of science are social relations that are fitted to the experiences of men and a hierarchical social world. At the most visible level, images of science and of masculinity are mutually edifying: Both are signified through language as tough, rigorous, unemotional, rational, independent, competitive. This gender symbolism is now entrenched in contemporary psychology. (p. 166)

I found a counter-story for this idea in the Taviani brothers' eloquent movie *Kaos*. At the beginning of the movie, which dramatizes five stories by Pirandello, you see a blackbearded Sicilian shepherd in the act of finding a male crow sitting on a nest on the ground. Lifting the bird, he sees that there are eggs in the nest. They are warm. He calls to his fellows, who come running. "Look at this crow," he says, "It's a male—a male who broods." The other shepherds look on in amazement, then they begin to chide the bird: "What's wrong with you? You're a male. You shouldn't be sitting on a nest!" They laugh, taking the eggs from the nest and throwing them at the bird. Then one of the shepherds grabs it. He draws a small bell from his pocket and ties it around the bird's neck, pushing it off into the air. The movie shows the bird flying over the crags and hills of Sicily, with the bell ringing every time he flaps his wings. Between each story he appears again, flapping and ringing. The "male who broods" ties the stories together with the sound of his bell.

This bell has not been ringing very loudly. I recently heard about a psychologist in Rhode Island who gave to a sample of third graders across the state a hypothetical question that read: "If you were to wake up tomorrow morning and find you had become a girl (to the boys) or a boy (to the girls), what would you feel and what would you do?" The girls were enthusiastic and spoke of the many projects they would immediately undertake. The boys' reaction was summed up in the statement: "I would kill myself."

Nevertheless, I was inspired by my own version of the ringing bell. I began to interfere with the formats of conferences and workshops, seminars and classes. Noticing how quickly a seminar would divide into Lions who did all the talking, and Lambs who remained silent (in mixed groups, usually women), I would set up a circle as if I were holding an AA meeting. Everybody would have a space bubble in which to speak. Or I would divide the group into pods and ask each pod to talk together while the rest listened in. This last device harnessed the observation that many women, and some men too, will feel more free to speak in a small group than in a large one.

The down side of this activism was that I was often perceived as imposing my own preferences. At one large conference, I asked my fellow panelists, both male, to help me move the table with the microphones from the
stage to the floor. Next, I placed the chairs in a semicircle on the platform
so that we could talk with and look at each other when being asked questions by the audience. I objected to the usual "swallows on a telephone
wire" format because it makes the speakers compete with each other for
audience approval. On that occasion, one of the panelists was Ericksonian
therapist Bill O'Hanlon, and after we had given our panel speeches and
opened the conversation to the audience, he drew himself up cross-legged
on his chair and announced, "I hate being collaborative." I said to him later
that, after years of putting up with hierarchical arrangements at male-ori-
ented conferences, it was now my turn.

In looking for formats that supported a "different voice," my concern
was not about the oppression of one gender by another, but about widen-
ing the choice of communication styles. It is not true that a relational
vocabulary belongs to women or that a hierarchical one belongs to men.
Women have been more apt to learn how to respond to the nuances of
relationship than men, but socialization is not destiny. Why not acting
classes for women in male behavior, and acting classes for men in female
behavior? I was delighted that gender was turning out to be such a myriad
affair, and wished to refine and illuminate the concept of a different voice
in family therapy for all sexes.

This was not a reassuring time for me. I did not agree with the political
stance of feminist family therapy, and I had become uncomfortable with the
instrumental stance of many of family therapy's pioneers. It wasn't until I
left Ackerman that I got up enough courage to publish an article that challenged both positions. In "Beyond Power and Control" (1985), I made my
case. I was worried that I might draw upon myself the wrath of the establishment, as Keeney had done, so I published the piece in *Family Systems
Medicine* rather than a family therapy journal. To my relief, the article provoked little notice. However, it contained guidelines for a style of family
therapy that later became widely accepted, so I will repeat them here. They
were far more prescient than I could have known.

1. An "observing system" stance and inclusion of the therapist's
   own context.
2. A collaborative rather than a hierarchical structure.
3. Goals that set a context for change, rather than specify a change.
4. Ways to guard against too much instrumentality.
5. A "circular" (non-causal) assessment of the problem.
6. A non-pejorative, non-judgmental view.

In the meantime, I struggled with valid objections to systemic concepts by feminists like Laurie McKinnon and Dusty Miller. In an important paper on domestic violence (1987), they pointed out that the problem with doing family therapy in situations of battering or sexual abuse was that it put the victim and the victimizer on the same level. Systemic ideas, by assigning equal weight to everyone in the system, were clearly unjust. However, using therapy to further an ideological agenda rather than the goals of those who consulted you seemed wrong, too. And seeing that in the politicized atmosphere of the '80s any support for my different voice would be long in coming, I turned to a group of unusual researchers who seemed to have inherited Bateson's mantle. With them, at least, I felt safe.

The Constructivists

Starting in the '50s, due to advances in artificial intelligence and computing, a group of scientists came along who were redefining the nature of knowing. Among those persons were the visionary biologist Umberto Maturana, the computational genius Heinz von Foerster, the radical constructivist Ernst von Glasersfeld, and the late logician Francisco Varela. These researchers thought of themselves as "constructivists." Their writings supported an attack on the notion of objective reality that was often confused with social construction theory (of which more later), but in their case had roots in the biology of cognition.

The position that had most implications for therapy was Maturana's idea that human beings were barricaded behind the sensory architecture of the brain. This led to the belief that we can never really "know" the reality of the world or of another person, hence Maturana's famous statement: "There can be no instructive interaction." Another of their ideas was "second order cybernetics," meaning a system where the loop includes the observer, as opposed to a "first order cybernetics," where the observer is left out. This was important because it undermined the assumption that the researcher, or therapist, could ever claim objectivity in dealing with human affairs.

This skepticism about "the truth" had always existed in philosophical discourse, but these four researchers challenged it in a novel way: they pointed to the shaping power of the mind's eye. From then on, one could never refer to family dynamics but only to an observer's *perception* of family dynamics. Maturana dramatized this position by placing the icon of an eye in a corner of the blackboard whenever he lectured. This signal cued us to remember that our ideas about the things we saw were not necessarily the way they really were. All we could pick up was a kind of negative knowledge, the experience of the pilot of a plane who lands his craft safely in a fog at night using his autopilot. Even though he knows his knowledge was adequate for the task, all he has really done is to align his indicators correctly on his instrument panel (Maturana & Varela, 1980).

I had first met von Foerster in California in 1982, during a conference sponsored by the MRI called "Maps of the Mind, Maps of the World." Von Foerster was an engineering genius from Vienna and a nephew of the philosopher Ludwig Wittgenstein. He came to the U.S. after the war to take part in building the first generation of computers and became a secretary for the legendary Josiah H. Macy conferences, which started after World War II. During these meetings, rocket scientist Norbert Wiener (1954) introduced the newly named field of cybernetics to an interdisciplinary world. Gregory Bateson and Margaret Mead were among those who took part in these conversations, which went on for ten years, feeding indirectly into Bateson's research project in Palo Alto in the '50s.

With his characteristic effervescence, von Foerster invited me to come to a conference he was planning with Maturana, Varela, and von Glasersfeld in New Hampshire. It seemed that they had got money from the Navy to hold a Gordon Conference (a small meeting on a narrow scientific specialty) on cybernetics, except that their aim was to design a Macy-style cross-disciplinary event. Family researchers Carlos Sluzki and Paul Watzlawick had originally been asked to speak on family therapy but were unable to come at the last minute, so Von Foerster asked me to substitute. Not wanting to do this alone, I asked a few family therapists from the Amherst area to go up with me. I knew that my band of colleagues would help me out.

Suffering intensely at the prospect of having to speak in front of so many credentialed individuals, I prepared my talk carefully. I took the position that the strategic schools of family therapy were founded on first order "input-output" models used by cybernetic engineers. I argued that we had to find second order models that would include the observer. I promoted doubts about the idea of the therapist as a "change agent." I attacked the belief that we could ever fully understand "the world out there," let alone the structure of a family system. My talk, like a few presentations in my life before, had aspects of what I thought of as "channeling," the sense that a spirit is speaking through you. Whoever was giving this talk (the Persistent Shade?), it was received with interest, and I felt that I had passed an invisible test.

This Gordon Conference was followed by several more, bringing some of us family therapists into a wider intellectual world. I remember Haley saying, "Reading rots the mind," and stating that new ideas only get into the universities ten years after they surface. Even Bateson was what a colleague of mine once called a "vertical genius," meaning someone who seems to drop out of the sky fully formed and rarely cites anyone else. But the people at the Gordon conferences were from every country, had illustrious degrees, taught or composed or painted or invented, and many represented the cutting edge in artificial intelligence and computer science. It was at one of these conferences that I first heard the term "postmodernism," introduced by a young literary theorist who was brimming with the ideas of a French philosopher called Jacques Derrida. Her talk seemed so pretentious and obscure that I dismissed it out of hand.

After attending these conferences, I wrote two articles relating ideas like second order cybernetics, autopoiesis, and observing systems, to the world of the family therapist. These pieces appear in my book *Exchanging Voices* (1993), and contain most of the information about constructivism that any family therapist would ever want to know. As it turned out, however, the most important concept I stumbled on during those years had to do not with philosophy but with an ancient Irish story about the Fifth Province. This turned out to be the philosopher's stone for which I had been searching, and it came to me indirectly through a phenomenon I called the Milan teams meetings. Let me explain what these were.

The Milan Teams Meetings

After *Foundations of Family Therapy* came out in 1981, I began traveling. My book was translated into several languages, including Japanese, and I became a worldwide lecturer on family therapy. My trips often coincided with the summer conferences organized in the Italian lakes during the '80s by Luigi Boscolo and Gianfranco Cecchin, which offered an idea exchange for family therapists from many countries. North Americans may have helped to start family therapy, but the Milan teams movement created an international presence that is still expanding today. Many of the people who attended these meetings not only started systemic teaching centers of their own, but also became the purveyors and initiators of some of our best new ideas.

One of the earliest of such teams was the one at Ackerman to which I referred earlier, consisting of Peggy Penn, John Patten, Jeffrey Ross, and myself. But we were only one of many. In London, Ros Draper and David Campbell started a program in systemic therapy at the Tavistock Clinic. Martin Little and Peter and Susan Lang created a program at the Kensington Center based on the communication-oriented model of Barnett Pearce and Vern Cronin (1980). Brian Cade, Bebe Speed, and Philippa Seligman held forth at the Family Institute in Cardiff, Wales, and John Burnham and

Queenie Harris designed a training program in Birmingham. Tom Andersen and his team brought systemic ideas to the University of Tromsø in Norway and Mia Anderssen, Klaus Grevelius, and Ernst Solomon started a research group in Stockholm. There was Michael White's innovative Dulwich Center in Adelaide, South Australia, and Karl Tomm and Lorraine Wright's systemic collaboration at the University of Calgary in Alberta. Last but not least, Imelda McCarthy, Phil Kearney, and Nollaig Byrne began teaching family therapy at the Mater Hospital in Dublin. This list does not include the many other innovators in family and systemic therapy in the U.S., Canada, Australia, Europe and the U.K., but it does give some indication of the far-reaching influence of Boscolo and Cecchin.

It was around this time that Imelda McCarthy, Nollaig Byrne, and Phil Kearney, whom I first met when they visited the Ackerman Institute in 1981, asked me to Dublin to speak to a gathering of the Family Therapy Network of Ireland. I had been at a Milan conference on the island of Montisola in Italy, and getting to Ireland from there was easier said than done. After sleeping overnight on the floor of the Center for the Study of the Family in Milan, amid the ladders and paint cans of a renovation, I couldn't get to Dublin until the middle of the day of my workshop. In spite of the terrible Irish telephone system, however, I was able to warn everyone that I would be late and Nollaig and Imelda bravely improvised until I appeared.

When I arrived, I was immediately thrown into the lion's den of a clinical interview. Here, I was told, was a classic Dublin family: a pair of poor, struggling parents and their two little boys. The terrible thing was that their Dublin accent was as impregnable as a fort, and I couldn't make out a word. So I sat and pretended to understand while the mother, a very expressive woman, went on and on about something that upset her very much. Finally, out of the fog came a word or two, something about "relations" and "six weeks." I said, "You haven't seen your relations in six weeks?" And the mother said, very loudly, as if to a deaf person, "No, *sex relations*, we haven't had *sex relations* for six weeks." At last I understood. But much to my horror, from the adjoining room, where the entire conference was watching the interview on closed circuit TV, there came the unmistakable roar of muffled laughter.

I don't know how I got through the rest of that interview and don't remember anything except the end, when I shook hands with the parents and thanked them. Then I bent down to say goodbye to the two little boys and wish them well. The older one gravely shook my hand and said in the sincerest possible tones, "And the best of luck to you too, Mrs. Hoffman." Hearing the room next door boiling over with new hilarity, I couldn't wait to get the family on its way. The family told the clinic later that they had enjoyed the interview very much. I wish I could have said the same.

As if to make up for this fiasco, Nollaig, Imelda, and Phil took me to a pub with an old fashioned snug (a corral of solid oak to protect females and clerics), and then to supper at the "Surf 'n Turf." It was a pleasantly bohemian place, with an Irish piper playing in the corner and a poet rising occasionally to declaim his verse. Nollaig immediately took me under her arm and we performed a jig between the tables. After I sat down, badly out of breath, the poet rose to make a satiric Ode to the Irish Telephone System. In fact, he was the same square shape as an Irish telephone box. Next we persuaded Phil's girlfriend to sing a romantic Gaelic ballad, which she did in a high sweet voice. Finally, just as our meal arrived, the Irish poet stood in the doorway and said he was going to recite one more poem before leaving. He announced the title: "To Masturbation!" As usual, I could make out very few of the lines, but I did hear one couplet, which began: "Does the friar pull his wire?" and I think implicated the Pope. As soon as he had finished, he rushed out, the piper struck up again, and we finished our food.

But this story is really about the Fifth Province. Imelda was a self-appointed channeller from Ireland's mystic past to family therapists of today. It was she who gave each visitor a tour of Joyce's Dublin. It was she who acquainted me with the work of Louis Le Broquy, an artist who painted white-on-white ghost faces of Irish writers like William Butler Yeats. And it was she who acquainted me with the literary journal *The Crane Bag*, edited by one of Ireland's brightest lights, Richard Kearney. She showed me where, in a piece in that journal, Kearney had written about the legend of the Fifth Province. But perhaps I should explain why it became so important to me.

The Dublin group often encountered family problems, like incest, that in Ireland usually fell between the legal system and the priests. In their effort to find a frame that fit these dilemmas, the group adopted the story of the Fifth Province (McCarthy & Byrne, 1988). It seemed that in the ancient days Ireland was divided into four provinces, each ruled by a king. However, there were often issues that no single king could rule on. To address this problem, or so the story goes, one day a year a place was set aside called the Fifth Province. There the kings could meet to solve conflicts on equal ground. True or not, this story proved to be of enormous help to Irish family therapists when working with families beset by abusive and illicit behaviors. If such things were dealt with at all, they were often left undefined and murky. The idea of a Fifth Province provided a way to get above the limitations of both justice and morality, and find a place where everyone could be heard.

To depict the structure of their work, the group created a diagram in the shape of a diamond. On this diamond they placed the different situations that a family therapist might expect to meet. Each of the four angles would represent one of the parties: this could be a person, a group, or an abstraction, like the legal system. The sides between the angles could be named differently too, according to the character of the relationship between each set: blame, protection, repentance, support. The entire politics of the situation could be represented on this simple map. I will give one example to show how it worked.

In the case of incest, which carries heavy penalties in Ireland and is heavily denied, the Dublin group would not speak of the "system of incest," which would be traditional family-therapy-speak, but the "system of disclosure." Disclosure, they said, often creates two warring camps. If incest is denied, this is either in protection of the family or of the father. If it is admitted to, this is usually in protection of the child. If a meeting were attended by the mother, father, daughter, and social worker, each angle of the diagram could represent any one of these persons. A "symmetrical" (equal) version of the diamond would be mother and father versus daughter and the social worker. A "complementary" (unequal) version would be mother, daughter, and social worker, with father excluded.

Whatever the configuration, the diamond showed clearly that the therapist could not side with any of the parties without pulling the family further apart. So the group drew a Celtic spiral in the middle of the diamond that signified the fluid position of the team. For instance, by focusing on disclosure rather than truth, the team stayed at a hovering level that allowed possibilities rather than judgments to be explored. They might bring up a question like "Is incest a crime or is it a sin?" This ambiguity offered a range of solutions from legal punishment to religious expiation, but most importantly it allowed a forbidden subject to be discussed.

The most striking impression I got from watching Byrne, who was a powerful interviewer, was the overwhelming importance of culture. Ireland, the group had told me, is "the country of no clear statements"; the collective Irish mind is "an ambivalent batch." Since poetry's medium is ambiguity, the group's reliance on what one could dismiss as Celtic fairytales seemed very necessary to me. I felt that my own culture could benefit by using this language of ambiguity, if only to counteract our tendency to demand solutions couched in terms of right or wrong. It seemed to me that because we were bonded to a technical-rational code of justice, our legal system had not done well with any kind of family violence, and that we too needed a Fifth Province.

I held this powerful story close to me in the days to come, when it seemed as if incest, molestation, battering, and abuse were raining down on the heads of all family therapists and our collective search for solutions was going nowhere. In the next chapter, I want to introduce a major ally in this predicament, Harry Goolishian. It was Goolishian and his partner, Harlene Anderson, who tied my ideal of a different voice to practice. It was they who rescued me from the dilemmas of family justice. In fact, in their concept of "not knowing," they seemed to offer a Fifth Province of their own.

8

The New Paradigm

The Flybottle

In this book, I have been trying to document particular examples of work with the persons and families who have been my teachers over the years. However, I have also had to struggle with the paradigm I was born into. My encounter with the Bateson Project in Palo Alto convinced me that a huge barrier to knowledge in the field of human suffering was not practical but conceptual. The means we used to fix our positions were flawed, so our conclusions were flawed. Certain errors of thinking operated to convince us that we could research emotional problems as if they had "causes" similar to physical ones, or as if they were "contained" within an individual or within a particular family structure. Since entering the family therapy field, I had felt an eerie succession of displacements that suggested that these mechanical trappings were weakening. More and more it seemed that a new framework was building itself around me as the old one faded away.

In fact, all through the past half-century there have been sightings of what Harvard philosopher Thomas Kuhn (1962) called in his great and original book, *The Structure of Scientific Revolutions*, a "new paradigm." Kuhn describes a paradigm as a compelling conceptual framework widely accepted by a community of knowers. For instance, in the educated Europe of the Middle Ages, an overarching theory evolved that was built around St.

Augustine's notion of the City of God. It was a closed system of congruencies: "As in the Heavens above, so on the Earth below." Ideas that did not fit, like those of the astronomers Galileo or Copernicus, could not "take" until a new framework evolved in which they were no longer anomalies.

The Enlightenment of the 18th century was another such paradigm, fed by the dazzle of scientific discovery and the explosion of technological invention. More and more areas of life became systematized, and more and more areas of work were professionalized. In the beginning of the 20th century, what social philosopher Kenneth Gergen (1994) calls a "neo-Enlightenment" framework ushered in the modernist movement in technology and the arts. Positivism was its philosophy, justified by extraordinary achievements like getting people to the moon. Then, in the second half of the century, like a slap in the face to modernism, the postmodern movement was born. And now a bewildering number of terms are vying for the status of "new paradigm": not only postmodernism, but postpositivism, poststructuralism, deconstructionism, constructivism, social constructionism, to name only a few.

When this barrage of abstractions first hit me, toward the end of the eighties, I knew I would have to read an army of books and my spirit quailed. I got some comfort from *New Yorker* writer Adam Gopnik (1998), who refers to "the never-never land of poststructuralist discourse where everything must be understood as a social construction but all the social constructions end up looking more or less the same, like corporate headquarters on Sixth Avenue." Nevertheless, there are some important differences between these corporations that have important consequences for family therapy.

The main distinction, as far as I can see, is that what I think of as the postmodern trunk line of family therapy seems to have bifurcated. One arm is represented by the collaborative therapies that have taken postmodernism as their larger frame and social construction theory as their operational guide. The narrative therapies represent the other arm. Their original spokespersons, Michael White and David Epston, draw inspiration from poststructuralism and deconstructionism, categories that are indebted to the work of French philosophers Jacques Derrida (1978) and Michel Foucault (1972).

Here I must give due credit to ongoing conversations with psychologist Lois Shawver (2000), who has attempted to clarify for me the tributaries that fed into the larger river of postmodernism. She once said to me that postmodernism is like atheism. There are Jewish atheists and Christian atheists and it matters which kind you are. In the same way, there are different kinds of "posts." There are post-positivists like Wittgenstein (1953), who argued his way out of the entrapments of logical positivism, and post-structuralists like Derrida (1976), who amended the rules of structural linguistics. Postpositivism gets its force from its challenge to positivism, which is the tradition of research psychology, operationism, and behaviorism. Poststructuralism gets its force from its challenge to structuralism, a theoretic veil that some think has obscured every field in the humanities for at least a century. Shawver sees Wittgenstein and Derrida, as two pathfinders, each starting from a different intellectual setting but arriving at a similar place.

In this chapter, I will begin with Wittgenstein, as he was one of the earliest philosophers to expose the scrim of language that, in his view, interprets and distorts our efforts to understand the world. People find his work difficult because he put no title on his ideas and so there is no School of Wittgenstein. All he left on his struggles with language was a set of intellectual exercises and musings which were collected under the title *Philosophical Investigations* (1953). They have bedeviled and fascinated students of philosophy ever since.

The story of Wittgenstein's conversion is quite amazing. While in the British trenches in World War I, he wrote a treatise on logical positivism called *The Tractatus-Logico-Philosophicus* (1961). At this time, he was a disciple of the famous logical positivist Bertrand Russell. After the war, he decided that what he had been working on was an illusory edifice. Going to a remote, rural place far from the world of the university, he hammered away at the claims of philosophy, saying, "What we are destroying is nothing but houses of cards and we are clearing up the ground of language on which they stand" (1953, #118).

To achieve his goal, Wittgenstein felt he had to use something other than didactic language. Partly he fell back on Socratic questions to himself, which he then answered in the same cryptic style. He also took advantage of the one element of language that seems to transcend the medium of words: the metaphor. To describe the situation he found himself in, he came up with the wonderful analogy of the "flybottle" (1953, #309). The flybottle symbolizes the plight of the mind when it cannot find a path out of confusing linguistic traps. In exercise after exercise, Wittgenstein struggled with the constraints of language and the opaqueness of conventional concepts until he could "see" this flybottle and make it evident to others.

Let me give you the context for this effort. Wittgenstein's original circle had challenged the notion of "ideal forms" that Plato said were printed on the mind as a seal is printed onto wax. According to Plato, when we perceive something from the outer world, we have only to compare it to the impression in our minds to know what it is. These mental impressions have also been called "essences," "universals," "natural laws," and so forth. Language was said to operate the same way, in the sense that for each word there was a corresponding essence that it named. The dream of the logical positivists was to escape from this Platonic system of ideal forms by drawing on the rules of logic. Wittgenstein had tried to use these rules in his *Tractatus*, but decided that the whole attempt was bankrupt and gave it up.

It must have been hard for the young philosopher to turn his back on everything he had built, and on Russell, his mentor. Nevertheless, he set out all over again, this time to show how our verbal frameworks deceive us. Shawver (2000) uses the analogy of "a mental prison without visible doors, a space where our thoughts can only echo prior thoughts." To work his way out of this enclosure, Wittgenstein invented a series of exercises that challenged the assumptions hidden in our language. He even coined a phrase, "the bewitchment of our intelligence by means of language" (1953, #109) to describe the power that these assumptions have over our minds.

Now let me try to explain the derivation of the term postmodernism. Shawver says that it was French philosopher Jean-Francois Lyotard (1984) who tried to bring the various "posts" under a single roof. Although Lyotard's later writings were intellectually closer to Wittgenstein than Derrida, Lyotard was initially a Saussurian structuralist (Readings, 1991) who moved away from this position later on. He had to be aware of Derrida's similar views, but the club of public intellectuals in France was nothing if not competitive. The invention of a meta-term saved Lyotard from having to place himself under anybody else's banner. In 1979, in the French edition of *The Postmodern Condition*, he explained that the term "postmodernism" was already in use in social and literary circles in the U.S. However, he gave it his own spin. Calling it "an incredulity toward meta-narratives," he went on to describe a "metanarrative" as:

> any science that legitimizes itself with reference to a metadiscourse of any kind, making an explicit appeal to some grand narrative, such as the dialectics of Spirit, the hermenutics of meaning, the emancipation of the rational or working subject, or the creation of wealth. (1984, Introduction, p. xxiii)

It is interesting to note that Lyotard was a Marxist himself early on, but left the movement after the failure of the Paris uprisings of 1968. You could say that the invention of postmodernism gave him and others intellectual cover for moving out from under the Marxist umbrella, a doctrine that was arguably the most long-lasting political religion of the 20th century.

Among recent philosophers who have delivered fatal body blows to the corpus of modernist thinking, there is one more, Richard Rorty. He is known primarily for his deconstruction of a popular and widespread myth: the representational theory of knowledge. In *Philosophy and the Mirror of Nature* (1979), he writes these famous lines:

> The picture which holds traditional philosophy captive is that of the mind as a great mirror, containing various representations, some accurate, some not—and capable of being studied by pure nonempirical methods. Without the notion of mind as mirror, the notion of knowledge as accuracy of representation would not have suggested itself. (p. 12)

Rorty further points out the importance of the ocular metaphor and the mirror image to Western philosophical thought. The belief that words have a one-to-one relationship to that which they name is another version of the Platonic essence idea. That is why "representationalism" is a key target for postmodern thinkers, and why many abstract concepts in the social and psychological sciences that supposedly mirror nature are also under fire. I will return to this argument when I talk about social construction theory in Chapter 12. And rather than trying to explain deconstructionism and poststructuralism here, I will postpone these considerations to Chapter 13, where they will make a bit more sense.

If the reader is already getting her head whirled about by these competing abstractions, let me comfort you with Shelf Theory. This theory is my own invention. It holds that the only way to escape from one ledge of confusing concepts is by finding another ledge on which to stand. I am using a spatial metaphor, which indicates I am still trapped within the flybottle of Western grammar, but never mind, I only need a device that acts as another shelf. Once safely there, I can see the limits of the parameters that formerly enclosed my entire universe. Then I can say, with Alice, "Oh, you are nothing but a pack of cards."

For people who are still puzzled, I would recommend reading the elegant work on comparative linguistics by Benjamin Lee Whorf (1956). Whorf laid bare the structural bias of English usage by showing how totally it is suffused with spatial metaphors (examples: "I grasp your point," "I rest my case," "I take my leave"). He contrasts this framework with the process grammar of the Hopi Indians, whose language emphasizes the world of "eventing" rather than "events," and "becoming" rather than "being." Along with Wittgenstein, he was one of the early linguists to call attention to the way grammar shapes our views on "how it is."

Finally, there is always that wonderful book by the Victorian grammarian Edwin Abbott called *Flatland*, which gives the reader a personal experience of the different apprehensions of reality that constitute Euclidean geometry. If you are a point in Flatland, which is a world of one dimension, you cannot grasp what it would be like to be a line in a world of two dimensions, and even harder to be a square in the three-dimensional world of the cube. Not only what you can see but what you can imagine is drastically changed by each step that you take in this geometric progression. After you read this book, understanding the implications of postmodernism should be a snap.

Looking back, I think that Bateson was on to this idea. He used to say that his students complained behind his back, "Bateson knows something that he won't tell us." But how could he tell them? Like the Loch Ness Monster, it never came out while one was looking for it, and only betrayed itself by a smudge on a photograph or a blur on the radar. Bateson too was trapped on a shelf: the shelf of cybernetics, which was a source of reified spatial metaphors like "system" and "homeostasis" and "feedback." When he moved to an ecosystemic shelf, he escaped that flybottle. In fact, he alerted us to the ongoing destruction of huge contemporary ecosystems and in the process made us think twice about the implications of technology and expertise. His struggles with his own flybottle became an eloquent foreshadowing of the "new paradigm" we are now beginning to see.

One curious fact about the evolution of a paradigms is that a number of false Messiahs materialize first. During my decades of involvement in the family field I kept parsing through various theories, always thinking, "Maybe this is it." There was New Age physics (Capra, 1982), there was Prigogine's "order through fluctuation" (Prigogine & Stengers, 1984), there was chaos theory (Gleick, 1987). Sometimes I declared for one particular theory and then had to do some embarrassing backing down. I remember a cybernetics conference that I left early because two figures in the field whom I knew personally, Ernst von Glasersfeld (1987), representing radical constructivism, and Kenneth Gergen (1994), representing social constructionism, had been set up by their followers to debate each other, i.e., tear each other apart. They didn't, but rather than witness such a spectacle or show disloyalty to either, I fled.

As I have said earlier, all through this confused period I found Galveston psychologist and family therapist Harry Goolishian to be an unfailing mentor and friend. He also became a primary source of clarity on the subject of psychology and its relation to all these new ideas. Let me explain how our early relationship evolved and how he and his partner, Harlene Anderson, folded me into their endeavour. It was they who filled out the connection between the abstract concepts of postmodernism and the practices of the relationship therapies I was trying to describe.

Harry

Harry Goolishian, or Harry, as everyone called him, was an endlessly humane family therapy pioneer who lived and worked in Galveston, Texas. I had met him in the mid-70s at a conference in Birmingham, Alabama, where I was showing a reel-to-reel tape of an interview by Harry Aponte. To my dismay, the machine refused to work. I knew the fault couldn't be in my tape, because I had just played it the day before, but the technicians on hand said it was. Goolishian came up behind me and with a clumsy swagger pushed his way to the machine, "accidentally" bumping a button on it as he did so. It began to play my tape. "I don't know what was wrong, but it's okay now," said Goolishian, smiling at the technicians in a friendly way. This was his "Columbo" act, designed to get past the experts by playing dumb.

After this meeting, Goolishian began weaving me into his web of students, friends, and colleagues, and I felt in some wordless way that we were part of the same trajectory. His collaborator, Harlene Anderson, had moved to Boston, and he was always popping up to New England to see her and stopping by Amherst, or having me down to his corner of Texas for a conference. I remember sharing with him that instead of saying "the system creates a problem" you should say "the problem creates a system." He agreed, and we found that we both were moving away from the idea of the family system as a unit. He and Anderson objected to sociologist Talcott Parsons' (1951) normative view of social systems, one within another like Chinese boxes, because it was an "onion theory" that demanded that the lesser systems adapt to the needs of the larger ones.

People connected to Goolishian were infected by his fascination with new ideas. While he was still at the University of Texas Medical School in Galveston in the '50s, he was part of a team that hospitalized whole families of troubled adolescents, working with different groups over an entire weekend. The book about this work, *Multiple Impact Therapy with Families* (MacGregor et al., 1964), lay dormant in the soil of the family therapy field for many years. In a personal chronology, Anderson tells of joining the Galveston team in the early '70s and being impressed by the way the MIT approach, as they called it, constructed an encompassing cocoon within which families and helpers could both experiment with change. Having no conventional theoretical models to turn to that addressed this way of working, the group became interested in Watzlawick's writing and the interactional approach of the MRI. I remember when Goolishian, together with his genial colleague George Pulliam, came out to Brooklyn in the late '70s to show me some interviews that had the gentle, quizzical quality of the work of the late John Weakland.

At the beginning of the '80s, Goolishian showed me an article he had written with Paul Dell called "Order through Fluctuation" (1979). The authors used the ideas of physicist Ilya Prigogine to question the validity of the homeostasis analogy in family systems theory. I think Goolishian wanted my feedback because of an article I had written called "Deviation-Amplifying Processes in Natural Groups" (1971). This article, a paper for a human behavior class at the Adelphi School of Social Work, got me more attention than anything else I had done. I composed it while sitting on a beach on Martha's Vineyard and watching my children swim. It was another of those times when I felt that some ghostly spirit was writing through me, challenging the concept of homeostasis in family theory for reasons of its own.

Dell and Goolishian thought that homeostasis was a poor explanatory principle, preferring Prigogine's idea of a "system far from equilibrium" in which a chance stimulus could set off an exponential shift to a new configuration. Chaos theory, with its saying, "If a butterfly flaps its wings in Tokyo tonight, there will be a hurricane in New York tomorrow," was another version of this view. I had ended *Foundations of Family Therapy* (1981) with speculations on where this "rivers in time" thinking would lead us, as opposed to the "timeless circle" of the steady state. At that moment, I was again picking up the scent of my prey, and I felt drawn to Goolishian because, like Bateson, he had some kind of superior night-vision.

Over time I came to realize that Goolishian was abandoning a strategic approach and beginning to practice in an increasingly laid-back fashion. As he was in Texas and I was in New York, I became aware of this shift only gradually, but I remember one early clue. In 1982, the Galveston Institute of Family Therapy put on a big conference in Houston called "Epistemology, Psychotherapy and Psychopathology." Over four hundred people attended. Along with Goolishian and some members of the Institute staff like Paul Dell, the presenters included Humberto Maturana, Brad Keeney, Gianfranco Cecchin, Luigi Boscolo, Carl Whitaker, and myself. Whitaker was the first speaker. However, shortly before this event took place, Paul Dell had fallen under the spell of a psychologist named Robert Shaw, who was part of Werner Erhard's EST movement. At the last minute, without telling anybody, Dell invited Shaw to be on the panel.

Goolishian's behavior during the conference surprised me. During a pre-conference meeting of the panelists, Shaw insisted that Dell be the lead speaker because he had a vision to share. We looked to Goolishian to oppose Shaw, but he did not, and Whitaker backed down. Shaw was relentless in his purpose, and Dell seemed off in a dream. Keeney and the Institute staff were outraged, as was I, but we felt powerless. During the entire event, Harry became more and more detached, as if all this time he were going through the belly of a snake. No strategies, no standing up for our beloved Carl, no nothing.

My frustration led to an incident when I threw a button into the audience. Shaw and Keeney had begun arguing on stage and getting into what I call the male moose dance, and it was my turn to speak. Goolishian nodded at me, but the two men went on escalating. Annoyed, I got up, unfastened my button and read aloud its message: "Women who compete with men lack ambition." I then threw the button into the front row, saying, "I want some woman to pick this up. I have been unable to get the floor for the last twenty minutes, and Harry has signaled that he considers it hopeless." I got a fan letter from the woman who caught the button. If subsequent feedback is to be believed, a surprisingly large number of those attending remembered the meeting mainly for that event.

Later, I complained to Goolishian. I said that his behavior during the conference had reminded me of an experience with a leaderless group. It made me feel crazy. Why did he refuse to stand up to Shaw? It was then that he told me about his brief involvement with the A.K. Rice group in the U.S., which was an offshoot of British psychologist Wilfred Bion's research on leaderless groups at the Tavistock Clinic in London. I have wondered whether this experience might explain Goolishian's later move to a hands-off style, in striking contrast to almost everybody else in the field. Alas, I never asked him.

The Greek Kitchen in the Arctic

It wasn't until 1988, at a conference convened by Norwegian psychiatrist Tom Andersen called "A Greek Kitchen in the Arctic," that I saw a videotape showing Harlene Anderson and Harry Goolishian putting their new ideas into action. Andersen's conference was based on an image he had of Greek hospitality, where interesting strangers might be invited into someone's house and asked to sit at the kitchen table and talk while the villagers stood against the walls and listened to the conversation. As this event took place during family therapy's constructivist period, Andersen invited a group of "epistemologists" to speak: cognitive scientists Humberto Maturana, Heinz von Foerster, and Ernst von Glasersfeld were among them, and the rest included one or two social researchers, and myself. Segments of taped interviews by Goolishian and Anderson, Boscolo and Cecchin, and Tom Andersen and Anna Margrete Flam would be shown, and the epistemologists would then link what they saw in the tapes to a constructivist point of view.

Since I was the only epistemologist who was a woman, the only one without a Ph.D., and the only one who was a therapist, I was in an odd place. Most of the audience were therapists too, but there was a huge gap between our language and the language of the academics and I felt like a frail bridge. Somehow, the conference bogged down in the Greek kitchen metaphor: the strangers got stuck talking at the kitchen table, and the villagers got stuck listening in. The stalemate was exposed during one of the feedback meetings that had been usefully structured in by Andersen, and the audience decided to break into small groups to devise questions for the epistemologists to answer the next day. This decision brought the two worlds together and loosened the conversational purse strings.

Whatever the frustrations of the event, I felt that trying to look at therapeutic conversations through an epistemological lens was a richly fascinating thing to do. I was watching hawk-like for congruences between the practices of systemic therapy and the world view of constructivism. This was easy to do with Boscolo and Cecchin's interview. Not only did the Milan group agree that reality was an interactional construction, but the approach that had flowered into the interactional, strategic, and systemic models was built on that common intellectual base. However, Anderson and Goolishian's work took a right-angle turn in a very different direction. Instead of a therapist operating on the reality of a person or family from the outside, you had something closer to therapists putting themselves almost bodily into a family's or person's private world. To show the difference, I will describe two of the interviews: the one done by Boscolo and Cecchin (briefly), and the one by Anderson and Goolishian (in detail).

In the tape Boscolo showed, he was brought in as a consultant to a therapist who was seeing the father and stepmother of a fourteen-year-old boy. The boy had spent two years in a residential institution for molesting a younger child, and after he got out his mother sent him to live with his father and stepmother. When he was found to be stealing small sums from his stepmother, they went to a family therapist. Several sessions had already taken place by the time of the taped interview. In the consultation, Boscolo ascertained that the stealing episodes seemed to take place after phone calls from the biological mother. The boy said he wanted to visit her, but he seemed to be getting mixed messages about this wish from everyone. Although he looked forward to his mother's phone calls, his stepmother said that these calls just stirred him up and that recently his mother had stopped calling at all. In the tape, the boy seemed like a confused but well-meaning adolescent who was trying to find his way.

Hypothesizing with the team behind the screen, Boscolo surmised that the boy was not only caught between the two families but was being whiplashed by his biological mother, who kept pulling him toward her, then pushing him away. I had noticed in the past that Boscolo often departed from strict Milan neutrality to make room for feelings. During the interview, he had given the boy the opportunity to say that he loved his mother and believed that she loved him. It was a touching moment in an interview that was heavy with the stepmother's complaints.

In the intervention, which he crafted together with Cecchin, Boscolo praised the family for working so hard to become a new family and positively connoted the boy's troublemaking. If the boy were to be perfect, that would mean that his stepmother was a better mother than his real mother. A ritual was suggested to help him out of this bind. They were to choose one day a week during which the boy and the family could talk about his mother. On that day he could call her, write to her, and so forth; on the other days they were to only talk about the other family. The transcript of the session ends here and I have not saved my notes, so I don't have the family's reaction to this message, but I do remember that they found the interview helpful.

Anderson and Goolishian's presentation seemed to come from a different universe. Before they showed their tape, they explained their postmodern outlook, proposing a language-based point of view instead of the systems one we had been using. They made three points: first, the complaint that brought people in was a "problem-organizing story," not a condition or a disorder located within any person or group; second, therapy was a "problem-dissolving conversation," not a direct attempt to solve anything; third, the job of the therapist was "to act as co-author of a new text through the art of questioning." The goal of therapy was simple: a conversation in which the complaint no longer figured. Their ideas about the interview also broke from tradition in emphasizing the collaborative quality of the therapeutic relationship (Anderson & Goolishian, 1992) and presenting what they called a "not-knowing" stance.

Anderson and Goolishian explained that the reason for not-knowing was that in imposing a pattern on "the series of accidents we call life," the therapist could too easily predetermine the outcome. She had to counter the tendency to impose a pattern from her previous learning and instead to immerse herself in the client's story. Goolishian and Anderson believed that one could not know beforehand what should be changed or what a new story would be. The therapist's role was different too; she was a "momentary guest," a "therapeutic visitor," whose job was to deconstruct the "already known." Very importantly, Anderson and Goolishian declared, it must be the therapist who is willing to change, because one cannot change another person without changing oneself.

Later I asked Anderson how the term not-knowing had come about. She told me that in the mid-eighties their group was fascinated with the newly revived discipline of hermeneutics and with the writings of philosophers like Hans Lipps (Wachterhauser, 1986), who talked about "the circle of the unexpressed," and Hans-Georg Gadamer (1975) who spoke of "the infinite resources of the 'not-yet-said.'" Anderson and Goolishian first attempted to write about this elusive concept in 1985, when Goolishian put together some notes that were published in German first but ended up as an article in *Family Process* (Anderson & Goolishian, 1988). In these notes, Goolishian says,

> Within this [hermeneutic] framework, there are no "real" external entities, only communicating and languaging human individuals. . . . Thus, there are no facts to be "known," no systems to be "understood," and no patterns and regularities to be "discovered."

From a hermeneutic point of view, therapists were not seen as the possessors of expert knowledge, but as learners. Instead of coming up with solutions to problems, they were to engage in the development, through dialogue, of "the new" and "the not yet said."

Anderson told me that once the group in Galveston started incorporating these ideas into a way of doing therapy, they ran into all sorts of objections. Students would say, "Surely you must have a hypothesis or a clinical judgment in the back of your mind." Anderson and Goolishian would explain that they were only interested in the client's hypothesis and that the client's story overshadowed any pre-knowing of their own. Their goal was to be as accurate as possible in understanding what it was like for their clients, what they wanted them to do, what they wanted them to know. As time went on, they found themselves explaining that they were less interested in "knowing" than in "not-knowing," and this phrase came to characterize their stance.

While reading Gaston Bachelard's *The Poetics of Space* (published in French in 1958 and reissued in English in 1994), I was struck by a quote from a book by the art critic Jean Lescure, pointing out that the term "non-knowing" is interestingly different from "not-knowing." Lescure says:

> Knowing must be accompanied by an equal capacity to forget knowing. Non-knowing is not a form of ignorance, but a difficult transcendence of knowledge. This is the price that must be paid for an oeuvre to be, at all times, a sort of pure beginning, which makes its creation an exercise in freedom. . . . In poetry, non-knowing is a primal condition. (p. xxxii)

This fragment, although written for a different context, seemed to tie Goolishian and Anderson's work to a framework of social poetics that I will speak about in the next chapter. For now, here is an account of the "not-yet-said" story that evolved during the videotape Goolishian and Anderson showed to the audience in Norway.

The Young Bag Lady

Let me start by describing the setting for this interview. Harlene (I will use first names here, as in doing therapy we were used to a familiar basis) was living and working in Boston but came down periodically to Houston to consult with Harry. During one of these occasions, they taped a session with a thirty-six-year-old woman, Patsy (not her real name, of course), who had been seen a few times by Harry and Paul Millea, a family therapy fellow at a local family practice clinic. Patsy complained of painful "eye muscle imbalance problems" as well as a "boredom sensation" that sapped her will and kept her from looking for a job. To get relief, she would sit in her closet for hours, even days. Because she always brought a large shopping bag full of notes and eye exercise cards to therapy with her, Paul had described her to Harry as "a budding young bag lady."

Harry and Harlene explained to us that Patsy's problem was exacerbated by a conflict with the helpers. Since she was a chronic clinic attender who believed that her complaints were physical, while the people who treated her believed that they were psychological, the two sides had gotten into a standoff. Compounding the difficulty, the stories she told about her problems were like bits of a jigsaw puzzle that floated about without any connecting links. What Anderson and Goolishian did was to acknowledge and appreciate these pieces, without judging or trying to impose coherence, and she herself then put the picture together.

Looking back on this interview, I began to notice what I thought of as the "word web." At the same time that Anderson and Goolishian placed themselves inside Patsy's story, using her own words, they introduced words that seemed to come from a different lexicon. To her repetitive descriptions like "boredom sensation" and "eye complaints," they added other descriptions like "being in a fog," "as if her mind disappears," as well as emotion terms like "frightening," "depressed," "unhappy," and "lonely." In the process, Patsy spontaneously came up with a suggestion that maybe she ought to go and live with someone for a while. When asked who she might live with, she started to talk about her family, from which she had been estranged. This conversation led to some practical ideas that started to move her life forward.

I should include some comments Harlene made after reading the above paragraph. She asked me to emphasize that what I call "introducing words from a different lexicon," she calls "checking out." She plays back to the person who is talking with her what she has heard, using the same words to make sure she is on target. However, she also introduces new words to offer contrast and comparison. She says, "I do not introduce the new words for them to begin to change something. What does happen in the process of checking out is a very important aspect of transformation. It is talking about the familiar in a different way. It is very 'dialogical.' " Her remarks made me realize that an outsider who looks at a transcript and then makes inferences is often likely to miss the therapist's real intent.

The interview opened with Harry introducing Harlene to Patsy and explaining that she was a colleague from Boston who was also on the faculty of the Houston-Galveston Institute. Paul was present too. Harlene asked to be filled in on how Patsy and Paul had become involved and was told that he was brought in by a family therapy resident who had seen Patsy when her general practice doctor could find nothing physically wrong with her. Her troubles were so perplexing that Paul then brought Harry in. Harry was concerned because Paul's fellowship was soon going to end and so he brought Harlene in. As in the story of the Golden Goose, one person after another got stuck to Patsy's situation. In this instance, part of the goal was to record some material to show at the Norway conference Harry and Harlene were going to later that year.

Harry began by saying to Patsy: "I know you've been down this road before, but I wonder if you would help Harlene to understand, in a way that she could have some input, what we're up to here—if you would kind of give her sort of a capsule summary of how this problem has been with you through your life—some times more intense than others, but basically it hasn't yielded to all the effort and struggle you've put into dealing with it." Looking back, I could see that this phrasing did two things: invited Patsy into a partnership and honored her previous work.

In response to Harlene's curiosity, Patsy shared many details. She pulled some eye exercise cards out of her shopping bag and explained them. It seemed that fluorescent light made her eye pains worse. She also spoke about a "boredom sensation," which was more mental than physical but still oppressed her. She said, "I always thought that there was a relationship between my mind and my eyes." As Harlene questioned her, she noted that both the eye imbalance and the boredom sensation happened more frequently when she was in the kitchen and also when she made phone calls. As for remedies, sitting in the closet relieved her eyes, and reading seemed to help the boredom. Harlene's response was mainly to repeat back what Patsy was saying and to check that she got it right.

Here Harry joined in, and together he and Harlene began to weave themselves into her story. Harry started by wondering if the boredom could get so severe that thinking would become difficult, and if she then would lose contact with herself. She agreed, saying that at these times she couldn't think about anything. Harlene surmised that she might "get so bored that she was out of touch with herself." Harry added, "It's almost as if her mind disappears." Harlene repeated, "as if her mind disappears." Patsy agreed again, saying, "I can't really think." Harlene repeated, "She can't really think . . . she doesn't see the psychological context."

At this point, Patsy said that even if she did try to think, it took a long time, and she had to force herself. Harry suggested that at those particular periods her thinking got so slow "it's almost like walking through molasses." Patsy agreed that "the words go real slow through my mind." Harlene put in, "like walking through molasses in a fog." Harry said that this had to be "extremely frightening" for her. She said this feeling was discouraging and made her so unhappy she would rather not exist. Harlene then suggested that she felt "bored" and "depressed." Patsy said, "I guess you could summarize it that way." Harry added, "at least unhappy," Harlene repeated the phrase, and Patsy came in with, "especially I think I get discouraged." This process may sound like a hypnotic induction, but I doubt that Harry and Harlene were doing anything consciously other than building the "word web" that brought them into her world.

Harlene now remarked on the effort Patsy had been making to try to figure everything out. Patsy said sometimes she couldn't even make herself get out of the chair. She was confused about what helped what, but said the boredom sensation seemed to be more mental than physical. Harlene asked if the problems had gotten worse recently. Paul came in to say they were so severe on Labor Day that she had to spend more than two hours in the closet, just to protect her eyes. Patsy said it didn't help completely, but after that she continued to go in the closet, even though the eye doctor told her to try to keep these episodes to an hour a day.

Harlene, joining Patsy in her imagination, surmised that the darkness there was probably more total than if she just put a bandana around her eyes. Patsy said no, there was still a bit of light. Harlene said, "Oh, coming through the keyhole and under the bottom of the door." Harry added, a bit gratuitously, "There's nothing in life that is perfect." Harlene said that being out of work must add even more stress, and Patsy agreed. Harry informed Harlene that Patsy had told him the rent was due at the end of the month and she had no money to pay for it and no money to live on either.

Then Patsy said something surprising, as if she finally saw her plight from a new point of view. She said, "You know, I am living by myself, and I found out that that contributes to the boredom sensation. Cause I walk in, you know, and there won't be anybody there and nobody will talk to me. So I

am not getting any stimuli there." Harry asked Patsy what she thought
about living with someone else, and she said perhaps her doctors could talk
with her father and stepmother. And then Harry and Harlene turned to
each other and had the following exchange:

> HARRY: I'm impressed and trying to understand the complexity of
>   the problem—I wish I understood it. There are so many dif-
>   ferent facts, and not both ends but an infinite number of
>   ends to understand.
>
> HARLENE: So you think that it's going to take some time to figure out
>   what all these little ends are?
>
> HARRY: Yes, and yet they all seem to center together in some way.
>
> HARLENE: All touching in some way.
>
> PATSY: (*interjecting*) Well, some of them do.
>
> HARRY: And I'm also impressed with the courage she has in facing
>   this all by herself. . . . She's come a long way despite this
>   handicapping condition—has been able to struggle with it,
>   live with it, and keep herself moving.
>
> PAUL: She's been to college . . .
>
> HARLENE: She's been dealing with this all her life, but somehow
>   recently it's become more difficult.

Harry then mentioned that Patsy was able to take a three-hour trip to
Austin recently, and Harlene said, "So, being able to go to Austin, and even
come here today, are examples of ways she's been able to pull herself out of
the chair and get through this molasses-like bog-down." Patsy for the first
time admitted to a small success: "Well, I had to do something."

This felt to me like a turning point, and it was no surprise that Harry
now asked Patsy about bringing her father and stepmother in. Patsy again
suggested "the doctor" call them, but Harry said her parents would probably be more impressed by an invitation from her. This sparked Patsy into
explaining that her father "didn't see the psychological context" and
believed the solution to the eye problem was another pair of glasses.
Harlene pressed her to talk a bit more about her family, and Patsy told her
that her mother had died two years before and that she had a sister in Austin
and a brother in Denver. She said that her father and stepmother did not
think she "deserved things," and that they were "distant" and "emotionally
inept."

During the final segment of the tape, Harlene asked about Patsy's
mother, who turned out to be the only person Patsy felt had ever understood her. Harlene observed that her vision and eye problems had isolated
her even further and asked if her personal characteristics of being a loner

and a private person had contributed. Patsy agreed. Harry then said to Harlene how impressed he was by Patsy's analysis:

> "When she mentioned that the eye exercises actually helped the eyes, but they end up also helping the mind, and how the reading sort of helps the mind, but also ends up helping the eyes, it's the unity of this that we are talking about, the physical problem of the eye and the incoordination of the psychological issue; even though they come from different ends, so to speak, they nonetheless meet."

Harlene then said to Patsy, "That seems to be the theme that runs through everything you are discovering, that they are all merging or connecting in some way." And Patsy said, "Yes, they do merge a little bit. Each one does a little bit different thing, but each one does, to a certain extent, the same thing." Harry added, "They affect each other through the whole spectrum." Harlene said, "Her personality keeps her isolated but the physical problems keep her isolated too." Here the therapists seemed to be describing two ends of the physical and psychological continuum as contributing to a single problem: isolation.

At this point, Harry brought in the helper context, saying that even though Patsy had worked hard on herself, her progress hadn't justified the effort, and the professionals had to take some responsibility for this, too. Harlene said that the people working with Patsy should make sure that they continually got input and feedback from her. Harry added, "So that we don't lose sight of the unity." Patsy now came in to remark, "Part of my eye problem has to do with lack of stimulation and with stress. Cause now I have discovered what part of the link is. Stress in the kitchen is what it is." Harry asked her whether some of the stress had to do with phoning in regard to getting a job, and Patsy said "Yes."

After this, things moved right along. Patsy said that she knew of a part-time job, but wondered if it wouldn't be better if she just took a break and stayed somewhere else for a while, perhaps with her family. Harry asked about contacting her father and stepmother, and she said that would be a good idea. Harlene warned Harry "not to go off on that path and miss all the other paths." The interview ended with Paul and Harry setting up a date for the following week and Patsy saying she would ask her parents if they could attend. Harlene asked Patsy to continue taking notes and watching for clues.

The taped segments ended here, but Harry and Harlene gave us a follow-up. In the next session, Patsy and her parents came in describing an attempted rape. A young neighbor, high on drugs, had assaulted her, but she had pushed him off and run out of her apartment while other neighbors called the police. Patsy's father was very critical of his "undisciplined" daughter and demanded that she do something about her unsafe, dirty apartment and poor choice in friends. He also said he had a low opinion of therapy. It turned out that he had been exposed to a lot of it, since mental problems "ran in the family." A sister of his had similar problems, and so did Patsy's brother and sister, although they had overcome them. Patsy was fascinated to hear these stories. The only person who had ever spoken to her about emotional problems was her mother, but she had never told her any of this.

In response to the curiosity that surfaced, the father agreed to another session and they invited Patsy's brother and sister to come, too. During this meeting, another family secret was shared. The father said that when Patsy was young, her mother had been abducted at gunpoint for several days and was sexually and physically abused. After she came home, she never went out again and her father took over many of the parental duties. In addition to this disclosure, which Patsy had never suspected, the siblings spoke of their own struggles with sexuality and leaving home. As a result, Patsy decided to visit each of them in order "to talk and explore experiences." Her father and stepmother suggested that they clean and refurbish her apartment while she was away, so that she could have a new start. The father said he was impatient to finish the job of "growing up" his lagging daughter.

At the time I saw this interview, I knew that Goolishian and Anderson were reading deeply in the new postmodern movement. They had already spoken to me and others of the ideas they were finding that cast doubt on "modern" concepts like the family system. They said that a not-knowing stance helped the therapist to step down from the expert position that a modern view endorsed. At the time, I thought I both understood and agreed with their view, but I have to confess that when I first saw it transmuted into the form of therapy, it was so different from what I was used to that its fine points passed me by. Accordingly, I used the term "imperceptible therapy" to characterize their work. In retrospect I need to apologize for this inaccurate description. It was only imperceptible to me.

To return to our Greek Kitchen conference, this event marked a break in the love affair between our particular group of systemic therapists and constructivism. It was Goolishian who led the way. He had been prowling around the outskirts of the conference room during the last day with a brooding look on his face. At the end of the afternoon, he came up to Harlene Anderson and me, very excited, and shared his dawning realization. In one of his talks, Maturana had declared that cybernetics was "the science of meaning and understanding." Goolishian said to us: "Maturana is trying to rescue cybernetics from its background in engineering. However, he won't succeed, because Norbert Wiener originally defined it as the science of communication and control."

As Goolishian and Anderson's theories became better known, the field's response to the concept of not-knowing was hostile, to say the least. Goolishian developed an unsuspected stubborn streak and stood his ground, but his detractors only got more irritated. It seemed so evident that he knew so much. "How can you charge people money if you don't know anything?" they would ask. "How can you teach what you don't know?" Despite these objections, Goolishian and Anderson persisted in writing, teaching and practicing their not-knowing point of view. Since Goolishian's death in 1991, their collaborative approach has taken a place at the front of the field, and is now ensconsed under the regime of Anderson and her colleagues at the Houston-Galveston Family Institute.

It would be hard to overestimate the importance of Goolishian's legacy. With all the reading in postmodern philosophy they were doing, Goolishian and Anderson brought a stunning new piece into the field. Six years later, Anderson applied these ideas to therapy in her intricate tapestry of a book *Conversations, Language and Possibilities* (1997). I myself was impressed with the revolution that was overturning ancient creeds in the academies and hallowed ways among the professions. I don't want to go into the effects of postmodernism on therapy here, except to say that family therapists who took it seriously faced a profound paradox. This was: if you ban what postmodern writers were calling "essentialist views," how can you teach any view at all? If you question all "metanarratives," how can you teach the one called "questioning metanarratives"?

This challenge brought back a memory of summer stock when I played the old Arab in William Saroyan's *The Time of Your Life*. My only line was: "No foundation, all the way down the line." At the time, I didn't know about the conversation between the English gentleman and the Arabian philosopher, which goes as follows:

Q: What does your religion say about the nature of the world?
A: We believe that the world stands on the back of a turtle.
Q: What holds the turtle up?
A: The turtle stands on the back of an elephant.
Q: What holds the elephant up?
A: Another elephant.
Q: And what holds that one up?
A: Oh, sir, after that it is elephants all the way down.

This became a huge problem for me. I could ask with the constructivists, "How real is real?" (Watzlawick, 1976). I could intellectually agree with

Goolishian and Anderson about not-knowing. I could opt for the different voice of Carol Gilligan. But how was I to put these ideas into practice? First, I had to find some local partners who thought as I did. Second, I had to find a stage on which to experiment. And third, I had to find a therapeutic format that would guide me in this new direction.

Here I was lucky. Almost as soon as I came to the Valley, I was sought out by psychologist Bill Lax and social worker Dario Lussardi, who were co-directors of the Brattleboro Institute of Family Therapy in Vermont. They had heard that I was moving to the area, and they planned to sit on my doorstep until I came. I arrived a year later than advertised, but they were still sitting there. I joined their teaching program, and we were working together when I first heard about Tom Andersen's reflecting team. This turned out to be the less-purposive format for which I had been searching. From then on, I began to find ways to link the abstractions of postmodernism to the practices of the everyday professional.

9

The Reflecting Team

No Backbone

When I first started at Brattleboro, we were using a Milan-style teaching team. Then, in 1986, Peggy Penn called me from New York to tell me that Tom Andersen (1987) was coming to Ackerman to demonstrate an innovation that he called a "reflecting team." Penn had been corresponding with Andersen since the days of the Milan meetings and a bond of heightened creativity had evolved between them. They often experimented with each other's new ideas, and Andersen had asked Penn and myself to seminars in Norway for several summers in a row. I immediately told Bill Lax and Dario Lussardi of the Brattleboro Family Institute and they decided to hold a workshop for Andersen in Vermont. Penn and her colleague Marcia Sheinberg had also been using the reflecting team idea, so we asked them to come too.

In a foreword I wrote for *The Reflecting Team* (Andersen, 1991), I said, "One could call this a book but one could also call it the description of a new flying machine." Andersen's idea was amazingly simple: he simply decided to switch the light and sound between the one-way room and the interviewing room, so that the family and therapist could listen in to what the team had to say, and vice versa. Even before I saw it in practice, I knew that its effect on the world of family therapy would be profound. In *Foundations of Family Therapy*, I had described a new technology of visibility—the one-way screen—that opened the therapy process to observing professionals. Now, nearly a half century after the mirror began to be used, this visibility was turned back upon professionals themselves.

When Andersen and a colleague, psychiatrist Magnus Hald, interviewed one of the Brattleboro families together with Bill Lax and a few of the staff, before our conference, I was amazed by how different their style felt. The interview had no structure apart from small groups commenting in turn, one after the other. There were no interventions, no lists of questions. No hierarchy, either; each group got to be the first horse on the merry-go-round. And the shock of no protection took my breath away. Suddenly it was clear to me what a conspiracy of silence our profession rests on. I found I began to shun not just clinical words but clinical thoughts, and psychological language, which came so easily during backstage exchanges between colleagues, now began to seem like a form of hate speech. But at the time, we had no inkling of the enormous influence this new format would have. Let me describe the interview that introduced it to us.

Bill Lax had been seeing a man, whom I will call Gabe, and his fiancée, Ruth, in couple therapy. A day before Andersen and Hald arrived, the man had collapsed suddenly at work, struck down by an intense anxiety. Lax went to see him in the hospital and found him barely able to speak, but he and his fiancée agreed to come in for a consultation with the Norwegians. We decided that our reflecting team would include Hald, Dario Lussardi, Judy Davidson (another staff member), and myself, while Lax and Andersen interviewed the couple. (Note: In describing interviews I took part in or watched, I will use first names.)

When the couple arrived, I remember being struck by Gabe's brooding heaviness. He was a stocky man in his forties who looked physically powerful but sat with his head down, staring at the floor. Ruth, his fiancée, was a lively, dark-haired woman who had met Gabe the year before at a Parents Without Partners meeting. After introductions and an explanation about the reflecting team and the taping, Tom asked Bill about the history of his work with the couple. Bill described the issues they had been working on and shared his present concerns. He had no explanation for Gabe's sudden collapse, nor did anyone else, and Gabe wasn't speaking. Tom now turned to the couple. He spoke of his origins in the North of Norway and asked where their families came from. Ruth, speaking for Gabe, said his family had been in Vermont for generations and that her own grandparents had come from Italy.

This regard for place was a hallmark of Tom's style. Before every workshop he would show videotaped clips of the mountains that surrounded his hometown of Tromsø, or play a tape he himself had made of wild bird cries from the nesting islands of the Arctic Circle. He believed that we should be forthcoming about our cultural and ecological context, and, like an anthropologist, held the idea that we only understand our own society by visiting another. He would periodically climb to the top of one of his favorite mountains so that he could come back to his home as a "small stranger."

I noticed that by talking separately with Bill in front of the couple, Tom gave them a similarly reflexive experience. Then when he turned to the couple, he put Bill on the outside. It seemed that this alternation of being on the edge and being in the center was another hallmark of this new process. In this case, it was mostly Tom asking Ruth her impressions about Gabe's situation while Gabe looked down and said nothing. All at once, Gabe burst out and said loudly, "I got no backbone!" He repeated this several times. Tom asked him what it meant. No further explanation was forthcoming, so he asked, "Who else in your family hasn't got a backbone?" Gabe said, "None of them. My father got no backbone. My brothers and sisters got no backbone." Ruth told Bill that on the day he broke down, he had run into his father, who worked in the same lumber business. It had apparently upset him, but Ruth had no idea why.

Now Gabe broke into heavy sobs. Tom sat quietly and said nothing for a long time. The sobbing finally diminished and Tom asked, "Who does have backbone?" Gabe replied, "My grandfather. He had backbone." Tom asked, "Is your grandfather still alive?" Gabe said, "He died ten years ago." Tom asked, "What do you remember about your grandfather?" Gabe seemed to go into a reverie. He said, "When I was a kid, we always used to go fishing. My grandfather had a bamboo pole with a safety pin on it and I had this fancy rig, and he always caught more fish than I did." A long silence followed. Finally Tom asked, "If your grandfather were still alive, what would he tell you?" Gabe said, "He'd tell them to go to hell. All of them."

At this point, we on the team changed places with the group in the room. I remember wondering what in the world a reflecting person was supposed to say, but I have also forgotten what we did say. I confess I was more interested in "what Tom did" than "what I did." I was still thinking in terms of a Milan-style operation and assumed erroneously that the only difference would be that we would share our thoughts in front of the family rather than behind closed doors. In any case, we talked a bit, then went back behind the screen while Bill, Tom, and the couple took our place.

Further efforts on Tom's part to get Gabe to talk only brought on more muteness mixed with anguished groans. Tom wondered aloud about stopping for the time being and asked whether Bill might want to meet Gabe alone. When Bill said "Yes," Tom asked when Bill thought that might be. Gabe inserted a loud "Soon! Soon!" So a date for Bill to see Gabe the following day was made and the couple agreed to come in the following week. The next day, Gabe told Bill that his father was a lifelong bully who

had abused and intimidated Gabe's brothers and sisters and that Gabe was
the only one who stood up for them. He was also in a struggle with his
divorced wife for custody of his children. Bill continued working with
Gabe over the next two years, and when last I heard, Gabe had split up with
Ruth but had gotten his children back.

When Tom came back for a visit the following year, Gabe came in to see
him. Despite his many family problems, he had not had another collapse.
After that, every time Tom and his team came to Brattleboro, Tom always
met with Gabe. It seemed that they had formed a deep attachment in that
first interview. I was surprised to see how much Tom's approach seemed to
encourage a realistic friendship, a possibility that was banned by most psychotherapies. The idea made a strong impression on my assumptions about
the nature of therapeutic boundaries, and I found that I began to work in
a more familiar fashion with the people who consulted with me.

During that first visit, we had many interesting discussions. One subject
we talked about was the beginning of the session. In our more strategic
days, when meeting a family for the first time, we used to ask, "What is the
problem in the family?" Tom said he now asked, "What is the history of
the idea to come to therapy?" This formulation changed the nature of the
inquiry. Instead of putting the problem front and center, the emphasis was
on the conversation: how it came about and how it could continue. Tom
had begun to invite Harry Goolishian and Harlene Anderson to Norway,
and many of their ideas were percolating about the Arctic Circle. One
thing was clear—that Tom was deeply devoted to Harry and much influenced by the idea of therapy as a conversation and the not-knowing point
of view.

What most impressed me about Tom's interviewing style was his attentive stillness and the way he held his body. He told us that when sitting next
to Gabe and speaking with him, he had been careful to inhale and exhale
in the same rhythm. Tom had worked for years with a body-work trainer
named Aadel Hansen, and he had recently written a book about her work,
so this was no surprise. Nevertheless, I was struck by the degree to which
Tom's bearing in the session showed what the English poet John Keats once
called "negative capability." Keats had defined this as "the ability to be in the
midst of doubts and uncertainties without any irritable reaching after facts
and reason."

Another surprising practice was the way Tom spoke. We knew that a
slow tempo and a long reaction time were characteristic of people of
Northern Europe, and the further north you got, the longer the time would
be between a question and its answer. Family therapy in Finland was especially famous for long pauses. But Tom's deliberate pace seemed unusually
marked, and his use of phrasings like "if," "perhaps" "maybe," "could it be?"

threw a veil of tentativeness over the proceedings. This tone was catching, and for a while we too began sounding like the bachelor uncles from Lake Woebegon.

Kneading Bread

The next day, Tom and Magnus did a reflecting consultation with a couple who were being seen by Bill and Mardie Ratheau, a staff therapist. We learned that when the family first came in a year before, the husband had been hospitalized for depression, the oldest daughter had dropped out of college, and the couple had separated. Since then, the couple had gotten back together and the daughter had gone back to school. The question now was whether to continue with therapy. Bill and the husband felt they should, while Mardie and the wife were less sure. On this occasion, Magnus was the interviewer and the reflecting team included Tom, Judy Davidson, and me. The couple, in their forties, was sitting behind the screen with us, while Magnus interviewed the two therapists.

I was fascinated by the layering that went on in this consultation. If it were a play, Act One would consist of Magnus speaking to the two therapists while the couple listened. In Act Two, the couple was interviewed by Magnus about what they had just heard, while the team and the co-therapists watched. In Act Three, the reflecting team went into the interviewing room while the therapists, the couple, and Magnus listened from behind the screen. In Act Four, Magnus, the couple, and the co-therapists commented while the team listened. Finally, in Act Five, Magnus took his leave and the couple and the therapists decided on another appointment. But this was no "well made play," with a beginning, middle, and end. The event consisted of a succession of dialogues, with participants alternating between listening and talking. There was no set goal beyond a general feeling that the conversation had reached a temporary stopping place.

If ever there were a nonpurposive format, this was it. More than anything else, it reminded me of kneading yeast dough. When I was a young faculty wife on the campus of Bard College, a kind neighbor had taken my culinary education in hand and showed me how to make bread. First you put the water and yeast in a bowl. Then you added flour. After it became a firm enough ball, you folded it over and over upon itself, to introduce air into the mix. Eventually, my neighbor told me, the dough would "come alive." I asked how I would know that. She said, "When it begins to resist you." Sure enough, at a certain point I felt the dough pushing back. When I poked a hole in it with my finger, the hole would close back up. Years later, it occurred to me that it was not just the activity of folding that was important, it was also the warmth of the human hand.

This metaphor helped enormously when I had to explain the difference between reflecting work and more conventional interviews. There were no direct links between what a therapist said and the outcome of any given session, and one had to get used to the general idea of expecting no solutions. The meditations of the reflecting team were similarly divorced from cause and effect. Since interpretations, suggestions, and tasks were ruled out, the comments we made were indeed very different from those of a Milan-style team. It seemed that the only things one could contribute would be stories from one's own experience or associations built on the conversations that had already taken place.

But there did seem to be a few rules. I had noticed that in Act One, when Magnus spoke with the therapists alone, only issues pertaining to the therapeutic relationship were addressed. Magnus wanted to know what perceptions people had about therapy: who wanted it; who thought they were stuck; what stopping therapy would mean; who would be glad, who disappointed; what issues remained to be resolved; to whom did they matter; which persons was each of the therapists most aligned with; how would the therapists feel if they stopped now? None of these questions were aimed at the couple's situation. In other words, the consultant was less interested in the story of the problem than in the story of the therapists.

Magnus's carefulness addressed the outer position of the consultant. After all, it was the therapists, not the family, who had asked for the session, and it was not the consultant's role to walk in and take over. This was a radically different point of view than any I had encountered before. One had to prevent oneself from becoming a supervisor to the therapist or discussing family dynamics. It was hard for traditionally trained people to understand this shift, and when I first demonstrated it, people actually walked out of workshops because I was failing to "do" or "show" family therapy.

The action in Act One was a telling example of what I mean. Magnus asked the therapists why they wanted the meeting. They said they felt stuck, although the family didn't seem to feel this way. Were the problems getting worse? Mardie said that the leaving of the adolescent daughters had inspired the wife to go off and "do her own thing," and now it seemed that the husband was speaking one language and the wife and daughters another. Magnus asked who most understood the wife's language and Mardie said she did; Bill said he understood the husband's language.

On the question of stopping therapy, there were also differences. Mardie said she wouldn't mind taking a break, but Bill, who seemed to be speaking for the husband, said, "There's still a question of who wants to continue and who wants to stop." It was clear to me, as I listened, that the split between the couple was reflected in a split between the therapists. However, Magnus made no effort to point out this obvious dilemma or base an interpretation on it, but let it float there on its own. I realized that when you had a reflecting team, you could leave such matters to the team. As I will explain later, Michael White found the reflecting process useful because it acted to "decenter" the therapist from the problem-solving position.

In Act Two, the wife agreed with Mardie's comments about the different languages. The husband said he wanted help in resolving their relationship, but the wife said they had to rebuild the foundation of the marriage first. She told Magnus it was particularly interesting for her to watch Bill and Mardie being interviewed. She also said that their twenty-three-year-old daughter, who had recently spent a year on top of a mountain, had announced that she was gay. She wanted her parents to accept her fully and not push her to go to counseling or to college. The wife seemed comfortable with this, but the husband said it was hard for him to agree to the request. At this moment, Magnus suggested we break for the reflecting team. Here was another example of the consultant deflecting conflict at the family level rather than taking it on.

In Act Three, when it was the team's turn to reflect, I said that I found it easy to identify with the family, having had three daughters myself. Judy commented on the respect and caring the therapists showed for the couple and the respect and caring the couple showed each other and their children. Clearly, we were playing it safe. But Tom was next to speak, and I admit I was all ears to find out what he would say.

Painted Language

Here I want to highlight a key element of Tom's work: his use of what Austrian psychologist Gisela Schwartz has called "picture language" and I call "painted language." This is the realm of sensory metaphors and parables. An example is the fantasy Tom builds up of a man who walks up a mountain to pick a bouquet of flowers. There are many pejorative orientations that would have fit this family: a psychiatric orientation, with the emphasis on the father's depression; a cultural orientation, with the wife running off on a New Age quest; a feminist orientation, casting the father as an out-of-date patriarch. Instead of these pejorative understandings, the bouquet of flowers story showed the way everyone was connected to the situation without invoking a vocabulary of blame.

The story also addressed something I call the "presenting edge." By this I mean the edge of feeling that seems to be calling attention to itself and which usually sets up a reverberation in the therapist too. Bateson used to say that the other end of the probe the researcher sticks into the human material sticks into the researcher himself. I believe that some sense of this two-way probe must be acknowledged in an interview, otherwise nothing will go forward. In my mind, this is what Tom did by finding an analogy for the father's sense of fear and his longing for connectedness.

TOM: I wonder if I should share a metaphor—the metaphor grasped me and took me away and then I came back—[it] was a bouquet of flowers, the flowers were in a big bouquet, many flowers, beautiful colors, beautiful smells—and each flower represented an experience or a meeting or a friend, in going away and coming back to say "I'm still liked"—even going to the mountain and coming back with a grasp of the wind on top of the mountain. So I saw a lot of flowers in a big bouquet.

And I saw at present the father holding the bouquet, saying, "Please come," and I thought he said that he had the job at present, and the women went and came back with flowers—I thought that must be a very ambivalent feeling, saying, "Please go and come back with flowers," but would they really come back? And I thought that there's always a risk that when people go, they learn a new language, a new dialect—the person having the job to hold the bouquet is back there, and the other people come with a new language, a new dialect, and the person is staying there with his language, which every person understands, but he has a problem understanding the new language, the new dialect.

So I wondered what would happen if another person took hold of the flowers for a time saying, "Go away and find new flowers for the bouquet and maybe you'll learn a new language, which we shall learn." Would that be possible? Who could hold the bouquet? And if he should have the task to hold the bouquet, would it be possible to learn the language and the dialect from those going away. This seems so crucial, to be able to deal with all the tasks of going away and coming back with new flowers, to understand the language and the dialects—that was my metaphor. It took me away and I was away for a long time. And I thought what was the tendency of the metaphor to move the person smelling it and watching it, or is it to make new ideas, or what? That was my thinking.

JUDY: Yes, I was wondering if the father trusted that if he stopped holding the bouquet, there would be anyone else to hold it—and it seems so important for him.

LYNN: Or if he holds the flowers—those are flowers that are already picked and could fade, and then he'll be left with a bunch of

faded flowers, while these other people are going off and finding new flowers. Will they come back and bring him these new
flowers?

At this point, I fell into the familiar problem-solving mode and mentioned the differences that had emerged in regard to therapy. Instead of
picking up on this subject, Tom noted that the parents spoke different languages and observed that, while the daughters seemed to share the mother's
language, the father didn't. He said: "So perhaps each should tell more about
the way they've created their language and how they use their language."
Still holding to my idea, I asked, "Should they continue in therapy?" Tom
said he believed the couple had a strong feeling about what to do and did-
n't need our advice. I finally got his point and shut up.

Act Four was the scene in which the couple, the co-therapists, and
Magnus commented on the reflections, while the team went back behind
the mirror. Magnus asked if there was anything that the couple particularly
liked. The wife said she liked Tom's metaphor, and felt that if the language
problem could be dealt with, this would go far to improve their communication. She added, "That was so true about my husband hanging onto the
bouquet." Magnus asked her to expand, and she explained that their marriage originally had a "Christian" basis. Her husband's role was to be the
head of the house and her role consisted of "a healthy submissiveness." She
felt he had a hard time adjusting to her when he got sick and she had to
become more assertive.

Tearing up, the wife then said that when her husband went away to the
hospital, she had to hold the bouquet, even though she didn't do it very
well. The metaphor had made it clear to her how much the family meant
to her husband. She was now crying openly and saying how touched she
was at the thought that he wanted them—his wife and daughters—to come
back. She hoped he would want them back even if they didn't conform to
the way he wanted them to be, saying, "If we hold the bouquet too tight,
they won't find out what they like, they'll only know what we like."

Before the husband could respond, Magnus turned to the co-therapists.
Bill picked up on Tom's flower metaphor, but changed it to perennials that
bloom, then come back the next year. Mardie hoped that the husband
might eventually join the wonderful conversations his wife and daughters
were now having. The couple began again to argue, but Magnus stopped
them, saying how special this experience had been for him. Remarking that
it was not his job to give advice, he thought he should withdraw. The wife
thanked him "because you brought the four of us back together again with
new ideas." Magnus then left the room. I must include one last appreciation
of Magnus' work. Even in leaving, he left the major question hanging in the

air: should therapy continue or not? I asked myself how the simple layering of reflections could possibly have any influence on issues like that. I had to live with that doubt until reassured by my own experience that this novel approach could succeed.

This interview was an important marker for me because this was the first time I had seen Magnus interview or Tom reflect. It interested me to see how their different contributions to the work hinged together. Tom's image of the bouquet had the effect of hitting all the little facets at once. One feature of painted language was that it so often created a place for feelings. In this interview, the wife teared up at Tom's description of her husband holding so desperately to the bouquet. Tom himself would sometimes tear up, moved by the story he was hearing. I believe that the images he used allowed him to reach beneath the surface and touch people as he himself was touched.

The Artful Schemer

An objection can be made that a reflecting process can't be used in situations of crisis. In reply, I will briefly describe another interview that Tom did at Brattleboro. Bill was about to do an intake with a sad and difficult family situation. The family consisted of an airline pilot, whose divorced wife had just died of cancer, and his three adolescent children, who were now living with his ex-wife's mother. His new fiancée was there too, along with the grandmother, who referred to the fiancée as "the artful schemer." They had come to therapy because the thirteen-year-old son was having problems in school. Tom joined Bill in this first session, and I was behind the screen with a number of other staff.

While the father explained to the therapists what was going on, the grandmother sat on one side of the room, darting hate looks at the fiancée, who sat next to the father on the other side. The fiancée was a determined-looking, mature woman with dyed blonde hair and heavy gold jewelry. She stared straight ahead, ignoring the grandmother. The father, also mature but equally resplendent in an airline captain's uniform, looked as if he wanted to disappear. The son told Tom that he had gone back to their house that morning to find that his father's fiancée had just recovered the living room furniture and had his cats declawed as well. In a voice that cracked with indignation and nearly weeping, he said, "When I came in this morning, my cats were bouncing off the sofa like cotton balls."

Things heated up very fast. The grandmother was yelling at the fiancée, the fiancée was shrieking back, and the father was trying vainly to placate both of them. I confess that in my heart I was saying, "Good. Let's see what Tom can do with this one." To my surprise, Tom sat there as peaceful as a

Buddha, letting everything break over his head. Finally he turned to Bill, and observed, "Perhaps we can't have a conversation right now. I am wondering if we should ask the family to go home. Maybe the father could call you later and tell you which persons would be able to talk together most easily, and you could make another date." Bill agreed with Tom, and the family members, who had suddenly become silent, filed out.

The father called Bill the next day, suggesting that he come in alone with his three children, and they had a successful meeting later that week. The reason I wanted to include this anecdote is because it so well illustrated Anderson and Goolishian's ideas about therapy as a conversation during which problems would not be "solved" but "dis-solved." As a result, the well-made play of conventional therapy went out the window. No assessments, no interpretations, no interventions. You didn't ignore threats to life or limb, but an added rationale for taking care of them was so that the conversation could be continued.

Poetic Activism

Since I first watched Tom Andersen work so many years ago, an emphasis on bodily feelings has come to the fore in the family therapy field. John Shotter (1993b, p. 15) has described communication as an in-the-moment, almost visceral activity, saying that people "see and act through their use of words, just as much as through their use of their eyes and limbs." He ties his position to the work of Russian philologists Mikhail Bahktin (1981) and Lev Vygotsky (1978), since these two were among the first to call attention to the "tool-kit" nature of language and the idea of "images as prosthetics."

Kenneth Gergen (1999, p. 49) describes this use of language as follows: "If we long for change, we must also confront the challenge of generating new meanings, of becoming *poetic activists*." Scholar-therapists James and Melissa Griffith, in their book *The Body Speaks* (1994), agree, stating that the suffering that brings people into therapy can often be tied to "unspeakable dilemmas" that cannot be expressed, and describing the aim of therapy as helping people find a way to communicate the "not-yet-said." It is clear that a therapy that rests on this philosophy cannot use words in the sense of imparting information, but must treat them as quasi-physical events. U.K. family therapist and poet Kieran Vivian-Byrne suggests what I mean in lines like, "As actual as waiting to be body-searched," and "There's something in a handshake."

German psychologist Klaus Deissler (2000) describes just such an instance: the significance of an actual handshake with a man who was consulting him. This man, who needed unemployment insurance while looking for another job, complained that his workplace was "too noisy" and he wanted the opinion of a professional to back him up. Deissler felt the man was not telling him the whole truth. In addition, his handshake was so strong that he crushed Deissler's hand. The next time they met, Deissler made his own handshake even stronger. The man was surprised and impressed, and said, "You have a firm handshake!" After that, Deissler said, his suspicions disappeared along with his client's evasiveness, and their work in therapy prospered.

Deissler applies the term "social poetics" to such moves. In another instance, Deissler found that a woman's grief after her mother died was mixed with anger at her husband and brother. They had abused her when she was small, and her mother had covered up for them. She told Deissler how much she would have liked to stand up at the funeral and expose them, showing all the mourners her middle finger. Rather than do "grief-work" with this woman, Deissler listened to that angry finger, and the woman's grief mutated into a more useful kind of action.

Following along the same path, researchers Arlene Katz and John Shotter (1996) have written about "social poetics" in medical interviews. They describe watching for "arresting moments," by which they mean the sense of surprised clarity that indicates to them that something important is going on. Katz was supervising a medical intern who was conducting an interview with a young woman from Haiti. While the patient was complaining about chest congestion, an almost incidental line, "It's not like it is back home," alerted Katz to suggest that the intern inquire further about how the woman's condition would have been treated had she fallen ill in her own country. Back home, she said, her mother would have massaged her and her whole family would have gathered round. This conversation created a closer connection between the intern and her patient and deepened the context of the complaint, which now included a social as well as a medical explanation.

The trouble with these examples of "social poetics" is that it is hard to distinguish them from the strategies therapists already use: Let us bomb you with a paradox, confuse you with a task, cue you with a suggestion. Such anecdotes are wonderful tributes to therapist brilliance, but they do not usually well up from the connections, the currents among the players. Instead, they are consciously hatched in the therapist's mind and used instrumentally. I don't want to declare this form of influence not useful. Many strategic tasks and interventions are behavioral metaphors that give permission and invite change at the same time. It is just that they do not grow out of the "joint action," as social theorist John Shotter (1993b) puts it, between the persons in the room. An example of this difference can be found in Chapter 13, in which a therapist consults his inner voices and finds the image of a white mother wolf. When he shares this picture with his client, also a mother, they come up with new understandings that bring their relationship to another place.

This is a good time to bring in the voice of French philosopher Gaston Bachelard (1964). This unusual writer makes the statement that poetry belongs to a different universe than that of cause and effect:

> To say that the poetic image is independent of causality is to make a rather serious statement. But the causes cited by psychologists and psychoanalysts can never really explain the wholly unexpected nature of the new image, any more than they can explain the attraction it holds for a mind that is foreign to the process of its creation. The poet does not confer the past of his image upon me, and yet his image immediately takes root in me. The communicability of an unusual image is a fact of great ontological significance. (p. xvii)

In other words, there is a kind of interpersonal transmission that is instant, like a chemical signal. This effect comes from analogies that are jointly achieved rather than taken from a storehouse of prior knowledge. Researcher Harold Raush has remarked that there is a difference between a skill and a modality that might lead to an opening. In the sections below, I will describe the contributions of Tom Andersen and Peggy Penn, who honor this modality by attending to the conversations that people have with one another on the body level, and the voices that these bodies use.

The Double Helix

Penn and Andersen have influenced each other over time in the manner of a double helix. Both of them employ language in the interest of relationship, and base their current work on Bahktin's (1981) concept of "dialogism." As Bahktin says,

> The exact sciences are a monological form of knowledge: the intellect contemplates a thing and speaks of it. . . . But the subject as such cannot be perceived or studied as if it were a thing, since it cannot remain a subject if it is voiceless; consequently, there is no knowlege of the subject but dialogical. (quoted in Todorov, 1984, p. 42)

Bahktin clarifies his point further by comparing Tolstoy with Dostoyevsky. Tolstoy's universe is monological because "there is no second voice alongside that of the author" (Todorov, p. 62). Dostoevsky's novels, by contrast, are dialogical. Bahktin says that they contain "a plurality of consciousnesses, with equal rights, each with its own world." (Todorov, p. 104). Penn and Andersen try to gain access to the worlds of consciousness that people bring to them through bodily sensing and listening, through playing back images, and through asking people to draw or write about the experiences they wish to share.

In describing her approach, Penn (2001b) sees "acts of metaphor" as a powerful subterranean language. For example, Penn said to a couple where one of them had an illness, "You are like two tall trees that have endured many storms without breaking." Or, to a suffering man, she said, "There is a part of you that has a lion's voice. How can we invite it to speak for you?" Again, when a woman talked about having terrible stomach pains, Penn asked her for another way to describe it, and the woman said, "It's like a fight going on inside my stomach." A member of the reflecting team suggested that Penn ask whether that fight were going on outside her stomach as well, and if so, with whom, and about what. This question uncovered an important context that until then had remained concealed.

Andersen uses underground communication in the same way. During one workshop I attended, he showed a taped interview with an older couple who had fallen in love and married late in life. Although the husband was a Buddhist and the wife was a born-again Christian, they showed a remarkable tolerance for their religious differences. However, they fought about other things. As they described their disputes, many explanations suggested themselves: a struggle for control, a clash of loyalties, individual stubbornness. Andersen, who was on the reflecting team, surprised us by not even mentioning the fighting. All he said was that the couple reminded him of "two beautiful, smiling suns." Then Andersen added, as if he were speaking a mantra: "As I watched these two smiling suns, I kept thinking: Let come the sun, let go the sun; let come the sun, let go the sun." He repeated this phrase several times. Leaving aside the hypnotic effect, I decided that Andersen might be trying to portray the difficult situation of a solar system with two suns. The implication was that it would be best if they didn't try to occupy the same space at the same time. However, Andersen never spelled anything like this out. We learned later that the couple was very pleased with the interview and referred to Andersen as "that nice man who talked about the suns."

A more somber example of a "dialogical metaphor" comes from an article by Penn (2001a). She and Andersen have been doing reflecting consultations with each other in the U.S. and abroad, and on one such occasion they were asked by Swedish psychologist Judit Wagner to do a consultation in a prison where Wagner worked. Penn told me that they spoke with a man who was in jail because he had assaulted his wife. As she began to engage him in conversation, the man said he was glad to speak in English because it was a "softer" language than Swedish, and this would help him to talk about his son. The boy's mother would not allow him to visit or write his father and the man's feelings of isolation and despair were intense.

Penn then asked him if he thought words were stronger than bars. When he agreed, she suggested that he might write a diary for his son to read sometime in the future. Andersen added, "as a way to send a touch." Then Andersen asked the man, "Would it be possible for you to ask your son to pick an autumn leaf and send it to you? The most beautiful one he can find the next time they are outside in nature?" The inmate agreed to do this. By using words in this way, Andersen and Penn were going directly to where the feelings live. The images of the diary and the leaf set up resonances in my own mind between the father and his son, between inside the prison and nature, and between present and future time. The prisoner was touched too. Wagner told Penn that he asked about her for over a year, and kept wishing Wagner to give her his regards.

It is too simplistic, of course, to suggest that "a metaphor a day keeps the doctor away." Penn believes that therapy is about moving from monologues that are dominated by accusations against oneself and others to dialogues that include more varied and hopeful voices. In describing chronic illness (2001a), Penn says that it is "a form of incremental trauma characterized by an insidious silence." To interrupt this silence, which she believes is upheld by the pejorative culture of illness, she has pioneered an approach that alternates between writing and speaking. This recursion, she says, creates a therapeutic narrative which she and Frankfurt have called the "participant text." Her goal is to break the silence: "Once the family's voices are reconstituted through writing, the emotions that have been displaced by the illness are restored to their conversation" (2001a, p. 33).

To illustrate her point, Penn tells the story of the work she did with a family where the dilemma was expressed as how the parents could best help their son. They either overwhelmed him with support or withdrew it entirely, and this was confusing to him. Penn described the family's plight in terms of the father's wish to rescue everybody when it was really he who wanted to be rescued. She said the father should write a letter to his own deceased father, who had been an alcoholic, and the son should write to his not-yet-born, out-of-wedlock son. The father read out his letter, in which he said he realized how much he longed to be fathered. He wept, and his wife and son, moved by his vulnerability, wept too. The parents were equally moved by the son's letter, in which he vowed to stand by his own son. In this emotional crucible, Penn said, the family's idea of the father-son relationship changed to include ideas of tenderness as well as disappointment.

If Your Hand Could Speak?

Andersen has been doing new work that gives an imaginary voice to bodily actions. Recently, I saw a tape of a second consultation with a South

American family where the father had misbehaved in several ways in the presence of his five year old son. The wife urged that the family come to therapy, which the father hesitantly agreed to do. Unwilling to see the family around a problem that so negatively connoted the father, and wanting to decrease the tension between the father and the son, Andersen kept the focus on the son's noisy behavior. This meeting was attended by father, mother and son, along with the psychologist who was working with them. A year later, Andersen met with the family a second time. The mother said that the boy had changed a lot in the previous year. He was on Ritalin and was able to go to school, and relations in the family had improved.

However, in this second meeting, the boy's behavior still seemed out of control. He was running, crawling, hitting. Andersen asked the father, "If his crawling behavior could speak, what would it say?" The father said, "That he wants attention." Tom said, "No, what would his *body* say?" The father looked confused, but finally said, "Give me your attention." The mother said that the boy would try to get the father's attention at home, when he did his school work, but that the father got impatient too easily and often beat the boy. Tom asked, "How would you beat him?" The father said that he beat him with his right hand, but said he did not know if the hand was closed or open.

Then Tom turned to the boy, asking him if his father beat him with a closed or an open hand. The boy said, "He hits me with the closed hand and pushes me with the open one." Tom asked, "What hurts you the most, the closed hand or the open one?" The boy said, "The closed one." Tom then asked the father, "If your hand, when it is moving to hit your son, stopped its moving and could speak, what would the words be?" The father was silent. After Tom helped him in the search for words, he said, "That my son should stop doing what he is doing." Tom said again, "If it could speak, what would it say?" Again, silence. The mother then broke in to explain that the father often found it hard to find words. She said, "I would talk to our son calmly." She said, "My husband speaks to his head; I speak to the heart."

The boy was now asked to leave the room. At this point, the mother shared the fact that she too was often hit by the father. She said she had only become aware of this during the past year, after the noisiness of the son had decreased. She recalled a recent incident when he pushed her so hard that she "flew through the air." Tom asked what that was like for her. She said that it made her realize what a thin line there was between life and death. Tom asked how that made her feel. She said, "That I wouldn't like to grow old with someone who treated me like that."

Tom then asked the father, "Was that hard to hear?" The father said, "No, it's true." Tom said, "One part of you seems to be violent. Is there another part that wishes something different?" The father said, "Yes, but I can't control myself." Tom asked, "What if that part had a voice and could speak?" The father said, "It would say, you only have one family and it should be protected." Tom now asked the father where in his body the voice that was activated in the violent moments should go. The father answered "In my head." Tom asked, "If this voice could move, where would it go?" The father said, "I wish it could stay in my head." Tom asked, "If that voice that says, 'Think of your family,' could find a new place in your body, where would you like it to be?" The father said, "In my heart."

The father now asked Tom, "Are we going in the right way?" Tom said, "Yes, a right way. There are many right ways. I noticed that your son could accept me much more easily than last year; I heard your wife speak of the difficulties she discovered in the family during the past year; and I heard a lot about the changes with the boy." Then the father got eager and said, "Since last year, he is happy in school, and able to go wherever he wants to go. Before he was never happy." Tom said to him, "And the talk you and I had in the last few minutes, where you were able to be open without defending yourself, that is a big step."

The therapists reported later that the father had stopped beating the boy and that he continued to improve. The father had told the psychologist that he still remembered Tom's voice. Tom's last comment to our group as we were watching the tape was that people must be given the chance to be moved by the conversation. He added, "Voices must have homes. You must always ask where in the body they might choose to live. The therapist must not side with one voice against another, or encourage one voice to control another. They must be given the chance to live side by side, as in every work of peace."

The Maroons

Here I want to say that the most lasting effect of Penn and Andersen's work, at least in its influence on me, has been the literal posture they assume during an interview. I was once talking with a statuesque family therapist from the island of Jamaica who told me that her ancestors were slaves called "Maroons" who had run away into the mountains to escape their white owners. Sharing a memorable phrase, she said that her people always knew when someone was a Maroon "by the way they carried their soul." And she took a pose, quite unconsciously, which reminded me of the way both Penn and Andersen hold themselves when they are in a therapeutic conversation.

To show what I mean, here is a story from a piece by Peggy Penn and Marilyn Frankfurt called "A Circle of Voices" (1999). In it, Penn describes one of Andersen's occasional visits to the Ackerman Institute, during which he and Penn interviewed Chris and John, two married gay men who each had AIDS and with whom Penn and Frankfurt had been working. Penn explained in her part of the article that when the couple found out that they had HIV, nine years before, they had decided to marry. Now John wanted to separate, although Chris felt they could change enough to stay together. Penn asked them if Andersen might join the interview and they agreed. Andersen's first question to them was: "How would you like this meeting to be used?" Penn wrote:

> I saw Tom lean in toward the men and keep that position almost for the entire interview, either supporting his chin on his hand or folding his arms and leaning toward them in strong concentration. I was touched by this message from his body; it was as though their suffering was being written on him and he accepted it patiently.

Penn explained that in this type of consultation, the conversation is open-ended and there is no set plan except to take in what the family says and does, their silence as well as their words. As the two men spoke of how their bodies were doing and how they felt, Andersen seemed very moved. A sense of loss and mourning permeated the room and Penn noted that her eyes occasionally filled with tears.

Then Andersen asked a question: "Is it possible that your relationship could last forever?" After a moment of silence, Chris said he wanted their ashes to be mixed together and placed under the roots of an azalea bush, so that their families would have a single place to go. Andersen asked, "If the azalea bush could sing a song, what would it sing?" Chris chose Vivaldi's "Four Seasons" and Beethoven's "Pastoral Symphony," but John wanted a memorial party with wine, food, and sex. Maybe he would prefer a sturdy oak. John added that his current wish was for something more than just to stay alive. Penn commented to him that she was touched by his wish, and commented in her article that this thought had stayed with her for a long time.

At the end of the meeting the two men asked Andersen, "What are your thoughts?" He said, "I can't find words; certainly there would be sad words, and words of beauty." Chris worried that they had hit him with a lot of problems. Andersen replied, "I don't feel hit; I am touched. Hit is a small word; touched is a much longer word. I know I will always remember this meeting." Peggy wrote: "It was raining outside but when we left our room, it felt bright, not from the video lights but from all four of us being able to move together." As the couple had given Andersen permission to show the tape, Penn suggested that they each write something about the experience, so that when the tape was shown, they would have the last word.

I have included this story, although somewhat amputated, because it summarizes the feeling tone of what I had experienced as a new kind of work when I first saw Andersen in Brattleboro. The attentive listening, which occurred as much on the body level as on the verbal level, was absolutely different from anything I had yet experienced. In the above case, I also saw that the question Andersen asked not only reflected back feelings, it embraced a future. Frankfurt, who contributed the second part of this article, says,

> Such communicative events are performative because they make things happen. For this couple, given John's need to create an independent space for himself within the relationship, their differing visions of themselves after death are affirmed in the dialogue. (p. 177)

The Arctic Circle

Before I end this chapter, I want to describe the beginning of Andersen's northern network (see Chapter 14). In 1986, Andersen invited myself and Peggy Penn to a seminar in a tiny fishing village called Gryllefjord near the Arctic Circle. This event was the start of a training program for groups from the north of Norway who were interested in practicing systemic work in their own settings. At the end of this first meeting, Tom presented to Peggy and me a one-of-a kind object that he had made by finding chunks of weathered wood, gluing them together, then hollowing the block into the shape of a large bowl. Before we left, he also organized a small fleet of fishing boats to take us on a five-hour trip at midnight to a remarkable wooden structure sitting on stilts in the sea off a deserted beach. Called Crow House, it had been built by an industrialist seeking solitude. There we had a late-night supper of barrels of North Sea shrimp, piles of homemade bread with fresh butter, and casks of beer.

As you can imagine, these trips were memorable. I remember one that took place in the village of Solveig, at the end of a long, mountainous peninsula called the Westerollen. When Andersen took Penn and myself to our lodgings and opened the door onto a barren room furnished with a cot and a chair, we gazed around silently until he remarked, "It's not very fashionable." We broke into peals of laughter, and another venue was arranged. The next year, the speakers and participants stayed in local fishermen's houses with showers that did not always work. But despite occasional hardships, these events, like the Milan team meetings before them, kept the field of family therapy unrolling like a carpet before our feet. I have already described the impact of the Greek kitchen conference at Sulitjelma, and there were others that were just as powerful.

A few years ago, when Andersen invited me to give a workshop at one of his more recent meetings in the North, I found that the reflecting process had turned into what I was now calling a "rolling conversation" (see Chapter 13). Small groups would reflect in front of the larger group in a kind of daisy chain, or simply converse in parallel. I found myself attempting to organize a reflecting consultation with one of the participants, but the effort curled off into space like smoke. I thought again of Bateson's endless stories. Only after you had gone home did you suddenly see his point, and even then you wondered. Here, to end this chapter, is an example.

Long ago, at a seminar at South Beach Psychiatric Hospital on Staten Island, where Bateson was giving a talk, I asked him how he would describe a "single bind." He stared off, with his cigarette ash as usual getting longer, and began to tell me about a tank where he used to keep two octopi, a big one and a small one. The small one had got hold of a shrimp, and the big one slowly propelled itself to the other side of the tank where the small one was clutching its prize. The big octopus settled its large bulk gently over the head of the small one and stayed there for a minute. There was no sign of a struggle, but when it sailed up and back to its corner, you could see that the shrimp was firmly ensconced in one of tentacles. At the time, I was mystified, but many months later I realized that my question had been answered. Faced with a choice between being engulfed and giving up the shrimp, the small octopus had recognized a "single bind" and acted accordingly. Stories are a form of poetic activism too.

10

You Tell without Telling

Death Is Better Than Parting

After Andersen's visit, the Brattleboro approach to both clinical work and teaching went through a period of confusion. We were betwixt and between expert and collaborative postures, but while the back feet of the inchworm were fastened firmly to the leaf, its front feet were waving in the air, searching for the next good spot to land. We did agree on a few things. Instead of either instructing or manipulating people, we were trying to step back, make space, evoke. We no longer made systemic assessments and avoided giving tasks and interventions. In this way, we tried to stay true to the objectives of continuing the conversation and taking a not-knowing stance.

However, we had picked a bad time to do this. There was beginning to be criticism in journal articles and at conferences about the moral relativism of the social constructionist position and the ethical deceptiveness of not-knowing. We believed that making therapists into society's policemen was counterproductive and distanced us from the people we were trying to help, but ours was not the received wisdom of the time. Then along came two persons who tested our position: a white American woman with an American Indian husband came knocking at our door and put their story of violence in our lap.

Let me set the context for this story. The Brattleboro staff therapists—Judy Davidson, Mardie Ratheau, Dario Lussardi, and Bill Lax (again, I will use first names)—had decided to use a reflecting team format for all intakes. One particular interview became a type example for us all. Mardie was in her Brattleboro office one day when a woman called up and asked if anyone there could see her. Mardie gave her an appointment for that afternoon, and Paula, a thin, attractive woman with long black hair came in and announced, "All the psychiatrists in this town are out to lunch." She meant it literally because she had tried calling them at lunchtime. The next thing she did was to stand on her head. Explaining that this was the way she cleared her mind, she said, "I used to be a contortionist." Mardie has a high threshold of imperturbability, but even she was surprised.

Paula told Mardie the following story: six weeks before, her husband of only a few months had gone without her to a party at the next-door apartment. They had quarreled, and she was so angry with him that she shot three bullets through the door—all through the same hole! She was a very good shot. Her husband, Mel, was a building contractor who drank too much, and their frequent arguments and her mounting anxiety had prompted her to seek help. In the meantime, she said, Mel had quit drinking. Mardie gave the couple an appointment, and the other three members of the Brattleboro group were present as a reflecting team. I was not there, but I watched the teaching tape that was made of this interview many times. I should add that not everything in the session was included in the tape, so there are a few gaps in this version, but nothing substantial.

The couple were in their forties and carried on like the newlyweds they were. Mel was a short, thickset man, and very humorous. Paula flirted and joked with him the whole time, and he, in turn, seemed like an affectionate bear with a teasing princess on his back. Mardie asked Mel how he had taken to Paula's idea of marriage counseling, and he said this was a first time for him. He said he probably didn't need it but "every idea is a good idea." Mardie filled in, "Every new idea is *possibly* a good idea," and Paula added, squeezing Mel's neck in the crook of one arm and laughing, "Anything new is too weird for him." Mardie asked Mel what he had perceived about Paula's state of mind before the shooting incident. He said he knew something was coming on because she kept snapping at him. He added, "I watch every move she makes."

Mardie asked what had decided Mel to come in for couple counseling and he said that Paula had told him that their marriage depended on it. Mardie asked him to describe what Paula thought were the issues between them. Mel mentioned Paula's temper and the fact that he was "wicked jealous." Mardie asked if things were better since he had stopped drinking, and he replied that this had cut down on the violence. When Mardie asked him to describe what the violence was like, Paula replied for him, saying that it would be easy for him to kill her. He agreed, saying, "I'm powerful for my size. Grabbing her is like grabbing a paper bag. I don't want to kill her, but the power in me probably could." Paula said, "It's not like me to call the cops except to save my life—I'd rather beat the shit out of you." During this exchange, she was giggling and giving Mel playful shoves.

Mardie observed that they hadn't been married long, and asked when they had realized there was "a violence factor." Apparently, it was on the occasion of the first time they had gone away from home together. They took a bottle of liquor with them, and Mel got angry and began "beating up on" Paula. Paula said philosophically, "Alcohol is a catalyst for anger." She had forgiven him for this episode and for a number of similar incidents, explaining that after she divorced her first husband, who had also hit her, she had lived alone for twelve years. She said, "I waited a long time to be with Mel."

Mardie asked when Paula had first thought of calling in outside help. Apparently, even before the shooting, there had been an incident when she asked Mel to go to couples counseling. Mel said he had resisted the idea, and added, "I've always done things on my own. Me going for help means someone's better than me. I've got that bad attitude: Why should this guy help me? Means he's smarter than me." Paula lunged toward Mel's neck in another mock attack, asking, "What if he is?" Mardie then said to Mel, "I can't imagine you've lived your lifetime without giving help to someone." Mel was taken aback, and said, "I've helped a lot of people but . . ." He paused, then added, "I never thought of it that way, that me helping somebody means I'm any better than them."

Watching this piece of the tape, I was impressed with the way Mardie had turned Mel's remark around; it seemed to have got him thinking. Mardie then asked him, "What was the difference between the time before New Year's, when the shooting happened, and now?" Mel explained that Paula was more mixed up then: "She was like an up and down person and now it's like she's going in a straight line. She seems to be feeling better about herself lately." At this point, Mardie decided to take a break and see what the team had to say. They switched rooms, so that Mardie and the couple could listen from behind the screen.

Judy spoke first, remarking on the warmth between the couple and how much physical affection they showed. Dario agreed, saying that they were a touching couple and also that "As much as she touches him, he eats it up." But he had one question: "As loving as they can be, how do they go from being a loving couple to one where they could literally threaten death to one another?" He wondered about the gun incident, but was more concerned with what could trigger "that kind of flip." He also wondered which of them would be more likely to kill the other. Bill then said that he was particularly struck by the poetry in Paula's language, citing her phrase "that vale of tears called Brattleboro," and her statement that she "couldn't show any diminished responsibility," an allusion to her upcoming court appearance. Bill pointed to the issues around control—who controlled whom, or who was out of control. Finally, he commented on how important the marriage seemed to both of them.

At this point Dario asked what it was about Mel that made Paula take such a big leap of faith in marrying him. He wondered if this were due to the strengths she saw in him. He also brought up the question of "Who's the Indian and who's the Chief?" and said he'd like to know how the couple divided up these roles. Bill spoke next, commenting on Mel's wish to stay in control, even though he sometimes lost control because of drinking. He remarked that perhaps Paula was more in control in regard to therapy, but even she couldn't control the situation when she tried to get help, because no one had been immediately available, and Mel gave away some of his control just by showing up.

The group launched into a discussion of issues like reaching out versus doing it yourself, the honeymoon problem of deciding how to be a couple, and the question, "Is it going to be your way, my way or a third way?" Bill suggested exploring how the couple's differences could lead to fights. Judy noted that if Paula and Mel were too different, that might mean they couldn't stay together. And Dario ended with a somber question: "Given the investment in the relationship, particularly on Paula's side, is death better than parting?"

The groups exchanged places again, and Mardie asked Paula and Mel what rang a bell for them. Mel said, "Control—it's all about doing things my way or her way." Paula said, "I can bend," and Mardie remarked, "She can bend a lot—she's a contortionist." Then Mel said, "Who's the Indian, who's the Chief? A lot of our conflicts are like that. You do everything I say, we get along good." Paula said, "You wish." Mel said, "I can bend a little," and Paula said, "Like a teepee." Ignoring Paula's teasing, Mel went on: " I tell her everything that goes my way goes good. She's always fighting against me like that." Mardie remarked, "You've had quite a history of things going like that." Mel agreed: "Everything ran smooth till I ran into Paula." Paula said, "Everyone who runs into me it's the same thing. I thought I warned you; if there's a maniac in the neighborhood, it's me he'll walk up to; if there's a famous person in the neighborhood, I'll be the only one to see him. There's something in my soul that attracts the unusual. All I have to do is breathe in and out."

Mardie turned to Paula for her impressions. She said she liked Bill's comment about the poetry in their relationship and was also struck by Dario's idea that death was better than parting. She said to Mel, "I've thought of that many times. I feel that strongly about you, that if we couldn't work it

to our new format, we started by asking about the history of the
come to therapy, and learned that the mother had heard of the insti-
m her sister, who had a good experience there. I remember we spent
time gathering information: the history of Bridey's sleeping pattern,
uence of worries about the serial killer, concerns about the health
grandfather, and so on. True to our self-imposed mandate, we
d from trying to change the "family system" by giving messages or
e simply asked questions and listened—and as far as I was concerned
ed aimlessly all over the map. This was so contrary to my therapeu-
ringing that I was ready to go back to the old conscious purpose

aps due to our inaction, the father came in after three sessions say-
he was fed up with coming home at midnight and having to sleep
laughter's bed. He accused his wife of giving in to their daughter.
as the first time we had seen this mild-mannered man take a stand.
ult, the mother told Bridey that she would have to sleep in her own
t week. The father went on to complain about their social life, since
casualty of the sleeping problem was that the mother always had to
nd for Bridey's bedtime and they could never go out. The mother
to go out for dinner, too.

e next session, they came in without the children, but they had
o report. Bridey had managed to sleep in her own bed for several
t on the evening they went out, she waited till they had left and
er grandmother, who sympathized with her fears during a lengthy
ht chat. The next day the grandmother called her son and asked
could leave his children with a babysitter—what about the killer
as still on the loose? The father told his mother that she must stop
ing with his family. After he told us this, he remembered that when
a boy, he too had night fears and had slept in his mother's bed until
nine and was sent off to boarding school. We were used to finding
that repeated across the generation lines and took hope from the
success in overcoming his problems.

sleep problem disappeared in Bridey's family, too, except for one
ckslide. When her grandfather died, Bridey temporarily went back
ing in her parents' bed. We saw the family through that crisis, and
pped coming in and got on with their lives. But I was baffled.
our decision not to try to change the family, many changes had
lace. The father had stood up to his wife. The parents had got
r as enforcers. The father confronted his mother. The daughter
leeping in her own bed. Best of all, the daughter got to go to a
r party before she hit thirteen. All this happened without any con-
lan. But I was particularly struck by the way in which Bridget at

out, I wouldn't want anything. I think you probably do too." Mel nodded
but said, "I'd hate to think of that happening." Mardie now asked, "If things
were to get so complicated and difficult between the two of you, and if that
ended up as the unthinkable solution, who would be most apt to take that
solution first?" Paula said, "Probably me." Mel said, "I don't know—I don't
even like the thought of it." Mardie then said, "Maybe it's too unthinkable
to talk about, but perhaps we could just talk about it and say, well, it's been
talked about." In retrospect, I saw that Mardie's remark was a wonderful
example of the "telling without telling" the couple brings up at the end.

After a moment of silence, Paula said, "I don't see that there's anything
you can't talk about—if you've thought about it, you can talk about it.
That's why we're here." She said to Mel, "I've thought about it, and I think
if it were to happen I would get you first." She lunged at Mel and pulled
his glasses off, saying, "See, you look away, you're naive, so I get your glasses
every time." Both were laughing uproariously. Mardie tried again. "What
you say makes me think of what happened six weeks ago, the shooting I
mean, when things heated up." Paula said, "He did the unthinkable so that
made me do the unthinkable. My temper was aroused to the point where
I don't think I would have cared until afterward. When I lost it, I lost it. I've
never picked up a gun against anybody." This statement segued into an
account of when she once picked up a hammer to hit her sixteen-year-old
son, but refrained from using it.

Mardie asked them, "Who do you think is more apt to be able to stop
the other from his or her own violent outburst?" She caught herself, saying, "That's a pretzel," but Mel said he understood. He thought that she
would have a better chance of stopping him than the other way round.
Paula put in, "Unless you've been drinking," while Mel said, "Nobody can
control her when she gets mad," and Mardie asked, "If she passed over that
fine line, and you were drinking, would it be very hard for her to stop
you?" Paula answered, "He doesn't know what he's doing or care what he's
doing. I've never seen anyone lose control as much as Mel when he's drinking. He's reached such a high tolerance level that any alcohol at all pushes
him over the line. " Mardie asked Mel whether he had given up alcohol on
his own or had sought the help of AA. Mel said he had stopped drinking
on his own.

Mardie now broke for another team reflection. Judy started off by
remarking on the couple's amazing honesty, and their recognition of the
problems around drinking and control. Dario said it was a good sign that
the couple were able to talk about personal and even embarrassing things.
He wondered if they could go any further today, but said they seemed to
have started and that the team would be glad to be there for them. Bill
wanted to know their thoughts about continuing with Mardie and asked

whether everyone was reassured that drinking wouldn't become an issue before the next meeting. Dario added, "Or that there might be another episode of violence." After a short pause, during which "the unthinkable" hung heavily in the air, they got up to leave and the two groups switched places.

Mardie asked for the couple's impressions again. Paula said that everyone was afraid of another violent episode, but she felt that the meeting that day would probably defuse things. Then she surprised Mardie and the team with the following compliment: "I liked your approach. It tells without telling, says without saying. That's good for both of us because neither one of us wants to be told what to do." Mel said it felt very new to him too, and that he would have to think about whether to come in again.

Mardie saw the couple the next week and Paula alone the week after that. It was only then that Mardie found out that Mel was not the only person with a drinking problem. Paula was a habitual drinker and had been drinking during the sessions, including the first one. She agreed with Mardie that her habit was definitely not helping and told Mardie that she had decided to join AA. As there were some weeks before her case was to be heard, she went down to Florida to visit a friend, leaving Mel behind. Six months passed, during which time Mardie never heard from her. When she did come back, she came in to see Mardie and told her that she and Mel had broken up for good. She and Mardie had a few more sessions around her drinking problem, and after that she vanished.

However, none of us ever forgot either of them. There was much affection in this work, and much life and wit between the couple. The use of the reflecting team, if only for that one session, took us far away from our previous concerns with making hypotheses and delivering messages and interventions, and seemed a much more collegial and spontaneous enterprise. In view of the life and death issues the couple presented, I remain in admiration of the balancing act everyone took part in, and the fact that the only casualty may have been the marriage. At least we hope so. Mel and Paula (not your real names), wherever you are, thank you.

Teaching without Knowing

In regard to instructing others how to practice a reflecting team approach or, as Goolishian had suggested Andersen call it, reflecting process, we were in the country of experiment. Rules were minimal and how-to's were scarce. We were trying to let go of the extremely knowing mind-set of the Milan approach and adopt the not-knowing stance of a more Egalitarian style. The reflecting format was an ideal teaching arrangement for this pro-

ject because, as our couple had pointed out, it
without telling. However, we were a little nerv
with trainees and so at first stuck to our old fo
us over the edge. What happened was that Dar
Milan-style team that included two trainees w
Dario and one who had been working with m
tion for the interviewer and Dario would hav
one message to give the family, and Dario wo
made for a very bumpy ride.

One day a trainee of Dario's was the therap
and I again came up with conflicting messag
between us that she went mute and couldn't say
switch to Tom's reflecting team. We were both
simple move. All voices were welcome. The sup
pete. Most importantly, the family was drawn i
active way than ever before. I could see whe
improve therapist morale, but I was flabbergaste
sion, the families began finding solutions to the

But it was Bridey who convinced me. Bride
who, because of night fears, had become used t
ents' bed. Her mother would sit with her unti
move her back, but if she woke up, she was ca
up until she got her way. So the parents took
The mother put Bridey in their bed and shared
who worked till midnight, went into his dau
home. Then Bridey, because of her sleeping
invitation to a sleepover. The mother saw that t
with her growing-up, so she decided to call the
myself, and a reflecting team of four trainees beg
also included a six-year-old brother.

What I remember most clearly about our fir
the reflections one of the trainees wondered abc
name. If it was a nickname for Bridget, did it m
of bridge? Although Bridey's little brother pou
learned later that a bridge did feature in the s
been closed down, so that a lengthy detour wa
the grandparents' house to the family's house. T
too poor for them to drive such a long distanc
only saw her grandchildren on state occasions.
killer in the area had recently hit the papers. Be
mother and grandmother shared their fears dur

idea t
tute fr
a lot c
the in
of the
refrai
tasks;
wand
tic up
ways.
Pe
ing th
in his
This
As a
bed t
anoth
be a
agree
In
much
days,
calle
late-
how
who
inter
he w
he w
patt
fath
T
brie
to s
they
Des
take
toge
star
slee
scio

least temporarily took the place of the missing bridge as the grandfather's health declined.

The Vow

In this period, when new models seemed to be popping up all the time, therapists could often move at cross-purposes. This problem was highlighted when Bill and I started to make some training tapes. In one instance, a handsome young couple came in because the husband, in a fit of anger, had thrown his wife's bookbag at her. This was doubly upsetting because of a "vow" the wife had made some ten years before. They were out driving and the husband had become angry and "elbowed" his wife. She had told him that if he ever hit her again, she would leave him. They went on to have three children, who were now all under the age of six, and in the previous year she had left her job to get a teaching degree.

The trigger for the recent incident, the husband said, was that she had gone to a weekend workshop, leaving the children with him. When she came home later than she had promised, he got mad at her and hit her with the bookbag. Of course, as the husband pointed out, there were extenuating circumstances: the fact that they were sleeping in separate bedrooms since the birth of their third child; the fact that he had lost his job due to a downturn in the economy; his feeling of being deserted when she went back to school. After the incident, he had driven away in the car while she just waited. On coming back, he said he expected to find that she had thrown all his clothes out on the lawn, but instead she sat, paralyzed, excoriating herself for her failure of nerve. That was the dilemma they brought in.

I didn't know this, but Bill had just come back from a workshop on solution-focused therapy and wanted to try some of its methods. He decided to focus on the vow—a word you could just as well associate with a marriage as with a threat—and take the conversation in a more solution-oriented direction. So he wondered aloud if it wasn't time to change that old vow to a new one. I remember being struck by the defeated, downcast look of the wife when she heard this, so when Bill looked to me for my response, I embarked on a tangential association of my own.

I said that when the wife described how she sat in the house after her husband drove off, I pictured one of those Victorian heroines who jump into the sea, or are shipwrecked, and are weighed down by their long, wet skirts. I said that when I was an unhappy wife with three young children, I had felt them dragging at my legs and weighing me down in the same way. The wife, beginning to weep, began to talk about how betrayed she felt, both by her husband and by herself. Later I went back to the meaning of the bookbag: was the husband "throwing the book" at his wife? This gave him a chance to air his own grievances, which he did, but at least she had a chance to present her side.

In that session I did something else that moved away from Milan neutrality. During the nineties, family therapists often found themselves handling domestic problems with legal implications, and were often pressured to become an adjunct to the courts. I was in a serious bind. I continued to think that taking sides in a family was usually not productive. Children, in particular, often had deep loyalties to family members no matter what those persons had done. In addition, family therapists usually had no legal means to keep families in therapy, and if we came on like moral arbiters, families tended to drop out. We were up against Satir's old bugbear, the Morality Play. My solution was to make a 180-degree turn toward subjectivity but a *situated* subjectivity. As long as I tied my opinions, suggestions, biases, to their appropriate contexts, I thought I would be home free. I would frame an objection to some behavior as "my own bias" or "conventional wisdom," or I would bring in authorities, like "the clinic director" or "the state."

Further on in the session I am describing, the husband began to blame the bookbag episode on his wife. It seemed that after the birth of their third child she had asked for separate beds. He had three theories about what he described as her physical rejection of him. One, she was frigid. Two, her mother didn't like sex. Three, she was a covert lesbian. His wife was mournfully agreeing with all this, so I interrupted him and said that I was going to make a "citizen's protest." I said that I felt so strongly that I was going to break in here, despite the fact that as a therapist I didn't generally feel that giving advice or delivering personal judgments did much good.

So I said to the husband that I felt it was important to share some information of which they apparently were unaware. I said that when I was a young wife, I too blamed myself for the difficulties in our marriage. I went to all the bookstores in the city where we then lived, only to find accounts that treated my disinterest in sex as an indication of "genital immaturity." However, as the years went by, research on couples told me that another reason for becoming turned off to sex was when disagreements between partners went underground. By framing my account as "only my story," I was not handing down a judgment, or at least I hoped I wasn't. The husband accepted this alternative explanation and the wife seemed glad to be off the hot seat. The couple came in one more time and after that Bill saw the husband alone. The upshot was that they got divorced.

However, after our session, Bill and I discussed how we came to be at cross-purposes on the matter of the vow, and he told me about the solution-focused workshop he had attended. This explained everything. I still thought we had moved too quickly to the what-to-do and had not given enough attention to the how-it-felt, but my idea of including emotion-talk was still in bud at the time, so I didn't mention it. I showed some of that interview at a small gathering sometime later, and writer-therapist Virginia Goldner mentioned the "heavy skirts" story and said that my demeanor had struck a chord. She felt that I was doing something different, although she couldn't say what. I think it was the fact that with my metaphor of the drowning heroine, I had attempted to play back a picture of what might be going on emotionally inside the wife.

But now I want to move to an event that surprised me. At this late date in my therapeutic education, I saw for the first time a videotape of an interview by Carl Rogers. It was shown by psychologist Maureen O'Hara at a conference on brief therapy in New York. I was shocked to realize that if you set aside Rogers's (1961) person-oriented, humanistic theories, and watched the work itself, it would bring to mind the style of attentive, quiet listening that I described in the last chapter.

The Stillness of Carl Rogers

When I saw this tape of Rogers doing a consultation with a young woman at a workshop, I was amazed to see that the way he held himself resembled what I recognized as a reflecting posture. He leaned toward his interlocutor as a sailor might lean into the wind, but remained nearly motionless as he questioned and reflected back. As a result, his style differed vastly from the impression left on me by phrases like "active listening" or "unconditional positive regard." The interview was taped in 1984 during a conference on humanist psychology. On this occasion, Rogers was speaking with a young married woman who had miscarried and lost a set of twins. This event haunted and obsessed her. Now she was pregnant again and didn't know what to do. She was asking herself, "Did I make a mistake? Did I start having babies too late?"

Rogers said that he thought she might be the kind of person who liked to win, and that in this case she had played and lost. The woman agreed with him. She said she tried hard to please other people. Rogers remarked that she must feel cheated, since she had lost something that would please other people. She replied that she hadn't even told her husband or mother about the miscarriage. Rogers responded, "That must be very hard." There was a long silence, and Rogers didn't move. The woman finally said, "If you don't tell anybody you lost it, you lose it alone."

Rogers then said, "You think, 'Could I have done something differently?' You were the keeper and you did lose it." The woman responded that part of her really wanted to have the child, and that she felt she had everything but that one important thing. Rogers commented that at some level she must feel like a failure. He said, "Some things one can control and some things one can't." The woman said, "Well, there must be something wrong with me." Rogers said, "So this body of yours, in one respect, you can't control." The woman agreed, saying that even if her doctor said that her body was doing fine, she would still worry about control.

After a silence, Rogers said he believed that if there were any sacrifice she could make to have a child, she would certainly make it, but that she was still grieving over what might have been. She answered that she had thought of visiting the grave that Christmas. He asked, "So the grieving is still there?" She said, "It comes and goes." There was another long silence. Finally the woman said, "You've made it easy to talk about. I guess I've come to the conclusion that I have to let go." To which Rogers remarked, "But you still feel you've failed. That something could have been done." The woman said, "Yes," and placed her hand across her chest.

At this point Rogers said, "It's a bodily feeling." She again said, "Yes." He said, "You're not really fulfilled." She said, "Not completely." He said, "It's a real sadness." At that point, there was a palpable shift. The woman suddenly went on a new tack, saying, "But some good things emerged. I saw a side of my husband that was strong." I was struck by the unexpectedness of this remark. Previously, the woman had given the impression that her husband not only failed to help her during her travails but also added to her burdens because she feared disappointing him. Now she seemed anxious to give him credit.

After the interview ended, before the moderator turned the discussion over to the audience, the woman and Rogers reflected together on the stage. During this exchange, the woman said she had found it easy to talk with Rogers because she didn't feel that she was being judged. Rogers said that at first he felt clumsy getting into her world. He spoke of being privileged to enter into her feelings of loss, but the most important clue to him was when she put her hand over her chest, because this meant to him that something had shifted. He had just commented on her feeling of failure, and she had said that some good things had happened.

Rogers said that his intention throughout was to be a companion to the woman in her own world, with the hope that she would feel released enough to go forward. She confirmed his observation, saying, "I got in touch with the good parts when we were talking about failure. That's when I put my hand on my chest." Someone in the audience later asked about the silences, and Rogers made this statement: "Silences are okay, they can be working silences. But if it's a safe place, a person may say something significant." I was struck by the similarity between his use of silences and Tom Andersen's, as well as their parallel use of bodily attentiveness.

Looking these notes over, I was amazed at how much this small piece of work contained. It seemed to express what a good reflecting conversation might aspire to. First of all, Rogers's stillness encouraged the woman to share what she felt. Second, in the words of the philosopher Jean-Francois Lyotard (1996), he "spoke in order to listen," as opposed to "listening in order to speak." Third, by joining the woman in her frustrations, Rogers may have amplified them until she finally let them go. Haley used to say that a "reductio ad absurdam" could push people to such a far edge that they would have to bounce back. But I think this is what White (1995) would call a "thin description."

Which brings me to Rogers's much-vaunted empathy. As I watched the interview, I found his manner static and quite dry, despite its compelling quality. He made no positive remarks, betrayed no personal sentiments, was never affirming. He reflected what his respondent said, but did nothing to try to change her attitude. However, when she was asked about her impressions later, she said that while speaking with Rogers she experienced a feeling of enormous compassion and warmth. She seemed to be taking on this compassion herself by the end of the interview, when she finally found something good to say about her husband.

This consistent attention to body process is an aspect that links Rogers to the therapists whose work I have described in this chapter, as well as James and Melissa Griffith, who wrote that impressive book, *The Body Speaks* (1994). I went back to my notes to see what had happened just before the woman touched her own body. At that moment, as the woman was acknowledging her feelings of failure, Rogers continued to reflect back what she said except for one idea that he put in himself: her disappointment at not being able to exert control. As far as I remember, the word "control" was his. When she then said she was going to stop trying to control things, that was when her hand went to her chest. It could have been an instance of suggestion on his part, but there was no hint that it was deliberate.

In sum, Rogers's video reminded me that the history of therapy contains many treasures buried in plain sight. We are often kept from using them because of an old feud in the field or because disciples have worn out the freshness of the ideas. In Rogers's case, I think it is because the language of humanism is so oriented to the individual. But as I looked beyond the context Rogers operated in, beyond his personal theorizing, and beyond the writing of his adherents, I found that his practices, including the way he embodied his words, resembled what I think of as a collaborative working style.

Tekka with Feathers

I should mention one other milestone while I was teaching at Brattleboro—the start of my work with writer and therapist Judith Davis, who became an important friend and partner. Judy's doctoral dissertation at the University of Massachusetts was on ritual in families, carried forward in her book, *Whose Bar/Bat Mitzvah Is This Anyway?* (1996), which is the best application of systemic family theory to a contemporary social ritual that I know. After she finished at the Brattleboro training program, she and I began to see families and write about them together. On one occasion, we asked a family to collaborate with us. As we have published this article in another book, I will only outline the story here, but I do want to highlight one unusual feature. This article marked the first time we had asked families not only to reflect upon their experience at the time, but also to comment on the accounts that Judy and I wrote later on. I thought of this writing scheme as postmodern because it was composed of (1) personal voices rather than the passive voice of scholarly research; (2) a linked sequence of stories rather than an imposed coherence; and (3) multiple perspectives rather than a God's eye view.

This article, "Tekka With Feathers" (1993), was about a young woman artist whom we called Tekka, not her real name, but suggested by her. She had been hospitalized for seemingly crazy behavior after she apparently tried to walk through the back wall of a subway station. After she recovered enough to return to college, her mother and stepfather asked Bill Lax to see all three of them because they wanted to get Tekka off medication. The fear of suicide was also in the air, as Tekka had dangled some clues that were alarming. Judy was the interviewer for the four sessions we had with them, and Bill and two of our trainees acted as a reflecting team. I joined the team during the last interview. Rereading the article, I am pulled in all over again by Judy's description of Tekka:

> The most striking thing about Tekka was her hair. Long and strawberry blonde, it was piled high on top of her head and cascaded down around her face in a combination of curls and matted dreadlocks that were interspersed with beads, bits of colored ribbon, and feathers. Dressed in a tie-dyed jump-suit with a fingerless black glove on one hand, and her nails painted with black polish, Tekka looked to me both exotic and exhausted.

What I remember most about the session (I sat behind the screen) was the fear expressed by Tekka's mother, a social worker who worked with suicidal teenagers. She was worried that Tekka would take her life, and Tekka had a way of hinting about such things, as when her mother discovered that she had hung a "recovery doll," noose and all, from the knob of the door to her room. In my reflection after that disclosure, I remember saying that nobody tells parents that every child they have is a hostage to the universe, and that they are vulnerable for the rest of their lives. Tekka's mother said in her written reflection that this thought stayed with her during the following year. Luckily, all went well. Even though Tekka voluntarily went for a brief time back into the hospital, she was able to handle this event herself and it did not interfere with her year-end graduation.

Tekka's written reflections on this experience were eloquent. In a critique of society's ways of dealing with young adult anguish, she said:

> To respond to the idea of a suicide rather than the act of expression gives the suicide even more power. For example, I felt very violated to have the topic of my "recovery doll" even be a topic. To me it was a very sensitive personal thing to begin with (the doll, that is) and to hang it on the door was my way of consciously expressing how I was feeling in relation to others. To have the "others" then react to it only perpetuated the feeling: the feeling of violation, oppression, infringement. So where does one go with that? It can become a vicious circle very quickly. (Hoffman & Davis, 1993, p. 195)

She then asked, what would happen if, when the black slaves sang of freedom, the white people's response was gratitude or hopefulness rather than repression? Instead of reacting with horror to ugliness, why couldn't they agree that it was real but do something about it. She ended by saying that if every artist who dealt with suicide or death were put on a suicide watch, we would be missing out on much of our culture.

I was grateful to her for putting our concerns into such a passionate framework. I was also grateful that events justified her optimism. That next spring, Judy and I were invited to the art exhibition at Tekka's graduation. We decided to go, as we felt like substitute mothers by that time, and both Tekka and her mother welcomed us. It was a vivid event. We were stunned by the beauty, originality, and humor of Tekka's work. But most amazing of all was Tekka herself. Instead of the tangled dreadlocks, she was wearing a yellow satin pillbox on top of a short boyish bob and a yellow satin tunic and trousers. She looked like the Russian boy from the firebird legend. I thought to myself all over again how stilted our descriptions become when we enter the clinical world and forget about the beads and feathers in the tangled hair.

11

Sharevision

The "Bambi"

In this chapter, I want to argue that the field has been evolving toward a more communal set of practices for therapy. Michael White and David Epston had begun to use the reflecting team as an audience for the project of re-authoring someone's story. I, too, had been struck by the way a reflecting team could fold in persons who were not originally part of a troubled situation but might change its outcome beneficially. I found confirmation of this idea in social constructionist Kenneth Gergen's (1994) comments on the interactional context of meaning. Finding the idea that meaning originates within an individual mind to be deeply problematic, he writes:

> Words (or texts) within themselves bear no meaning; they fail to communicate. They only appear to generate meaning by virtue of their place within the realm of human interaction. It is human interchange that gives language its capacity to mean, and it must stand as the critical locus of concern. I wish then to replace *textuality* with *communality*. This shift allows us to restructure much that has been said about meaning within texts as a commentary on forms of relatedness." (pp. 263–4)

I resonated to this outlook. In coming to New England, I had set myself the task of finding places where family therapy was hard, if not impossible, to do, and where problems resided in complex social envelopes. This search led me to a child protection agency in the hills of Northern Massachusetts called People's Bridge Action. It had started in the '70s as a street-front outfit and still had the flavor of a renegade brigade. They weren't looking for a consultant but an anti-consultant, and I saw that any effort to project expertise on my part would be taken as a dare. On the other hand, what better place to hone my search for a less hierarchical way to teach and practice?

I initially learned about PBA from a colleague named Lisa Thompson, who worked there until she decided to get a degree in social work. She wanted to bring me together with the Director, Richard Baldwin, figuring we would hit it off, and she was right. It seemed that he was as disestablishmentarian as I was. He had a background in fine arts and was a bona fide painter to boot. With the consent of his staff, he offered me the job. However, it only paid $35 an hour, for a total of two hours a month plus a commute of an hour each way. So the staff generously decided that what they really needed was to come down to Amherst once a month, have their two-hour consultation at my house, and eat a crunchy lunch at an alternative eatery called Daisy's.

This fit my subterranean purpose well. From talking to the group, I discovered that they liked the idea of doing a case consultation along reflecting team lines. We agreed on the need to depathologize our work and found the emphasis on stories rather than problems immediately helpful. Of course, one hazard of a staff that bright and democratic was that everyone was equal but not all were the same. Case discussions could be like religious debates, as the tensions between individual orientations and relational orientations played themselves out.

I suggested we try something new: we would go round the room and, instead of trying to give suggestions or advice to the person presenting a case we would come up with an image, a play, a movie, or a book. Personal experiences that resonated with the situation were encouraged. We would not engage in back-and-forth arguments, and we outlawed so-called constructive criticism, along with advice and suggestions of any sort. Baldwin was interested in narrative theory and other ideas that were coming out of the increasingly influential postmodern movement, so at first we called our process "narrative supervision." Then Baldwin came up with "sharevision" (being something of a software nut, he was inspired by the computer term "shareware"), and it stuck.

The reflecting process turned out to be a process that actually did dissolve problems. Many of the dilemmas aired in agency case conferences were no-win binds where fixing a situation in one place only caused it to break down somewhere else. There were many cases where, for instance, an alcoholic husband would keep beating his wife, she would get a restraining order or go to a shelter, he would reappear sad and sorry, she would take him back, and everything would return to the status quo. The staff would bombard the therapist with suggestions, but she would often reject them, saying that she had tried each one. The group would then suggest that she refer the family to another therapist or agency. The therapist would refuse, the tension level would rise, and an argument over whether the therapist was "codependent" would break out.

This kind of scene was guaranteed to produce the well-known occupational hazard called "burnout," but once I began to use a reflecting process, these tense escalations stopped. I began to think that burnout was an understandable side-effect of ineffectual help. In fact, the most pressing task of case conferences was often to upgrade the morale of the discouraged therapist. Once she felt more hopeful, she could often find new ways to deal with her intractable clients, if only to bear witness and "be there."

When I first introduced a reflecting process, I noticed it had an amazing serenity effect. For one thing, everyone had his or her own space bubble. Unlike the case conferences of the past, there was no chance of being interrupted or not being able to get a word in edgewise. An anticipatory quietness prevailed; people would go off on riffs that were often inspiring and had the rest of us in trance. I remember Shakespeare being invoked in reference to an alcoholic mother whose children were about to be taken away by the state. The therapist felt angry, useless, sad. In an unlikely comparison to *Romeo and Juliet*, someone said that even though the Bottle of Poison was threatening the Cause of Love, it had not yet succeeded, so despite the manifest dangers, she must be doing something right. This idea, while a bit ludicrous, gave the therapist some space and calmed her down.

To those who would say that this approach was not aggressive enough for child protection, I can only answer that this staff knew all about protection. Two young female social workers told me about their fears when they went alone to rural homes to check on reports of child abuse. I was struck by the name they used for themselves: Bambi. The enemy's name was The Men in Orange, because every fall the hilltowns were full of hunters in orange hunting suits. The Bambis, quite logically, thought of themselves as prey, especially those who were bisexual or gay. They had entered the child protection field out of their own commitment to human rights, and to them it was personal.

To illustrate, here is a story I heard from a young social worker at another outreach agency where I consulted. She had gone to the house of a family where a daughter had been running away from home. The mother and daughter were out, so the father answered the door. He was clearly not glad to see the worker. As she sat down to wait at the kitchen table, he picked up a knife and began flourishing it suggestively while buttering a piece of bread. At the same time, he told her about an upcoming pig slaughtering ceremony that his community looked forward to each year. He said that his six-year-old boy loved to drink the blood. At this point, the worker told me, she decided to leave. Thinking to myself that consultants can do very little with pig slaughtering, I concentrated on every possible way to dignify the work of this young woman, acknowledge how assaulted she must feel, and tell her not to lose heart. I don't remember what I said to her, but it probably had something to do with Joan of Arc.

The Wild Turkey

Another story was told me by one of our own "Bambis," therapist Jean Flegenheimer. She was working with a young woman, Lorna, who was refusing to leave her house. She had no friends, no activities, and wouldn't come to see Jean at the clinic, so Jean had to drive to her home. Lorna had asked for help because her mother had recently died and she was afraid that she would "fall off the line" or "go crazy." Her mother had been agoraphobic, and her death was due to complications from self-starvation. Her father was no help; he was a World War II veteran who suffered from flashbacks and, during these spells, would hold his family at knifepoint. Lorna said that he had sexually abused her younger sister, who was now bulimic and suicidal but would not admit to the abuse. Married for the second time and raising two young children, Lorna blamed herself because she had not been able to prevent her mother's death.

In our meeting, Jean told us that she had felt stymied in trying to help this paralyzed young mother. She took to going over and sitting in her kitchen and just talking to her. One day, the woman told her about a wild turkey that had come to the field in back of her house. She put out some seeds and bread crumbs. The turkey began to eat the food she left for it. Soon it came regularly and became tame enough to wander close to the house and to Lorna. Jean felt that she, too, was trying to connect with a wild creature. The story of Lorna and the wild turkey symbolized many things: the preoccupation with food that was such a problem in this family; the fear of becoming too close to other humans; the need to nourish and be nourished; the problem of "wildness." All these issues were contained in the group's reflections about the turkey and Lorna's efforts to care for it. Not only were we touched, but our collective conclusion was that Jean's attempts were paying off.

Lorna did indeed begin to show signs of moving out of her slump. She enrolled her three-year-old in a playgroup; she got the children's father to take more responsibility for them; she began to reconnect with her sisters; and she even mulled over the idea of going to church. She was now driving to the agency to see Jean. As Jean continued to speak about the case, it changed from another hopeless-sounding situation to an inspirational fable. Lorna had used the story of the wild turkey to communicate about a dilemma of loneliness, and Jean used it to describe a dilemma of connection. Janine Roberts later included it in her book, *Tales and Transformations: Stories in Families and Family Therapy* (1994), but it was such a special story that I wanted to retell it here.

The PBA group, too, felt like a "wild turkey." Some of the staff's ways sounded more New Age than I was used to, but my agenda was to learn their language, not to impose mine. Eventually, I hoped, we would arrive at "our" language. The format that we jointly came up with for our consultations was very simple. We would start with a moment of silence, then go round to share what had been going on for us during the past month. During this segment, we acted as a support group. The second half of the meeting consisted of a reflecting process. Someone would present an issue which could be a clinical dilemma, a personal matter, or a crisis in the agency. Everybody would offer an association, after which the presenter would comment back. As this meeting was only held once a month, the group set up pods of three or four persons who would meet in a peer supervision format during the other three weeks. Saving money was imperative, because the staff only had a small amount that they used for all consulting services.

During the next seven years, the agencies that served the poor in Massachusetts came under increasing pressure to become more cost-efficient. This meant that larger agencies began swallowing smaller ones and that professionals who lacked reimbursable degrees were at risk. Many of the staff at PBA had no such degrees. During the last three years of my service, there was a new upset each month: directors were being replaced, staff was being let go, services to families were being disrupted. Finally, PBA was engulfed by North Central Human Services, a large community mental health agency in the neighboring town. The caseloads got bigger and morale dropped lower, but our small staff kept meeting. And what was so amazing was the creativity of this particular group in the face of a collapsing professional world.

I remember a meeting in 1992 when we began to brainstorm against the inevitable. The agency had long been an outpost of reformers, feminists, and idealists, many of them graduates of the UMass School of Education. PBA's offerings consisted of art therapy with families, children's music groups, anger classes to transform low self-esteem into protest and ropes courses to build strength and trust. Individual therapy was available for persons in crisis, but the major emphasis was on repairing networks and creating community. Chief among the agency's projects were a program called Mak-It, designed by Ellen Landis and Deborah Muyskins for a group of young, poor mothers, and a group called Mosaic, directed by social worker Catherine Taylor, for mothers whose children had been sexually abused and whose families had been torn apart by the judicial system.* Here I want to tell the story of Mosaic and our entry onto a larger stage.

New Voices

Mosaic represented a collaboration between Taylor, videographer Carlos Fontes, and a group of unusual mothers. The title was an acronym for Mothers of Survivors Are Interested In Children. They had first met in one of Taylor's anger classes, and all of them had daughters who had been abused by a husband, boyfriend, or male relative. Fontes, originally from Portugal, had extensive experience in the popular video movement, which used video to help marginalized people tell their stories. Taylor suggested to Fontes that he help the group make a videotape of their struggle to recover from their collective nightmare. The subsequent document, "Not Alone," was a powerful and moving set of images, shot by Carlos and edited by the Mosaic mothers, who also wrote the script.

But this and other projects were now endangered. As the staff met and pondered how it could take hold of its future, it seemed to me to be answering its own question. We looked around and saw that there were many unusual and colorful programs gathered under our leaky circus tent. Somebody suggested we have a one-day fair at which we would present our ideas to our colleagues in the Valley. So, under the title of "Transforming the Story of Trauma," we held an event to acquaint local agency people with examples of the way we had been using drama, music, art and games to change the context of help. The hope was to move people from a framework of pathology to one of play and imagination. Emboldened by the success of our collective story-telling, we decided to have a national conference in Northampton on a similar theme the following year.

This second conference was called "New Voices in Human Systems," and it was the first time I had ever tried to design such a meeting. I had the resources of North Central Human Services, then directed by organizational consultant John Szivos, to back me up, and the artistic services of Dick Baldwin, who designed our brochure and poster. The presenters were outstanding writers, teachers, researchers, and practitioners like Mary Catherine Bateson, Mary and Kenneth Gergen, Sheila McNamee, and the late Donald Schoen. When I made up a list of recent books and articles by

---

* The Mosaic group originally included Karen Lenois, Arlene Meyers, the late Jane Sampson, and the late Colleen Leslie, joined later by Theresa Melanson, Mary Thiboult, Sharon Powell, Ann McKinney, and Dorreen Gallien.

all the speakers, reflectors, and facilitators, I came up with sixteen titles, all published since 1990. At the end, the Mosaic group covered themselves with glory by showing their video, "Not Alone."

The three days of this conference were attended by 250 persons representing human services, teaching, and organizational consulting. In shape, the event was reflexive and collaborative. Each presentation flowed into and fed back upon the next. The two daily speakers contributed what I called starter dough, giving brief talks that were then commented on by two reflecting panelists. After this the audience commented, and then the ball was passed to twenty small discussion groups, each with two facilitators. Basically, this was the reflecting process writ large and transposed to the level of a conference. To my surprise, not only was it a success, but it actually broke even.

At this time, I joined with systemic therapists Ros Draper and Margaret Robinson from the Tavistock Clinic in London, and Jim Wilson and Geoff Faris of The Family Institute in Cardiff, to organize a small conference in Devonshire called The Dartington Event. At the suggestion of Cathy Taylor, representatives of both the Mosaic group and the Mak-it group attended and presented their ideas at the first meeting. It was unusual in British conferences to mix professional psychotherapists with peer advocates who had once been "clients." However, their heartfelt stories moved many of the people who heard them speak, and the Mosaic Mothers became a tradition at that conference for several years.

When PBA finally closed its doors in 1996, few of the original staff were still there. All the people I knew had found new employment, and in some cases had started consulting practices of their own. I remember the ritual we used when the end was in sight. I was living in a retirement community in Northampton, on a hill above the community's meetinghouse. One of the staff members, social worker Akiba Mermey, was a practicing Sufi, and he, with Lisa Thompson, organized a leaving ceremony for us. I bought two dwarf Golden Delicious apple trees and planted them beforehand in front of my cottage. Lisa started us off by burning the usual mixture of cedar and sage while we held hands, then Akiba led us in a Sufi dance and we all whirled in place. We offered appreciations of our long connection to each other, hugged each other, and took our leave. Later, when I went down to the meetinghouse to get my mail, I ran into a group of puzzled neighbors. They asked me, "Who was that group of crazy people on the hill?" I tried to explain, but what could I say? That we were therapists doing a rain dance? So I left it vague. In the six years since the demise of PBA, one of the two apple trees was sliced off by a mowing machine, but the other one blooms every year in the spring and bears wormy but golden apples in the fall.

In looking back on these experimental days, there seemed to be no end to the uses to which Andersen's reflecting process could be put. I also used it to teach family therapy seminars at the University of Massachusetts and the Smith School of Social Work, and was struck by the way it changed the dynamics of the class. Left to its own devices, a mixed gender seminar of more than 12 people would evolve into two groups: people who raised their hands (usually male) and people who didn't (usually female). The first group, which I called the Lions, would begin to feel smarter and smarter, and the second group, the Lambs, would feel dumber and dumber. Soon this latter group never raised their hands at all. Changing to a reflecting format insured that every voice would be heard.

Naturally, there were complaints by devotees of "open and honest" debate, but I explained that I was interested in affirmative action for shy people. For instance, in a large group, I might ask smaller pods to take turns talking together while the others listened in. This seemed to provide the safer environment I was looking for. Sometimes I would join the pod that was speaking, adding my protective status to the mix. This seems like a contradiction to the project of not being an expert, but I took care to set things up so that ideas would come out of other people, not just me. I also began to think in terms of moving in and out of hierarchy, because it is too simplistic to believe that a therapist or a teacher can ever be status-free. But the most important discovery I made during these years was that a reflecting process, applied to different venues and to different contexts, was one way to influence the emotional atmosphere of any group toward more openness and comfort.

Jack and the Beanstalk

My most successful example of a reflecting process in therapy is the story of Jack and the Beanstalk. After I left Brattleboro, Judy Davis and I continued to do consultations together. On one occasion in 1994, when I was doing a joint consultation for PBA and North Central Human Services, I asked her to join me. Present were twelve-year-old Jack and his mother, Lori; Jack's therapist, Jeanne Ingress; and two new therapists, one who would work with the family's two other children and one who was going to work with the whole family. David Haddad, the Clinical Director of North Central, and about twenty-five staff members from both agencies, were also there. Dick Baldwin, fascinated by media affairs as usual, was acting as our camera man.

I have many ways of doing these theaters-in-the-round. Here I began by introducing myself and Judy and explaining to everybody about the reflecting team and how it was going to work. I told them it was "like a beehive or a big brain, like many, many brains buzzing together." The next step was to introduce the four people who would be our team and to ask the rest of the participants to listen "as if" they were the professionals in the case (see Chapter 12 for a discussion of Harlene Anderson's interesting "as if" exercise). Judy and I then thanked Lori and Jack for being willing to come to this consultation. Lori, the mother, was a big woman in her forties, comfortable-looking but with signs of strain in her face. Jack, who was sitting next to her, meek and hunched-over, reminded me of an endearing puppy.

In a reflecting consultation, I always start with the person who has asked for my help. Because the family has usually never heard of me, I weave myself to them through that person. So I turned to Jeanne and asked, "What was it about this family that inspired you to ask them to come?" Jeanne explained that they were so friendly and outgoing that she was sure they would not object to such a crowd. Lori had called her earlier in the day and said she had been crying all morning because her son Jack was in trouble again. Jeanne had told her about our meeting, and how the family we were going to see had cancelled, and Lori had jumped at the chance.

I then asked Jeanne what her concerns were, and she said she was worried about Jack, whom she had been seeing for two years. She asked him if he minded her talking about him, and he said he didn't care. She then went on to ask Lori whether she or Lori should tell the story, and Lori invited Jeanne to do so. Jeanne told us that Jack got into another fight at school, and the teacher had found a knife in his pocket. The school said that if he got into one more fight, he would be suspended for good and there was also a threat of a CHINS petition, which meant that the state would take custody of Jack.

Jeanne then described a childhood heavy with violence. After Lori divorced Jack's father, she had a boyfriend who used to beat her. In order to get the boyfriend out of the house, Jack told the police that this man had sexually abused him, even though he later said this was not true. Jeanne said to us, "Jack is a protector." Jeanne also told us that when Jack was small, three adolescent girls who lived in the same house had sexually molested him. Then one of their boyfriends found out he had AIDS and cut his wrists at Jack's kitchen table, spilling much blood. Jeanne said that as a result of seeing and experiencing so much violence, Jack had a lot of anger in him. In fact, the fights at school had gotten so bad recently that he was sent for three weeks to a hospital for observation. After being put on medication, he was allowed to come home, and, except for this latest incident, he had been doing well.

At this point, I was hearing the "cascade of violence" theory: the idea that if a boy is victimized as a child, a cache of anger will build up that will spill over into violence to others when he is bigger. A social picture to that effect was already forming, backed by health professionals, agencies, the school. So, looking consciously for an emotional connecting point (see Chapter 14), I cut in to ask Lori: "Is that why you were crying?" In response, Lori said she had phoned Jack's father to tell him about the incident and he had told her, "My girlfriend says we're going to court for full custody and you're not going to see Jack anymore." I asked Jack, "Did you know why your mom was crying?" He didn't, so Jeanne explained that his dad had threatened to take him away from his mom. He replied that if this happened, he would sneak out at night and run home from the city where his father lived. He was a sparky little fellow.

The conversation went back to the fight. Jack said he had gotten mad at a boy who had kicked one of his friends in the face and was always sitting on his little brother. Lori said that the presence of the knife in Jack's pocket was an accident. The night before, Jack and his older sister were bothering the mother's boyfriend and he was yelling at them, so she sent them upstairs. While there, they decided to run away to Maine, and Jack had put the knife in his pocket because they were going to use it to catch fish. I asked Lori what of all of this had pushed her to come in that morning, and she said her worst fear was losing Jack. She said, "I've had him since he was inside of me. I don't want to lose this kid." Caught on video was the loving look she gave him.

We broke now, and our reflecting team of four, led by Judy, seated themselves in a circle. Judy started, saying that Lori and Joe were so different from what she had expected. After having heard about a family where so many terrible things had been going on—abuse, violence, hospitals, police—she said she had an image of an adolescent boy who was "really tough, really angry," and who was probably being dragged in by his mother. "What I saw instead," she said, "was this sweet looking boy. What came across the most for me was the love that was in this family. His love for his mother and his mother's love for him, just permeated everything. So I was struck by the difference between the story I made up in my head and the story I now have after meeting them."

David Haddad, the clinic director, commented on how resilient and alive Jack and his family were. He had expected to see a family that was more beaten down. He commented on how far Jack was willing to go to protect his mother, brother, and friends, and how his mother was willing to go to any ends to get what she needed for him. He wondered how they were able to maintain such resilience. Ellen Landis, a dance therapist, spoke of the mother's "sense of knowing and caring," and how she and Jack protected each other. Then another therapist said that what came up for her was the sense of justice. She noted that Jack had figured out a way to get rid of this man who was abusing his mother, and that when he saw his brother getting hurt he went after the attacker. In other words, his sense of justice got him into trouble. She wondered what it felt like to be in the other systems that stand for justice, like the Department of Social Services, and how the different concepts of justice fit together. She commented on how everybody is trying hard to do what Mom and Jack are trying to do—make things work.

Judy came in again, saying how helpful the word justice was. She noticed that a story about the family had evolved that had to do with anger, but somehow that word didn't fit for her. She said, "There's a piece that's anger, but maybe that's not the title of the book. It might be a little chapter. But justice, wow! He's this little crusader for justice." David commented again on Jack's resourcefulness and added, "He has a message for kids that often doesn't get talked about. Many kids his age are dealing with insignificant things in comparison with the kind of struggle that Jack has gone through. It's not always easy being a kid. It's not just going to school, it's all these other things. And we who are adults and work as teachers and caregivers have to listen to these messages and give kids a voice. We don't often do that very well."

The team now went back to their seats in the larger circle, and I asked Lori and Jack what their thoughts were. Lori, nodding her head, said, "They care." Jack only shrugged, so Judy asked him, "Is this what you expected to hear?" and he said "I didn't expect this," gesturing to the assembled crowd. Everyone laughed, and Lori explained that Jeanne had said that just a few people would be there and to her this was a few. She said that her mother had 40 grandchildren, and when they all got together she didn't even know who everybody was. Jack said his class at school had 24 kids in it, so he was used to it too.

At this point, I asked Jack an out-of-the-blue question: "Did you ever want to be an actor?" Sometimes an idea or image will come up from the "deep well," as I call it, and I will have to decide whether or not to go with it. In this case, I did, whereupon Jack surprised me by saying "Yes." When I asked what kind of actor he'd like to be, he said, "I'd steal Knight Rider's acting kit." Later I learned this is a James Bond type show for kids where the hero goes around helping people. What was fascinating was that Jack's hero image of himself, though at odds with the school's perception, was corroborated by later evidence.

Judy then asked Lori if the team had said anything that surprised her, and she said she liked David Haddad's comment that kids ought to be listened to. She said that Jack had a teacher with a "strict voice"—the same teacher she had had when she was Jack's age—who made him feel "this big," so of course Jack was going to take out his anger on other people. Jeanne said she thought that Jack must have been surprised by the reflections because he was so often reprimanded at school for being a bad boy, and here he heard people say that he was a seeker after justice.

Building on my previous hunch, I said to Jack, "Well, I have a feeling that if we did a play, it would be called Jack the Giant Killer." I asked him if he knew the story. He said yes, he had the book, but his brother had stolen it, and when he gave it back, it was "scribbled on." He made a disgusted face. I would have asked him more about his impressions of the book, but I suddenly realized I had left the new social worker, Norma, out when asking about reactions to the team, so I turned to her instead. She said she wanted to hear from those persons in the group who had listened from the point of view of the teachers and other professionals.

When I went to the "as if" professionals, a number of corrective points were made. People talked about the need for safety and the concern for protection. One of the speakers made the sensible point that there is a difference between a DSS worker's job and what therapists are supposed to do. When we had gone round, I turned to Lori and asked her to give this whole experience a grade. I said she didn't have to give it an A plus, but asked that it "not be below a B." Lori smiled and said, "Well, really, above a C." I turned to Jack and asked the same thing, and he said, "A plus." When I asked why, he said "Because you care a lot." I thanked him for taking us so seriously.

Here Judy came in again. She asked what it would be like for Jack's teachers if they were introduced to this story through the idea of justice. She said, "This child is the Giant Killer who, when he feels there is an injustice, acts in a way that looks to other people like anger. If this other piece of the story were given to them, would they interact differently with him and his family? How do you and everyone involved enlarge this picture that has so much more richness than the original story?" "And more goodness," I added. Lori looked hard at us. She said, "Do you mean there is more bad showing than there is good? And you see good, so why doesn't that come out more?" When Judy nodded, Lori said, "I don't know if this is what you're talking about, but people see the wrongs, hear the wrongs, so they're not going to want to know nothing about you." How true, I thought, and how important it was for her to say it.

So I asked Lori whether it would be helpful for people who might not know the whole story to see the tape. Lori said she would like her fiancé to see it, and Jack said he'd like to include his brother and sister. Norma wanted to show it to some of the other therapists she worked with, and Lori suggested setting up a meeting with the principal and the teachers at the school. Jeanne said that a meeting was already arranged with the school. Judy turned to Jeanne and asked if it was all right with her to show the video to them and she said, "Absolutely, I feel very good about this."

Then Lori did a double take, saying, "I just hope Jack's teacher won't take what I said in the wrong way. She's a really nice person." I said, "You can tell her yourself when you show her the tape," and Lori said, to much laughter, "That's the God's honest truth." I said that our idea about the videotape was that it was not just a record but something that could add power to everybody's voice. And that it did not just document the past but could affect the future. Dick Baldwin was still taping at the far end of the room and I knew he had the same opinion, so I said to him "Right, Dick?" and he said, "Right."

Then I stood up to say goodbye to Lori and Jack, but to my surprise Lori just sat there and pointed to Dick. "He never got in the picture," she said. I felt a little shocked. How could I have forgotten to include him? This was another example of the way this method seems to spread ownership: if I left someone or something out, another person would so often remind me. So I asked Jack if he wanted to hold the camera. He nodded and walked briskly up to Dick, being photographed all the way, and Dick walked back to our group, being photographed all the way back. Watching the tape later, that sudden switch as Dick and Jack exchanged roles spoke volumes. Judy, in an article she wrote about the case later (Davis, 2000), noted how Jack looked all at once taller and prouder. She said that this moment seemed to her like a small coming of age ceremony and that it was similar to the Bar-Bat Mitzvah ritual that she had written so much about, despite it being in the context of therapy. In this opinion, she agreed with Michael White, who has often used the ritual of therapy is to create a public validation of a person's worth.

I then asked Dick what his thoughts were, and he gave a very eloquent reply. He said that he was trying to follow the conversation rather than just taping the individuals as they spoke. He was asking himself, "If I were Lori, what would I want to see?" Whenever possible he had included Lori and Jack in the picture, pointing out that in most taped interviews the family members are separated from the team and one can't see their reactions to what the team is saying. He ended by sharing his impression of how "loving and powerful" they were as a family.

I liked that word "powerful," as it was a description that specifically described this family and was not just positive in a general way. To reinforce the different story that the video captured, I suggested we have a screening at PBA. Dick agreed and said it would be good to hear a conversation that moved from "a family experiencing problems" to "a family in collaboration with others trying to change something." He said, "It was exciting to see something growing like this." I said, "Like a Beanstalk." Then we relieved Jack of his duties and he turned the camera off.

When I looked at the tape, I saw that many of its images confirmed what Dick had hoped to show: the intensity in Lori's face when she said "I don't want to lose this kid"; the knowing look between Lori and Jack when the team spoke of the way they protected each other; the interest and surprise in their faces during the introduction of the concept of justice. The whole family did come in to watch the tape later, but Jack told us that Lori's fiancé started talking after the first few minutes and so they never saw more than a bit. I was pleased anyway; we were honoring the new picture of Jack by making it public.

A year later, Judy and I were going to our conference in Devonshire and we wanted to show this tape as an example of a reflecting process. We arranged with Jeanne to meet with Jack and Lori again, to get their permission and to check in with them. I was expecting that Jack would be the same hunched-over, subdued person, and to my surprise in came a tall young man who had shot up about six inches. He was indeed a Beanstalk! He was also alert, funny, talkative, and alive. We learned that he had been given antipsychotic medication while in the hospital and was still taking it when we first met him. Lori told us he had stopped using it shortly afterward because it made him feel like a zombie.

Jeanne told us that she and Lori had fought to get Jack into a new school and that he had responded well to the change. He was getting better grades and had developed techniques for walking away from fights. Lori was looking especially attractive, having cut her hair in bangs, and told us that she was marrying her fiancé in a few weeks. The children from each family were going to give their parents away, and Jack had already picked out his tuxedo. Continuing on this future track, I asked Jack what he hoped to be when he grew up, and he said "a bus driver or a lawyer." Judy then asked what his biggest wish would be if he had a million dollars. In true Knight Rider style, he said, "I would buy houses for all the homeless."

One of the things that was beginning to impress Judy and me was the halo effect of bringing people together to witness and support Jeanne's efforts. A staff worker at PBA had said admiringly to Jeanne that she had never known a family to get so many services. One way we kept this halo effect going was by showing the videotape at workshops and bringing back sympathetic messages from the audiences that viewed it. I had been at a conference where Michael White said he had asked a reflecting team to do the same thing. It had occurred to both of us that the reflecting team was a natural agency for creating what he called a "community of concern," and I was calling an "attending community."

The following year, I showed our tape at teaching events in Britain, Australia, and Mexico. One young Mexican psychologist, Jania Quintero, was particularly touched by the Beanstalk story and gave me a postcard and a letter to take to Lori and Jack. On my return, Judy and I once again arranged with Jeanne to meet with the family. Jack was taller than ever.

Jack's little brother Danny came in, too, and entertained us with somersaults. Then I read aloud Jania's postcard, which had a picture of the volcano called Popocatepetl on the back. It said:

> Dear Lori and Jack, Lynn Hoffman came to my city this year and showed us a tape about your family. This is to tell you that the echo of the mountains brought your voice and love to many hearts around the world and especially to mine.

While I was reading, I noticed that Jack was busy scribbling, seeming not to pay attention to Jania's message. When I asked what he was doing, he showed us a letter to Jania. We found it hard to read, because Jack's handwriting was not of the best, but here it is:

> Hi. I am doing good. I hope all you people like my video. I see myself as a good role moddle. I see myself as a very popelar person. I hope my family is doing a lot better. I do hope people will see this video and see what I have to say because I do like to save my mom and brother. Now that my brother is older he is being a little brat. But I do like what I have and I do hope you will all listen. Jack

When we asked how things had gone with the family, Lori told us a startling story. Their landlord, one of the richest men in the area, had tried to molest Jack. He was well known in the neighborhood for sexually abusing children and had been getting away with it for years, but Jack and Lori took him to court. Even though the family lost their apartment, they succeeded in getting their landlord registered as a sex offender. Our young giant killer was still on the job and although Lori's husband had been fired from his job, he found a new job in a relocation company, and the family found a new house in a better area.

However, not all the news was good. Jack was doing well at the new school, making As and Bs, and continuing to keep himself out of fights, but he was facing a court hearing the very next day. One evening recently, his mother had gone over to "pop a zit" on his face, and he became very agitated and struck out at her. This led to a fit that was so violent that the mother's husband had to sit on him; in fact, it sounded like some kind of neurological episode. After he calmed down, he had no memory of what had happened, but his sister was so frightened that she called the police before anyone could stop her. His mother didn't want to press charges, but the police took Jack to the station anyway and gave him a court date.

This was alarming, so we asked Jeanne what she was going to do, and although she didn't go to court, she did call the lawyer and social worker who were involved with the family and encouraged them to be there. At the hearing, we heard later, the judge gave Jack a lecture about how he shouldn't hit his mother and followed it up with twenty hours of community service. When Jeanne told us this, Judy and I gave a sigh of relief, but the incident showed the power of the record. The police knew all about Jack, even though it was three years since he had been in a single fight.

After this meeting, we sent Jeanne a Certificate of Appreciation commending her and the family for all their good work and listing their joint and individual accomplishments in detail. In this we were copying White and Epston (1990), who had been using similar documents as part of their effort to create "counter-stories" for people. Not long after that, PBA suffered the fate of many agencies serving poor families in the Massachusetts hilltowns: it closed down. Jeanne lost her job, which left her in a difficult situation because her degree did not allow her to be reimbursed by insurance. She also lost touch with Lori and Jack, because the family had no telephone and had moved. However, Judy sent a copy of her article to Jeanne, and Jeanne wrote a letter back, thanking Judy and saying,

> You also made it sound like my work had meaning, even if it wasn't immediately apparent (for how will we know how Jack turns out until he's fully grown?). I'm so grateful to you for evoking the warm feelings that originally went with this work. By the time it was over, the chaotic dysfunction of the agency & the inhumane demands of managed care, covered what was once sacred & good with a veil of such negativity that it became impossible to see if anything we did or thought had any value whatsoever. There are so many lost boys like Jack in the world. Your paper gives a real sense of hope that there are answers that can be evoked.

In ending this story, I want to repeat what I said above about the idea of using the reflecting process to further a new kind of communal work. Our team was not attempting to influence the community in a social action sense; instead we wanted to make a more communitarian event out of therapy. Conventional psychotherapies—individual, group, family—seemed to distance people rather than bring them together. Jeanne's letter reminded us of "the loneliness of the long distance therapist" and made us glad that we had become witnesses who could appreciate her work.

12

Unforeseen Speech

The Social Web

Harlene Anderson's *Conversation, Language and Possibilities* (1997) was one of the first books that attempted to link the ideas of the postmodern philosophers to family therapy practice. In this book, Anderson is like a gifted painter who has built a beautiful gallery to house the work of a larger community. This community includes the revolutionary thinkers in social psychology and linguistic philosophy who are leading the challenge to the essentialist outlook of modernism (Gergen, 1994; Harré, 1984; Shotter, 1993b). Anderson's book has joined this conversation, providing an account of how the Houston-Galveston group has translated concepts like postmodernism and social construction theory into what she and Goolishian have called a collaborative language systems approach.

The questions of postmodernism put words to many of the doubts I had about the field of psychology. Having grown up with a background in the arts, I intuitively felt that there was something wrong with the flatness of psychological language. I loved Haley's early (1963) examples of meaningless descriptors like "needs," "drives," "affect," and so forth, which he wanted to ban from the vocabulary. Psychology itself was a mystifying term: what was a "psyche" anyway? How could the "logos" of a "psyche" be treated? I had long thought that therapy of the psyche was an especially meaningless descriptor, and that just as no self existed outside its intimate community, there was no psychotherapy that was not social.

This is why social construction theory appealed to me. Not only did it challenge psychology's love affair with the freestanding individual, but it also validated the idea that therapy was always about relationship. Or rather, it did and it didn't. Anderson points out that the move in therapy from the individual to the family merely shifted the unit one level up; you were still looking for disorders and dysfunctions and you were still the expert who knew how to cure them, but the role of the professional was now itself being deconstructed. Under the circumstances, it seemed natural to turn to a new metaphor. Instead of the "system," with its assumptions of stability and functionality, we were looking at interactions that were constantly in motion, from the stylized motions of a country dance to the more random passing of strangers in a city street. If there were "patterns" in this flow, they were products of our social and linguistic negotiations, not forms or essences existing on their own. Kenneth Gergen's *Invitation to Social Construction* (1999) explores the history of this challenge to "essentialism" in a particularly friendly way.

As a branch of philosophy, Gergen tells us, constructionism came out of the American practical philosophy movement called pragmatism. Its ancestors were social thinkers like William James, Charles Pierce, and Herbert Mead, but it was Peter Berger and Thomas Luckmann's book *The Social Construction of Reality* (1966) that turned a loose group of theories into an intellectual movement and now into a candidate for a paradigm. My own opinion is that constructionism, which has taken shape around a socio-linguistic template, is a better basis for a postmodern psychology framework than cognitive theories like constructivism, which may cast doubt on the possibility of being objective, but are narrowly located in brain biology. To show the difference between essentialism, constructivism and constructionism, here is the well-known Three Umpires joke.

FIRST UMPIRE: I calls 'em as they are. (essentialism)
SECOND UMPIRE: I calls 'em as I sees 'em. (constructivism)
THIRD UMPIRE: They ain't nothing till I [or we] call 'em. (constructionism)

Translated into therapy, the essentialist looks for the cause of the problem, which exists in "the world out there," and tries to fix it. The constructivist says that the experience of a problem is always filtered through the nervous system and tries to change the way it is perceived or acted upon. The constructionist moves to the social web, believing that she is at the same time one of the weavers and one of the threads. Her hope is to set up the conditions that evoke, as Schoen puts it (1984), "the situation's potential for transformation."

If constructionism is indeed a useful metatheory, we might feel that the word "psychology" has outlived its usefulness, being too weighed down by its attachment to the individual mind. In that case, the newcomer field of communication could be the area that constructionism might represent. Its research arm would be represented by forms of qualitative research (Leeds-Hurwitz, 1995; Olson, 2000). Its applied methodology would include post-modern therapies like the collaborative and narrative approaches, and would find further applications in organizational consulting and mediation. Kenneth Gergen and his research partner, Sheila McNamee (2000), have been pushing for this extension of constructionism to many kinds of relationship counseling (see chapter 15). Of course, constructionism might also end up as just another corporate structure on Sixth Avenue, but whether it does or not, it has been very useful to me. In this chapter, I hope to tell you how.

Two Sleeping Beauties

With the demise of my niche in the Massachusetts hilltowns, I began to take my reflecting theater all over, and wherever I went I would use its participatory format. I stopped showing videotapes because they were "dead" material, preferring the impact and unpredictability of the live experience. I was at this time attending "The Dartington Event" in England each year, and from there I got invitations to give workshops in many countries. For the first time, I felt that I was bringing something of my own rather than a product invented by someone else. The reflecting process had set free my improvisatory gifts in a way other methods never had.

The first time I experienced this particular lightness was in Thessaloniki, where I had gone to take part in a seminar on cultural genograms (Hardy, 1995). I had not used genograms in some time, not since leaving New York, because I didn't know how to weave them into a postmodern approach. However, the seminar leaders who were expected by the workshop leader failed to show up, so I was pressed into service. I simply turned the cultural genogram into a reflecting consultation, asking people from the audience to serve as my reflecting team. In addition, I set up a group of "as if" listeners, an idea that Harlene Anderson used in her presentations and had shared with me. My version was to ask several people to become "floating identities," that is, to move in and out of the viewpoints of persons in the story that was being told, and then report on the experience.

I did my first cultural genogram with a woman of Greek ancestry whose family had suffered at the hands of the Turks in Albania and who had recently moved back to Greece. This went so well that the other seminar asked me to perform for them too. When I asked for a volunteer, an

American woman came forward and introduced her sister as well. I suggested that we do a "relational genogram" (an invention of the moment) and I would interview the two of them together. In a way, I was seeking to deconstruct the genogram as I knew it. Then Luigi Boscolo, who was one of the faculty, came in to watch. I was a little nervous, because I was not sure how he would react to my new not-knowing style.

The interview was intriguing. The sisters were in their forties—cultured, intelligent, handsome, both with families of their own. The younger of the two already had an M.A. but said that she wanted to go back to get a doctorate. On the minus side, she would have to commute to the university and her daughter was only sixteen, so she worried about spending so much time away from her family. The older sister had not one but two M.A.s, and she too had dreams of becoming a Ph.D. They told me that if either of them had been born a male, they would have gone on to higher education, but in their Jewish family, the daughters weren't expected to aim so high. They had already pushed the envelope with their three M.A.s.

This was a cultural issue right there. However, instead of pursuing it directly, I took a right-brain tack and asked the older sister what legend or fairy tale came to mind in regard to the other one. She said, without skipping a beat, "The Sleeping Beauty." I asked the same question of the younger sister and got the same answer. So I had twin Sleeping Beauties. One reason for working in this more associative way was to elicit images for us all to work with. I had been finding that painted language served to expand the power of connection, and I wasn't disappointed here either. The reflecting group acted as thoughtful voices in representing the dilemma of the sisters and used the Sleeping Beauty story in their comments. But it was the "as if" listeners, speaking out of their floating identities, who threw in the wild card.

In this instance, they brought in a big charge of energy. The woman who listened as the mother said she was torn about her daughters' ambitions, since it was unusual in her milieu for women to aspire to academic degrees, but she wanted whatever would make them happy. The "father" regretted not having had a son, but said his daughters more than made up for that and that they had his blessing to go forward. The "daughter" of the younger sister came on strong, telling her mother that if she got the Ph.D., she would set a pioneering precedent for her daughter. All of a sudden there appeared one more floating identity who said he was the unborn Jewish son. He thanked both women, saying that in pursuing their dream of higher education, they were giving him life.

The reaction of the sisters was interesting. The younger said the reflections from the "as if" persons made her feel much more positive about going ahead with her plans, but the older one, despite staunchly backing her sister, held a sadness in her face. I thought to myself that, since their age-difference was so small, they might well feel as twins often do: if one moves on too fast, the other will be left behind. That could hold back both of them. So I asked her, "Do I have to worry about you?" She looked startled, then reassured me, saying, "I'll be okay." She said she was keeping her options open. Both sisters said they enjoyed the way I worked and that it felt very congruent with their own ideas. I said I would call them in Chicago in the fall to see where they were.

I subsequently lost these sisters' phone numbers, and I regret that. In doing consultations away from home, I usually promise to do a follow-up. I like to think that the future layering of a phone call reinforces my effect as a witness. But there was an immediate coda to the event. I had asked Luigi Boscolo to comment on the interview, explaining that he had been one of my teachers. So he gave a beautifully reasoned, systemic interpretation of the situation. I wasn't surprised at what he said, but I was surprised at my reaction to it. Boscolo, whom I admire enormously, had superimposed a knowing template on my not-knowing interview. This experience acted like growth markings on a doorway, showing how drastically my therapeutic attitudes had changed. I saw in a way I never had before how different from conventional therapy a not-knowing conversation really was, and to what degree I was beginning to escape the flybottle of my own training.

The Wings of Stone

In the late '80s, Goolishian and Anderson were often invited to conferences in Norway by Tom Andersen, and many ideas were passed back and forth. Although Anderson does not use a reflecting team per se, she sees her innovation of "as if" listeners as filling a similar space. First, she will select a trainee to present a case. Then she will ask who is in the "cast of characters" and divide the listeners into groups representing each role: mothers over here, fathers over there, and so forth. Next she asks the presenter what she wants from the listeners. The listeners' mandate is to listen to the presenter and, when she is done, to tell her with the voice of the character they inhabit what they would like her to know and what they would like her to do.

Anderson refrains from maintaining a heavy presence during the exercise and gives the presenter ample time to tell the audience about the family she has been working with. If she thinks the audience wants to see her in action, she herself will interview the presenter, but if she does so, her aim is only to clarify her agenda, which is to treat the family as the source of knowing. After this stage, the participants will then move into the "as if" clusters and decide what it is they want to say to the therapist. The consultant will put these ideas down on a flipchart. This procedure gives a professional audience the experience of thinking outside of the expert position and in this sense does the same job as a reflecting team.

I was fascinated by Anderson's invention and began to adopt it in my own workshops. A particularly compelling example was a reflecting consultation I did at a conference in Mexico at the end of the '90s. The day before, I had attended a workshop given by Anderson and her co-presenter, psychologist Sylvia London. I had heard about, but had never seen, an "as if" exercise, and thought it was a brilliant way of deconstructing both professional and client roles. So I told her I would like to use her idea at my workshop and asked her and Sylvia London to join me at the end and comment on their experience.

On the morning before my workshop, an elegant psychologist from another city in Mexico had come up to me and introduced herself. Her name was Maria Eva. I had mentioned Virginia Satir in a positive way during a talk I had just given, and Eva (her preferred name) told me that she had met Satir when she came to Mexico and had attended some of Satir's workshops in the U.S. At the end of our talk, she said she was coming to my workshop, so it did not surprise me that when I asked for someone who would be my partner in the consultation, the person who offered herself was Eva. I was glad she came up, despite my worry that she might be expecting another Virginia Satir.

Next I asked four people to be a reflecting group, and another three to be "floating identities." I had already explained the job of being members of a reflecting team in my earlier talk, but the "as if" exercise was unfamiliar to most of my audience. I told them that I wanted them to listen while Eva told her story and then comment as if they were speaking in the voices of one or another of the persons that she had talked about. But this was not a role play. The "as ifs" were to respond to what they heard Eva say, and then tell the consultant (me, in this case) their reactions to what they had heard. I also assigned "as if" roles to the audience, as Anderson and London had done the day before, so that everyone there would have a chance to feel, speak, and be heard. We had four audience groups: mothers, fathers, brothers, and aunts. I told the "as ifs" that they could float in and out of these identities as they wished, but the rule about floating did not apply to the large groups, who were assigned static roles.

After the hand mikes were distributed and the translator was in place, I started. I usually take a moment to arrange my mind, so there is a bit of silence. After this, I tell my partner that the way I begin this process is to think of a bowl with very wide sides, a bowl that can hold whatever falls into it. Alternatively, I will imagine that I am a big beach—the waves will come up but they will also go down, and the beach will still be there, except maybe for some new pebble or shell.

Then I looked at Eva and asked her if there were some issue or concern she wished to tell me about. She said that someone had asked her how she was feeling during the break, and she said that she had felt calm, like that big beach. Then she said she wanted to thank me for being "the woman you are, a woman I like, admire." Referring to herself, she said she was trying "to be more fluid, to have less fear." She said, "Today I started to feel more spontaneous, to function in each moment instead of asking, 'How can I do this?'" I asked her, using an image that comes from what I call the deep well, "As if you might not have your safety wings on?" She said, "Yes. I haven't spoken about my family, but I do want to go there. Just now, when you said wings, I thought 'wings of responsibility,' as if they were made of stone, like the ones on a Greek statue."

This was such an unusual, kinesthetic image that I decided to leave the world of talking. I asked Eva to place her hands in my palms, and I held them gently, as if I were weighing them, and said, "Yes, they are very heavy—I can't lift them." I dropped my hands to show the weight, and hers followed. After a while, I lifted her hands up again and said, "I wanted you to know I can tell that you are under a real weight." Truth to tell, I surprised myself by this gesture. I wondered if it was because Eva had made Virginia Satir the link between us. It was as if I had asked, "What would Virginia do?" and the answer had come at a body level. In any case, my idea was to do something that would confirm the heaviness, so that Eva would know that I knew what she was experiencing.

Eva then said, "In the break, something small but significant happened. I was talking to Harlene and she asked my name and then asked where Eva came from. I told her that I was named Maria, after my mother, but chose the name Eva when I was six years old because my father's family was in the war, and he and his sister, who was called Eve, were the only survivors. I asked my father, 'What is Eve in Spanish?' and he said 'Eva.' I didn't meet my Aunt Eva until I was age 12." I asked Eva what the name meant to her father, and she replied, "It meant that my father lost everybody and had only his sister left." I said, "You became another Eva?" She said yes, and that what she, the second Eva, meant to her father was "the only piece of life." She said, "My mother never understood what it meant to my father to be Jewish, even though she knew it was frowned upon in a Mexican Catholic society, because she had to get permission from the church to get married."

Eva continued: "I felt I carried my father. I needed to have very big wings to give my father life, so I was a good student. I danced, I was gracious, I did everything well." I said to her, "I have the image of a stream that is being joined by other streams until there is too much water and it overflows its banks." I think I felt that the image of the stone wings was too solid, so I changed to a more fluid one. Then I asked, "How long have you been feeling like this?" She answered, "Until this morning. I am now feeling more relaxed."

This initial conversation had taken only nine minutes. However, many weighty (pun intended) issues had surfaced in a very short time, and I wanted to move us out from under. First I asked her if there were any other people I should know about. She said, "My father, who is dead, was named Abraham. My aunt is dead too. My mother is alive, but she doesn't share in my sorrows, and I'm ten years younger than my older brother." I said, "So in your generation, you are alone. Are you a practicing Jew?" She said, "No, but I'm religious." At this point, I asked her if it was all right to break for the reflecting team.

Why did I choose to break so early? Again, I was puzzled. Michael White (1995) has come up with something that might explain it. He too is bothered by the hierarchy built into the therapeutic relationship, but instead of asking therapists to deconstruct their expertise, he offers the concept of decentering (see chapter 13). One way to decenter is for the therapist to hand off some of her activity to others. I think that is partly why White found the reflecting team so valuable and it was perhaps why I turned to it at this moment. The wings of stone were on my shoulders too. I think I wanted the reflecting group and the "as-if" persons to share it with me.

The Reflections

With the help of a translator, I now joined my reflecting group, all four of them women, and asked them for their impressions. I had previously told them about my wish to move away from clinical language toward associations that were more personal or story-like. All the same, I was surprised by the directness and freshness of their responses. The only time I had to meddle was when the first reflector spoke directly to Eva, who was sitting outside their circle. I said it was important that the reflector direct her comments only to us, so that Eva could overhear but would not have to respond.

The first reflector said that she knew Eva personally and admired her courage in coming forward. She said that what Eva had told us about her part in carrying the stories of her father and mother, as well as being the daughter of a mixed marriage, explained why she was so flexible and open to new ideas.

The second said that she started crying while listening to Eva's story. She said she had tried not to think, only to find out what Eva was feeling. When I took Eva's hands, she felt that Eva was with someone safe, who could help her, and she began to feel less anguished herself. She said, "Now I feel peaceful and I see her peaceful—I see that it is possible for her to feel better."

The third reflector said that what impressed her was this weight that Eva had borne for so long, and how in this session, "when the talking was removed," Eva could feel how heavy it was. Now, after living with this hidden pain, she could begin to open her heart. She made a big change when she changed her name, when she was so young, too, and that was when she decided to live her life as a survivor.

The fourth reflector said that she could identify with Eva's story. Her father too was a survivor of the war. She felt that a part of Eva's heart had been taken away, so she had gone into her head. The problem was how to recover those fragments, those little parts of her heart. Now, at last, she could begin to put them back together and recover her identity. In doing this, Eva was honoring her father, and also honoring herself.

After thanking my reflectors, I went and sat with the small group of "as if" listeners (two men and a woman), and asked which voices they were choosing to speak in. The first woman spoke as the mother, saying that she regretted the distant relationship she had with Eva but explained that she had been jealous of Eva's closeness with her father. One of the men spoke as the older brother and said that he often resented Eva because she got more attention and favors than he did. Then the other man spoke as the father, or at least I thought he was going to, but instead he launched into a long, emotional account of having lost his own son.

This production, though sincere, threatened to take over the event. I remembered White once saying that if reflecting persons get too carried away with their own story, it will compete with the story of the persons who are the focus of the consultation. So I broke in and apologized for misleading him, but said that I meant to ask him to speak in the voice of Eva's father. I asked, "What message would you give your daughter now?" So he told Eva how grateful he was to her for her support and love. He reminded her that he had been strong enough to survive the war and that he was proud of her for showing so much courage. I then asked if he could speak for the aunt, and in doing so he gave thanks to Eva for being a standard-bearer for the lost family. At this point, I thanked everyone and we had a break.

The Lost Sister

After this second break, Eva and I sat together in front of the audience and debriefed each other. When I was listening to those negative statements from the "as if" mother and brother, I had some trepidation about the effect on her. I asked her, "What was the most hopeful thing you heard?" and then added quickly, "or the least?" She answered, "All that was said by each person today was for me silence. Listening, I felt that a little piece of me was always going around inside me, in my inner thoughts." I asked, "The silence was in you?" and she said, "Yes. In my house, nobody talked. When I was growing up, people criticized my father because he was strange —a Jew. Even though he was a good friend of the Bishop, even though he was well respected, there were social occasions we couldn't go to. I've held all these things in my head. There were times I couldn't sleep, when the voices I heard expressed here visited me at night in my dreams."

She continued, "I believe that today I understood what this social constructionism is. When you asked people to talk, I felt at ease. I thought, they will tell me many things, but all are pieces of the puzzle in my mind or heart. In the past, if I felt like crying, my tear ducts were blocked. This experience unblocked them. Before, I felt I had to live my life keeping the pain inside. The role you played here meant that I didn't have to feel it alone." I asked, "What were you able to take away?" She said, "Everybody put in a clear piece of my reality so that I didn't have to bear it in silence. They said very important things and it didn't matter if some of them said they resented me or hated me, the whole event was like a collective unconscious.

Eva continued: "One coincidence was when a person in the audience talked about a sister who died. All at once I remembered that my father wanted to give me the name of his own mother, but he couldn't because it had been given to my sister, who died before I was born." Surprised by this new information, I asked, "What was the name of your sister?" She said, "Rachel, the name of my father's mother. I couldn't be named that, so I was named after my mother. And here, when the colleagues were crying and sympathizing, I started to miss Rachel and wish that she were here. I felt that many of the people who spoke were sisters of the soul, very pure and tender."

Eva went on to say to me, "There were many things you did that were tender, too. For instance, I heard you trying to speak Spanish with some of the groups. I thought, 'Lynn is making a great effort.' In the break, you said, 'I will bring you a glass of water.' I felt that you brought me freshness." I asked Eva, "If you could bring one person back, or if you could bring Rachel back, where would she be in the club of your life?" (another one of Michael White's ideas; see chapter 13). Eva said, "The club of my life is here today. I feel a very deep peace. I am very thankful." We stood up and I hugged her. I said, "For the moment, I will be Rachel."

It was now time to ask the audience to take part. I asked them to stay in their groups and share with each other what they wanted me, and indirectly Eva, to hear.

This small group exercise was important, not just because it allowed the audience a face-to-face experience, but because they could speak in Spanish. I had no other way to honor their language, since I was communicating via a translator. I gave them about twenty minutes, then asked the spokespersons to tell us the ideas of each group. I wrote these comments down, but clumsily, on a flip chart, with my back to the audience, mistakenly thinking this was the way Harlene did it. I didn't keep these notes, but gave them to Eva to take home, and she told me she still has them.

After all the groups had spoken, it was time to for Harlene and Sylvia to come forward. The three of us now sat together in front of everyone. Harlene said, "The first thing that comes to mind is unpredictability. You never know where a conversation is going and how important it is to take every conversation seriously. I'm thinking of the very casual conversation Eva and I had at the break, in terms of what that meant for Eva." Harlene then told us that that her grandmother had died when her mother was seven years old, and that in response to this death her mother had also changed her name. To my surprise, I saw that Harlene was struggling with tears. I was afraid I had upset her in some way, but I said nothing.

After she recovered, Harlene went on: "So it's the multiple conversations, people speaking from their own experiences, the many voices, that is so powerful. You used the word 'cumulative.'" (She was referring to my term for the layering effect of the reflecting process.) "I would use 'generative.' The process is not so much additive as transformative. The powerful experience of the listening position is that you're on hold, you can talk with yourself, or with the voices inside you. Anytime you are having a conversation, you never know what the other person is doing with that. That's what's so interesting." At this point, Harlene talked about my struggle with the flip chart, telling me that she usually asks someone else to do that because it interferes with her connection to the audience. I thanked her for the suggestion because she was only too right.

Sylvia then said that she was interested in Eva's idea of the silence and how the voices of the speakers represented the spaces taken by the silence— as each voice came in, the silence went out, and when the silence went out, the pain went out. She said she was reminded of how many women have been silenced, and how the stream I had talked about was like the community Eva carried with her from the past. The silences had flowed into the community we created here, so there was a link between the past and the future. Listening to Sylvia, I was interested that my stream metaphor, which had not been picked up before, had resurfaced here.

Sylvia went on to say that she noticed that I became a shield for Eva. She said, "It is so different when people are not looking at you. You are free to connect with the inner voices; then you can connect later with the voices outside." She also mentioned the words Eva used to describe my role as a therapist: "tenderness," "freshness," and "caring." I added that when the "as if" listeners used loaded, negative words to describe their relationship to Eva, I was amazed that this didn't upset her. Sylvia said, "Because she could go in or out, or play with it." Harlene said, "Because you're not having to defend yourself or comment," and Sylvia added, "You're free to be what you want to be." I then said that the consultant can do the same thing by handing over the work to the community. Harlene said, "I call that shared responsibility," and Sylvia said, "You don't have to control the discourse, you can let the process flow."

A Rolling Conversation

For me, this was a watershed event, as it seemed to express so many aspects of the improvisatory, layering kind of work that now interested me. Six months later, the Houston-Galveston Institute held a Galveston Symposium (called that because Goolishian had organized the first one in a Best Western Hotel in Galveston in 1991), and Eva and I both came to it. I played the tape of the interview we had done in Mexico City while Eva presented a running commentary, and Harlene and Sylvia contributed their own impressions. I thought of calling this extended exchange a "rolling conversation." Eva had sent her comments on the tape in a letter to me before the conference, so I will summarize some of the points she made.

Speaking about the first conversation we had, she said her confidence in me was an echo of her confidence in Satir. She was also extremely surprised to find that she only had to talk about herself for a few minutes, in contrast to her many years of therapy, where she had always had to talk a long time to be understood. In thinking about the reflecting team, she was glad that it was composed of women, because the gender support meant so much to her. She had heard their voices as if she were listening to her own unrecognized voices, and she was amazed that they were able to give her their thoughts without any effort on her part; it was like a present.

Eva said that this first group gave her enough security to hear the "as if" members. She liked my asking the "father" or "aunt": "What would you say to Eva now?" She also liked it when I clarified the statements of the "as if" people or asked them to reword their reactions so that she could "hear" them better. She said that hearing words of gratitude and forgiveness from her imagined father and aunt left her with a deep peace. She felt appreciated at last and could stop feeling guilty.

She was also glad when the "as if" family members told her honestly what they were thinking, in contrast to the silence from her family in the

she gave each cluster some questions about how they perceived their work. She and two of her colleagues sat in on these small groups while the participants spoke together. Then, during the debriefing in the larger group, she wrote down the ideas each cluster came up with on a flipchart.

Anderson told me that she was amazed at how energetic and positive the responses were. For instance, one of the therapists told of taking his dog with a backpack full of supplies like magic markers, pads, and a water bottle, to a school he was visiting, and introducing the dog as his co-therapist. When Anderson got home, she collated all the comments and sent them back to the agency with some new questions. These were answered in writing by some of the participants, and Anderson collated them and sent back the responses as before. I was struck by the layering of viewpoints that this format allowed, so similar to a reflecting team.

Then Anderson decided that her presentation needed a story and got permission from the director of the agency to attend and videotape the meetings of the next new case Victor was assigned. The first interview, attended by Anderson and one of her colleagues, included Victor, an adolescent boy called Mike who was in trouble for setting fires and robbing a school, his grandmother, and two psychology interns, Andre and Fabienne, who were asked to be observers and do the taping. During the first interview, Victor asked the boy to do a drawing, but he had his writing arm in a sling and his grandmother suggested that maybe one of the interns could help him. Andre went over to assist Mike, and they got into a conversation about the Swiss watch Andre wore. At the end of the meeting, Andre and Fabienne were both asked to reflect, and did so, even though they said they had assumed that this was against the rules.

During the next session, Victor and the boy were playing a "feeling cards" game and the boy asked the interns to join in. Mike had refused to cooperate with three previous therapists, but he spoke so positively of this session that the grandmother said she wanted to attend the next one. The result was that she too joined the "feeling cards" game. One day the boy arrived to find the interns picnicking across the lake from the site of the meeting. He suggested to Victor that they join them, and they all ended up having the session, and future sessions as well, by the lake. Home and school visits were made, too, involving some of the other persons connected with the case. Mike's behavior improved strikingly in a relatively small number of sessions.

While this went on, Anderson told me, she was on the sidelines, coaching and observing and getting feedback. At the same time, she was trying to shift herself out of the central role. Her aim was to make everybody researchers. When a producer of documentaries she had just talked with suggested that the boy videotape and narrate a documentary of the case himself, she went ahead with this idea. She had noticed how much interest Mike took in the taping, and he was only too happy to oblige.

As background to his narration, the boy shot views of the interns' car, the parking lot, the lake, and questioned the various participants on their views. The grandmother said in her interview how happy she was that the therapists felt comfortable enough to come to their house. She was glad that they didn't just concentrate on her grandson but tried to help the family as a whole. In listening to this story, I saw that a key feature of Anderson's work was to open the doors to the resources that were implicit in the scene and let them do the work.

World Building

This brings me to a favorite idea of mine that I call "world building" (distinguished from Nelson Goodman's [1984] "world making" by the fact that his is a cognitive operation and mine a systemic one). I got this concept from the writings of architect Christopher Alexander (1979) who, in *The Timeless Way of Building*, invokes a time when there were no blueprints or architects and the art of building depended on a "pattern language" going deep into the past. He says that these patterns have a folk feel and are intuitive rather than mechanical. As examples, he cites elements like "farmhouse kitchen," "child caves," and (for the garden) "sunny corner."

Alexander then asks, "What is the difference between a place we instinctively enjoy, and one that seems empty or sad?" He notes that there is a "quality without a name" that gives a house, a town, or a courtyard its sense of beauty and worth, but he cannot put his finger on the exact description. After considering attribute after attribute—"whole," "eternal," "exact," "comfortable," "free,"—he finally chooses the word "aliveness." A house we enjoy visiting is in some mysterious way "alive."

I liked this emphasis. Even though I never believed I could or should predict a specific outcome for therapy, I did have one goal: to build together the kind of small local world where everyone feels "more safe, more free, and more alive" (Hoffman, 1993). Let me end this chapter with one of Alexander's attempts to explain "the quality without a name":

> It is never twice the same, because it always takes its shape from the particular place where it occurs. . . . In one place it is calm, in another it is stormy; in one person it is tidy; in another it is careless; in one house it is light; in another it is dark; in one room it is soft and quiet; in another it is yellow. In one family it is a love of picnics; in another dancing; in another playing poker; in another group of people it is not family life at all. (p. 26)

I have included this passage because it is so close to the way the Houston-Galveston group has always worked, deferring to a particular guiding quality, rather than following specific methods and techniques.

13

The Christmas Tree Village

Counter-Narratives

I first met Michael White in Adelaide back in the mid-1980s. I had been asked to be one of the speakers at an international conference on children and the family in New South Wales, and to give a workshop in Adelaide. White offered to be my guide or, the way I saw it, my "Nanny." It turned out that he and his wife, Cheryl, had a newborn of their own, and I was going on trips to the wine country and posing with kangaroos, so I didn't get to spend much time with him. However, I was intrigued with Adelaide and the group of bright and original-minded family therapists I met there. It didn't surprise me when White came up with the kind of right-angle ideas that baffle futurologists, because they do not follow a straight line of progression.

White and his New Zealand colleague David Epston (1990) were among the first persons in the field of family therapy to be inspired by the critical writings of French philosophers Michel Foucault (Hoy, 1986) and Jacques Derrida (Norris, 1991). Blending these ideas with offerings from cultural psychology (Bruner, 1990) and anthropology (Geertz, 1973; Myerhoff, 1980), they created a rich new tapestry that they called narrative therapy. The first time I saw White work in this way was in 1988 at a family therapy conference in the U.S. He showed us the tape of a session with a little boy with a soiling problem that illustrated a technique called "externalizing." The intention was to personify the problem so that it could be seen as an outside hostile force and then to form an alliance with its victims to defeat it. Using what they called "relative influence questions," they would ask how the problem influenced the person's life, and then how the person's life influenced the problem. This idea acknowledged the person's status as a sufferer, but also introduced the possibility of agency.

Pursuing this goal further, White and Epston might give the problem a name, like Trouble, or Mischief, or Sneaky Poo, depending on how the child or the family described it. Monster Busting and Fear Taming were other strategies for fending off threats to children's peace of mind. This technique had an instinctive naturalness and charm that appealed both to children and to the adults who came with them. They appealed to me, too. I felt that this was a way in which therapists could draw upon the language of the people they saw instead of the language in which they had been trained. The technique also undermined the tendency of psychiatric terms to locate emotional and behavioral disorders within the person.

The next time I saw White at work was on a videotape in the early '90s in which he was using a version of Tom Andersen's reflecting team. His interviews now included a reflecting team, transposed, following Myerhoff (1986), into a "definitional ceremony" that could provide witnesses for change. Using the metaphor of re-authoring lives, White (1995) would try to find a "preferred outcome" to serve as the basis for a counter-story. A teenager who was living in a detention home would mention that he had taken a shower that morning. White would ask, "Does this mean that you have begun to be your own caretaker?" If the young man nodded assent, he would turn to the father and say, "Were you surprised to hear this news about your son?" The "news" would then be echoed and built on by the reflecting team. Not surprisingly, the family members would become engaged in this optimistic procedure, and begin to add other evidence on their own.

While at first finding White's teaching practices too structured, I have come to admire what he does more and more. He is extremely personal in his style, constantly checking with the people he sees, picking up their language in the most careful way, while never being more than an inch away from their experience. I began using the adjective "tender" in watching his tapes, and I had never used that word to describe a therapist's work. There was something new here, something to do with the way a therapist might acknowledge her own emotions, as opposed to manipulating the emotions of those who consulted her. I also came to admire the intellectual consistency of White's theory-building. I felt that no other practitioner had succeeded in making such useful links between the poststructuralist wing of the postmodern movement and therapeutic practice.

But before I go into the details of White's work, let me go back to where I left off in Chapter 8 and sketch the intellectual journey that led to the allied concepts of deconstructionism and poststructuralism. Unlike the philosophical conversation out of which postmodernism emerged, this new strand became closely entwined with American literary theory. I will try to lay out its complicated history below.

The End of Structuralism

Looking back, you could say that the 20th century was a palace of structuralist thought. Every field offered an internal armature that explained its doings. Psychoanalyst Sigmund Freud gave us intrapsychic structures; psychologist Jean Piaget gave us cognitive structures; anthropologist Claude Lévi-Strauss gave us myth and kinship structures; sociologist Talcott Parsons gave us the normative structure of the nuclear family; linguistic philosopher Ferdinand de Saussure gave us structural linguistics; the New Criticism described the symbolic structures of literary works; and family systems theory introduced the idea of the family structure. So if you want to talk of poststructuralism, you must imagine all these London Bridges falling down at once.

I was alerted to this change by the buzz around narrative theory. Just as the New Critics had made a fetish of symbolic structures, the next wave of literary theorists seemed to be looking for laws of form similar to those of structural linguistics (Berman, 1988). Then came the encounter with deconstructionism. Dazzled by Derrida's invention, these theorists swerved away from the structuralist project and began to doubt the existence in a given text of any patterns at all. Scholars began to say that the meanings in a book were not placed there by the author but were created by the encounter between the reader and the work. An approach to literary criticism evolved known as reader response theory (Fish, 1980). In essence, this meant that every time someone read *War and Peace*, it was a different book.

With my early indoctrination into the New Criticism, I came into family therapy with a structuralist bias intact. New critics believed that literary works contained systems of meaning determined by the work's immanent structure (Berman, 1988). From my college days, I knew that poet T.S. Eliot thought of these structures as "objective correlatives," or concrete embodiments of abstract ideas. For instance, Melville's Great White Whale might symbolize a man's obsession or his struggle with evil. As these systems of meaning were usually not spelled out, a class of literary specialists arose whose life work was to discover and comment upon them. Nobody ever doubted that they were sitting there, in that poem, or in that novel, waiting to be found. I spent four years of college trying to do just that.

But this was pre-Derrida, whose ideas were instrumental in dismantling this whole empire. Although he grew up in the structuralist tradition of de Saussure, Derrida set out to revise it through a textual practice he called deconstructionism. He preferred this term to poststructuralism as a way to categorize his work, but the two cover similar ground. Gone was the belief that each text contained a core of meaning the way a bowl contained an apple. The text had not one but an infinite number of meanings, and the dominance of any one meaning was only an illusion because all other meanings had been "suppressed" or "deferred." Derrida called these suppressed meanings "traces," and pried them out in close readings of works by Nietzsche or Marx or Freud.

It was not Derrida's intention, however, to attack the ideas of any particular philosopher. He said, "Deconstruction does not consist in passing from one concept to another, but in overturning and displacing a conceptual order" (Derrida, 1982, p. 329). In fact, it was only in the moment of deconstruction that one could "see" beyond the boundaries of the conceptual order that was being displaced. In a wonderful image reminiscent of the flybottle, Derrida spoke of "trying to find a crevice through which the yet unnameable glimmer beyond the closure can be glimpsed" (1976, p. 14). Like Wittgenstein, Derrida was aware of the need to see beyond or through the linguistic structures that color what we think is real.

Then where did the term poststructuralism come from? As far as I can ascertain, Derrida's ideas about deconstructing texts spread like wildfire across the intellectual landscape. No literary monument was safe, and the demigods of Anglo-European social and literary theory were being pushed off their pedestals. In the U.S., with its strong tradition of literary criticism, a group of American critics (Berman, 1988) developed their own deconstructionist outlook, which they called poststructuralism. Here is one description of its provenance (Poster, 1989):

> The term poststructuralist, local to certain intellectual circles in the United States, draws a line of affinity around several French theorists who are rarely so grouped in France and who in many cases would reject the designation. . . . Americans have assimilated Foucault, Derrida, and the rest by turning their positions into "poststructuralist theory." (p. 4)

By the end of the 20th century, these ideas had begun to shake the foundations of American social thought.

In the field of psychology, not surprisingly, a similar un-doing was going on. Psychologists were deploring the concept of an essentialist self that grew hydroponically without reference to context. A major proponent of this view was cognitive researcher (and charming writer) Jerome

Bruner (1986). Influenced by the Russian linguist Lev Vygotsky (1978), Bruner stated that culture was constitutive of self and self was situated in culture. He was also a key person in bringing narrative theory to psychology, pushing the idea that the narrative mode, not the truth or logic mode, was uniquely suited to the study of human life (1986, p. 13). He also believed that the organizing principle of folk psychology was story-like, and that "what does *not* get structured narratively suffers loss in memory" (1990, p. 56).

Psychoanalysts Roy Schafer (1981) and Donald Spence (1984) were among the first clinicians to attack the "truth" approach to emotional problems. The idea of the psychoanalyst digging for the the buried city of Troy was a persuasive one, given the modernist belief in hidden structures, but Spence and Schafer declared that the archeology metaphor was wrong. They argued for a "narrative retelling," not an excavation of pots and shards. The therapist's job was to help his client create a story with aesthetic appeal and ability to persuade, not to find out what was "really there." In one bound, these pioneers used narrative theory to leap over the modernist views bequeathed to them by their predecessors. Of course, there was one modernist aspect they overlooked: the idea of the "better story." This immediately introduces hierarchy and puts the therapist in the position of editor-in-chief.

Although Spence and Schafer described the territory, they did not capture the name. White and Epston (1990) took the term "narrative" for their own approach and made it stick. One great strength was that they brought in an anthropological mindset. Bruner (1990) had pointed out that you cannot study the mind without studying the nexus between mind and culture. This resonated with White and Epston's multicultural, gender-sensitive point of view. Where psychology locates problems within the person, postmodern anthropology focuses on the specific idiom of each culture and calls into question the universals on which modern psychology is built.

Reconfiguring Foucault

It is a short step from Bruner's world of cultural psychology to the view that we are shaped by the conventions of institutional discourse. Enter the work of French philosopher Michel Foucault (1972). White and Epston drew many of their best ideas from the writings of this gifted reconfigurer. If Bruner calls attention to the idea of cultural narratives, Foucault calls attention to institutional narratives. Haunting the dusty archives of the Bibliothèque Nationale in Paris, he pulled out firsthand accounts that made visible the evolution of each institution he studied. His inquiries into the changing discourses of madness (1965), justice (1979), sexuality (1978), and medicine (1975), from premodern to modern, laid out "the disciplines of the self" through which modern institutions stamped out subversive behavior before it even began.

In his book *Discipline and Punish* (1979), Foucault researched back to a time before the existence of the modern penal system and found an account of a botched attempt to draw and quarter a condemned man. In a scene out of Monty Python, the man kept trying to give pointers to his bumbling executioners. Foucault contrasted this grisly event with the orderliness of 18th-century French prisons and the efficiency of the guillotine. By taking what he called a "genealogical" approach to the development of modern bureaucracies, Foucault raised our consciousness about the taken-for-granted structures and procedures that control our lives. Unlike the old days, when centralized authorities like kings and judges supervised the conduct of their citizens, often brutally, this new type of governance operates so invisibly that we obey it without thought.

White and Epston (1990) apply a similar consciousness-raising to the received truths of psychiatry. For them, diagnostic categories are a way the culture imposes its "dominant narratives" on people's "lived experience." But instead of simply pointing out the flaws in the canon, which is what the anti-psychiatry movement has so often done, White and Epston come up with useful alternatives. The practice of externalization makes individuals aware of the powerful narratives that are running their lives. A similar idea is contained in the "telling and re-telling" processes of reflecting teams. Such techniques help people to stand outside the situations they are caught in and see them in a different light.

One psychological myth that White (1995) cheerfully beheads is the belief in "essences" that lie below the surface of the psyche. Individually-oriented therapists have claimed that what they do is superior to short-term therapy because the latter only treats symptoms and not the underlying cause. Mirroring Jay Haley's (1963) long-ago objection, White questions this surface/depth dichotomy. As a substitute, he proposes the anthropological distinction between "thick" and "thin" description (Geertz, 1973). White says that to speak of individuals in terms of traits, needs, or attributes is to rely on the "thin" identity categories of modern culture rather than the "thick" descriptions of narrative practice. These terms are a helpful substitute for categories like functional/dysfunctional or normal/abnormal, and many clinicians have adopted them with relief.

In another departure from the canon, White rejects the idea that attributes like "identity" or "authenticity" are traits that can be ascribed to the individual. For him, they are always the product of social negotiation. In helping people to discover "who they really are," he says, modern therapies rely on a process of private introspection guided by an expert. In contrast,

White believes that nothing is authentic until it has been acknowledged in a public space. He draws upon ethnographer Barbara Myerhoff's (1986) term "definitional ceremonies" to describe such rituals. A definitional ceremony is any made-up procedure that allows people to bear witness to and give significance to persons or events that would otherwise go unnoticed.

White has also taken from Myerhoff (1982) the concept of "re-membering." Myerhoff talks of a special type of recollection, one which highlights the important presences that have graced a person's story, whether they are alive or not alive, nearby or far away. In the same vein, White asks people he is working with, "Who would you want to have in the club of your life? He describes his invention as follows:

> The membership of this association of life is composed of the significant figures of a person's history and those figures of the person's contemporary circumstances of life whose voices are influential in regard to matters of personal identity. Re-membering provides an opportunity for persons to engage in a revision of the membership of the association of life. (1999, p. 66)

In his workshops, White says that these re-membering practices correct the distortions caused by the Western belief in a coherent or unified Self. White suggests we use a multi-voiced concept of identity instead. I think one reason the format of the reflecting team appealed to him was because it so graphically embodied a perspective with many heads.

White (1997) deconstructs other structuralist terms like hierarchy and boundaries. He feels that these concepts do little except protect the power of professionals over the people who consult with them. Deploring the fact that a therapist whose life is affected by the life of a so-called client can be faulted for losing boundaries, he says, "We have an obligation to identify how conversations with those who consult us change our lives." After years of secretly rebelling against the fetish of the boundary in my work, and resenting the way it threw up walls between myself and the people who consulted me, I found in White's blunt statement a refreshing truth.

Poststructuralism and Beyond

And now, here comes a question. In his criticism of traditional psychotherapy, White (1997) leans on the insights of poststructuralism rather than postmodernism. Why does he prefer this term? Why does he no longer use the idea of deconstruction, which appeared in an earlier essay (Epston & White, 1992)? I don't know, but I have an idea. Wittgenstein and Derrida believed that the accepted canons of philosophy and social thought had been influenced by the essences and structures of Platonism. They both tried to make the familiar strange by pulling conventional concepts out of their usual sockets. Under the banner of poststructuralism, White has simply applied the same "outing" maneuver to the shadow architecture of modern psychotherapy.

Then what about Foucault, the Great Original, who neither took a clear position nor aligned himself with anyone else's position? Unlike Wittgenstein and Derrida, he had in his cross-hairs not the deceptions of language but the discourses of disciplinary institutions. He set out to expose the "capillary" nature of power and the way it pervaded the most ordinary exchange. In the past, activist meta-narratives like Marxism pitted a generic "us" against a generic "them." Foucault did not lead us to the barricades, but he did something perhaps more useful. He gave us the tools to first recognize, then take action, against what has been called the micro-fascism of everyday life.

Perhaps this was why White and Epston took Foucault as their guide. In a manner of speaking, Foucault was one of the first persons to use externalizing techniques as a means of making visible the practices of oppression. By staining the germs on the slide, so to speak, he offered us the ability to first perceive and then resist them. The discourse of mental health is permeated with dynamics and essences that colonize and degrade personhood, and part of the narrative therapist's mission is to flush this operation out. One thing White does particularly well is to deconstruct humanistic language, showing, for example, that concepts like "self-actualization" and "personal growth" dissolve as soon as you begin to question developmental metaphors for identity and container metaphors for the self.

At this point, I asked myself about the similarities and differences between the collaborative and narrative approaches. These two schools do agree strongly on one theme: the therapist takes a back seat. For Anderson and Goolishian, it is important that the therapist defer to the family's expertise, allowing the presumption of knowledge to be more fairly distributed throughout the conversation. For White (1995), the task is not to deny the therapist's knowledge but to decenter it. White hands off much of the work of re-authoring to other persons in the family or community, perhaps aided by members of a reflecting team. One other thing Anderson and White have in common is that they are both improvisational theater directors. They may set the scene for a transformative event, but they let it unfold on its own.

There are also many differences. Despite the fact that White and Anderson both take aim at the essentialism of modern schools of psychotherapy, Anderson's theorizing stays at the level of the general stance (the emphasis on not-knowing) and the therapeutic relationship (the emphasis on collaboration). She is clear about her distrust of essentialist ideas, but she offers general, not specific methods for dealing with them. In contrast, White and Epston actively counteract the myths of psychotherapy that put people into belittling categories. They give people documents of self-worth or certificates that testify to courage. They set up "leagues" for people with common conditions or handicaps. Some of their best deconstructive questions challenge professional hierarchies: patient to psychiatrist, "How does this new medication you are prescribing for me fit into your plans for my life?" In that sense their stance is very "knowing" indeed.

Anderson seems to feel more at home within the framework of postmodernism, which outlaws the representational view of reality along with modernist "meta-narratives," but makes no other claim that can be translated directly into practice. By adopting the framework of Poststructuralism, on the other hand, White not only challenges psychotherapy but also hits at the disciplinary discourses and procedures clarified by Foucault. Since day one, the narrative school has promoted an "ethic of accountability," emphasizing the duty of therapists to counteract, or at least make people aware of, the consequences of harmful interpersonal myths. As a result, the narrative approach is becoming a larger consciousness-raising movement for persons whose position of privilege has protected them from noticing the effect of this privilege on other peoples' lives.

What differentiates the activism of poststructural approaches from plain vanilla activism is its emphasis on a Foucauldian consciousness. The enemy is not any single person, group, or ideology, but the pejorative language games that haunt our ordinary exchanges. Here the enemy is the flybottle, which stands for the culturally accepted ways of thinking and talking that control our postures and beliefs.

Communities of Concern

What seems radical to me about White's approach is the way he creates small, local communities as witnesses for suffering and change. These bodies function as a kind of therapeutic Greek chorus, or attending community. As I said above, they can be composed of persons from an audience or from a reflecting team, but they can also consist of friends or relatives who are already in the picture. White has begun to keep an "outsider witness" registry on which he will put names of persons he has worked with who are willing to help others with similar problems. These outsider witness groups have proved to be enormously effective in bringing their perspectives to bear on someone else's life. I will offer one or two examples here of such ad hoc communities by describing two of the videotapes White has shown in workshops over the years. The first interview was with the family of a ten-year-old boy who would probably be called in the U.S. a "conduct disorder."

The social worker who was trying to work with him described him as "never speaking to therapists" and "leaving therapists in tears." It was she who had brought the child and his parents in for a consultation.

The boy was a robust, ten-year-old charmer whom I will call Greg. He initially lived up to his billing as a non-talker, but each time he shrugged off a question, White merely turned to the parents and asked the same question of them. They would answer and White would turn to the boy and ask if he agreed. Greg would nod or shrug and in this way he began to be threaded into the conversation. His mother told White that he had recently begun to behave better at school but was still doing alarming things at home. She recited a number of incidents, like coming at her with a knife and pushing his brother off a bike. She was particularly worried by the bad headaches he was having.

White asked Greg if he worried about these things too. He said "Yah." "You worry about dangerous situations?" "Yah." "Why?" "So I don't get hurt." It turned out that he didn't like the "aggression" he encountered at school. His mother told White that he was having less trouble at school than before, so White asked him if he would rather bring his school achievement into the home or his trouble at home into the school. No answer. White stopped the videotape to inform his workshop audience that this was not a good question. Then, on the tape, he took a piece of paper and asked Greg to draw a picture of home as "Trouble's home territory." Would he like to "squeeze Trouble out of Trouble's home territory?" Greg said, "Yah."

White then asked the parents how Greg had kept Trouble from "ruining things at school." His parents spoke of several ways he did this, like telling himself to walk away from fights. Then White asked him, "Is this idea of being an adviser to yourself new or recent?" Greg said he'd had the idea for about a year. White got him to agree that this was part of "caring more for his life." Then he asked the parents if they were surprised to hear this. When they said they were, he asked Greg if it was good for them to know this. Greg answered, "Yah." White asked him why he thought this, and he said, using a whole sentence, "So they'll know what I'm up to."

Greg's newfound loquacity astounded everyone, and he kept it up. Toward the end of the interview, White asked Greg if he'd ever been asked so many questions, and Greg said no. On a scale of one to ten for answering questions, where would he put himself? "Ten." When asked if that was good or bad, he said "Good." When asked if it made him feel better or worse about himself, he said, "Better." White asked the parents if they approved of the idea that their son was developing these "skills in caring for his life," and they said they did.

This is where other therapists might stop, but White went on to ask who else in the family had these skills. The answer was Greg's grandparents and a couple of cousins. Would they make a good audience for hearing about the skills Greg was developing? Yes. Everyone then agreed with White that it would be useful for him to ask some of these relatives to a future meeting and listen to their thoughts on this subject. The feedback from that session and the later one with the relatives was that Greg's behavior changed dramatically for the good. The parents told White that they were amazed at how much their son had talked in the interview and that he was behaving much more reasonably at home.

Following this general tack, White (1997) has gone on to create "communities of concern" out of many other kinds of presences: imaginary friends, stuffed animals, even people who are dead. In another taped interview, which White (1997) has also written about, he was meeting with a woman whose husband had just died and who was overwhelmed with grief. The woman was proposing to take her own life so that she could be buried beside her husband, and she had indeed made one unsuccessful attempt. White had helped her to overcome some feelings of depression a few years before and she had come back to see him.

In this very shortened account of the session that I saw, the widow had told White that her friends would be angry if she took her own life, but that her husband would understand. When White asked her to describe the behavior of these friends she said, "Exceptionally egotistical." When he asked what her husband would say to her, she said he would want her to "be herself." White then asked if it was positive or negative to bring her husband's voice into the conversation, and she said it was positive. She added, "He was with me downstairs." White then asked the woman when her husband was with her most, and she said, "When coming here." In fact, she said, he was sitting right next to her at that moment. White asked her if his presence helped her "get on with her life," and she said, "Yes." She said that he often came and sat with her at moments when she was thinking about him. White said he would like to help her bring her husband more frequently into her life and she said she would like him to do that.

Before she left, White asked if there was anything in his room she would like to take with her. She pointed to a stuffed bear sitting on the windowsill. This was a bear called Rupert that she herself had made some years before and "gifted" to White. White thought of him as a "stuffed team member" and had often sent him out to stay with children who wanted "to break free of the problems in their lives." Rupert had come back from his latest adventure with a torn ear, so the woman said she would take him home and fix it. White asked if she knew why he was so well worn, and she said, "Because he's been loved." White added that Rupert was not only very accepting but able to keep wisdom to himself. The woman replied, "Like

Bill." Hugging the bear, she said, "One of the things I miss most is touching Bill."

In a subsequent interview, she told Michael that when her granddaughter came to visit, she overheard her talking about Bill to Rupert. Shortly after that, when she went out to rake leaves, which she hadn't done since Bill died, his voice came to her. She also heard him when she went out to the back garden. White found out that another voice in her life was her father's, who had died when she was quite small. White asked her an interesting question: "If you could keep Bill's voice in your life as long as you have kept your father's, how old would you be then?" He also asked how it was that her granddaughter could speak with Bill too, and wondered whether she had passed that ability along.

In the discussion after the tape was shown, a member of the audience asked White about the fact that he had paid so little attention to helping the woman "work through her grief." White said that during the first couple of interviews she had been weeping copiously, and that he had been weeping right along with her. It is not hard to imagine him doing that. What is hard to convey is the sweetness that pervades these conversations. In addition to their lightness of touch, one is struck by the intense emotional connections that arise spontaneously and affect everyone who is there.

The Christmas Tree Village

During the late '90s, I was interested in creating documents that acted like reflecting teams in print. "Tekka with Feathers," a series of commentaries on the work we had done with one of our families in Brattleboro, was one example (see Chapter 10), but I wanted to do more of these pieces. You might say that in those days I went about with my butterfly net looking for stories with wings, like the one depicted on the cover of one of Michael White's books. The next example that fluttered into my life came out of a project the Family Institute of Maine had been funded to do. The Institute had received a grant for working with families who were struggling with AIDS, and the director, Cindy Osborne, asked me to join one of their cases as a reflecting team member.

Michael White had come a few times to the institute to give intensive workshops, and Osborne and Chris Behan, a narrative therapist on the staff, were particularly interested in experimenting with White's version of a reflecting team. So I joined their team during an interview that Behan was conducting with a gay couple he had been seeing for several months. The younger of the two men had AIDS and was failing fast, so I suggested that I try to create a document that would testify to their story and also address the question of what effect a reflecting team had on the therapy process.

Here is an account of the situation as I became aware of it and of the inter-view in which I took part. As I have done before in describing these events, I will use first names.

Meeting with us beforehand, Chris told the team that he had been see-ing Bob and his partner Mark for about a year. Now that Mark's health was declining, his family wanted him to come back to live with them, but he preferred to stay with Bob in the home they had created together. Early on, the couple had drawn for Chris a series of concentric circles on newsprint. Mark said that when he came to the end he wanted Bob to be in the inner circle, his parents in the next ring, and his grandparents and brother in the ring outside that.

Chris had explored the effect of the "dominant discourse" of homo-phobia on the couple, and found that Mark's relations, especially his grand-mother, were having a hard time honoring the couple's relationship. Complicating matters, Mark had become a born-again Christian at age 13 and had come out as a gay man at age 20. He felt torn between the dictates of his faith and being active in the gay community. Gradually, Chris said, the couple had begun to be more open about their relationship. They had begun wearing matching gold bands and were now planning Mark's funeral. Chris had helped Mark to deal more directly with his family, with the result that Bob was no longer in the middle.

Chris filled in the picture with more detail. For many years, at Christmas time, Bob and Mark had hauled pine trees down from northern Maine, where Mark grew up, and sold them at the side of the road. Mark, disap-pointed that this year he was too sick to help run the stand, busied himself setting up the miniature village they placed each year under their tree. This village had grown over time to include houses and shops, a tiny skating rink, and a diminutive railroad whose train regularly passed through town. The little village and its train had become an important symbol of Bob and Mark's relationship.

The session I sat in on was made up of Chris, Bob, and Mark sitting together in the middle of the room, and the team sitting against the wall. Chris introduced us. The team that day consisted of Cindy, the director, psychiatrist Tony McCann, psychologist Eric Aronson, and myself, with social worker Penny Backman sitting in. Chris explained to Bob and Mark that the five of us would later be commenting on what the three of them had said, and that Penny was acting as an observer. This team had a floating membership and had met with Chris and the couple once before. At that time, some of the team members did not want to use a reflecting format, preferring to talk to the couple face to face. As those persons were not pres-ent this time, we decided to follow the usual procedure where the team reflects and the family and therapist listen in, then switch places.

In the beginning of the session, Chris asked the couple what was going on for each of them. Mark described feeling as if there were two people inside him, a gay man and a born-again Christian, and that he had to keep them from offending each other. He said, "The two people inside of me have agreed to get along even though they don't agree." Bob said that he had accepted Mark's right-wing affiliations, even though he didn't share them. He felt that in a couple, each person had to make compromises in order to make the other person happy. I was impressed by how each partner put his love for the other ahead of the personal ideologies that divided them.

Chris then asked Mark to read a letter he had composed to be read at his funeral. In it he declared his faith in Christ and said that he did not believe that God was punishing him and that he knew he was going to Heaven. It ended: "Thank you all for being part of my life. It may have been briefer than most, but I assure you that I enjoyed every day and lived it to the fullest. I love you and will see you again soon."

Chris now asked the team to share their thoughts. We had agreed to speak not as professionals but as persons who had been allowed into a very private space. Cindy and Tony both remarked on Mark's depiction of the two people inside himself. Tony said he was reminded of how well gay people keep secrets, because they get so much practice being one way at home and another way in public. Cindy was reminded of the time she was visiting the Holocaust Museum in Washington and found out that Martin Luther was anti-Semitic. As she had been brought up Lutheran, she said, this shook her to the soul. What was different from the usual clinic-speak was that they talked about the issues that had been raised in the interview with reference to their own lives.

When it came to me, I said that I found it hard to deal with the idea that Mark was dying, despite the fact that he was the same age as my own grown children. I said I was touched by his saying that he would be in Heaven waiting for us and I also thanked Bob for his part in taking care of Mark. Eric said that as he listened to Mark's letter for the funeral he found himself asking, "What is Bob's place in that funeral?" He commented on Bob's statement that he had to hide his feelings for Mark in public and wondered if that might change. Mark had previously asked whether he should edit his speech, so Tony said passionately that he did not believe anything should be cut at all.

After listening to these comments, Chris, Bob, and Mark got back into their small circle while the team moved back to the sidelines. Mark related strongly to Tony's description of gay people being better at keeping secrets and described how difficult it was to put on a different face depending on whom he was with. Bob's associations were to the movie *The Remains of the*

Day, where Anthony Hopkins passes up the chance to show his affection for Emma Thompson. He said that he himself never showed emotion, so he was glad when Tony expressed how strongly he felt about Mark's speech. He also said that it was important for Mark to tell people, especially the older people in his birth family, what his beliefs are, and to say that even though he's gay he still believes he's going to Heaven. Then Bob shared the fact that it was hard for him to accept a compliment for something that a person would do automatically. If he took care of Mark, it was because it came from his heart, and he didn't think anyone should thank him for it.

Chris now asked Penny, who was listening as an outside observer, for her thoughts. She said that she had been asking herself if there were enough energy coming from a format like a reflecting team to make a difference to a couple seeking help. What she found was a theme about dichotomies. She noted how each reflection placed one view in opposition to another, with both views being held "in the same breath, in the same person, in the same way of thinking." She ended by saying, "So I felt that the idea of holding these oppositions was what caught energy." I liked Penny's phrasings, but noticed that her assignment required her to operate from a "metaposition," while the rest of us were trying to inhabit a more horizontal space. White uses the term "experience-near" for this latter posture.

The two groups now sat together and exchanged reactions. Cindy asked the couple what difference it made having the two groups speak separately rather than face to face. Bob and Mark said there were advantages either way. The large group felt "more like family," but not having to respond immediately was seen as helpful too. Tony wanted to hear from Bob and Mark how it felt to be asked to comment on what the consultants said. He told them that from the viewpoint of his own training, asking a client to answer the question "What had an impact on you?" would seem like heresy. Bob and Mark said they were very comfortable with the question and thought it made sense. Chris made a date with them for two weeks later.

This was the last time any of us except Chris saw Mark alive. Chris told me later that the couple only met with him a few more times, but that, toward the end, the two of them were able to draw a magic circle around their relationship. After he was hospitalized, for instance, Mark allowed Bob to give him a foot massage in public. At this point, the question of who would be with Mark at the end took center stage. Mark's relatives, especially his grandmother, assumed that it would be limited to the family. Aided by Chris, Bob was able to arrange a parting ritual that included everyone. He got the family members to agree that, when it was time, they would go one by one into Mark's room and say goodbye. Bob would then rejoin Mark and would be with him when he died. And this is what happened. I was deeply impressed by this outcome, and told Chris that I felt it might never have happened if it were not for him.

After Mark died, the team met one more time. Chris told us that Bob and Mark had asked him to say a few words at Mark's funeral and that he had considered not speaking because of his concerns about confidentiality and overstepping professional bounds. However, he had thought better of it. He said, "I needed to acknowledge how I had been touched by Mark in this life. I needed to ignore what Lynn calls 'the fetish of the therapeutic boundary.'"

Chris's eulogy to Mark is too long to quote verbatim, so I will condense and paraphrase it. He spoke about the strange position he was in of being Mark's therapist, because he felt that if clients knew he might speak at their funeral, they might not tell him much. So he said he wouldn't tell any secrets about Mark. However, he did want to mention Mark's enormous capacity to love. The proof was that Mark was able to love both the family he was born into and his family of choice, despite their differences. Chris went on to talk about what a gifted teacher Mark was, and what he had taught Chris about courage and dignity and honesty. He talked about Mark's sense of humor and the jokes he cracked in the hospital. He said that Mark was "the kind of man who could contain complexity" and that he had an incredible ability to bring opposites together.

Chris then said that he knew how sad the people there were feeling, and that it was okay to feel sad, and also to feel relief that Mark was no longer suffering. He said: "All those feelings are okay, even anger is a normal feeling to have. Anger because he's gone, anger because his life was too short. He was 33 years old." Chris commented on how many funerals he had gone away from angry because nobody there had been able to say the word AIDS. He noted the many people there wearing red ribbons, which stands for AIDS awareness, and talked about the courage it took to say, "I am not going to be silent about this." Chris praised Mark for having the courage to stand up to the employer who fired him from his final job and to say how wrong that was. He commented on the loss for the world that "someone so young and so brave and so handsome and so funny and so sweet" was gone.

Then Chris told his audience about the idea of "saying hello again," a concept he had learned from Michael White. He wanted to join Mark in his belief that we would all say hello again in the hereafter. Another way people could say hello was by seeing Mark in themselves. Chris said, "Every time you realize you are sticking up for justice and fighting discrimination, every time you have a sense of humor against incredible odds, that's the way you can say hello again to Mark." A final way to say hello to Mark was to think of a wonderful memory of him right then. And Chris produced one, saying:

> We'll be able to remember Mark when we see a tiny train and a miniature village beneath a glimmering Christmas tree. I don't think any of us will ever be able to see a Christmas tree, for whatever reason, again, without thinking of Mark. We will be able to say hello again to Mark, even though we have said goodbye.

After reading this eulogy, I went out and bought a Christmas tree ornament in memory of Mark—a shiny colored-glass engine that hangs on my tree each year. It has now graced several trees, and it will go down to my children, together with a copy of the story, when I die.

Coda

In the months after Mark died, Bob felt the loss bitterly and kept very much to himself, but Chris saw him alone a few times to round things off. I was now finishing the document we were calling *The Christmas Tree Village*. I felt throughout as if I were a scribe composing a history as it ran parallel to my own. This was inevitable, I suppose, since I had come in as a stranger to sit in on a team that was only just getting itself together. It was presumptuous to think that I could have any kind of relationship to the couple. I think Cindy wanted me to be a consultant, but that would have been inappropriate. As a result, I kept a respectful distance and leaned on long-distance channels like transcripts and the phone.

I did have some influence on the materials we used. As Chris and Bob's meetings were tapering off, I asked Cindy if she could sit in on one of these meetings and get some feedback on the couple's experience with us. Bob agreed to the meeting. In the audiotape of this conversation, he said that he had thought a lot about our comments in regard to his being "giving" and wondered if they were really true. He finally decided that if they were true, it was Mark who made this possible, because Mark himself was so giving. In regard to the reflecting team, he was ambivalent. He said that he didn't hold with counseling but that being in a one-on-one with Chris, whether there was a reflecting team or not, made it easier to open up and talk. He said that Mark's being the kind of person he was made it more comfortable, too.

Cindy commented on Bob's idea that Mark may have helped him to be more giving and asked what he would do with this description of himself now that Mark was no longer in his life. Bob said he had learned to open his mouth a little more. In the past, he would bite his tongue rather than jeopardize his job, but now he hears Mark's voice in his head saying, "Come on, Bob, speak up." He talked about two new employees at his job who were gay and another who was very open in her hatred of them, and how he was trying to deal with the situation himself, without involving his boss.

Cindy then asked if Bob were beginning to define himself as "a man who opens his mouth," and Bob said yes, that he was beginning to speak up to people who were being discriminating or vicious, "otherwise nothing would change." Cindy remarked to Chris that the idea of Bob being "giving" was larger than it looked. Chris answered that he was hearing how Bob kept Mark alive by standing up against discrimination and homophobia. Something else that kept Mark alive was the idea that being a caring person was not just being gentle and sweet but strong and powerful too.

Chris then asked what effect, if any, the team had on their immediate relationships. Bob said that the team had helped Mark to be more open with his mother and to express his feelings about the people in his family who couldn't accept his being gay. As for the two of them, it had drawn them more closely together and helped them talk about hard issues like religion. Chris asked about Mark's allowing Bob to touch him in public, and Bob said that Mark had let Bob nurse him during the final days. Finally, Cindy asked Bob about his reaction to the entire process, and he said he thought that on the whole it was a good idea, as long as the people involved were comfortable with each other. He said that sometimes, at the end of a session, a team member would ask if there were any more things they wanted to comment on, and they would say no, but as soon as they got outside they would talk non-stop.

Bob had one criticism about the reflecting team, which was that he wished they would have met more often. He said that Mark missed the group when he was in the hospital. The team was an important social contact for him, because toward the end his connections had dwindled down to only his mother and Bob. Cindy turned to Chris and asked for his final comments too. Chris said that even though he was proud to have been involved in this experience, part of it didn't feel real to him. He didn't know whether that was because Mark wasn't there anymore, but there was a dreamlike quality to it. Cindy asked if that might be because when they stopped working with Bob and Mark, the AIDS project stopped too. Chris said, "So then I woke up?" and everyone laughed.

This story, with a color photograph of Bob and Mark smiling in front of their Christmas tree village, was published privately in January 1999 by a group of generous sponsors who wished to support Bob and Mark and Chris. Many copies went out and I shall always treasure mine. But before I end this chapter, here are two afterthoughts. First, Bob's objection to being complimented was an important message for me. White has criticized the "culture of applause," as he calls it, and its unfortunate influence on the comments of reflecting teams. An unthinking addiction to the positive has dogged many therapy approaches, raising suspicions of insincerity and manipulation. Even though I have been one of the addicts, I was glad that White came up with such a useful alternative, the move to "thick description."

Second, I want to say something about the concept of "saying hello." This is one of White's most gifted understandings, not only for dealing with situations of loss and grief, but for challenging psychological dogma. First, it feels intuitively correct (think of all the cultures that vivify the spirits of the dead). Second, it offers an alternative to the idea that people must free themselves from negative feelings by "working through them" with a trained professional. I thought that the way Chris described "saying hello" in his eulogy was profound. Here was yet another example of a way of thinking that sees each dilemma as an opportunity for community. I believe more and more that effective therapy is not individual but communal, even when the individual is the focus of the work.

This might also be the place to note that "saying hello again" may come in many shapes and sizes. Remember, reader, when I told you that my dream was someday to be on the same stage with Haley at an important conference? That dream came true, but not in the way I imagined. In 1995, Haley and I were invited to be on the faculty of a conference organized by the Milton H. Erickson Foundation called *The Evolution of Psychotherapy*. Present were legendary figures like Thomas Szasz, Joseph Wolpe, and James Hillman, and some of the stars of family therapy as well. As the conference was attended by thousands and was held in a vast barn of a place, I only glimpsed Haley in passing. Then the time came for a faculty picture. I was shown to a room where a series of rising platforms had been set up. Haley had been placed on the top platform on the left and I was directed to the bottom platform on the right. The picture was taken. I had to leave quickly, but when the picture came to me a few weeks later, I was surprised. Haley and I were standing next to each other on the top row, shoulder to shoulder. When I asked Jeffrey Zeig, the organizer of the conference, how this could be, he merely told me, "Computer Magic."

14

Knowing of the Third Kind

The Worrybox

The paradigm shift that led to concepts like postmodernism allowed therapists to break out of the ocular metaphors of the past and engage with other sensory channels. When I first encountered the Bateson group in the '60s, the main modality was that of vision, perspective, view. In the '80s, I moved out of this channel into one of listening and voice. Carol Gilligan's work supported this more connected style and a new politics of voice, which spread to any silenced group, came into play. I also became aware of the limits of what linguist Walter Ong (1982) has called "the consciousness of literacy," as opposed to "the consciousness of orality." I began to question the "three Ts"—teachers, training, and texts—that academic and professional fields have built on since Aristotle.

Now I am aware of another shift. I find that I am using a channel that has to do with sensed feelings and emotions—not the within-person kind bequeathed to us by individual psychology, but something more like an underground communication system. Being touched or moved, sending signals, receiving images, this is the vocabulary that keeps beckoning to me now. When I first saw Tom Andersen work, I knew that we were going into a more kinetic space, and I began to shape my work in that direction too, but there weren't many people putting this into words.

For this reason, I was grateful to John Shotter (1993a) for tackling this problem head on. Shotter was inspired by a passage by 18th-century thinker

Gianbattista Vico (1968), who wondered why philosophers were so concerned with nature, which only God knows, to the neglect of civil society, which is something men should know. Shotter, looking for a way to describe what goes on in our day-to-day social life, struggles for a language that as yet does not exist. Into this space, he launches the concept of "knowing of the third kind":

> It is not theoretical knowledge (a "knowing that" . . .) for it is knowledge in practice, nor is it merely knowledge of a craft or skill ("knowing how"), for it is joint knowledge, knowledge-held-in-common with others. It is a third kind of knowledge, *sui generis*, that cannot be reduced to either of the other two, the kind of knowledge one has from *within* a situation, a group, social institution or society . . . (1993a)

Shotter states that the experience people have when performing together on a ouija board is typical of the joint knowledge he is trying to describe. It is "an unbroken flow of responsivity," all the more difficult to study because it relies on "oral, preliterate (but not pre-linguistic) non-conceptual, non-logical, poetic, rhetorical forms of communication . . ." (1993b, p. 63).

To clarify further this third kind of knowing, Shotter refers to Vico's (1968) example of the experience of thunder in a preliterate society. One person feels afraid and sees that other people show the same emotion. It occurred to me that what Shotter calls a "moment of common reference" resembles the signals that occur in species like the slime mold, which can send out a simultaneous directive to all its individuals to form a fruiting stalk. Another example is a nest of fire ants, which can sting in unison. I asked myself what a good example would be from my own field. Prompted by Vico's thunder, I decided that the story of the worrybox might fit here very well.

This story was told to me by family therapist Amy Urry in Devonshire, England, and the family involved gave their permission for me to retell it here. During a session with an little boy of eight, whose family had brought him to see her because he was fearful and anxious, she said that everyone has "worryboxes." The boy said he would like to make a drawing of his own worrybox, and drew a figure with a box inside its chest. Then he looked dissatisfied and said that there was something missing. He said, "I have to draw my Mum because she has a worrybox too." So he drew his mother and her bigger worrybox, and then he said, "There's a channel that connects our worryboxes," and drew a kind of pipe between them. He then said, "The problem is that my Mum's worrybox doesn't have a lid on it and when it gets filled up, it overflows into mine." Urry asked him about his dad's worrybox, so he drew his father standing between him and his mother and said, "My Dad's worrybox is in his throat—that's why he coughs so much—he can cough his worries out, but it's very high and there's a tight lid on it, so I bypass his and go on to Mum's." His mother and father didn't have a channel between their worryboxes, but the channel that linked him and his Mum was a very thick one and it detoured up over his father's head like an arch.

That is all I remember of the story, but the "worrybox" idea began to haunt me. It seemed to me that this child had an intuitive understanding of the nature of social communication. Perhaps he was right, and we all have worryboxes linked by pipelines. I began to have the image of underground rivers flowing between people when they connect. I was always trying to break free from my individually-oriented background and find some way to describe the transactions that go on between people as if they were light displays.

This is why I was so glad to run into psychologist Janet Bavelas and her group at the University of Victoria in British Columbia. She is one of the few researchers I know who has zeroed in on this area. After co-authoring *Pragmatics of Human Communication* (Watzlawick, Bavelas, & Jackson, 1967), she didn't rest on her laurels but went on to test some of the book's insights empirically (1992). One of the aspects of her work that resonated strongly with me was her assumption that emotions are better described as performances people take part in, rather than experiences within them. Let me describe two of the experiments she showed me the first time I visited her in the early '90s.

In the first one, Bavelas (Bavelas, Black, Lemery, & Mullett, 1986) wanted to test whether an empathic response was an instinctive inner reaction or a response to social cues, so she videotaped two students who carried a heavy television into the room and placed it upon a table in front of students waiting for a class. One of the students had a splint on his finger, and he purposefully dropped the television on it. The next four seconds were the crux of the study. In Version One, the apparently injured student made eye contact with one observer. The split-screen videotape showed that this observer immediately demonstrated empathy with him by wincing and showing a pained expression. In Version Two, the bandaged student held his head to one side and made no eye contact. The observers either presented no reaction or suppressed their response. Bavelas and her colleagues concluded that the observers in Version Two had failed to get an appropriate social cue for showing empathy. They were very aware of others seeing their responses, confirming the idea that empathy is cued by social process.

In the other experiment, Bavelas, Coates, and Johnson (2000) videotaped two strangers in split-screen, one of whom was asked to tell a "close-call" story to the other. In Version One, the listeners acted naturally. They gave many responses that encouraged and supported the speaker's narrative—nods, smiles, mock horror, interjections, and so on. In Version Two, however, Bavelas and her colleagues deliberately distracted the listener. They asked her to press a hidden button every time the speaker used a word that began with the letter "T." The button caused a light to flash, which was picked up by another camera, so that the experimenters could see whether the listener was doing the task.

What happened was striking. In contrast to the seamless cooperation of Version One, as soon as the listener started "punching the T," the whole production more or less fell apart. The listener offered general responses, but not specific, finely tuned ones. As a result, the speaker began to fumble words, hesitate, and say things like "I guess you had to be there," and "I thought it was a good story at the time." Deprived of social partnering, the narrator's story fizzled out and ended lamely. Together, these two experiments showed the degree to which we call "tuning in" is a mutual event.

Remembering these experiments and reading some of Bavelas' articles, I realized how much meaning Bavelas had given to that dry word "communication." I thought back to my experience of being supervised by phone-ins from behind the screen or knocks on the door, and how disruptive I found them. I saw that every time I had asked myself, "What circular question should I ask next?" or "What task shall I give this family?" it was as if someone had "punched the T." Furthermore—and this is strongly seconded by Tom Andersen—anytime someone interferes suddenly with the channel between the therapist and the family, the effect can be like cutting an unseen artery.

As a result, I began thinking about an expanded lexicon that would express an emotion language that was socially, not individually, based. I came up with some ordinary phrasings based in part on my own experiences and in part on some Internet conversations with psychologists Lois Shawver and Gisela Schwartz. Let me start with a word I made up, "tempathy," and go on to the terms "generous listening," "connected speaking," "reverberation," "embracement," and another two categories: "the emotional main chance" and "knowing how to go on." Any of the anecdotes offered below could probably fit under several of these titles; I have merely matched case to category in the best way that I can.

Tempathy

I made up this word because "empathy" was too focused on the individual and bore too much humanistic baggage. I was convinced that the empathy we were dealing with in relationship work was not a trait but a form of transpersonal communication, so I began to call it "traveling empathy" or "tempathy" for short. Since a friend of mine had said that the term made him feel uncomfortable, I decided not to go public with it, but colleagues in the field began to pick it up and ask me about it. As a result, I began to wonder how to more fully describe it.

First, I want to propose a channel that is closer to animal communication than to human speech. After all, the consulting relationship begins on a kinesthetic, almost proprioceptive level. Language adds another layer (unless you define communication and language as identical, which I don't, believing that communication is larger than language). What takes place between me and someone who comes to see me for the first time seems almost sublingual, like those medications you put under your tongue so they go directly into the bloodstream. When Bateson used the term analogic communication, I think this was what he meant.

In my practice, after I had adopted the reflecting team format and the stance of "not knowing," I began to encounter more and more unusual effects. Coincidences for which I had no explanation cropped up all about me. A young Japanese woman in a workshop asked me if I would sign a book for her. She said her name was "Keiko," so I wrote "To Keiko, of the White Birds." I didn't know why I wrote that, so I asked her if there were white birds where she lived, and she said, "Yes, I come from Nagasaki, the city of the white cranes." A few months later I was giving a workshop in Tokyo and there she was, saying, "You remember me, from the city of the white cranes?" I wish I could say that this prefigured some transcendental event, but as far as I know it didn't. So the effect could be quite trivial.

It could also be helpful. A social worker who was consulting with me in a workshop told me that she was struggling with a horrific case involving child sexual abuse. While listening to her story, I found myself thinking of the movie, *The Loneliness of the Long Distance Runner*. I asked her if she knew the movie and, without missing a beat, she said, "Yes, I run the marathon." A little while later I said, "I have this image of Blind Justice," and she nodded and said, "I am a Libra." I thought of this as a confirmation: "Am I understanding you? Is this what it is like to be you?" This search for confirmation was an important first step.

However, just to show that this kind of channeling can't always be trusted, let me relate an incident that happened when I first started a private practice in Amherst. I was seeing two gay women who were having trouble with their relationship. Our conversation became stilted and I wondered whether my being straight was inhibiting them, but didn't wish to ask. Then, to my horror, I heard myself say, "You know, you remind me of two neutered cats." There was a dreadful silence, during which I pondered whether I should become a bank teller. Suddenly, both of them broke out laughing and one of them said, "That's it." They proceeded to give me a lecture on "bed death," and the effect on lesbian couples of loss of desire, and the session flowed again. Luckily, I had a good enough relationship with them to carry the weight of my unfortunate remark.

I had a happier outcome while giving a workshop in Marburg, Germany. I had been speaking of stepfamilies, so one of the participants asked me for a consultation around the issue of stepmothers. She said that her father had remarried when she was six and took her away to live with him and his new wife. The stepmother kept the child from seeing her mother and grandmother, although they lived together in the same town. She continually scolded and harassed the little girl, sometimes making her sit all day in front of a plate of food because she hadn't finished it.

The girl bided her time until she was around 12 years old, then made a plan to escape. Waiting till night, she climbed down to the roof under her window, jumped to the ground, and ran away to find her grandmother's house. She struggled through the city, on foot and in the dark, and at last she and her mother and grandmother were reunited. After this incident, she said, her father relented and allowed her to stay with her mother. I said to her that, in addition to having a mother and a grandmother who loved her, she must have had the help of a guardian angel. She said, "How did you know? My mother and grandmother believed in guardian angels and they said the same thing."

I had the same kind of experience in many shapes and circumstances, but the sequence was always the same: I would be listening, almost idly, not moving toward any goal, deliberately holding myself away from any conclusion, when an idea or phrase would float up from the "deep well," as I thought of it. I could imagine myself literally sitting on that steaming cleft in the rocks at Delphi, probably hallucinating from some drug. And I would usually not know why some particular thought was knocking at my door until I shared it. If the other person confirmed its relevance, that would be an example of tempathy.

Generous Listening

In 1998, I finally got a computer good enough to handle an Internet connection, and this was when I went online and joined Lois Shawver's Postmodern Therapies List. This discussion group has been going on for quite a few years and Shawver distills from the posted conversations enough material for a monthly *Postmodern Therapies Newsletter*. In reading the many exchanges dealing with philosophers like Ludwig Wittgenstein and Jean-Francois Lyotard, I noticed that the phrase "generous listening" kept cropping up. Shawver explained to me that Lyotard was the source of this term. He had described a kind of conversation where a person listened with the aim of understanding what the other person was saying, rather than pushing one's own opinions or disproving other views. To show me what Lyotard meant, Lois sent me a passage from *Just Gaming* (1996) in which Lyotard discusses the characteristics of different kinds of "language games" (a phrase invented by Wittgenstein):

> For us, a language is first and foremost someone talking. But there are language games in which the important thing is to listen, in which the rule deals with audition. Such a game is the game of the just. And in this game, one speaks only inasmuch as one listens, that is, one speaks as a listener, and not as an author. It is a game without an author in the same way as the speculative game of the West is a game without a listener, because the only listener tolerated by the speculative philosopher is the disciple. Well, what is a disciple? Someone who can become an author, who will be able to take the master's place. This is the only person to whom the master speaks. (p. 71)

What Lyotard was doing, Shawver said, was making a distinction between "listening in order to speak" as one did in a philosophical debate, and "speaking in order to listen," which was what we did as therapists. I was electrified. In talking about "the game without an author," Lyotard was describing something like a not-knowing position. When he said that this game was "a game of audition," he seemed to be supporting my version of a different voice. And when he added: "Such a game is the game of the just," bells went off. This was what I had been trying to say all along. At the same time, it amazed me that Lyotard, despite being one of the great male bluestockings of France, was able to turn and look critically at the masculinist tradition of argument he himself stood for. Of course, he was quite conscious of this irony. In another passage he says: "One day a UN vote will denounce as male sexism the primacy accorded theoretical discourse, to the great scandal . . . of us all" (1989, p. 70).

But I still didn't understand how Lois got the phrase "generous listening" out of Lyotard's words. I kept at her until she remembered that a more immediate inspiration was a passage in a book by Donald Davidson (1984) where he spoke of "charitable listening." Lois had transposed that phrase into "generous listening" and then ascribed it to Lyotard. I felt that she, not Lyotard or Davidson, should get full credit for a phrase that naturalized a common aspect of therapy. At the same time, I liked the idea that this type of listening had been so grandly legitimated by an important French philosopher.

As an example of generous listening, here is the story of Darrah, a social worker at a day treatment program with whom I did a consultation a few years ago. I asked her early on where her name came from and she said it was Scots dialect for oak. I remember saying to her, "That's a strong name." She then told me that she had spent the morning trying to persuade a divorced woman in her fifties not to commit suicide. This woman, Mrs. S., had hung a rope with a noose from an oak tree next to her house and told Darrah that when she went home that day she intended to hang herself. She had been in the day program the previous year and had just come back to it again because she was so depressed. Apparently, this was not the first time she had made such a threat. Darrah told me that some of her teammates thought that she had become too enmeshed with this woman, and she worried that she might be colluding with the client's "dependency needs."

So I asked Darrah what she had said when Mrs. S. told her about her plan to go home and kill herself. She said she had asked her why she wanted to do this. Mrs. S. responded, "Because being alive is too painful." Darrah asked, "How do you know it won't be just as painful after you are dead?" The woman became very quiet. They talked some more, and finally the woman said she wasn't going to kill herself that day. She asked Darrah to call her disabled adult son, who lived with her, and tell him to take down the rope. I had asked two members of Darrah's team to be in a reflecting group and some other participants to be "as if" persons. They had not known about Darrah's comment to Mrs. S. and were impressed. Then, one of the "as if" persons said that she had decided to listen as if she were Mrs. S., and told Darrah how much their connection had meant to her over the two years. She said that if she lost Darrah, it would be a disaster. When Darrah and I turned to speak to each other at the end, I said I thought that she was living up to the strength of her name.

In retrospect, here was a young line worker who was suffering from her own feelings of failure, amplified by the understandable anxiety of her colleagues. When I stumbled on the meaning of Darrah's name, it felt like a gift and hopefully could double as a counter-charm. Finding out the meaning of Darrah's name and linking it to an action that added another dimension to the over-all story did not cause anything to get better or worse, but it set the slice of bread butter-side up. Therapy is often a matter of building on such accidents.

But was "generous listening" anything new? Many people would say it is the same as "active listening." It interested me, therefore, that Bavelas, McGee, Phillips, and Routledge (in press) described a research study by Armstrong (1998) on how people feel about active listening techniques.

Armstrong asked some university students to recount a bad academic experience to two different listeners, also students. One of the listeners was trained in active listening; the other was a person who was told to just listen naturally. When the students telling their stories rated their listeners afterwards, they described the active listeners as significantly more weird, unnatural, phony, and unrealistic than the untrained listeners. They said the trained listeners were more likely to misunderstand and to interrupt at odd times. The implication is that training in active listening may actually remove our natural ability to listen and replace it with a style that others find artificial.

Of course, it is not enough, if you are a therapist, to be "just natural." I liked Shawver's formulation of "speaking in order to listen." My own guidelines for this kind of listening involve a slower pace, a bottomless patience, and (when I watch myself on videotape) an odd kind of earnestness. To put myself in the right frame of mind, I often use special metaphors like the bowl or the beach I mentioned before. I will also make a conscious effort to resist the pull of goals and structures that still remain from previous training. At times I will use an expectant silence, as if waiting for something to fall into my lap. What often happens is that into this space come very unusual thoughts, leading to unusual remarks, and not necessarily by me.

Connected Speaking

Tom Andersen (1998) has written about the conversation that goes on among the "inner talks," the private dialogues inside the self that take place concurrently with the "outer talks," the dialogue with others. He even makes a drawing of this process, which consists of two outlines of persons facing each other. Directional lines come up from the belly and through the mouth of each, then into the mouth of the other, down and around in the belly, and back and forth in a recursive loop-the-loop.

I appreciated Andersen's focus on inner voices. The generous listening I had begun to do was very different from the formalized questions of my earlier training. It gave me the space to pay attention to associations of my own. Ideas and observations began to form in my head, which I sometimes shared. But what to call them? They were so different from the clinical speaking I was used to, which usually took the form of interpretations or tasks. Finally, I decided to use the phrase "connected speaking." You had to listen generously to establish the conditions for the underground channel to flow and when it did, you spoke from that connected place. It is wrong to break up this two-way process into speaking and listening. The beauty of

Andersen's picture is that it shows how intricately these actions are entwined.

In any case, when an odd idea would surface, I would first sift it through my own mind for relevance. It was not always clearly linked to the conversation, but if I did decide to share it, I would often get responses of surprising depth. An experience during a workshop in Mexico remains for me a vivid example. In this instance, I did a reflecting consultation with a very sensitive, bright psychologist named Elena. She was working with a teenage boy who had taken an overdose of pills, and she was worried that she would not be able to help him. In a consultation, as I have said, my job is to concern myself not with the crisis in the family but with the relationship of the therapist to the situation. I think of this as "the dilemma at the crossroads." In this case, no matter how many questions I asked, there was no dilemma. Elena had covered all the bases as far as I could tell. So I shared my "finding" with her, namely that there was nothing to find.

Then an out-of-place question welled up. After mulling it around and feeling that it might be too personal, I nevertheless decided to risk it. I asked, "Do you have any children?" Elena stopped short, as if caught off guard, and then said, "No." I immediately thought to myself, "Maybe she can't have children, and here I am, asking her about it." To my consternation, she began to weep. The tears kept rolling down her cheeks. After waiting to see if she would tell me why, I asked her, "Was that an inappropriate question?" She shook her head and brought me back to the topic of the family. Even while talking, she continued to weep. I decided to just accept the tears, no questions asked. When I asked the reflecting team to take over, the tears dried up. We finished the consultation on a hopeful note, as she was really doing a wonderful job.

However, I was left wondering what raw nerve had been exposed, and went up to Elena afterward to ask if something I had said or done had upset her. She told me that I had indeed hit on a sensitive topic but that it had nothing to do with either me or the case. Another teenage boy whose family lived next door to her had overdosed on drugs three days before the workshop and died. She was very close to this family and had known the boy for many years, but she didn't want to derail the consultation by sharing the story with the audience. She was relieved that I was willing to accept her tears without explanation.

I still don't know if I should have suppressed that question. If I had been working in the old way, I probably would have, but I have recently begun to accord more weight to these intrusions from the underground river. I did have that inner dialogue, and I did decide to take my chances. In retrospect,

I am glad that I did, because if I had not, my guess is that I would not have connected as personally with Elena as I did.

Reverberation

As an emphasis on language has taken center stage in therapeutic theory, there has been an upsurge of interest in image and metaphor. There has also been much speculation about how such wordings can effect any kind of change. French linguist Gaston Bachelard, whose work I have already cited, comes closer than anyone else to explaining this puzzle when he says that the power of poetic images is reverberatory rather than causal: "Very often, then, it is in the opposite of causality, that is, in reverberation, that I think we find the real measure of the being of a poetic image" (1994, pp. xvi).

This is a wonderful point. Poetic language, while not literally instrumental, has its own kind of influence, as a stone dropped in a pond creates ripples along the shore. The work that many relational therapists do seems to me to be noncausal and reverberatory in exactly this sense. Psychiatrist Mony Elkaim (1997), who lives in Belgium, places the kindred concept of "resonance" at the heart of his method, and two French philosophers, Jacques Deleuze and Felix Guattari (1985), expand further on this kind of influence by comparing the strategy of the tree to the strategy of the rhizome. The tree is characterized by hierarchy and sequence, where the rhizome is horizontal and generative. Poetic approaches to therapy, relying on reverberation, would be closer to a rhizome form.

Michael White has also been influenced by Bachelard's notion. Here is a passage from *Narratives of Therapists' Lives* that refers to the practice of "decentered sharing" in connection with a reflecting team. He says:

> I believe that Bachelard's account of the "image" is helpful to the development of these practices of decentered sharing. His interest was with the images of one's life that are evoked by states of reverie and how these images set off reverberations that reach into personal history. In response to these reverberations, certain experiences of the events of one's life light up through resonation. (1997, p. 102)

White recommends that members of reflecting teams share images that come up during the process of listening and also share the effect of others' images on themselves. He goes on to say, "For outsider-witness group members, the reverberations that are set off by these therapeutic conversations frequently touch on many experiences long forgotten, and, as well, endow previously remembered experiences with a new significance."

As an example, let me tell a story about image-sharing in an article by Belgian psychologist Peter Rober (1999). Rober agrees with Tom Andersen that it is not enough to concern oneself with the "outer conversation" of the therapy; one must also look to the dialogue that goes on in the "inner conversation," and to the images, moods, associations, or memories that the conversation has evoked in oneself. It is true that the periods of silent listening afforded by Andersen's style of interviewing and by the reflecting team foster the production of such ideas.

In his story, Rober describes a consultation with a mother of two children whose husband had left her for a younger woman. While she was sharing this painful situation, Rober made empathic comments, but she pushed him off, as if keeping him at bay. Consulting his inner voices, Rober came to an image of a white wolf who lay in the snow, wounded and bleeding. He decided to share this image and began telling the woman a story about a white mother wolf who encountered a grizzly bear and was attempting to lure it away from her pups. Two Indians happened to come by who admired the courage of the wolf, and followed both of them. At last the bear gave up and fell back. The Indians continued on, hoping to rescue the brave mother wolf, but she mistook them for the bear and kept on running. By the time they caught up with her, the Indians found the mother wolf dying in the snow. Their help had come too late.

After Rober finished telling this story, the mother said, "I don't understand what you mean." Rober said he didn't either but hoped that it might mean something to her. They took some time to talk it over. Finally the mother said, "I realize now that if I start to need your help, you might leave me as my husband did. Maybe that's why I keep you at a distance, like the white mother wolf." Rober said that he had realized something too—that he had chased her away with his attempts to help her. As they spoke, the mother kept coming back to the image of the wolf, and at one point explained that she had learned in her own family to distrust offers of help. "In fact," she said, "we are a family of white wolves."

Another example of reverberation happened to me during a workshop in Crete. I was doing another reflecting consultation, this time with a psychotherapy trainer I will call Malina. One of the trainees in the experiential therapy program where she taught told her that he had learned all he could from the program and wanted to leave. She felt he wasn't ready and refused to let him go. He had apparently been influenced by a systemic trainer who had criticized the long-term model taught in Malina's institute. Worse yet, some of her other trainees were agreeing with him. This put Malina in a very bad spot. I was in a dilemma, too. I couldn't agree with my young colleague, because I had reservations about her approach. On the other hand, I wanted to find a way to comfort her.

What came to my rescue was the memory of a dream I had when I was a young mother living in a dark house on a small college campus. I decided to tell this dream to Malina. In the dream, I told her, I was in my bedroom. I went down the stairs of my house and found strangers in the rooms. In one was a small child, in another an old man, neither of whom I knew. Then I went into the kitchen where my husband was standing. I called to him as loudly as I could, but he could neither hear nor see me. I realized with horror that I was in a different time warp. I woke myself up by calling out his name.

Malina stared at me for a few seconds, and then told me that a week before, a woman she was seeing had told her a similar dream, only it was about Malina herself. Ordinarily, Malina said, she would explain that the dream was really about the person telling it, as psychoanalytic theory directs, but for some reason she encouraged the woman to tell the dream as she experienced it. The woman said that the dream-Malina had gone to her house only to find that the people living in it were strangers. The dream-Malina looked very sad, and the client said that she too had a strong sense of foreboding. Malina heard her out and made no comment except to thank her. The session then went on as usual.

Malina was silent after she told me this. There were many things I could have said, but all I did say was, "It's terrible to think that you might lose your home," and I took hold of her hands. From my travels, I knew enough of the politics of therapy in Greece to realize that Malina's world was indeed changing, and that new approaches to therapy were displacing the psychoanalytically oriented schools that had reigned there for so long. I had a sense of foreboding too, but I hoped she would feel that I had understood her situation. It is always difficult when the "presenting problem" includes the consultant herself.

Embracement

On my way out of the world of paradox and positive connotation, there was something about it that I did not want to lose. I looked for a word that would describe this feeling. "Acceptance" was close but didn't click. "Unconditional positive regard" was close but came from an individually-oriented vocabulary. Finally I decided on "embracement," clumsy as that sounds. It had to have a bodily feeling associated with it, because one way I knew I had found it was that my body said, "That's it."

One illustration of embracement is the Russian folktale, "The Magic Mitten." Once upon a time, a peasant was walking through the forest and dropped his mitten on the ground. A mouse came along, moved into the mitten, and turned it into a snug dwelling. Then came a frog, who joined the mouse. Then a hare arrived, then a fox, then a boar, then a bear. As each creature moved in, the mitten expanded. Soon it was practically an apartment house, and the animals were snug and happy. But then the peasant came by looking for his lost mitten. The animals heard him coming, got frightened, and rushed away. The story ends with the peasant picking the mitten up, putting it on, and walking home. This story is not only about a literal embracement (a mitten that fits all circumstances), but about embracing a contradiction: the idea that a mitten could house all those animals at one moment and at the next be back on its owner's hand.

After struggling with this idea of embracement for a long time, I finally found someone else who was groping in the same direction. Some years back, during a workshop I did in Norway with possibility therapist Bill O'Hanlon, he told me about his idea of "inclusivity therapy." He seemed to mean the same thing I did. Naturally, I was very interested to watch him while he did an interview with an American graduate student in psychology. This man told O'Hanlon that he had a poor opinion of himself as a father because he was often irritated with his kids. His wife constantly criticized him for this, and he felt starved for affection from her. O'Hanlon asked the man if he were willing to try a meditation exercise. He agreed and O'Hanlon launched into a hypnotic induction: "You can focus or not focus; your eyes may close or they may open; you can trust or not trust." This seemed like fairly standard hypnotic technique, and the man seemed to go into a kind of waking trance.

Then O'Hanlon said something that seemed right to me. He told the man that beneath his irritation at his kids lay a love that was always there. He said, "Hold that in your heart toward yourself when you experience one of these encounters with your wife, feel that sense of okayness, bring love and acceptance toward yourself, and you'll have more resources to handle criticism from your wife." The man nodded, and a tear trickled down his right cheek. After the session, he seemed somewhat calmer than before, even though he stoutly denied he had been in a trance. (O'Hanlon told me later that in these inductions there is usually one tear and it is always from the right eye.)

All well and good, but I was still puzzled by what O'Hanlon meant by "inclusivity," so after the workshop, he gave me an example. He recalled the time he had been doing hypnotherapy with a man who kept seeing a rectum floating in front of his face. O'Hanlon said he did a trance similar to the one I had seen. Afterward, the man said that he no longer had the obsessive thought but didn't feel that it was the trance experience that had helped. What was crucial was that O'Hanlon had said that whatever he did or didn't do, it was okay. That had apparently given him enormous relief.

Pondering this later, what came to me was the phrase "embracing the Y." The one thing common to these stories was that they seemed to be about including both horns of a dilemma. This had also been true of all the paradoxical injunctions I had observed or been trained in. If you positively reframed a problem, you added the hidden half of a polarity. This was one form of embracement. Another was the positive connotation, which did the same thing but at a systemic level. The problem, which was bad, was placed in the service of an aspect of the situation that was good. But where I parted company with these tactics was that they left the therapist in an instrumental position. The goal was to get beyond the merely instrumental.

So I looked for an example of embracement from my own experience, and decided to write about a consultation I had done with my colleague, Judy Davis. She had asked me to visit one day when she was meeting with a group of psychology interns at her home. During this meeting, one of her trainees presented a videotape. The situation of a college student of nineteen, whom I will call Jon, was being discussed in his presence by a reflecting team made up of Judy and two other trainees. This original group, plus myself, sat and watched the tape together.

The story was that Jon, an excellent student, began missing classes because he kept going home to take care of his divorced mother. She had lost her job and was becoming depressed to the point of illness. Jon's grades went downhill, and he began to talk about dropping out of school entirely, but there was a Catch-22. He was no longer a minor, and if he weren't in school, his father's support check would stop and his mother would have nothing to live on. In the video, Judy's team had pointed out to the young man how his effort to help his mother was jeopardizing his career. In our meeting, Jon's therapist told us that she had an individual therapy supervisor, who had commented on the "manipulative" nature of the mother's illness. That didn't help matters either.

So Judy asked me and the two other trainees to join her in some ad hoc reflections. Judy wanted to make a videotape that the therapist could take to Jon to watch later. In the earlier tape, Jon had been very defensive about his relationship with his mother. When it came time for us to reflect, Judy said with honest feeling that she and her team had been in no way suggesting that Jon abandon his mother, and that they knew how much the two of them loved each other. The other two trainees agreed fervently. Then Judy turned to me, explaining that I was a colleague and friend, and asked me for my thoughts. I remember wondering how to avoid saying anything critical.

So I started out with the safe observation that Jon had a beautiful face (which he did). Then there came to me the image of two hearts that shared the same blood supply. Offering this picture, I wondered what would happen if the blood supply were cut off. The mother lived with Jon's grandmother, so she shared in the blood supply, too. I said that there was a serious issue about how people could separate in this family and still maintain the life-sustaining allocation of nutrients. I also said that the family was trying to find a way to have separate agendas and yet nourish each other, because at some level they were only one beating heart. Judy added that Jon and his mother were trying to learn a way of living beyond sacrifice, and wondered in turn how they could hold this beating heart, this connection and love, between them, and still have individual lives.

Three weeks later, the therapist wrote Judy and the team a letter in which she said that Jon had been struck by the metaphor of the beating heart and called it a beautiful example of his relationship to his mother. He said that he and his mother were very entwined with each other, and that they helped each other in many ways, but they hurt each other too. He said, "Much of what I want to do is find a place in this relationship with Mom that isn't so extreme." Jon also talked about an email from his father, who complained that Jon never wrote him. The father was a compulsive gambler whose child support was deducted from his paycheck. Previously there had been an incident when Jon had to call the police because his father was physically threatening his mother over money. In the email, the father said that he had felt angry enough to kill her. While recounting this, Jon began to weep. He feared that his father would quit his job in order not to have to pay his mother anything. He wondered if he should write his father back and continue to maintain the relationship until he graduated.

The therapist said that this was a positive session. It was the first time Jon had talked about his relationship to his father, and the first time he had allowed himself tears. It was also the first time he had acknowledged the hurtful ways he and his mother communicated. Since he did not show up for any more therapy sessions, the story stops here, but it still shows what I want to emphasize. The more the therapists tried to give Jon insight into his self-defeating behavior, or his mother's manipulative illness, the more defensive he became. If I, as a consultant, had pointed out the equally self-defeating intervention of the therapists, they, too, would have become defensive. The beating hearts offered a way to embrace these layers of self-contradiction without putting anyone in the wrong. Also at stake, needless to say, was my relationship with my partner, Judy, who could have felt put on the spot. So do not believe anyone who tells you that this work is not a high wire act. They are really wrong.

The Emotional Main Chance

As I wandered through this ever-changing family therapy field, I often felt that I was looking for some grail. However, as I got near enough to see the shape of the grail, I was struck by its likeness to a tin cup sitting by a natural spring. As with my mother's ashes, it was never the container that mattered. And here I point not to any great new thing, but only to what the deconstructionists have been maintaining all along. After all my efforts to learn techniques, theories, formats, and the like, I began to see how easily they could become components of the flybottle. It was important to break out and sense what was beyond the essentialist structures of modern psychotherapy, and that included family therapy as well. In any interview, in fact, the most important thing was to look for, find, and have confirmed what I now think of as the "emotional main chance."

What do I mean by this? In a previous chapter I talked about "the presenting edge," meaning whatever during an interview seemed to be calling attention to itself most insistently, like an emotional hot spot. As I went toward it, an image or metaphor would surface inside my head, and if I played it back, I would often receive some kind of validation. This was important. If I couldn't offer some simulacrum, some concrete analogy for this edge, and receive a confirmation, I felt that I couldn't go any further. Techniques and methods can be helpful, but they can also get in the way. You have to find the worrybox, the channel, the place where body and emotion meet. You have to find the underground river and launch yourself upon it.

This is sometimes very simple. The image of two hearts sharing one blood supply was one example. Asking the mother in the Beanstalk story why she was crying was another. At other times, it was a matter of paying attention to what came up from the deep well: the White Birds, Blind Justice, the Long Distance Runner. Those were like testings; something might spark off from them or it might not. At other times I would use familiar legends: Jack the Giantkiller, the Sleeping Beauty. These folk tales acknowledged people's interest in transformation and suggested what the prospect might be like. Sometimes, as in the Magic Mitten story, the image bracketed mutual contradictions; at other times, as with the Wings of Stone, only the longing behind the dilemma could be discerned. Penn's "blue lightning" questions turned confused depictions into connected ones. Then there were mirror stories, like the dream about the house full of strangers that reflected Malina's situation at the feeling level and let us both know that we had touched.

I want to make clear that the feeling level I am talking about has nothing to do with the theory of emotions underlying so much popular psychology. This view holds that we have to "get out" anger, "vent" frustration, "work through" grief. If you can get an angry person to weep or a depressed person to put their sadness into words, the idea is that their suffering will dissipate. But a relational theory of emotion sees the expression of feeling as something different: a reverberation that has the power to touch and often change. In describing the effect of his definitional ceremonies, White (2000) has revived the Greek notion of Katharsis. He suggests that the original meaning of this term has less to do with purgation and more to do with moving people collectively from one place to another in an experience of transformation. I couldn't agree more.

"Now I Know How to Go On"

I want to end this chapter with an idea that comes from Tom Andersen (1998). Andersen was struck by a crucial (and famous) paragraph in *Philosophical Investigations* in which Wittgenstein asks how we know when we have understood something and says, "Try not to think of understanding as a 'mental process' at all. . . . but ask yourself: in what sort of case, in what kind of circumstances, do we say, 'Now I know how to go on'" (1958, #55). In what I consider an elegant move, Andersen (1998) applies that phrase to the therapeutic process, saying,

> I see it myself as a question of knowing how we can go on from this moment to the next moment. There is more than one way to know, and I will mention three ways, each belonging to different realms of life; i) to explain, ii) to understand and iii) to be sensible of. . . . This third kind of knowing, to sense the situation, leads to how one relates to the situation. One might relate well to a situation without being able to explain it or understand it.

I was immediately struck by the thought that here we had the answer to an abiding puzzle. I had long wondered how to describe the goal of a therapeutic conversation. Set against the usual treatment/cure framework, our stance seemed cavalier, if not outrageous. How could you charge people, or get insurance companies to pay for therapy, if you didn't cure them? But after a long experience with the difficulties of cutting suffering into commercially tidy pieces, to fit commercially tidy treatments, I felt relieved at finding an alternative.

Looking back on my own practice, I realized how aptly this phrase, "Now I know how to go on," described my own mode of operation. People I had seen for a period of time would drop away and then show up for a session from time to time. Sometimes single sessions were all I did. Whatever the situation, it seemed that what we were dealing with was unfathomable emotions or unexplained behaviors, and that our main job had to do with relieving fear, dispelling confusion, restoring hope. That was the big difference between us and the physicians. They could prescribe medications, which sometimes work wonderfully, but the relational therapies needed a lexicon that was not necessarily based on change.

As an example, let me tell you the story of Helen (not her real name), a sensitive, attractive woman in whom I saw a younger self. Many years ago, Helen and her husband Mark had come in to see me around developmental problems with their adolescent son. Things worked out after a few sessions and we stopped. Then, after a period of years, Helen came in alone. The two children were grown and out of the home, but Helen said she felt somehow cut off from them. It seemed that neither child shared the parents' cultural interests, and Helen felt especially at a loss with her daughter, who did fund-raising for feminist causes. Helen worried because this daughter was not yet married. She would try to find men to go out with, but the most recent eligible male had dropped her because she fell asleep on a date.

Helen's basic puzzlement seemed to be that her children did not play the same part in her life as she did in her mother's. In effect, she had been in love with her mother, and her mother had been in love with her. Her marriage was happy, she told me, because she and her husband were also in love, but she did not have the same happiness with her children. I told her I knew what it was like to feel that one had lost one's children. I added that I had tried to make up for this feeling by finding "spirit daughters," young women in my field whom I admired and tried to help. Since Helen had taken a degree in art history and now directed her own department at a small college, I wondered whether she could take one of her students to a conference in the field. She said she had always hung back from too personal a relationship with them, but she was intrigued.

I continued to share tips in the name of female solidarity, despite my lack of faith in suggestions or direct advice. I commented that I had recently taken to pasting family pictures in those frames with cutout holes as a record for my children. Helen didn't think her children would be very interested in that kind of thing. She went on to say that she had become much more involved in Catholicism, her cradle religion. It at least offered her spiritual sustenance, although she didn't take part socially.

The next week, Helen was going to visit both children, who were living in a city where Rob had gone back to school and Carol worked. She described how she used to love it when her mother would take a hotel room in that same city and share it with her. Helen said her own daughter would never dream of doing such a thing. The upshot was that Helen dreaded this visit; she was afraid both of disappointing and of being disappointed. Yet I found out that only four years before Carol had put her arms around her mother, saying that because Helen had given her so much love as a child, she could love her back as a grown-up. I asked Helen in what ways Carol disappointed her. Helen said she was a bit sloppy, seeming not to care about being feminine. I asked what activities they liked to share together. Helen said that her daughter liked to go shopping with her, and at one time used to enjoy getting "make-overs" at department stores.

At this point I told Helen that I thought she was suffering from a broken heart. She agreed. However, I knew that sympathy was not enough and cast about for some "gift" she could take with her. So I asked whether she and her daughter would be shopping together. She said yes, that Carol liked Helen to buy her clothes, but that these were just "things"—cheap, material things. I said that because Carol so obviously valued her mother's taste and looks, these things were for her like blessings. She might feel blessed. Helen was struck by this idea. "Oh," she said, "I never thought of it like that." She teared up. She kept saying how grateful she was for that idea and kept weeping while repeating, "Yes, just like blessings, like benedictions." This was the end of the session.

I then left for a trip abroad. After I came back, Helen called me. The visit to her children had been a huge success. Carol had apparently enjoyed the shopping and the make-over. The striking thing, however, was that Carol had found among some old photographs a picture of herself as a baby on a bed together with her brother and her mother. She and her brother had framed it and given it to Helen as a Christmas present. We both marveled at the coincidence.

At the time, I had not yet read Wittgenstein, but in retrospect I see that both Andersen and myself were searching for a way to describe a different type of end goal. If Schoen were alive, I think he would say that this was a good example of the evolution of a theory based on use. Helen came back to see me at intervals; each time we had only one meeting, but each time this was enough. All she needed was to get to a place where she could say to herself: "Now I know how to go on."

15

From Wisdom
to Responsibility

The Legacy of Systemic Thinking

During my long journey alongside the family therapy movement, the direction it was taking felt right, but the obstacles were many. Some of them were political. After all, family therapy did not even take off until the middle of the last century. When it did, it faced established fields that covered the same territory, so it had to engage in the game of "professional dominance" (Freidson, 1972). First, it had to develop a reasonably coherent theoretical position. Second, it had to offer a tested set of practices, legitimized by respectable research. Third, it had to have a set of ethics. All this had to be done within the technical-rational code of modernism in the 20th century.

But within family therapy, there was always an element pulling in the opposite direction. If, as Bateson and Ruesch (1951) indicated, communication was "the social matrix of psychiatry," this was the seed of the flower to come. Out of the Bateson group's studies of communication came the early research on the family, which quickly moved to a focus on larger systems. Even though some of this research stayed within a modern framework, it was family therapy's systemic wing, inspired by its Palo Alto beginnings, that began to move beyond essentialist assumptions about what was true and what was real.

At present, the incredulity to meta-narratives that Lyotard described has begun to challenge the field of psychology at its deepest core. There have been many studies on the cultural specificity of the emotions (Harré, 1984), many critiques of the concept of the "self" (Gergen, 1994), many doubts about developmental stages (Burman, 1994), and many challenges to the idea of universal cognitive goals and strategies (Rogoff, 1990). Richard Nisbett, a social psychologist at the University of Michigan, is about to publish a study (Goode, 2000) claiming that the cognitive habits we think are universals—like logical reasoning, cause and effect, and rules of classification—are cultural, not natural, givens.

Nisbett's controlled experiments suggest that East Asians "think differently" in these respects from Westerners. In reacting to his protocols, East Asian respondents were more apt to apprehend a picture as a whole than Westerners, who tended to focus on the largest or most imposing part. East Asians were also more comfortable than Westerners with accepting contradictions. Another difference was that the East Asians placed a high value on experiential knowing, while Westerners were more apt to value analytic reasoning. I had always associated Bateson's systemic ideas with non-Western traditions, but up to now the connection was more of an aesthetic one. I was glad that the analytic view our culture has enshrined was beginning to seem like only one among others.

Of course, there are limitations to a systemic view. The insights of critical feminism had a powerful effect on me, making it clear that systemic therapists had to drop a number of wrong ideas, some of which I have already mentioned. One was the belief in a neutral observer with an all-encompassing God's eye view. Another was the notion that a family was like a system where all the parts contributed equally. Finally, the ecological metaphor was misleading. Applied to human groups, it condoned the sacrifice of the individual for the harmony of the whole. As Bateson (1972) has observed, Nature looks at the death of one of her species and says: "Just what I needed for my ecosystem."

But for me, one part of the Batesonian heritage never dimmed: the idea of "systemic wisdom." Bateson defined this quality as an awareness of the interlocking circuits that connect the elements of the natural world. In *Steps to an Ecology of Mind*, he warned about the dangers of not taking this reflexive picture seriously:

> Purposive consciousness pulls out, from the total mind, sequences which do not have the loop structure which is characteristic of the whole systemic structure. If you follow the "commonsense" dictates of consciousness you become, effectively, greedy and unwise—again I use "wisdom as a word for recognition of and guidance by a knowledge of the total systemic creature. (1972, p. 440)

Bateson pointed to the wounding of the ecology by shortsighted applications of invention and technology. Sounding at times like an angry Jehovah, he declared that any species foolish enough to quarrel with Nature would be punished. He also deplored our tendency to believe in words like "crime" and "power" and "play" as if they were independent of the context that gave them meaning. Bateson was an early postmodernist in the sense that he saw the consequences of our habit of reifying abstractions. Somewhere I got the impression that it was he who was responsible for the bumper sticker "Stamp Out Nouns," a postmodern idea if there ever was one.

Bateson also attempted to describe transgressions against the integrity of relationship systems. The concept of the "double bind" (Bateson, 1978), which depicted a stressful relational tangle, was a start, but in the hands of professional helpers it too was reified and became another way to put families in the wrong. Another essay, "The Cybernetics of Self" (in Bateson, 1972), dealt with the premises that support the no-exit world of the alcoholic, illuminating the cycle of addiction and isolating systemic characteristics like "alcoholic pride." Again, in the hands of family therapists, Bateson's contribution devolved into the concept of the "alcoholic family," another term that some think ought to be stamped out. But despite what the world made of his ideas, Bateson should be honored as an early poser of the question: what would be the counterpart to systemic wisdom in the human world?

Relational Responsibility

As if in answer, social constructionists Sheila McNamee and Kenneth Gergen have come up with suggestions for a relational set of ethics. In the anthology *Relational Responsibility* (McNamee & Gergen, 1999), the authors and their associates (including spouses Jack Lannamann and Mary Gergen, themselves gifted researchers), comment on what shape this ethic might take. A companion book (Gergen, 1999), is called *An Invitation to Social Construction*. In my mind, these two works make an impressive contribution to an understanding of both postmodernism and social construction theory, and go far to rebut those critics who have accused social construction theory of moral relativism.

Reading Gergen's book first, I saw many commonalities between Bateson's and Gergen's ideas. Even though Bateson's arguments mostly refer to the world of nature, and Gergen's concerns are with the way humans connect, their views both overlap and complement each other. Bateson uses systemic ideas to reconfigure the boundaries between the creature and its world. Gergen uses postmodern ideas to critique psychology's separation of the individual from the social context. Let me list some of the points of agreement.

1. Gergen states that Western society ties accountability to the individual, who is the possessor of the impulses that lead to good and bad. This narrow view of individual agency, Gergen says, is a modernist idea that supports a host of shaky assumptions about moral order. Our legal codes are based on these beliefs, likewise our system of democracy and our devotion to free enterprise. These beliefs are not universal to all cultures, but because they form a heritage to which we are deeply attached, questioning them is dangerous. "Meddle with the self," Gergen says, "and all the bones of tradition begin to rattle" (1999, p. 16). Bateson makes similar points about distinctions that separate parts from wholes, one part of an ecology from another, and parts of speech, like nouns, from their context. As I explained previously, Bateson felt that these separations lead to errors, like speaking of power as if it were a substance or criminality as if it were a trait.

2. Gergen speaks of the blind spots that prevent us from respecting the traditions of cultures whose habits are strange to us. Because we think of our ideas as universally good and true, we do not always understand the values of others. Gergen refers to the work of Edward Said (1993), who showed us how deep our blindness is to colonialist traditions in Western literature: witness "Orientalism" in France, and the "Great Game" in 19th century British India. Bateson (1958), who studied and compared many cultures, felt that we would all be improved by being anthropologists. Many of his most important ideas came to him by trying to look through the eyes of people who lived in places like Bali and New Guinea. Where would the influential concept of symmetrical versus complementary escalation be without the Iatmul people? Where would the understanding of the connection between trance and running amok be without the Balinese?

3. Gergen objects to the enlargement of the "cycle of infirmity." He notes that the number of deficit terms in the psychiatric nomenclature has reached more than 300, and that between 1900 and 2000 the number of registered psychiatrists in the U.S. jumped from 400 to 40,000. Bateson, too, deplored conventional psychiatry, which he described as "the study of

pathology." In fact, he created a list of what we would now call its modernist features. This list includes many elements that postmodernists have been attacking: the belief in pathological structures, the splitting of social ecologies, the emphasis on the individual, the focus on systems that do not include the observer, the omission of the social context, the idea of objectivity. The last item on his list was, "Striving for absolutist theories" (Bateson & Ruesch, 1951, p. 259). If he could have looked ahead to the vocabulary of postmodernism, he might have changed that to "upholding meta-narratives."

4. Gergen challenges our emphasis on the self as the basic unit of analysis. He says: "We evaluate, judge, measure, heal and incarcerate separate individuals. As a result, we give little attention to relationships" (1999, p. 18). Repairing this lack, of course, was one of the purposes of the Bateson group, whose close attention to communication began an inquiry that is still unfolding to this day. As I mentioned previously, Jan Bavelas (1992), a survivor of the original MRI, has continued to extend and deepen this tradition, and her group at the University of Victoria in B.C. has been devising experiments that show that social interaction can better be described as melded interplay than as the reciprocal response of one individual to another.

5. Gergen believes with Bateson that our orientation toward mastery fosters an often myopic preference for instrumental relations. I agree wholeheartedly. I have often spoken of my unease with forms of therapy that hide the real intention of the therapist, and give pride of place to ingenuity. It was Bateson's warning about "the dangers of conscious purpose" in *Angels Fear* (Bateson & Bateson, 1987) that pushed me to break with the preoccupation with control of much of early family therapy and to search for a more transparent and collaborative alternative.

6. Again lining up with Bateson, Gergen deplores the pillaging of natural resources in the name of private gain. As globalized investment sees the world more and more in terms of the bottom line, less and less attention is paid to public welfare. As health care is increasingly rationalized as a business, it more and more departs from older standards of humanity. The field of psychotherapy is a stellar example. Gergen complains that the medicalized stance toward "behavioral health" (note the new dormitive principle) promotes practices of labeling and measurement that chop up medical services into reimbursable quantities. Gergen's culture of deficit continues to reign and, in the

triumph of the term "dysfunctional family," even the hopeful field of family therapy has been co-opted. Luckily, there are countermovements and opposing trends, and it is those that I have concentrated on here.

After writing this section, I began to think of the concepts of systemic wisdom and relational responsibility as if they were bookends. "Systemic wisdom" was the bookend that held my early inquiries, and "relational responsibility" the bookend that propped up the later half. Like these bookends, the metaphors favored by Bateson and Gergen also dovetail. One of Bateson's metaphors is the ecosystem. We are only just beginning to face the consequences of violating the conventions that sustain the natural world. The down side of this metaphor is that, in favoring stasis, it can obscure individual need. One of Gergen's metaphors is the dance, an analogy that gives honor to each person as well as to the participants' common achievement. This image too has a down side: it bans the dissonance that may be a necessary part of creation. As long as we remain aware of such provisos, we can use these metaphors to counter the focus on the individual that has held such a long monopoly over our minds.

The Fingertip People

Despite all my reading, there remained a crucial blur in regard to what postmodernism might mean for family therapy. I owe my big moment of enlightenment to a visit from my friend Lois Shawver, who has made her appearance in earlier chapters. Sitting across the kitchen table from me, she attempted to explain the enormous contribution of Ludwig Wittgenstein to the postmodern banquet. The more she spoke, the more I felt that I was drowning. Like many students of Wittgenstein, she had spent twenty-odd years studying his attempt to expose the platonic shadows pervading the Western language game, so how could I possibly "get it" in one short evening? I sat there feeling baffled and put upon.

Finally she said, "But you have been doing the same thing as Wittgenstein!" This roused me pretty quickly. "What on earth do you mean?" I asked. She said, "You too have been trying to think outside the prison of words." Somehow I was shocked into seeing what Lois meant. She was telling me that the dilemma the great Ludwig Wittgenstein had struggled with was the same one I had been struggling with. I saw that not just the postmodernists but many of the important theorists in the family therapy movement were part of this effort too. In our big and small ways, we had all been trying to get free of what Wittgenstein called "the bewitchment of language" (1953, #109).

Author Walker Percy (1996) talks about trying to make oneself aware of the linguistic frame as "something like wearing gold eyeglasses and trying to see gold." Now it seemed that we had to see beyond and past this frame. We were, to repeat Derrida's wonderful phrase, "trying to find a crevice through which the yet unnameable glimmer beyond the closure can be glimpsed." Only then can we begin to recognize how deeply the so-called human sciences have deceived us, and how serious are the consequences for the professions we work in.

If we were to treat relational practice as a similar enclosure, this would mean that we would have to "see through" the theoretical descriptions in which we have been immured. I have already cited Schoen's (1984) opinion that in the "soft" sciences, researchers should turn to hands-on work as a source of theory, rather than the other way round. When I first came to the University of Massachusetts in 1983, I was amazed to find that Sheila McNamee and Jack Lannamann, recent graduate students in the Department of Communication, had been writing articles that used Milan-style paradoxes as illustrations of relational impasses (Tomm, Lannamann, & McNamee, 1984). From that time on, McNamee and her associates never lost touch with the front-line workers who were struggling with problems of communication and relationship. In fact, it was her work with these people that led her and Gergen to the concept of relational responsibility, which they jointly fine-tuned later on.

I brought in this bit of history because Gergen and McNamee have drawn so many of their examples of relational responsibility from teaching, mediation, social research, and organizational consulting. When they themselves organize conferences, they include hands-on people from all these areas and not just other academics. They have long had an abiding interest in conferences that mix both species, like the one I did in Northampton in 1984, and like many similar conferences, from the Macy Conferences after the war to the still-continuing conferences of the American Society of Cybernetics. Perhaps this is why Gergen and McNamee's writings felt so profoundly validating to me. In them, I read account after account of practices that were based on a connectionist point of view and congruent with the idea of a different voice. Many of the scholar-practitioners I most admired had been singled out, and I felt as though my ragged band of wilderness guides had finally found a home.

What was this home? As I have said before, I had long been thinking that the field of communication was the successor to psychology and social psychology. These latter fields targeted the individual packets we call "selves," or bunches of selves, instead of looking at what John Shotter (1993b) terms "joint action." Worse yet, they were hopelessly essentialist. I have decided that when I come back in my next life, I will look for a degree in postmodern communication. Under its aegis, I could perform the switch that Schoen describes of going from experience up rather than from theory down. The term "relational responsibility" might not have been coined if what I call the "fingertip people" had not been brought into the equation early on.

Relational Responsibility in Practice

What, then, is involved in the "doing" of relational responsibility? McNamee and Gergen's respective volumes overlap on this subject, but I will pull out three main points. One seems to be a preference for affirmation, whether by witnessing suffering or evoking strength. Both authors note that David Cooperrider's (1996) work in organizational consulting is based on a practice that he calls "appreciative inquiry." Instead of asking people to talk about the problems in an organization, he asks them to talk about the areas where things are going well. This has turned out to be an immensely useful direction, promoting confidence and inspiring imagination. Despite White's (1997) warnings about the "culture of applause," a gift for positive discovery seems to be favored by many of the new approaches in both therapy and organizational consulting.

Another feature cited is "polyvocality," meaning practices that expand the number of voices. Karl Tomm's (1998) idea of asking people to take on the voice of the "internalized other" is one example, and Tom Andersen's (1991) reflecting team another. The reflecting process, Gergen notes, "invites a dialogic, open-ended search for useful meanings," and "loosens the grip of professional authority" (1999, pp. 174–175). Both books cite the letters that Peggy Penn and Marilyn Frankfurt (1994) ask their clients to write to persons important to them, with the aim of opening up new inner dialogues. A central target of these methods is the reduction of blame through entering the reality of another.

One more facet of relational responsibility is its belief in the power of community. Gergen (1999) refers to the Public Conversation Project (Roth, Chasin, Chasin, Becker, & Herzig, 1992) in Watertown, Massachusetts, a group that sets up discussions between people of opposing views, like pro-life and pro-choice. In these experiments, each group takes turns speaking with a mediator while the other group listens in. The hope is to get people to hear each other out rather than trying to convert each other or the world. In this goal, at least, the project has succeeded. Adding to the list, Gergen mentions narrative therapists White and Epston (1990) and the interest they take in the power relations of ordinary life. I would also add the role of the ad hoc communities that White calls on in his "definitional ceremonies" and that have such a transformative impact.

It was striking to me to see how much thought McNamee and Gergen have given to the world of family therapy in their books: they mention, if briefly, the kinship work of family psychiatrists Murray Bowen (1978) and Ivan Boszormenyi-Nagy (Boszormenyi-Nagy & Sparks, 1973); the systemic methods pioneered by the Milan team (Selvini Palazzoli et al., 1978; Boscolo et al., 1987), and further developed by Campbell, Draper, and Huffington (1989) and Fruggeri, Telfner, Castellucci, Marzari, and Matteini (1991). Also included are solution-focused models (Berg, 1994, de Shazer, 1994), Anderson and Goolishian's (1992) concept of not-knowing, and the new "open dialogues" work in Finland (Seikkula, et al., 1995). I was glad for this attention to our field, because it felt as though, at long last, our hands-on experiments were being taken up and amplified by a scholarly and academic community.

The Ethic of Justice vs. the Ethic of Care

In the foregoing discussion, I have welcomed the concept of relational responsibility. However, I am aware of the doubts this position may provoke. Critics have long accused systemic therapists of being out of touch with social and political issues in the "real world," to the point of being unethical. These naysayers may well decide that the idea of relational responsibility is a sham. The argument seems logical in the context of reform movements that place a high value on cultural and attitudinal change. A number of schools of therapy have made the amelioration of injustice a primary concern.

But there is another way to look at this debate. I am referring to a research article by Newfield, Newfield, Sperry, and Smith (2000), called "Ethical Decision Making among Family Therapists and Individual Therapists." These authors developed a protocol to determine styles of ethical reasoning as shown in the work of individual and family therapists. To do this, they identified two well-known conceptual camps: the justice model of moral reasoning developed by Lawrence Kohlberg (1981), and the care model put forward by Carol Gilligan (1982). As I have said previously, Kohlberg's model is based on the rights and obligations of the individual and emphasizes abstract principles of fairness, equality and what is right. Gilligan's ethic of care finds moral decisions to be embedded in relational contexts and for this reason their possible impact on the relational field must be carefully considered.

Newfield et al. point out that Kohlberg's more traditional point of view has been the standard in regard to professional behavior. Examining the code of ethics as defined by the American Psychological Association, they say that it is based on the doctrine of individual rights. But since the arrival of family therapy, a more complex picture has emerged. If you work with families and side with one individual or group against another, you run the risk of worsening the situation for everyone. There are dual relationships to worry about and many dilemmas that center on conflicting interests and opposing points of view. The side-taking process itself intensifies problems or makes them more likely to appear. This is where Gilligan's ethic of care can be a good alternative. In the multi-layered field of loyalties that any family presents, the best course is the one most sensitive to those pulls.

The article goes on to state that there is presently a conflict between family therapy's focus on the systemic context, which mainly follows a care model, and the guidelines used by professional organizations, which follow a justice model. The authors cite Hare-Mustin's (1988) attack on family therapy on the grounds that systemic assumptions do not follow the legal/moral codes that protect the individual. In rebuttal, they quote Becvar and Becvar's (1996) statement that the assumptions underlying the APA code are "individualistic, absolutistic, reductionistic and supportive of the linear model of cause/effect thinking." The authors add that this situation puts family therapists in a bind. If they work from the systemic perspective most of them have been trained in, they risk offending the code of ethics of their professional organizations.

I was glad to have the struggle between a justice model, which seems to be allied with the black and white certainties of modernism, and a care model, which is closer to the shifting hues of a postmodern view, laid out in such a clear form. As a family therapist, I have frequently been caught in this bind but have not known how to describe it without seeming to collude with abuse. The authors of this study, being researchers, are in a different place: they only ask which ethic is most frequently used by both individual and family therapists, and what are the differences between these two groups on this score.

To answer this question, the authors set up a research project that included thirty individual therapists and thirty family therapists. They asked each group to respond to three ethically challenging dilemmas. One was a real-life situation. Each participant was asked to describe a case of her own that had presented difficult moral issues. The second was a description of a dilemma involving an individual client, and the third was a description of one that concerned a family. There was, as you might expect, a difference between the individual therapists and the family therapists in the matter of clinical approach. The family therapists were far more directive than their individually oriented counterparts. However, they were not asked to give their own opinions about which model they subscribed to. The transcripts were stripped of identifying signs, and each value statement was coded as either "justice" or "care" by outside raters according to a protocol prepared beforehand.

What surprised the researchers was that there were no significant differences between individual and family therapists as to ethical outlook. Analysis of the transcripts showed that most of the therapists, regardless of model, used an ethic of care. No difference was found between the hypothetical and the real cases either. This conclusion suggests that there is a reason for the concerns that many therapists have voiced in regard to the limitations of the "justice" stance taken by their professional organizations. As a result, the authors say that the guidelines that now exist should be modified to include a relational ethic as well. In their words:

> Guidance for considering relationship responsibilities [should] be provided by the addition of a *relationship-caring process.* . . [which addresses] the relationship complexities consistently identified by therapists as ethically challenging. (Newfield et al., 2000, p. 185)

This piece of research is useful because it sets out the clash between the individually-oriented justice ethic that prevails in our oversight bodies and the relationally-oriented care ethic which seems to be predominant in most models of therapy. However, polarities are slippery, and there can be disagreement about which formulation to choose. Sharon Welch (1990) prefers to speak of an "ethic of control" versus an "ethic of risk." Sometimes, she says, it is important to take a stand for justice, regardless of consequences. In addition, pitting justice against care sets up a no-win escalation. I can easily imagine a standoff between political correctness and cultural correctness, with political feminists on one side and cultural feminists on the other. The term "relationally responsible," in fact, could set up the same type of escalation. Mulling it over, I would prefer the phrase "relationally responsive," with the hope that it could equitably encompass justice and care alike.

Communal Practice

Throughout this book, I have been putting together arguments for a type of endeavor in the relationship therapies that I call "communal practice." In *Realities and Relationships*, Gergen links the word "communality" with forms of communication that he distinguishes from the purely linguistic realm. This is what he says:

> Words (or texts) within themselves bear no meaning; they fail to communicate. They only appear to generate meaning by virtue of

their place within the realm of human interaction. It is human interchange that gives language its capacity to mean, and it must stand as the critical locus of concern. I wish then to replace textuality with communality. This shift allows us to restructure much that has been said about meaning within texts as a commentary on forms of relatedness. (1994, pp. 263–4)

The first time I thought of therapy in terms of "forms of relatedness" was in the mid- nineties, when I was watching a videotape of Harlene Anderson interviewing a family. I have described this moment before (1998), but looking back it may have been more of a milestone than I realized. Anderson was listening to a daughter talking at length while the rest of the family sat back and said nothing. Haley used to call this format "individual therapy in the setting of the family," and dismissed it. However, in this case it felt like something different. I asked Anderson later about her perception of what she was doing, and she said that she thought that when she listened so intently to one family member, the others in the family began to listen more intently, too.

I saw that Anderson was not concentrating on the act of speaking so much as the act of hearing. By offering an experience of indirect listening, she gave those present a chance to overhear the speaker's story without needing to be defensive or to immediately respond. The way she created a context of listening seemed to act as a solvent that altered the feelings and attitudes, or what I began to call the "cloud of perceptions," that had come in the door. I also recalled the way some of the postmodern thinkers had begun to replace the usual vocabulary of units (the individual, the family, the community) with one that depicted the web of language that links people together in daily life.

Carrying this idea forward, social psychologist Edward Sampson (1990) observes that postmodern theory replaces the autonomous self of modern psychology with individuals embedded in "communities of belonging" or "ensembles of relationship." In the same vein, Lyotard (1984) suggests dropping "Newtonian anthropologies," like the ones based on structuralism or systems theory, in favor of "a pragmatics of language particles." This turn away from the Newtonian unit supported my belief that we had gone too far in trying to change a behavior, restructure a family, or intervene in a system. What if a problem consisted of a "swarm of participations," like a cloud of gnats? What if we decided that our task was to influence that cloud but that we had to do so from the lowly position of one of the gnats?

However, it was the theory-in-use of the reflecting team that brought the concept of communal practice most vividly to life for me. Wherever this team went, connection followed. It turned opposing voices into mutually respecting ones. It allowed the therapist to decenter herself. The "therapeutic boundary" began to melt and the intervention as I knew it became a thing of the past. Most amazing of all, the atmosphere of the session would become intent and focused, as if we were all experiencing the pull of a good mystery story. We were often rewarded by a denouement of unexpected beauty and force.

I had long been brooding on the social weaving that resulted from using Andersen's reflecting process. It was not the reflections themselves that so interested me but the fact that one group would comment on what another group said, then yet another group, juxtaposing layer upon layer of response. As I said before, Michael White does something similar in the "telling and re-telling" (1997) of his definitional ceremonies, which are his way of creating a "community of concern." I had noticed that White's work had taken a dramatic turn toward personal and communal transformation after he began to incorporate reflecting teams into his practice, and I too have found them to be the source of a remarkable intensification of experience.

It occurred to me that this communal perspective rests on a change in the definition of what needs to change. The target of the social therapies has moved from the unit to the situation. Social therapists, as opposed to psychological therapists, attend to the relational fall-out from emotional distress: isolation, division, fearfulness, mistrust, secrets. What comes through the door is always a pessimistic environment, and since an environment is communally experienced, the antidote must be communal too.

Open Dialogues

Together with psychiatrist Jakko Seikkula and others in Northern Europe, Andersen is now working from a communal perspective in an international setting. A tier of teams has evolved that includes over twenty-five groups from eight countries: Norway, Sweden, Finland, Denmark, Northwest Russia, and the Baltic States. They meet once a year in different locations to explore forms of dialogue that can, in Andersen's phrase, "meet psychotic crises without medication and hospitalization." Seikkula's group was one of the first to use the term "open dialogues" (1995) to deal with crises in acute care settings. These were conversational circles attended by all the persons who were involved in the story of a person's breakdown. Seikkula and his team (1995) subsequently published a research study showing that this way of working was more effective than hospitalization in lowering the incidence of hospital admission, the degree of recidivism, and the use of medication.

What particularly interested me in Seikkula's work was the emphasis on speech rather than symptoms. In a recent article, Penn (2000b) tells us that

Seikkula's definition of a psychosis is "a crisis in language." His teams meet with, as far as possible, everyone who is touched by the crisis. By listening to and exploring the wordings of the person who is at the center of concern, a common language starts to evolve. Over time, the wordings begin to change and their meanings become more transparent and shared. Seikkula feels that establishing this new shared language is crucial for the work's success.

Andersen is writing about the nature of these dialogues, too. In a brochure for one of his northern seminars, he says that there are three types of descriptions that we can call upon in the crisis of psychosis. The first is when we "know" and can "explain" what it is that confronts us. The second is when we can only understand it in terms of "how it might be" or "how it might be different." The third is when we confront something that we can neither explain or understand, and this is when it can only be sensed in our bodies. Andersen tells us that we can choose to respond to these dilemmas in either a monological or a dialogical way. A monological conversation, he says, is made up of "those who question and those who reply" and fits well with situations that can yield hard and fast answers. In cases where it is hard to know how to relate or understand, a dialogical conversation fits better.

I have been fascinated to watch this particular strand of the braid take shape. The reflecting process of Andersen, linked with the open dialogues of Seikkula, and swelled by a growing network of professionals, is bringing change to the acute settings of Northern Europe. These groups are certainly introducing a communal perspective on a large scale. What continually astonishes me about this field of ours is the way it moves and changes unpredictably. Just as one says "That's it!" another strand appears, or a new loaf goes into the oven.

Before ending, I want to include some anecdotes about the work of other therapists who are working on this communal frontier. Marcelo Pakman (1994) is a psychiatrist of the disenfranchised who works mainly with Hispanic families in Springfield, Massachusetts. In his article "Disciplinary Knowledge, Postmodernism and Globalization," Pakman (2000) points out that even when we have postmodern good intentions, our practices are not postmodern. Structured by our disciplines and our institutions, these practices have become "increasingly and enthusiastically part of a globalized system" that helps to maintain the status quo.

Pakman's answer is to apply Schoen's (1984) call for "a reflective turn" in both teaching and doing. Citing Foucault's studies of disciplinary knowledge, he says that we must pay more attention to "dividing practices" that separate the normal from the abnormal; "scientific classification," which details the traits of the abnormal; and "the objectification of the subject," which creates an identity or self that becomes the object of the discipines described above. Inspired by Schoen, Pakman makes a parallel between therapy and a "design studio," in this way counterbalancing the scientific image that has so far held sway. I like this analogy, so long as we do not create a rigid skills hierarchy to replace the medical one.

Pakman's work has a political side too. Calling what he does "critical social practice," he designs his words and actions to touch many systems at once. For instance, in one of the settings in which he works, he developed a "risk reduction" endeavor that invited each professional who saw a client to sign off on a list of risk categories. In this way, he tried to build a systemic bias into the record-keeping system. He will also create linkages—itself a political practice—by recruiting ad hoc players from the ordinary settings that present themselves. His interactions with the people who consult him are in this way a kind of invisible weaving—what I call "knit one, purl two." In tiny movements of the needle, he will catch up the loose ends of the skein and link people through himself to others.

For example, Pakman (1999) tells us about Marguerite who is depressed, refusing to eat, and on the edge of being hospitalized. Pakman connects with the "hard time" she has been having. She asks him for medication. He tells her he is not interested in medication but in "life." She does not answer, so he goes to "death." Is she willing herself to die? She says, "There is nothing left for me." Pakman refuses to enter the death watch role, saying that this is not his line of business. He says that nobody else in the room wants that role either, because they all care about her. He tells her to ask two of the staff members who have worked with her to tell her why this is so. They feed back to her a picture of courage in the face of adversity. Like starting a balky motor on a boat, the engine catches. A plan evolves where she agrees to participate with the people who care for her under a regime of recovery rather than one of force.

Another communal worker, Chris Kinman (1999), leans on a "language of gifts" in his work with First Nations families and their caregivers in Vancouver, B.C. Using vernacular documentation as part of his work, he has devised an alternative to case assessment forms. Instead of offering diagnoses or pathologized descriptions, his "collaborative action plan" collects anecdotes under "gifts," "potentials," "roadblocks," and "community contributions." Most recently, Kinman has used this formula to work with public health nurses, compiling their activities in printed booklets that represent their voices and those of the persons they see, a procedure that has done much to remoralize this group.

Not long ago, Kinman asked me to lead a workshop in Vancouver called "Honoring Community." During this meeting, I interviewed small pods of people who worked with children. Most of them were nonprofessionals, with pride of place given to a group of rough-looking but tender-hearted bikers. These men were running group homes for very troubled youths, and much to their amusement I gave them the name of "fairy godfathers." Striking a different note, psychiatrist Robin Routledge brought in an advocacy group made up of ex-clients from a hospital on Vancouver Island called "The Mood Clinic." I was greatly touched by this experience, and this kind of meeting has continued to be part of Kinman's work.

Finally, I must mention psychologist/coach Patricia Romney, an African-American consultant to agencies and businesses in the Valley where I live. She tells me that she is using the Black Love ideas of the late management consultant Leroy Wells (1999), who taught her at Yale many years ago. When Romney was initally asked to consult with institutions that were trying to break free of complex legacies of racism, she faced many barriers. It was in response to this these impasses that Romney, calling upon the memory of her mentor at Yale, began looking for the windows behind the walls and started to use terms like "wonder," "reverence," "respect," and "love." Her account of this experience, "Can You Love Them Enough?" is in *Feminism, Community, and Communication* (2000), edited by scholar-therapist Mary Olson. This volume contains several other articles that depict communal practices, including the one I wrote and drew on for the introduction to this book.

The virtue of the practices I am talking about is that they assume the possibility of a good city. I am reminded of Lake Titicaca, which is situated high in the Andes mountains and is surrounded by reeds. My mother, who had gone to Peru in 1942 to put together an exhibition of Mayan weaving, was the first person I knew who had ever been there. She told us that when the local people need a dwelling, they lay reeds on top of reeds until there is a floating platform six feet thick and then they build their houses on it, also out of reeds. White's term "thick description" comes to mind. Upon such platforms an entire village can be built.

The Other Bateson

As I started with a Bateson, I would like to end with one too. Mary Catherine, the daughter of Gregory Bateson and the anthropologist Margaret Mead, has been pursuing her own ethical odyssey across the boundaries of culture, class and race. The term "relational responsibility" seems to bring us from the ecological transformations we face as a species to the social ones we face as members of groups. Moving along a similar track, Catherine Bateson puts her spotlight on human relationships. Although she does not use labels such as "postmodern," or "social constructionist," her style of writing is strongly suggestive of the shifts I have been writing about.

Bateson's next to last book, *Peripheral Visions* (1994), starts with the metaphor of a Persian garden. Using its intricate design as a symbol for the connections between the elements of Iranian society, she tells the story of a small epiphany. It was Easter, and she had taken her two-year-old daughter, Vanni, to the garden of an Iranian family for the ritual slaughter of a sheep. Explaining the procedure to the child on her hip, she named the various organs as they were taken out of the dead animal: heart, liver, stomach. She was shocked to see how big the lungs were and realized that she herself had never seen a large animal being dismembered before. The names of the organs had been bloodless abstractions; now they suddenly became real. Building on this dissonance, she comments on the shock of cultural differences, and how important it is to experience life from another perch:

> There are truths to be discovered in looking at a butchered sheep and recognizing heart and lungs and death itself as common. We have work to do to make empathy an acceptable form of learning and knowing for people who are not poets and therapists. We have to make it possible . . . to admit empathy as a legitimate, conscious discipline . . . thoughtful empathy as a form of knowing, leading to effective action. (p. 141)

In this book, Bateson weds the spiritual concerns of her father to the cultural interests of her mother. She finds merit in a non-zero sum "unlimited goodness"; prefers a "mutable self" to a stationary one; and notes the genius of women in being able to attend to many pulls at once. She ends by describing an encounter between a group of Tibetan monks and a Sufi teacher, where a meeting of minds about a ritual dissolves the linguistic and cultural barriers between them in a puff.

In her last book, *Full Circles, Overlapping Lives*, Catherine Bateson writes about a life history seminar she gave at Spelman College to a mixed group of faculty and students. She describes how she used the membership of the seminar itself as a way to make her point. Before even beginning, she made sure that the group included people of different status (some members were undergraduates, some were on the faculty); different ages (some of the women had children the same age as the students); different ethnicities (the group included whites, Hispanics, and African-Americans); and different sexual orientations (one young woman was bisexual).

The participants, despite wide varieties of life experience, were fascinated and moved by each other's stories, and all, including Bateson herself, became comfortable in sharing them. After the seminar was over, Bateson had the idea of threading the stories that came out of it into a book. Some were told by her, some by the participants, and she fashioned them together like the quilt that graces the book's cover. Reading it was to experience the Persian garden of a relationally responsive world.

An important verb for Bateson is "to cherish." She feels that our task on earth is to take care of each other, to "mind" who and what is in our charge, to attend and be present to each other. My colleague, Mary Olson, used this point while teaching a class that contained a mixed group of white and African-American students, one of whom had earlier ties to the Black Panthers. Tensions ran high until Olson described a talk Bateson had just given at a local bookstore, and asked the question: "How can we cherish each other across these differences?" After that question, she said, the mood of the group lightened, the tension broke, and her students began to address the heartfelt issues that were raised.

To move to another level, Bateson's style confirms my interest in "spoken writing." Here I am talking about works that are not necessarily scholarly but are informed by scholarship. This kind of writing would have an informal tone, an acceptance of one's natural subjectivity, an attentiveness to context, and a place for the voices of others. The inclusion of "painted language" would be important too. Most of our communications derive strength from images, metaphors, anecdotes, and analogies, since these devices allow us to escape, momentarily at least, from our word webs. They are ideal for teaching and counseling because they do not depend on true or false, or right or wrong.

They are also "performative " (Newman & Holzman, 1996). After all, a metaphor "performs" rather than saying that something "is." Bateson's seminar was full of words, stories and activities that performed, and these performances had a strong joining effect on the group. The social therapy of performance philosopher Fred Newman (2000) and theorist Lois Holzman (1999) is a more venerable example of this process at its best. I visited their center at the East Side Institute in New York one evening, having been asked to speak to one of their groups, and was extremely appreciative when Holzman, who had helped to organize the event, thanked me in her final comment for "not giving them any truth."

This book, too, is a weave of stories, performance, and painted language. It, too, attempts to be a non-essentializing tale. Since my early discovery of the field of family therapy, I had a hunch that drove me in this direction. Other people felt it, too. Gregory Bateson sniffed it with his wise nose, Harry Goolishian and Harlene Anderson felt it in their not-knowing bones, Tom Andersen found it in his inner and outer voices, Peggy Penn held it in her poetic grasp, Lois Shawver saw it through the chinks of language, Michael White spied it through the cracks of discourse, and Kenneth

Gergen and Sheila McNamee found it in the way we build uncommon worlds.

These innovators, among others, have offered a connectionist position for the field of consultation. This movement has sometimes been called "systemic," sometimes "narrative," sometimes "postmodern," sometimes "poststructural," sometimes "collaborative," and sometimes "communal," but the conversation always keeps going and continues to evolve. My sense of this phenomenon right now is like the experience of a swimmer who is riding the waves: there is that moment of lightness when you feel the swell lifting you up and you hover there, weightless, knowing that the wave is just about to crash forward on the beach.

References

Abbott, E.A. (1963). *Flatland: A romance of many dimensions*. New York: Barnes & Noble.

Ackerman, N. (1937). The family as a social and emotional unit." *Bulletin of the Kansas Mental Hygiene Society, 12,* 2.

Ackerman, (1966). *Treating the troubled family*. New York: Basic Books.

Alexander, C. (1979). *The timeless way of building*. New York: Oxford University Press.

Andersen, T. (1992). Reflections on reflecting with families. In S. McNamee & K. Gergen (Eds.) *Therapy as social construction*. London: Sage Publications.

Andersen, T. (1987). The reflecting team. *Family Process, 26,* 415–428.

Andersen, T. (Ed.) (1991). *The reflecting team*. New York: Norton.

Andersen, T. (1998). One sentence on five lines about creating meaning. *Human Systems, 9,* 73–80.

Anderson, H. (1997). *Conversation, language and possibilities*. New York: Basic Books.

Anderson, H., & Goolishian, H. (1988). Human systems as linguistic systems. *Family Process, 27,* 371–393.

Anderson, H., & Goolishian, H. (1992). The client is the expert. In S. McNamee & K. Gergen (Eds.), *Therapy as social construction*. Newbury Park, CA: Sage.

Aponte, H. (1976). The family-school interview: An eco-structural approach. *Family Process, 15,* 303–311.

Aponte, H. (1985). The negotiation of values in therapy. *Family Process, 24,* 323–338.

Aponte, H. (1986). If I don't get simple, I cry. *Family Process, 25,* 531–548.

Aponte, H. (1996). *Bread and spirit*. New York: Norton.

Armstrong, M.N. (1998). *Active listener and the speaker: How does that make you feel?* Unpublished honour's thesis, Department of Psychology, University of Victoria, Victoria, British Columbia, Canada.

Auerswald, E.H. (1968). Interdisciplinary versus ecological approach, *Family Process, 7,* 205–215.

Bachelard, G. (1994). *The poetics of space.* (M. Jolas, Trans.). Boston: Beacon Press.

Bahktin, M. (1981). *The dialogic imagination.* Austin: University of Texas Press.

Bateson, G. (1958). *Naven* (2nd ed.). Stanford, CA: Stanford University Press.

Bateson, G. (1972). *Steps to an ecology of mind.* New York: Ballantine.

Bateson, G. (1976). Comments on Haley's "History." In C. Sluzki (Ed.), *Double bind: The foundation of the communicational approach to the family.* New York: Grune & Stratton.

Bateson, G. (1978). The birth of the double bind. In M. Berger (Ed.), *Beyond the double bind.* New York: Brunner/Mazel.

Bateson, G., & Bateson, M.C. (1987). *Angels fear.* New York: Dutton.

Bateson, G., & Ruesch, J. (1951). *Communication: The social matrix of psychiatry.* New York: Norton.

Bateson, M.C. (1972). *Our own metaphor.* New York: Knopf.

Bateson, M.C. (1984). *With a daughter's eye.* New York: Morrow.

Bateson, M.C. (1990). *Composing a life.* New York: Penguin.

Bateson, M.C. (1994). *Peripheral visions.* New York: HarperCollins.

Bateson, M.C. (2000). *Full circles, overlapping lives.* New York: Random House.

Bavelas, J.B. (1992). Research into the pragmatics of human communication. *Journal of Strategic and Systemic Therapy, 11*(2), 15–29.

Bavelas, J.B., Black, A., Lemery, C. R., & Mullett, J. (1986). "I show how you feel." Motor mimicry as a communicative act. *Journal of Personality and Social Psychology, 50,* 322–329.

Bavelas, J.B., Coates, L., & Johnson, T. (2000). Listeners as co-narrators. *Journal of Personality and Social Psychology, 79,* 941–952.

Bavelas, J.B., McGee, D., Phillips, B., & Routledge, R. (in press). Microanalysis of communication in psychotherapy. *Human Systems.*

Becvar, D., & Becvar, R. (1996). *Family therapy: A systematic integration* (3rd ed). Boston: Allyn & Bacon.

Behan, C. (1999). Linking lives around shared themes: Narrative group therapy with gay men. *Gecko, 2,* 18–34.

Belenky, M.F., Clinchy, B.M., Goldberger, N.R., & Tarule, J.M. (1986). *Women's ways of knowing."* New York: Basic Books.

Berg, I.K. (1994). *Family-based services: A solution-focused approach.* New York: Norton.

Berger, P., & Luckmann, T. (1966). *The social construction of reality.* New York: Doubleday.

Berman, A. (1988). *From the new criticism to deconstruction.* Chicago: University of Illinois Press.

Boscolo, L., Cecchin, G., Hoffman, L., & Penn, P. (1987). *Milan systemic family therapy.* New York: Basic Books.

Boszormenyi-Nagy, I., & Sparks, G. (1973). *Invisible loyalties.* New York: Harper and Row.

Bowen, M. (1978). *Family therapy in clinical practice.* New York: Aronson.

Boyd-Franklin, N. (1989). *Black families in therapy.* New York: Guilford.

Brown, L.M., & Gilligan, C. (1992). *Meeting at the crossroads.* New York: Ballantine.

Bruner, J. (1986). *Actual minds, possible worlds.* Cambridge, MA: Harvard University Press.

Bruner, J. (1990). *Acts of meaning.* Cambridge, MA: Harvard University Press.

Buckley, W. (1968). *Modern systems research for the behavioral scientist.* Chicago: Aldine Press.

Burman, E. (1994). *Deconstructing developmental psychology.* New York: Routledge.

Cade, B., & O'Hanlon, W. *A brief guide to brief therapy.* New York: Norton.

Campbell, D., Draper, R., & Huffington, C. *Second thoughts on the theory and practice of the Milan approach to family therapy.* London: Karnac.

Capra, F. (1982). *The turning point.* New York: Simon & Schuster.

Cecchin, G., & Lane, G. (1991). *Irreverence: A strategy for therapist survival.* London: Karnac Books.

Cooley, C.H. (1964). *Human nature and the social order.* New York: Schocken Books.

Cooperrider, D. (1996). Resources for getting appreciative inquiry started. *OD Practitioner, 28,* 23–34.

Chodorow, N. (1978). *The reproduction of mothering.* Berkeley, CA: University of California Press.

Crawford, M. (1995). *Talking difference.* Thousand Oaks, CA: Sage.

Davidson, D. (1984). *Inquiries into truth and interpretation.* New York: Oxford University Press.

Davis, J. (1996). *Whose bar/bat mitzvah is this anyway?* New York: St. Martin's Press.

Davis, J. (2000). Ritual as therapy, therapy as ritual. In M. Olson (Ed.), *Feminism, community and communication.* Binghamton, NY: Haworth.

Deissler, K. (2000). The social poetics of therapeutic conversations. Posted on Internet: w.w.w.california.com/~rathbone/diessler3.htm.

Deleuze, G. and Guattari, F. (1984). *Anti-oedipus: Capitalism and schizophrenia.* Minneapolis: University of Minnesota Press.

Dell, P., & Goolishian, H. (1979). *Order through fluctuation.* Presented at the Annual Scientific Meeting of the A.K. Rice Institute, Houston, Texas.

Derrida, J. (1976). *Of grammatology.* (G.C. Spivak, Trans.). Baltimore: Johns Hopkins University Press.

Derrida, J. (1978). *Writing and difference.* (A. Bass, Trans.). Chicago: University of Chicago.

Derrida, J. (1982). Signature, event, context. In J. Derrida (Ed.), *Margins of philosophy* (pp. 309–330). Chicago: University of Chicago Press.

de Saussure, F. (1983). *Course in general linguistics.* (Roy Harris, Trans.). London: Duckworth.

de Shazer, S. (1985). *Keys to solution in brief therapy.* New York: Norton.

de Shazer, S. (1994). *Words were originally magic.* New York: Norton.

Dillard, A. (1994). *The Annie Dillard reader.* New York: HarperCollins.

Ehrenreich, B. (1978). *For her own good.* New York: Anchor Books.

Elkaim, M. (1997). *If you love me, don't love me: Undoing reciprocal double binds and other methods of change in couple and family therapy.* Northvale, NJ: Aronson.

Epston, D., & Tomm, K. (1992). Internalized-other questioning with couples. In S. Gilligan & R. Price (Eds.), *Therapeutic conversations.* New York: Norton.

Epston, D., & White, M. (1992). *Experience, contradiction, narrative & imagination.* Adelaide, South Australia: Dulwich Centre Publications.

Falicov, C. (1998). *Latino families in therapy.* New York: Guilford.

Fish, S. (1980). *Is there a text in this class?* Cambridge, MA: Harvard University Press.

Foucault, M. (1965). *The history of madness.* New York: Pantheon Books.

Foucault, M. (1972). *The archeology of knowledge.* New York: Harper Colophon.

Foucault, M. (1975). *The birth of the clinic.* New York: Vintage.

Foucault, M. (1978). *The history of sexuality.* New York: Pantheon Books.

Foucault, M. (1979). *Discipline and punish.* New York: Random House.

Freidson, E. (1972). *The profession of medicine.* New York: Dodd, Mead.

Fruggieri, L., Telfner, U., Castellucci, A., Marzari, M., & Matteini, M. (1991). *New systemic ideas from the Italian mental health movement.* London: Karnac.

Furman, B., & Ahola, T. (1992). *Solution talk.* New York: Norton.

Gadamer, H-G. (1975). *Truth and method.* (C. Barden & J. Cumming, Trans.). New York: Seabury.

Geertz, C. (1973). Thick description: Toward an interpretive theory of cultures. In C. Geertz, *The interpretation of cultures.* New York: Basic Books.

Gergen, K. (1994). *Realities and relationships.* Cambridge, MA: Harvard University Press.

Gergen, K. (1999). *An invitation to social construction.* Thousand Oaks, CA: Sage.

Gilligan, C. (1982). *In a different voice.* Cambridge, MA: Harvard University Press.

Gleick, J. (1987). *Chaos.* New York: Penguin Books.

Goldner, V., Penn, P., Sheinberg, M., & Walker, G. (1990). Love and violence: Gender paradoxes in volatile relationships. *Family Process, 29,* 343–364.

Goode, E. (2000, Aug. 8). How culture molds habits of thought. *The New York Times.*

Goodman, N. (1984). *Of mind and other matters.* Cambridge, MA: Harvard University Press.

Goodrich, T.J., Rampage, C., Ellman, B., & Halstead, K. (1998). *Feminist family therapy: A casebook.* New York: Norton.

Gopnik, A. (1998, May). The invention of Oscar Wilde. *The New Yorker,* p.79.

Griffith, J., & Griffith, M. (1994). *The body speaks.* New York: Basic Books.

Habermas, H-J (1971). *Knowledge and human interest.* Boston: Beacon Press.

Haley, J. (1963). *Strategies of psychotherapy.* New York: Grune & Stratton.

Haley, J. (1962). Whither family therapy? *Family Process, 1.*

Haley, J. (1968). Control in psychotherapy with schizophrenics. In D. Jackson (Ed.), *Therapy, communication, and control.* Palo Alto, CA: Science and Behavior Books.

Haley, J. (1976). *Problem-solving therapy.* San Francisco: Jossey-Bass.

Haley, J., & Hoffman, L. (1967). Techniques of family therapy. New York: Basic Books.

Hardy, K., & Laszloffy, T. (1995). The cultural geneogram: Key to training culturally competent therapists. *Journal of Marital and Family Therapy, 21,* 227–237.

Hare-Mustin, R. (1988). The meaning of difference: Gender theory, postmodernism and psychology." *American Psychologist, 43,* 455-464.

Hare-Mustin, R., & Marecek, J. (1990). *Making a difference.* New Haven: Yale University Press.

Harré, R. (1984). *Personal being.* Cambridge, MA: Harvard University Press.

Hartman, A. (1994). *Reflections and controversy.* Washington, DC: NASW Press.

Hetrick, E. & Hoffman, L. (1982). The Broome St. Network. In Sanders, Kurren & Fischer (Eds.), *Foundations of social work practice.* New York: International Thompson Publishing.

Hoffman, L. (1981). Deviation-amplifying processes in natural groups. In J. Haley (Ed.), *Changing families.* New York: Grune & Stratton.

Hoffman, L. (1981). *Foundations of family therapy.* New York: Basic Books.

Hoffman, L. (1985). Beyond power and control. *Family Systems Medicine, 3,* 381–396.

Hoffman, L. (1993). *Exchanging Voices.* London: Karnac Books.

Hoffman, L. (1998). Setting aside the model in family therapy. *Family Process, 24,* 145–156.

Hoffman, L. (2000). A communal perspective for the relational therapies. In M. Olson (Ed.), *Feminism, community and communication.* Binghamton: Haworth.

Hoffman, L., & Davis, J. (1993). Tekka with feathers. In S. Friedman (Ed.), *The New Language of Change.* New York: The Guilford Press.

Hoffman, L., & Long, L. (1974). A systems dilemma. In R. Klenk, & R. Ryan (Eds.), *The Practice of Social Work.* Belmont, CA: Wadsworth Publishing.

Holzman, L. (1999). Life as performance. In L. Holzman (Ed.), *Performing psychology.* New York: Routledge.

Hoy, D.C. (1986). *Foucault: A critical reader.* Oxford: Basil Blackwell.

Imber-Black, E. (Ed.) (1993). Secrets in families and family therapy. New York: Norton.

Imber-Black, E., Roberts, J., & Whiting, R. (1988). *Rituals in families and family therapy.* New York: Norton.

Imber-Coppersmith, E. (1985). Teaching trainees to think in triads. *Journal of Marital and Family Therapy, 2,* 61–66.

Jackson. D. (1957). The question of family homeostasis. *Psychiatric Quarterly Supplement, 31,* 79–90.

Jordan, J.V., & Surrey, J. L. (1986). The self-in-relation: Empathy and the mother-daughter relationship. In T. Bernay & D.W. Kantor (Eds.), *The psychology of today's woman.* New York: The Analytic Press.

Katz, A. M., & Shotter, J. (1996). Hearing the patient's 'voice': Toward a social poetics in diagnostic interviews. *Social Science and Medicine, 43,* 919–931.

Keeney, B. (1982). Ecosystemic epistemology. *Family Process, 21,* 1–22.

Keeney, B. (1983). *The aesthetics of change.* New York: Guilford Press.

Keeney, B. (1986). *The therapeutic voice of Olga Silverstein.* New York: Guilford Press.

Kinman, C. (1999) *Honoring community.* Abbotsford, B.C.: Fraser Valley Educational and Therapy Services.

Kohlberg, L. (1981). *The philosophy of moral development.* San Francisco: Harper & Row.

Kuhn, T. (1962). *The structure of scientific revolutions.* Chicago: University of Chicago Press.

Laird, J. (1993). Family-centered practice: Cultural and constructionist reflections. In J. Laird (Ed.), *Revisioning social work education.* Binghamton: Haworth.

Lakoff, G. (1980). *Metaphors we live by.* Chicago: University of Chicago Press.

Leeds-Hurwitz, E. (Ed.). (1995). *Social approaches to communication.* New York: Guilford.

Luepnitz, D. (1988). *The family interpreted.* New York: Basic Books.

Lyotard, J-F. (1984). *The post-modern condition.* Minneapolis: University of Minnesota Press.

Lyotard, J-F. (1989). One thing at stake in women's struggles. In A. Benjamin (Ed.), *The Lyotard reader.* London: Blackwell.

Lyotard, J-F. (1996). *Just gaming.* (Wlad Godzich, Trans.). Minneapolis: University of Minnesota Press.

MacGregor, R., Ritchie, A., Serrano, A., Schuster, F., McDanald, C., & Goolishian, H. (1964). *Multiple impact therapy with families.* New York: McGraw-Hill.

Maturana, H. R., & Varela, F.J. (1980). *Autopoiesis and cognition.* Dordrecht, Holland: D. Reidel.

McCarthy, I.C., & Byrne, N. O'R. (1988). Mis-taken love: Conversations on the problem of incest in an Irish context. *Family Process 27,* 181–198.

McGoldrick, M. (1998). *Re-visioning family therapy: Race, culture and gender in clinical practice.* New York: Guilford.

McGoldrick, M., Anderson, C., & Walsh, F. (Eds.). (1989). *Women in families.* New York: Norton.

McKinnon, L., & Miller, D. (1987). The new epistemology and the Milan approach. *Journal of Marriage and Family, Therapy 13,* 139–155.

McNamee, S., & Gergen, K. (1999). *Relational responsibility.* Thousand Oaks, CA: Sage.

Mead, G. H. (1934). *Mind, self, and society.* Chicago: Chicago University Press.

Miller, D. (1994). *Women who hurt themselves.* New York: Basic Books.

Miller, J. (1976). *Toward a new psychology of women.* Boston: Beacon Press.

Minuchin, S., Montalvo, B., et al. (1968). *Families of the slums.* New York: Basic Books.

Minuchin, S., Rosman, B., & Baker, L. (1978). *Psychosomatic families: Anorexia nervosa in Context.* Cambridge, MA: Harvard University Press.

Mishler, E. (1986). *Research interviewing.* Cambridge, MA: Harvard University Press.

Myerhoff, B. (1980) *Number our days.* New York: Simon & Schuster.

Myerhoff, B. (1982). Life history among the elderly: Performance, visibility, and remembering. In J. Ruby (Ed.), *A crack in the mirror.* Philadelphia: University of Pennsylvania Press.

Myerhoff, B. (1986). Life not death in Venice: Its second life. In V. Turner & E. Bruner (Eds.), *The anthropology of experience.* Chicago: University of Illinois Press.

Newfield, S., Newfield, H., Sperry, J., & Smith, T. (2000). Ethical decision making among family therapists and individual therapists. *Family Process, 39,* 177–188.

Newman, F. (2000). Does a story need a theory? In F. Fee (Ed.), *Pathology and the postmodern: Mental illness as discourse and experience.* London: Sage.

Newman, F., & Holzman, L. (1996). *Unscientific psychology.* Westport, CT: Prager Publishing.

Norris, C. (1991). *Deconstruction: Theory and practice.* New York: Routledge.

Olson, M. E. (Ed.). (2000). *Feminism, community, and communication.* Binghamton, NY: Haworth.

Olson, M. E. (2000). Listening to the voices of anorexia: The researcher as an "outsider-witness." *Journal of Feminist Family Therapy, 11*(4), 25–46.

Ong, W. (1982). *Literacy and orality.* New York: Norton.

O'Hanlon, W., & Weiner-Davis, M. (1989). *In search of solutions.* New York: Norton.

Pakman. M. (1999). Designing constructive therapies in mental health. *Family Process, 25,* 83–98.

Pakman, M. (2000). Disciplinary knowledge, postmodernism and globalization. *Cybernetics and human knowing, 7,* 105–126.

Papp, P. (1983). *The process of change.* New York: Guilford Press.

Parsons, T. (1951). *The social system.* New York: Free Press.

Pearce, W.B., & Cronen, V.E. (1980). *Communication, action and meaning: The creation of social realities.* New York: Praeger.

Penn, P. (1985). Feed forward: Future question, future maps. *Family Process, 24,* 299–311.

Penn, P. (2001a). Chronic illness: Trauma, language and writing. *Family Process, 40,* 33–52.

Penn, P. (2000b, in press). Metaphors in regions of unlikeness. *Human Systems.*

Penn, P., & Frankfurt, M. (1994). Creating a participant text: Writing, multiple voices, narrative multiplicity. *Family Process, 33,* 217–232.

Penn, P., & Frankfurt, M. (1999). A circle of voices. In S. McNamee & K. Gergen (Eds.), *Relational responsibility.* Thousand Oaks, CA: Sage.

Percy, W. (1996). Shakespeare had it easy. *The New Yorker,* June 24–July 1.

Polkinghorne, D.E. (1988). *Narrative knowing and the human sciences.* Albany: State University of New York Press.

Poster, M. (1989). *Critical theory and postructuralism.* Ithaca, NY: Cornell University Press.

Prigogine, I., and Stengers, I. (1984). *Order out of chaos.* New York: Bantam Books.

Rabinow, P. (1984). *The foucault reader.* New York: Pantheon Books.

Rabkin, R. (1968). *Inner and outer space.* New York: Norton.

Raush, H. (1974). *Communication, conflict and marriage.* San Francisco: Jossey-Bass.

Ravich, R. (1974). *Predictable pairing.* New York: Peter H. Wyden.

Readings, W. (1991). *Introducing Lyotard: Art and politics.* New York: Routledge.

Rober, P. (1999). The therapist's inner conversation in family therapy practice. *Family Process, 38,* 209–228.

Roberts, J. (1994). *Tales and transformations in family therapy.* New York: Norton.

Rogers, C. (1961). *On becoming a person.* Boston: Houghton Mifflin.

Rogoff, B. (1990). *Apprenticeship in thinking*. New York: Oxford University Press.

Romney, P. (2000). "Can you love them enough?" In Olson, M. (Ed). *Feminism, community and communication*. Binghampton: Haworth.

Rorty, R. (1979). *Philosophy and the mirror of nature*. Princeton, N.J.: Princeton University Press.

Roth, S., Chasin, L., Chasin, R., Becker, C., & Herzig, M. (1992). From debate to dialogue. *Dulwich Centre Newsletter*, 2, 41–48.

Said, E. (1993). *Culture and imperialism*. New York: Random House.

Sampson, E. (1990). Social psychology and social control. In I. Parker & J. Shotter (Eds.), *Deconstructing social psychology*. London: Routledge.

Satir, Virginia. (1964). *Conjoint family therapy*. Palo Alto: Science and Behavior Books.

Schafer, R. (1986). Narration in the psychoanalytic dialogue. In T. Sarbin, *Narrative psychology*. New York: Praeger.

Schoen, D. (1984) *The Reflective Practitioner*. New York: Basic Books.

Seikkula, J. (1993). The aim of the work is to generate dialogue: Bakhtin and Vygotsky in family session. *Human Systems: The Journal of Systemic Consultation and Management*, 4, 33–48.

Seikkula, J., Aaltonen, J., Alakare, B., Haarakangas, K., Keranen, J., & Sutela, M. (1995). Treating psychosis by means of open dialogue. In S. Friedman (Ed.), *The reflecting team in action*. New York: Guilford.

Selvini Palazzoli, M., Boscolo, L., Cecchin, G., & Prata, G. (1978). *Paradox and counterparadox*. New York: Aronson.

Selvini, M., Boscolo, L., Cecchin, G., & Prata, G. (1980a). The problem of the referring person. *Journal of Marital and Family Therapy*, 6, 3–9.

Selvini, M., Boscolo, L., Cecchin, G., & Prata, G. (1980b). Why a long interval between sessions. In M. Andolfi & I. Zwerling (Eds.), *Dimensions of family therapy*. New York: Guilford.

Selvini, M., Boscolo, L., Cecchin, G., & Prata, G. (1980c). Hypothesizing—circularity-neutrality. *Family Process*, 19, 73–85.

Shadish, W., Ragsdale, K., & Glaser, R. The efficacy and effectiveness of marital and family therapy. *Journal of Marital and Family Therapy*, 21, 345–360.

Shawver, L. (1983). Harnessing the power of interpretive language. *Psychotherapy: Theory, research and practice*, 20, 3–11.

Shawver, L. (1996). What postmodernism can do for psychoanalysis: A guide to the postmodern vision. *The American Journal of Psychoanalysis*, 56, 371–394.

Shawver, L. (1998a). Postmodernizing the unconscious. *The American Journal of Psychoanalysis*, 58, 361–390.

Shawver, L. (1998b). On the clinical relevance of selected postmodern ideas. *Journal of the American Academy of Psychoanalysis*, 26, 617–635.

Shawver, L. (2000). Postmodern tools for the clinical impasse. *Journal of the American Academy of Psychoanalysis*, 28 (4), 619–639.

Shawver, L. (In press, 2001). If Wittgenstein and Lyotard could talk with Jack and Jill. *Human Systems*.

Shotter, J. (1993a). *Conversational realities*. Thousand Oaks, CA: Sage.

Shotter, J. (1993b). *The cultural politics of everyday life*. Buffalo, NY: University of Toronto Press.

Showalter, E. (1985). *The female malady*. New York: Pantheon Books.

Singer, M. (1997). From rehabilitation to etiology: Progress and pitfalls. In J. Zeig (Ed.), *The evolution of psychotherapy: The third conference*. New York: Brunner/Mazel.

Singer, M., & Lalich, J. (1996). *"Crazy" therapies*. San Francisco: Jossey-Bass.

Sluzki, C., & Ransom, D. (Eds). (1976). *Double bind: The foundation of the communcational approach to the family*. New York: Grune & Stratton.

Spence, D. (1984). *Narrative truth and historical truth*. New York: Norton.

Tiefer, L. (1995). *Sex is not a natural act*. Boulder, CO: Westview Press.

Todorov, T. (1984). *Mikhail Bakhtin: The dialogical principle*. Minneapolis, MN: The University of Minneapolis Press.

Tomm, K., Lannamann, J.W., & McNamee, S. (1984). No interview today—A consultation team intervenes by not intervening. *Journal of Strategic and Systemic Therapies, 2*, 48–61.

Tomm, K. (1998). Co-constructing responsibility. In S. McNamee & K. Gergen (Eds.) *Relational responsibility*. Thousand Oaks, CA: Sage.

Varela, F. (1976). *Principles of biological autonomy*. New York: North Holland Press.

Vico, G. (1968). *The new science of Giambattista Vico* (T.G. Bergin & M.H. Fisch, Trans.). Ithaca, NY: Cornell University Press.

von Foerster, H. (1981). *Observing systems*. Seaside, CA: Intersystems Publications.

von Glasersfeld, E. (1987). *The construction of knowledge*. Seaside, CA: Intersystems Publications.

Vygotsky, L.S. (1978). *Mind in society*. Cambridge: Harvard University Press.

Wachterhauser, B. R. (1986). *Hermeneutics and modern philosophy*. Albany, NY: State University of New York Press.

Walters, M., Carter, C., Papp, P., & Silverstein, O. (1988). *The invisible web*. New York: Guilford.

Watzlawick, P. (1984). *The invented reality*. New York: Norton.

Watzlawick, P. (1976). *How real is real?* New York: Vintage Books.

Watzlawick, P., Bavelas, J., & Jackson, D. (1967). *Pragmatics of human communication*. New York: Norton.

Watzlawick, P., & Weakland, J. (1977). *The interactional view*. New York: Norton.

Watzlawick, P., Weakland, J., & Fisch, R. (1974). *Change: The principles of problem formation and problem resolution*. New York: Norton

Welch, S. (1990). *A feminist ethic of risk*. Minneapolis, MN: Fortress Press.

Wells. L. (1998). Consultants as nautical navigators: A metaphor for group-takers. *Journal of Applied Behavior Science, 34*, 379–391.

White, M. (1995). *Re-authoring lives*. Adelaide, South Australia: Dulwich Centre Publications.

White, M. (1997). *Narratives of therapists' lives*. Adelaide, South Australia: Dulwich Centre Publications.

White, M. (1999). Reflecting-team work as definitional ceremony revisited. *Gecko, 2*, 55–82.

White, M. (2000). *Reflections on narrative practice*. Adelaide, South Australia: Dulwich Centre Publications.

White, M., & Epston, D. (1990). *Narrative means to therapeutic ends*. New York: Norton.

Whorf, B. L. (1956). *Language, thought and reality* (J.B. Carrol, Ed.). Cambridge, Mass.: Technology Press of MIT and John Wiley.

Wiener, N. (1954). *The human use of human beings*. New York: Anchor Books.

Wittgenstein, L. (1961[1922]). *Tractatus logicus-philosophicus*. London: Routledge and Kegan Paul.

Wittgenstein, L. (1953). *Philosophical investigations* (G.E.M. Anscombe, Trans.). New York: Macmillan.

Index